Graphics Programming with Direct3D™

Techniques and Concepts

Rob Glidden

Addison-Wesley Developers Press

An imprint of Addison Wesley Longman, Inc.
Reading, Massachusetts • Harlow, England • Menlo Park, California
Berkeley, California • Don Mills, Ontario • Sydney
Bonn • Amsterdam • Tokyo • Mexico City

Many of the designations used by manufacturers and sellers to distinguish their products are claimed as trademarks. Where those designations appear in this book, and Addison Wesley Longman, Inc. was aware of a trademark claim, the designations have been printed in initial capital letters or all capital letters.

The author and publisher have taken care in preparation of this book, but make no express or implied warranty of any kind and assume no responsibility for errors or omissions. No liability is assumed for incidental or consequential damages in connection with or arising out of the use of the information or programs contained herein.

Library of Congress Cataloging-in-Publication Data

Glidden, Rob.
    Graphics programming with Direct3D : techniques and concepts / Rob Glidden.
      p.   cm.
    Includes index.
    ISBN 0-201-56173-5
    1. Computer graphics. 2. Three-dimensional display systems. 3. Real-time programming. 4. Direct3D. I. Title.
T385.G587   1997
006.6—dc20   96-35943
                                                                                                CIP

Copyright © 1997 by Rob Glidden

A-W Developers Press is a division of Addison Wesley Longman, Inc.

All rights reserved. No part of this publication may be reproduced, stored in a retrieval system, or transmitted, in any form or by any means, electronic, mechanical, photocopying, recording, or otherwise, without the prior written permission of the publisher. Printed in the United States of America. Published simultaneously in Canada.

Sponsoring Editor: Mary Treseler
Project Manager: Sarah Weaver
Production Coordinator: Erin Sweeney
Cover design: Chris St. Cyr
Set in 11-point Times Roman by Circle Graphics

1 2 3 4 5 6 7 8 9 -MA- 0099989796
First printing, December 1996

Addison Wesley Longman, Inc., books are available for bulk purchases by corporations, institutions, and other organizations. For more information please contact the Corporate, Government, and Special Sales Department at (800) 238-9682.

Find A-W Developers Press on the World Wide Web at
http://www.aw.com/devpress/

Contents

Part I	*Essential 3D Concepts*	1
Chapter 1	**The New Metal**	3
	In the Beginning	4
	What Is Realtime 3D?	4
	3D on PCs: What's the Big Deal?	5
	The Case for the 3D Desktop Supercomputer	5
	The PC Revolution at Middle Age	6
	3D Gets Interesting	6
	Retooling the PC	7
	3D: Who Needs It?	8
	Free Code!	10
Chapter 2	**The 3D Infrastructure**	13
	Why Care About the 3D Infrastructure?	13
	The "Industry-Birthing" Perspective	14
	Infrastructure Component Overview	16
	The Frame Buffer and the Screen	17
	3D Hardware	19
	Back Ends	20
	3D APIs and the Scene Database	21
	3D Application Environments	21
	Rough Spots and the Future	22

Chapter 3	**The DirectX Architecture**	23
	DirectX: The Big Picture	23
	DirectX: Interface to Graphics Hardware	24
	DirectX: Where Media Types Collide	25
	Phase 1: The Game SDK	26
	Phase 2: DirectX as a Direct OS	27
	Phase 3: UI?	27
	HAL and HEL	27
	Overview of DirectDraw	29
	Direct3D and the British 3D Invasion	30
	Direct3D Overview	31
	The COM Model	31
	Standard Interfaces	32
	COM and Performance Programming	34
Chapter 4	**Fundamentals of Realtime Rendering**	37
	Key Concepts	38
	The Frame Tree	39
	The Rendering Pipeline	40
	Z-buffering	40
	Lights	42
	Shading	43
	Meshes	44
	LOD	45
	Color Models	45
	Texture Mapping	46
	Texture Filtering Techniques	47
	Point Sampling	47
	Linear (Bilinear Filtering)	47
	Mipmapping	48
	Mipmaps in Direct3D	48
	The Next Step: Progressive Transmission?	51
Chapter 5	**3D Hardware**	53
	Why You Should Care About Hardware	53
	The PCI Bus	54
	3D Thumbnail Calculations	55
	Accelerated Graphics Port	56
	The Permedia 3D Chip in Depth	57
	The Delta Chip	57

	Delta Programming Model	59
	The Permedia Rasterization	61
	The FIFO Pipeline	61
	The Rasterization Pipeline	62

Part II — Programming in Three Dimensions   67

Chapter 6 — Retained Mode Architecture   69

	The Retained Mode Scene Graph	69
	Retained Mode Components	70
	Standard Retained Mode Interfaces	74
	COM and Performance Programming	76
	The IDirect3DRM Object	77
	Devices	78
	Viewports	80
	Picking and Transforming	82
	Frames	82
	The Scene Graph	83
	The Local Transform	84
	Transforming Coordinates	84
	Visuals	85
	Moving a Frame	85
	Z-buffer and Sort Modes	87
	Lights	90
	The Mesh Component	92
	Groups	93
	MeshBuilder Component	95
	Face	98
	Material	99
	Shadow	99
	Texture	100
	Decals	100
	Wrap	101
	UserVisual	102
	Animation and AnimationSets	102

Chapter 7 — A Simple 3D Scene   105

	Getting Started	105
	Initializing D3D	106
	Creating the Device	106
	Setting Render Quality	108

		Creating a Camera Frame and Viewport	108
		Setting Up Lights	109
		Loading a Mesh	110
		Summing Up	110
Chapter 8		**Immediate Mode**	**113**
		Use Immediate Mode or Retained Mode?	113
		Overview of Immediate Mode	114
		The Immediate Mode and COM	115
		What Is an Execute Buffer?	116
		Transform Module	117
		Lighting Module	118
		Rasterization Module	118
		Immediate Mode COM Components	119
		The Big Picture	119
		IDirect3D	119
		Device	120
		The 3DDEVICEDESC Structure	122
		ExecuteBuffer Object	123
		The Rendering Loop	128
		UserVisuals and the Immediate Mode	128
Chapter 9		**World Management 101**	**131**
		The 3D Application Framework	132
		Why Not an MFC Wrapper?	132
		What About a World "on Top of" a Scene Graph?	133
		Traversal Engine	135
		Direct3D Traversal	136
		Limits of Traversal	137
		Actors as Things	138
		Building Actors in Direct3D	139
		Making Actors Persistent	140
		Events as Things	140
		Godforces as Things	141
		Orchestration	142
		The User: Bystander, Godforce, or Actor?	143
		The User as Bystander	143
		The User as Godforce	144
		The User as Actor	144
		Variations on a Theme	144
		So What's the Right Way?	145

Chapter 10	**The Zen of 3D Performance**	147
	Tips, Tricks, and Pitfalls	147
	Beware the Blame Game	148
	Get Humble	148
	Understand the Scalable Base	149
	Beware of Moore's Law	150
	Scale Image Quality	151
	Use High-Level Culling	151
	Scale Frame Rate	151
	Scale Texture Quality	152
	Forgo Mipmapping	152
	Beware of to-the-Metal Myths	152
	Understand Traditional Optimization	153
	Manage Your Resources	153
	Balance Your Pipeline	154
	Understand the Resource Big Picture	154
	Real Programmers Use the Immediate Mode!	156
	Can You Trust the Retained Mode?	157
	Use Fog	158
	To Z or Not to Z	158
	Know Thy Depth Complexity	158
	Avoid State Thrash	160
	Use Level of Detail	160
	Optimize Your Meshes	160
	Keep Texel/Pixel Ratio Near 1	161
	Use Hardware Stretch	161
	Minimize Palettes	161
	Seek the Fast Path	161
Part III	***Advanced D3D Issues***	163
Chapter 11	**Multiuser 3D**	165
	The Big Picture	166
	A (Very) Short Internet Course	166
	Distributed Interactive Simulation	168
	DIS for Nonmilitary Uses	169
	DirectPlay	169
	The Send/Receive Paradigm	170
	3D Design Implications in Creating	
	3D Multiuser Environments	171

Chapter 12	**Motion Capture**		173
	Motion Capture, Rotoscoping, and Art		173
	Motion Capture Data		174
		Overview of .bvh	175
		Sample File: Line by Line	177
	Building Motion Capture Data Structures		178
Chapter 13	**The DirectX File Format**		179
	The File Format Failure Syndrome		179
	Fundamentals of 3D Scenes		180
		Storing Objects	180
		Hierarchical and Associational Relationships	180
		An Object-Oriented Database?	181
	Goals of the .x File Format		181
	A Simple Example .x File: "Hello_Up"		182
		The File Header	183
		Header Template	184
		Data Objects	186
	Retained Mode Templates		186
	Retained Mode File-Loading Methods		190
	Future .x File Directions		191
	A More Complex Example File: A Cube		192
		Adding a Material	194
	Representing Hierarchy		195
		A Frame Hierarchy	195
	An Animation Set		196
Part IV	***3D Resources***		199
Chapter 14	**Essential 3D Math**		201
	What You Do Not Need to Know		202
	What You Do Need to Know		202
	3D Math Preliminaries		203
		Coordinate Systems	203
		D3DVALUE	205
	Vectors		206
		Retained Mode Vector Support	207
		Finding the Length of a Vector	208
		Vector Multiplication	208
		Vector Addition and Subtraction	209
	Dot Product		210

		Properties of the Dot Product	212
		Converting a Vector to a Unit Vector	212
	Understanding 3D Planes		213
		The Dot Product and the Equation of a Plane	215
		Distance from Point to Plane	215
	Quaternions		216
		Quaternion Support	218
Chapter 15	**Realtime 3D Resources**		219
	Information About 3D Accelerators and Boards		219
	Periodicals		222
	Books		223
	Conferences and Trade Shows		223
	Newsgroups		224
	3D APIs		224
	VRML		225
	3D Modeling and Animation Tools		226
	Realtime 3D Tools		228
	3D Models		229
	File Converters		230
	Motion Capture		230
	Web Sites		230
	Research		231
	Multiuser 3D		232
	DIS		232
Chapter 16	**3DS**		233
Chapter 17	**.dxf File Format**		249
	Overall File Structure of .dxf		250
		A Simple .dxf File	251
		Reading a .dxf File	253
	Binary Format .dxf		256
	Vertex Group		257
Part V	***D3D Reference***		*261*
Chapter 18	**Retained Mode Reference**		263
	Retained Mode COM Objects		263
	IDirect3DRM		264
	IDirect3DRMObject		265

IUnknown	265
IDirect3DRMAnimation	266
IDirect3DRMAnimationSet	267
IDirect3DRMDevice	267
IDirect3DRMFace	268
IDirect3DRMFrame	269
IDirect3DRMLight	271
IDirect3DRMMaterial	272
IDirect3DRMMesh	273
IDirect3DRMMeshBuilder	274
IDirect3DRMShadow	275
IDirect3DRMTexture	275
IDirect3DRMUserVisual	276
IDirect3DRMViewport	276
IDirect3DRMWinDevice	277
IDirect3DRMWrap	278
IDirect3DRMArray	278
All RM Objects	279
IDirect3DRMObject	280
IDirect3DRM	281
IDirect3DRMAnimation Interface	291
IDirect3DRMAnimation Set	293
IDirect3DRMDevice	294
IDirect3DRMFace	298
IDirect3DRMFrame	301
IDirect3DRMLight	314
IDirect3DRMMaterial	317
IDirect3DRMMesh	318
IDirect3DRMMeshBuilder	323
IDirect3DRMShadow	331
IDirect3DRMTexture	331
IDirect3DRMUserVisual	334
IDirect3DRMViewport	334
IDirect3DRMWinDevice	340
IDirect3DRMWrap	340
RM Arrays	341
Structures	343
Enumerated Types	347
Other Types	356
Retained Mode Functions	360

| | Callback Functions | 365 |
| | RM Return Values | 368 |

Chapter 19	**Immediate Mode Reference**	369
	IDirect3D	369
	IDirect3DDevice	370
	IDirect3DExecuteBuffer	371
	IDirect3DLight	372
	IDirect3DMaterial	372
	IDirect3DTexture	372
	IDirect3DViewport	373
	IDirect3D Interface	374
	IDirect3DDevice Interface	375
	IDirect3DExecuteBuffer Interface	380
	IDirect3DLight Interface	382
	IDirect3DMaterial Interface	382
	IDirect3DTexture Interface	383
	IDirect3DViewport Interface	384
	Macros	387
	Callback Functions	390
	Structures	392
	Enumerated Types	417
	Other Types	423
	Return Values	424
	Execute Buffer Instructions	425
	D3DTRANSFORMSTATETYPE	430
	D3DLIGHTSTATETYPE	430
	D3DRENDERSTATETYPE	431

Glossary		439
Index		456

Part I

Essential 3D Concepts

Chapter 1

The New Metal

The personal computer (PC) is undergoing a fundamental transformation that is changing the face of the planet's techno-landscape, and 3D is at the center of this sea change. The 3D-enabled desktop supercomputer will affect everything from entertainment and the Internet to multimedia and user interfaces. It will reshape both computerdom and consumer electronics.

Pretty bold claims, eh? Over-the-top hype to sell imagine-if-you-will 3D applications? Wait-til-you-see-the-next-gen 3D hardware and otherwise dry books on 3D graphics programming? Sure. Real-time 3D on PCs is a Next Big Thing, with all the promise, techno-cultural baggage, and flame-out potential that implies. As with any Next Big Thing, however, you will have to judge the claims and realities for yourself. You also can count on some blood in the street as the divergent strategies of early players meet the reality of the future.

Try this checkpoint: Go to the local game arcade. You'll be hard-pressed to find anything new that is not realtime 3D. Now imagine arcade quality doubling, or quadrupling, or more. Imagine higher screen resolution, more memory, more color depth, and richer textures. Recognize that the actual cost of arcade hardware is much more in the PC price range than in the workstation price range and add your own estimate of how quickly PC performance will go up and prices will go down. (A standard benchmark is performance doubling every 18 months. In 3D graphics, performance increases will likely be faster than that for the next two to three years.) Add to this the fact that the multibillion-dollar computer game industry, and particularly video game consoles, have completely embraced 3D, and you'll get some sense of what the excitement is all about.

In this chapter, I take you on a quick tour of the realtime 3D landscape, the habitat in which Direct3D resides. If you are interested in realtime 3D, a facility with this overview material is likely to be part of your stock-in-trade for years to come.

In the Beginning

3D is computing's first, and perhaps only, native media type. Although it is not new, it is just coming into its own. It is unlike sound, video, film, and pictures, which existed without computers, although computers have increasingly absorbed the role of creating and playback of these media. 3D is a uniquely computer-centric medium—a combination of algorithms and data to which is applied a big dose of computing power.

3D's roots go back to computing's earliest days. Over the years, it has been funded and nurtured primarily by government research and the development of flight simulators. More recently, 3D has had a high-profile role in entertainment, from film animation and special effects to video games. Silicon Graphics has built a cooler-than-cool reputation as the preeminent high-end 3D platform. The photorealistic rendering results of modeling and animation packages like Softimage, Alias, and Wavefront have become the common fare of TV show openings and commercials. 3D has long been used in CAD (computer-aided design) and architectural design and rendering, primarily on workstations or high-end PCs.

What Is Realtime 3D?

This book covers "true" realtime 3D—objects and scenes drawn quickly by a computer as if you were viewing them in 3D space and possessing depth, lights, and perspective. "Realtime" means rendering frames—that is, drawing individual pictures—enough times a second so that they look realistic. The goal is usually 30 frames per second, although 10 to 15 is common and in some circumstances even a couple of times a second could be good enough.

"True" realtime 3D is not two and a half D—layers of 2D images with the background moving at a different pace than the foreground. Neither is it stereo-vision 3D or BSP trees—precomputed, static structures used to simulate simple 3D scenes in games like Doom and Quake—although each of these techniques has important, even essential, uses in the context of "true" realtime 3D. And realtime 3D is not photorealistic prerendering of the type exemplified by the movie *Toy Story*. Although the quality of realtime 3D is improving rapidly, this level of photorealism is years away. But make no mistake, the image of a realtime *Toy Story* on your computer is a wonderfully powerful future vision that has gripped the popular imagination.

3D on PCs: What's the Big Deal?

So what is the big deal about realtime 3D on a PC? It is in part that you can have it at all at an affordable price. Also, the mass market likely will put 3D to interesting and innovative uses once the technology is out of the hands of the few and in the hands of the many.

But perhaps most important is the impact that realtime 3D could have on the PC itself: its design, its markets, its future direction. Direct3D and the DirectX family of which Direct3D is a member are very much about providing you, the 3D application developer, an enabling infrastructure to do things on PCs never before possible.

An even more fundamental dynamic is at work here. 3D on PCs has a way of encompassing other media types. Video becomes just another 3D texture; sound becomes 3D spatially oriented sound; and 2D drawing becomes a special case of 3D modeling. 3D is a stepping-stone for the PC's conversion into a visual computer.

The Case for the 3D Desktop Supercomputer

Here is the four-step argument for realtime 3D and the desktop supercomputer:

1. The relentless exponential increase in computing power both threatens to bring personal computing to a "good enough" plateau and enables the possibility of a new generation of capabilities.
2. The consumer, not business, has become the king of PCs, and consumers demand visually rich computing.
3. A fast ramp-up to a visual personal supercomputer capable of stunning realtime 3D, better-than-TV-quality video, and better-than-CD-quality sound will create a platform for a compelling new generation of consumer applications that eventually will spill into business uses.
4. Number 3 is technologically and economically feasible.

Versions of this vision have taken hold in many parts of the computer industry, from chip fabs to application development houses, from staid investment houses to fringe cybernaut outposts. If you are looking into realtime 3D application development, you have probably already encountered this vision in some form or another.

The PC Revolution at Middle Age

There is a thinly veiled secret that haunts the entire PC industry: By and large, PCs over the last decade have evolved into devices that are amply capable of handling the original bread-and-butter tasks of personal computing. For word processing, database management, spreadsheet development, and basic communications, new versions of software and hardware generally offer marginal, not major, improvements. If there is no longer a fundamental need for PCs to innovate, then a $500 Internet computer looks like a pretty good idea.

The specter of the "good enough TV" hangs over the computer industry. That is, people resist replacing their perfectly good TVs, even if there is a better one in the store, because the one they already have is good enough. PC sales have outpaced television sales, but what will happen when everyone has a "good enough" computer? Flat and declining sales and a slide into the commodity oblivion. The specter of this can strike fear in the heart of the growing computer industry. Note that nothing of the sort has happened yet. The trend for unit sales of computers has been relentlessly up, and all signs are that this will continue for years to come.

But the cycle of ever-faster computers each year seems a little more like the planned obsolescence of the automobile industry in its heyday. Certainly, each new computer model is demonstratively superior to the previous one, so things have not yet degenerated into fashion wars of fin and fender styles. But the personal computing industry is still hungry and restless. It is still run and inspired by its founding generation's drive, blessed with ever-improving technology and price/performance, and infused with the enthusiasm and drive of a new computer-encultured generation.

So the PC industry—the great predator industry of the late twentieth century—is at a crossroads. The easy conquests, like typesetting equipment and dedicated word processors, fell long ago. New versions of the same old things, once thought useful and lucrative, are beginning to face the uphill resistance of an installed base. The great "convergence" industries on computing's horizons—communications and consumer electronics—are formidable in their own right. It's time for something new. And a $3,000 computer that can imitate a $300 TV or a $200 video game is just not enough.

3D Gets Interesting

For many people, the idea of realtime 3D on PCs conjures up images of grainy, low-res 3D Doom-like twitch games and mesmerizingly slow mood adventures like Myst. These are cool products, definitely. But they may not provide a good enough reason to throw out your old computer and get a new one.

If you saw some of the early converter 3D graphics boards that hit the market in late 1995, you may have been underwhelmed. You may have wondered what the difference was between a 3D-enabled PC and a regular old PC.

Here's the real "3D deal." It is possible that something qualitatively different will start to happen with 3D at somewhere around a 200MHz MMX Pentium with a second-generation 3D graphics chip (minimum features: setup, texturing, and filtering) and good memory management (good PCI, fast memory, and perhaps an AGP bus). The image quality could start to improve; latency may drop so that there is more fluid and realistic interactivity. Polygon budgets might go up enough to allow for more lifelike characters. You could integrate 2D, 3D, and sound in interesting ways. And as screen resolutions exceed 640×480, one could even imagine the beginnings of a 3D user interface.

But are there the will and the way to bring this grand 3D vision to reality?

Retooling the PC

This tantalizing vision of ubiquitous, powerful realtime 3D on every computer faces a fundamental challenge. That is, realizing it requires not only a fast CPU but also some key redesigns of the PC itself. Any major redesign of PC architecture would require the cooperation and participation of CPU vendors like Intel, OS vendors like Microsoft, video and memory chip makers, and a large segment of the software industry. That is a tall order. Filling it requires a close alignment of technology, industry structure, and demand.

In essence, seven key elements are necessary for this realtime 3D vision to come to fruition. Here they are, along with my view of their status.

1. A 3D technology base. Already exists. The fundamental technologies and techniques of realtime 3D have been well established. Perhaps more than any other computer discipline, 3D is blessed by having a robust academic and research community. Workstation vendors have already worked through generations of issues relating to realtime 3D rendering. The weak spot is that this technology has to be adapted to the specific needs of a consumer market: low cost, accessibility, and ease of use.

2. New graphics accelerators. Underway, but off to a shaky start. Graphics and memory chip makers, as well as Intel, are perhaps the most enthusiastic backers of bringing realtime 3D to the PC. A kind of cycle of market stoking and resulting fear of falling behind is involved here. 3D represents a new generation of features, a way to add new value and to avoid commodity status, and an enormous potential demand for more memory and computing power. But once the race began, market share was in the balance, inspiring rounds of improvement in features, quality, and performance. The 3D race to the motherboard has become a billion-dollar proposition.

But 3D-in-a-chip is a very difficult proposition to bring about. There are design, cost, and practical issues that will take time to resolve. A fundamental problem is that 3D chips involve putting a lot of sophisticated software in hardware. This is risky and time-consuming even when there is a well-defined target. Add the evolving and competitive nature of the chip business, and you have a tough situation. When all is said and done, 3D-in-a-chip may look quite different from a traditional 3D pipeline inherited from graphics workstations. Just as PCs transformed the typesetting industry in a previous era, PCs will morph the traditional workstation 3D to fit the needs of the PC industry.

3. **More CPU power and memory.** Inevitable. Pick your time frame and place your bet.

4. **OS-level support.** Done, at least for the first round. Direct3D is the 3D graphics OS for Windows 95 PCs and will also be available on Windows NT. Other major computing platforms also now have support for 3D at the OS level: Microsoft (Direct3D), Apple (QuickDraw3D), and SGI (OpenGL). But the OS-level support for 3D will need to improve over time.

5. **An installed base.** In transition. Depends on your definition of "good enough." The pitch is usually something like this: 3D works in software only (no hardware acceleration) on some portion of the installed base, but wait until next year and there will be more-powerful systems. Grainy 3D is here today at consumer prices. But is there a sufficient base on which to evolve an industry?

6. **3D content and tools.** Partially available. An active field of 3D content development exists. It is focused primarily on developing "linear" 3D—prerendered commercials, promos, multimedia clips, films, special effects, and so on. Linear 3D is a close cousin to realtime 3D. Its main limitation is in the area of tools. Existing 3D modeling and animation tools are generally poorly equipped to create content for realtime 3D. The realtime tools that do exist tend to be quite expensive (typically $10,000 per user) and oriented toward workstation simulation.

7. **Compelling applications.** This is where you, the 3D application developer, come in.

In sum, there needs to be a PC 3D infrastructure.

3D: Who Needs It?

Ask a 3D fanatic what realtime 3D is really good for and the response you receive is likely to be something between a dumbfounded stare and a dressing-down for your lack of vision. It is easy to gush with enthusiasm about the many exciting but as yet untested product ideas and markets. But a largely unanswered question about realtime 3D is what new functionality and markets it will actually bring beyond arcade-like fight, race, and flight simulation games. Here are some candidates.

- **Games and entertainment.** It is fair to say that the computer game industry has fully embraced realtime 3D as a fundamental medium. 3D and games seem to go hand in hand. Visit an arcade, and you'll be hard-pressed to find any new games that are not 3D. On PCs and consoles, 3D is quickly becoming an integral part of game development. If you intend to work in game development, the message is clear: You better know 3D.
- **Multimedia.** Game developers call multimedia "bad games," but few multimedia developers seem to realize (or care about) this. But if realtime 3D is visually appealing enough, it will likely find its place in many multimedia applications.
- **Virtual reality.** Realtime 3D is virtual reality without the fashion accessories. But there is social tension between the traditional VR industry and the up-and-coming 3D crowd. Traditional VR places the immersive experience center stage, with headmount displays, force feedback devices, and so on. Realtime 3D supporters see all of this as a misplaced infatuation with gear of secondary importance, a kind of cult of cyborg envy.
- **Data visualization.** An obvious use of realtime 3D on PCs is simply as a consumer extension of professional fields such as architecture and CAM. Consumer home architecture programs are already a popular software category. It is easy to imagine that higher quality will make them more popular. A related field of data navigation is often touted, with 3D spaces as metaphorical places in which to walk around and do or discover things.
- **Virtual cities.** Some people want to build new worlds in 3D. Some just want a new view of the world we already have. Consumer GIS offers a potential realtime 3D content environment, although this field may require a large amount of memory and processing power to reach a critical mass.
- **Children's software.** Widespread belief is that realtime 3D will be a particularly good medium for children's software: 3D play sets; building, fantasy, and story environments; 3D creativity tools; and a setting for popular film and TV characters. Several efforts are already underway in this area, but it remains to be seen exactly what the successful formulas will be.
- **Net 3D.** With realtime 3D and the Internet both coming of age in the same general time frame, it was inevitable that the two would cross paths. Put 3D on the Internet, and how could you not have the mother of all Next Big Things? Online 3D games, 3D chat rooms, VRML—there is an enthusiastic

following for these possibilities. In fact, the image of 3D shared space has entered the popular consciousness far faster than practical solutions have appeared to match the popular imagination. This field requires far more than a file format or a standardized application environment. The practical limits of 28.8 modems require workarounds that will stall overly simplistic efforts.

But there is more at work in the area of Internet 3D than awkward walkthroughs of amateur 3D home pages and hokey avatars. The whole concept of shared space—everything from online versions of existing games to collaborative workspaces—seems to have an innate appeal for many people.

- **Medical imaging.** Although consumer and education 3D anatomy tour applications have already become established, these are only the tip of the iceberg. It is easy to imagine a new generation of applications that assist in health care training and visualization, surgical simulation, and eventually surgery. But this field is not for the fainthearted. The demands of volumetric representation, digital image processing, and anatomical correctness are likely to tax even the most powerful computers for a long time.

- **3D user interface.** Can the 2D desktop metaphor give way to a 3D version? Early efforts have been insufficient, offering cartoon-like desks, corny guide personas, and so on. But the 3D metaphor can go much deeper. Some people imagine applications and windows as panes floating in 3D space and file directories as places, not lists. Although 3D user interfaces will take a great deal of processing power, the idea is appealing that there may be something beyond the user interface paradigms of today.

Free Code!

Combine all of the above into the melting pot of strategic maneuverings by computer companies large and small, standards-setting gambits and counter gambits, and Internet-era multiplatformism. Add OS extensions to arbitrate between new hardware and software, and the result, to the delight of 3D application developers, boils down to two simple words: Free code!

Microsoft, Apple, SGI, and Sun all have plans to widely distribute at little or no cost 3D-enabling software in the form of OS extensions, playback tools, and API toolkits. Other companies have released free 3D viewers tied in subtly, or not so subtly, to their 3D products. Netscape put Live3D in Navigator; Microsoft and Apple added 3D to the OS; Sun launched Java3D. The reasoning is simple: Control the new graphics OS, and you will control the new generation of computing.

But contrary to the traditional maxim, you should look this gift horse in the mouth. To be blunt, it is not altruism that motivates major computer companies to invest millions of dollars in a free-code fest. Just as war is a continuation of politics by other means, all of this is a continuation of competition and profit-seeking by other means. Free code is your enlistment bonus, enabling tool, and care package in someone's strategic deployment strategy. Pick carefully. And since this book is about Direct3D, I assume you will be looking in this book for information as to why Direct3D should be your choice. Read on.

Chapter 2

The 3D Infrastructure

Life is short and 3D is hard. Hence the 3D infrastructure. If you think 3D is simply a do-it-yourself proposition of writing some rendering code, think again. There is already a 3D infrastructure you need to take into account. The 3D infrastructure is the combination of operating system functions and components, graphics hardware designs, realtime rendering software, authoring tools, and enabling standards that add up to making adequate 3D performance achievable on a particular computer platform. The 3D infrastructure is something like the computer image display infrastructure or the file saving and loading infrastructure. It is the starting point for application building. It is the net result of the efforts of different companies that have an interest in enabling 3D performance. And on PCs, it is still evolving. Assuming you can do all of this yourself is like assuming that the best way to write an application is to design your own hardware, OS, and supporting tools. Maybe you can do this, but most people would rather find a quicker way.

Why Care About the 3D Infrastructure?

Your first reaction as you pursue 3D application development may very well be skepticism. You may ask, why should you care about the 3D infrastructure? Shouldn't you just take it pretty much as a given, and build your applications on top of it? And if you are a to-the-metal graphics programmer, shouldn't you just "roll your own" 3D software in order to maximize performance? The answer to all of these questions is no, for three reasons.

1. **Concerns about its performance.** 3D performance is an overriding issue (perhaps *the* overriding issue) of 3D development. I address it more directly later in the chapter on 3D hardware and optimization. But for now, please try to take my word for it: 3D performance is a very, very tricky and complex beast. It has a lot to do with how effectively (and competitively) you manage to take advantage of the infrastructure available to you.

2. **Uncertainty.** As I hope will become clear to you by the time you finish this chapter, the 3D infrastructure on PCs is far from stable. It is undergoing its own establishing evolution. Although the general outlines of the different components are relatively clear, many fundamental aspects still are undergoing revision. You simply have to watch out. Today's cool 3D application feature may be given away free tomorrow in the operating system (and that may or may not make any difference!). Today's coolest software trick may be a set of gates in tomorrow's graphics chip! Spotting the weaknesses in the 3D infrastructure as it evolves and cleverly addressing those weaknesses constitute a major technical business strategy of professional 3D application development.

3. **Scalability.** Paying attention to the 3D infrastructure offers you a way to handle scalability. You will need some way for your 3D software to run on a variety of computers (from relatively slower to relatively faster) and hardware (from no 3D acceleration to 3D chips of various flavors and stripes). Managing these various environments will be, simply put, a nightmare. Very few if any 3D application companies are likely to tackle this problem alone. They will seek any help they can find. You should, too, unless you are willing to dedicate a huge amount of effort to support a dizzying array of strange and exotic hardware and accept the blame when things don't fit together as well as someone may have promised.

The "Industry-Birthing" Perspective

Before I dig into the components of the 3D infrastructure, let's step back for a moment for some perspective. Realtime 3D is a quest to push the limits of computer hardware and software design to create the visual illusion of the real world. If you think about this for a moment, it is obvious that the real world (and our visual interpretation of it) is infinitely complex. Creating an interesting simulation of it simply will not be a job for one person, one company, one application, or (any time soon) one chip. But an underlying movement spurred by perceptions of market opportunities and the capabilities of technology is driving a wide range of companies to participate in the construction of 3D infrastructure in order to advance 3D visual simulation. This is industry-birthing stuff. Chip makers, authoring tool companies, OS providers, and content creators are building the 3D infrastructure as they search for new business opportunities and compete with each other. So it is important to recognize that "infrastructure" is not something owned by a single company. Rather it is the result of the efforts of many companies and individuals.

Of course, on a particular hardware platform the key architect of any infrastructure that involves cooperation between hardware and software is going to be the operating system company. This means that Microsoft, Apple, and SGI are the leaders in architecting many components of the 3D infrastructure on their platforms. Sun, which with Java is launching something of a "multiplatform, Web-based, OS-like infrastructure," also is involved in 3D infrastructure building. Then take the "fight your wars on distant shores" strategies of companies like Apple and SGI to provide cross-platform 3D infrastructure solutions and combine them with products such as QuickDraw 3D and SGI's Cosmo. The result is a competitive stew of "open" standards (how open will depend on your perspective), cross-platform 3D infrastructures, and "free code" wars that (we can hope) will end up benefitting the 3D application developer.

But it is important to recognize that infrastructure-building does not take place in a vacuum or simply by fiat. (Companies like Microsoft may rule the software world, but they cannot dictate that graphics hardware should simply "arrive" to their specs and then actually be sure it will show up.) A complex behind-the-scenes dance is taking place. Can chip makers deliver a key hardware feature, or will the feature have to be written in software? How much middleware is necessary to make a graphics operating system usable on a cost-effective basis by thousands, or tens of thousands, of developers? Where is the line between application software and infrastructure software? Which components are platform-specific, and which are cross-platform? And perhaps most daunting, how does the industry grapple with what is sometimes delicately called the "installed base" problem (consumers probably perceive this more as the "planned obsolescence" problem). That is, how do companies convince millions of people that their current computers are hopelessly out-of-date and that a new generation of features is worth buying? The super-multimedia computer of the future may indeed be a compellingly different category of computer. However, the work-in-progress, almost-super-multimedia computer of today is not. The resolution of these kinds of issues is part practical, part technical, and part political.

So all told, computer infrastructure building is a messy business, much more like making legislation or sausage than building a house from a blueprint. If you are looking for certainty in your application development environment, you'll just have to wait a few years. But if you do, you'll risk that by then someone else will have suffered through the infrastructure-building era and already implemented your neat 3D application idea!

Infrastructure Component Overview

On to the specific components of the 3D infrastructure, as it is currently shaping up on PCs. Figure 2-1 shows a basic overview of the infrastructure. The infrastructure is a set of layers of components, somewhat overlapping and interconnected, each of which provides a more generic abstraction of the layer below it and adds some more application-oriented sets of features.

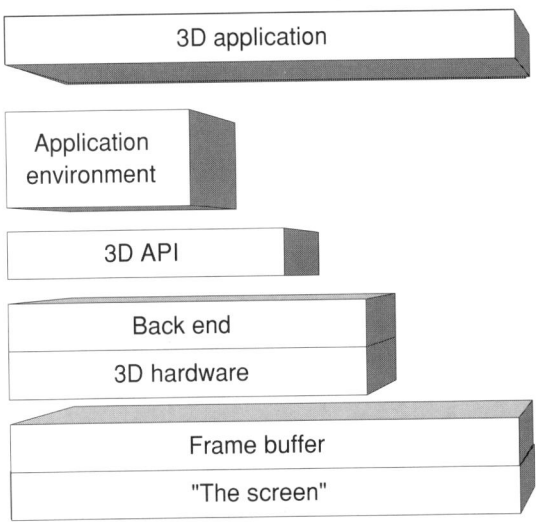

Figure 2-1. Overview of the 3D infrastructure on PCs.

Your first reaction may be, there are too many layers! How can true performance programming be achieved through such a cascade of components? Collapse this whole thing into a couple of layers. Then we'll start getting some real performance! Ah, patience, patience; this scheme actually makes sense (at least in an evolving ecosystem kind of way). Each component represents a core function in the process of getting from application-level concepts ("show a red ball and make it bounce") to actually putting those concepts onto the screen (put some red pixels here on the screen).

I'll put some more meat on the component skeleton. Table 2-1 gives a working functional description of the components of the 3D infrastructure.

Chapter 2 The 3D Infrastructure

Table 2-1. 3D infrastructure components

Component	Function	Key Concepts	Representative Products
Application environment	Authoring tool level interface for 3D application	Objects, behavior, and interaction	VRML, authoring tools
3D API	Programming interface to a 3D scene database	Scene graph/database, shapes and appearances, spatial and child relationships, visual culling	D3D Retained Mode, Open Inventor, Performer, RenderWare, BRender
Back end	The "graphics operating system": the standard interface to frame buffer and 3D hardware	Lists of display commands, geometry and lighting pipelines, rasterization	SGI's OpenGL, D3D immediate mode
3D hardware	Special-purpose graphics processing	Acceleration of rasterization and geometry, texture mapping	3D rasterizer chip, geometry accelerator
Frame buffer	Graphics memory	Memory management, blitting	DirectDraw

In examining the emerging 3D infrastructure, I take a bottom-up approach. I start with the frame buffer and screen, even though the top-down application perspective is probably going to be more important to you, the application developer. I do this because conceptually, each layer of the infrastructure presents an abstraction of the layer below it and each adds a new set of functions.

The Frame Buffer and the Screen

Think of a frame buffer as a graphics memory management system with specialized software and hardware support that speeds up the drawing of graphics data primitives. If you are a Windows graphics programmer, think of it as a good engine under GDI that you have direct access to. If you are a VGA graphics programmer, think of it as graphics memory explicitly unhooked from screen display, with lots of blitter and graphics primitives functions. But I'm getting a little ahead of myself.

The traditional to-the-metal view of graphics programming on PCs derives from a frozen-in-time concept of EGA, VGA, and SVGA registers and graphics memory. If this is what you have learned, then forget it. It's time to move on. If you don't already know about VGA registers, then don't bother to learn. The Frame Buffer era is here.

But to linger in the past for a moment, consider the "frozen-in-time" EGA/VGA era and how and why it died a slow death. Recall that long ago and far away, PC standards were set by fiat by IBM; each new generation of IBM PCs generated a compatibility race in the computer industry. Whoever could most quickly and most completely demonstrate IBM compatibility was almost automatically the winner of a significant business opportunity.

The last hurrah of the IBM era was 1987, which brought the last major efforts by IBM at defining the PC: the PS/2 computer line, the Microchannel bus architecture, OS/2, and the VGA board. Microchannel and OS/2, to summarize almost a decade of subsequent industry tumult, flopped, and the PS/2 computer line faded into an evolutionary, not revolutionary, role in PC history. But the VGA board, a minor upgrade to 1984's EGA board (itself a descendant of the original IBM PC's CGA board), quietly became the last major standard of the IBM era. (A more ambitious XGA standard from IBM drifted into oblivion.)

The core concept of PC graphics programming of the EGA/VGA was "blit and flip." You'd set registers and then use the CPU to cram as much data into graphics memory as fast as you could, hoping you didn't trip over the vertical retrace while you were at it. Graphics memory equalled what you saw on screen (although in certain resolutions you could flip a block of undisplayed graphics memory to the screen). A whole software subindustry was built around writing fast blitting code.

But without IBM as the standards leader, the graphics chip industry drifted and eventually fragmented into a collection of mutually incompatible SVGA (super VGA) chips. Advances such as hardware blitters lay dormant for lack of enabling standards. (A hardware blitter can move blocks of graphics memory around much faster than CPU-based "blit and flip" techniques that PC graphics programmers had to rely on.)

Windows 3.0, released in May 1990, was a major boon to the VGA chip industry. (It was also the beginning of the end of the VGA era, because it started a process of hardware-based graphics acceleration.) The first truly commercially viable release of Windows, Windows 3.0, had appallingly slow graphics performance. By early 1991, a new category of Windows graphics accelerator chips began to appear. Eventually that category grew into a substantial industry to include such companies as Cirrus Logic, S3, ATI, and Tseng. In 1995, over 50 million accelerated VGA chips of different flavors were sold—in essence, a zero to billion-dollar product category over four years.

However, the growth of this industry laid the groundwork for the death blow to the VGA era on PCs: DirectDraw, Microsoft's (initially) game-oriented frame buffer architecture, launched in 1995 for high performance, non-GDI graphics under Windows. Although this book is not about DirectDraw, from the 3D point of view the key point is that direct connections exist between DirectDraw and the 3D infrastructure. The connections are acceleration (both DirectDraw and 3D encourage graphics acceleration) and memory management (3D textures can be DirectDraw surfaces and 3D accelerators can render into a DirectDraw surface). In fact, DirectDraw folks see 3D as a subset of what they are doing and 3D folks see DirectDraw as a subset of what they are doing!

3D Hardware

The move to the Frame Buffer era has freed the PC graphics chip industry from the dreaded jaws of "commodity" status. At the same time, it has launched an exciting (read: risky) period of product innovation, differentiation, new entrants, and general panic, frenzy, and jostling. With hardware acceleration fully center stage in the field of performance graphics, the core issues have become what can and should be accelerated, how to decide this, and as a result, who will win, and who will lose. Add to this other turbulent forces: video games (built-in 3D acceleration is standard), video (a must-have for a graphics chip maker), Intel (what graphics features may appear in future Intel CPUs and motherboards?), and SGI (the master of 3D performance).

Enter the Great 3D Chip Race. By some estimates, as many as 34 companies have announced intentions to develop 3D chips. In addition to existing PC graphics accelerator companies, new entrants include venture-financed start-ups like Rendition, 3dfx, and NVidia and players moving down-market like 3Dlabs and Lockheed Martin. Of course, any market race worth watching is likely to produce some blood on the street along the way. Overall, however, the trend is toward providing a significant and useful amount of graphics acceleration.

What is the bottom line for you, the 3D application developer? You will need at least some understanding of how 3D acceleration works. You may or may not ever need to program directly to a particular 3D chip or board. But then again, you may.

You are likely to hear a lot of claims of "almost SGI-level" performance from purveyors of 3D on PCs, with gleeful musings about what will become of SGI now that PCs are "going 3D." Don't believe it, at least not at the high end of what SGI computers can do. At the low end of SGI's line, PCs (more accurately, NT-class personal graphics workstations) are sure to take a bite out of SGI's price/performance curve in the near term. But at the high end, systems like SGI's Onyx computers, with the RealityEngine2 graphics subsystems, still leave in the dust anything that looks like a PC, super-multimedia charged or not. If you've got the bucks, you can look at specs like 930,000 meshed, antialiased, textured triangles per second; fill rates up to 320 million pixels per second; 48-bit RGBA color; up to 24 CPUs; 160 MB of frame buffer memory; and 4 to 16 MB of texture memory. Certainly someday we'll all have something like a RealityEngine on our desktops. But by the time that happens, SGI should have also moved far up its own performance curve unless it falls catatonic on its own 3D switch.

Back Ends

Back ends exist because frame buffers and graphics hardware are a moving target, are too hard to program directly, and are missing essential generic functionality. A back end is the programming interface to the frame buffer and its supporting graphics hardware. Examples of back ends are SGI's cross-platform OpenGL, Microsoft's Direct3D immediate mode, the Rave 3D component of Apple's QuickDraw 3D, and Autodesk's Heidi interface for 3D Studio and part of AutoCAD.

In one sense, you could call a back end the "graphics operating system," since the core function of any operating system is to provide a software interface to the underlying hardware. But don't think of a 3D back end as an operating system in the do-it-all sense of something like Windows 95, Unix, and the Macintosh OS. Graphics back ends are more modest in scope. They are more like standardized driver interfaces to hardware. Some back ends are more ambitious than others: For example, OpenGL has a broader set of features than does Direct3D. However, this is primarily because OpenGL was originally aimed at higher-end and multiple-application categories, whereas Direct3D was originally targeted more toward games. But in the ecology of the 3D infrastructure, they occupy a similar niche.

Back ends are sometimes called "immediate mode" renderers. This means they do not retain a copy of the graphics data sent to them but simply process it and pass it on to the frame buffer. Direct3D's immediate mode, as you will see, has added another layer of complexity to the definition of a back end as an immediate mode. Actually, some people would call Direct3D's immediate mode nonhierarchical display-list retained mode, but I am getting ahead of myself.

On PCs, the HAL concept has played a particularly important role in the development of 3D back ends. HAL, the Hardware Abstraction Layer, is Microsoft's clever name for its standard-setting hardware driver architecture that reflects its role as the heir to IBM as PC standard setter. Since there are several 3D chip makers, with competing designs and various future plans, how can a back end know in advance what hardware features it should assume exist and so pass on as a generic feature? And what about future changes? How can the installed base be evolved to avoid the ossification that threatens any deployment of millions of systems?

It's not easy. The first two major efforts to create a generic PC 3D back end failed. These were 3DR (3D Render) by Intel Architecture Labs and 3D-DDI (3D Device Driver Interface) by Microsoft. 3DR faced opposition from chip makers who saw Intel as their competitor, and were concerned that 3DR might ultimately map out a narrower role for accelerators (rasterization only) than many chip makers wanted. 3D-DDI died because, unlike 3DR, it did not attempt to provide a minimum set of guaranteed functionality that would be emulated in software if the hardware did not provide it.

For many PC 3D developers, the key back end is likely to be Microsoft's Direct3D immediate mode. Direct3D immediate mode is the back end portion of RenderMorphics' Reality Lab 3D API. After Microsoft acquired RenderMorphics, Reality Lab's back end was broken out as a separate product, modified, integrated with DirectDraw, and then released as Direct3D retained mode and immediate mode.

3D APIs and the Scene Database

3D APIs exist because back ends are a moving target, are too hard to program directly, and are missing essential generic functionality (are you starting to see a pattern here?).

Perhaps the best way to think of a 3D API is as a 3D scene database toolkit with an input (the programming interface it presents to the 3D application developer) and an output (the commands that the API sends to the back end).

The emphasis here is on "3D scene database," the description of which will merit a good deal of attention later in this book. For now, think of a 3D scene database as an organized collection of 3D data that includes primitives (such as spheres and cubes) and shapes (such as meshes of connected polygons). It also contains information on the appearance of these primitives (color, texture, shininess, and so on) and their location within the 3D scene.

3D Application Environments

3D application environments exist because (you guessed it) frame buffer 3D APIs are a moving target, are too hard to program directly, and are missing essential generic functionality. Actually, it is an overstatement to say that 3D application environments "exist." More accurately, they are in an intense early era of development. Solving the 3D application environment is a challenging and overarching issue of 3D application development. It is attracting a wide range of virtual reality authoring tools and content export facilities for 3D modeling and animation tools. Also involved are academic research into shared virtual spaces, VRML design efforts, and the development of extensions to multimedia authoring tools.

Here is the fundamental problem of 3D APIs: 3D APIs think in terms of a 3D scene database or scene graph, organized in a back-end, performance-friendly format. People don't think like this. Finding the general-purpose abstractions of a 3D scene graph that work for a wide range of applications is the core challenge on the interactive 3D authoring and application front.

The fact remains that 3D database and scene graphs are simply not going to go away, to be replaced by some higher-order set of abstractions that you, the 3D application developer, may find more comfortable to work with. Remember, 3D APIs and their scene databases not only provide a programming interface but also abstract the back ends below them.

Rough Spots and the Future

I hope I've painted a reasonably coherent component view of the 3D infrastructure. Now it's time to describe a few of its complications, rough spots, and complexities.

1. Where does culling take place? **Culling** is the process of eliminating from further graphics processing portions of a 3D scene database that are not actually visible on the screen. Culling occurs at every level in the 3D infrastructure.
2. Which component really manages the database? Although in practice the scene database is a 3D API level function, some aspects of it spill over into the other components. For example, texture memory (the images that are wrapped around 3D objects when displayed) is probably best stored in graphics memory or a system memory extension to graphics memory, which is the domain of the frame buffer. Large scenes that exceed available memory may need some higher-order paging from disk. Is this an API function or an application function?
3. Is animation playback a function internal to an API and its file format? Or is it something that a 3D application or playback tool "does to" the scene database through API calls? Sometimes it is one, and sometimes it is the other.

These kinds of questions help to make 3D application programming complex (and hopefully interesting!). They all center around a fundamental premise: In 3D, performance is king, and the best way to do something is whatever provides the best performance.

Chapter 3

The DirectX Architecture

You may think of DirectX as just a set of game development tools. But it is evolving toward something much more fundamental, to a "direct OS"—an operating system in the classic sense of a bridge between the worlds of software and hardware. Only this time the environment for the OS is a much more sophisticated set of hardware and software functions that leads all the way up to connectivity with the Internet.

In this chapter, I examine DirectX and its implications for 3D application programming. In a nutshell, Direct3D is intimately integrated with the DirectX family, and this relationship will provide enormous benefits as you develop 3D applications.

DirectX: The Big Picture

The big picture of DirectX is deceptively simple, as shown in the first box chart view in Figure 3-1.

The DirectX family of technologies is a low-level interface to hardware through a layer of hardware abstraction and emulation. ActiveX technologies sit on top of DirectX technologies, providing a higher, more application-oriented set of functionality. If you are doing to-the-metal performance programming, you use DirectX. If you want application-level support, you use ActiveX.

Notice something missing? Where is the operating system in this picture? Hmm. . . .

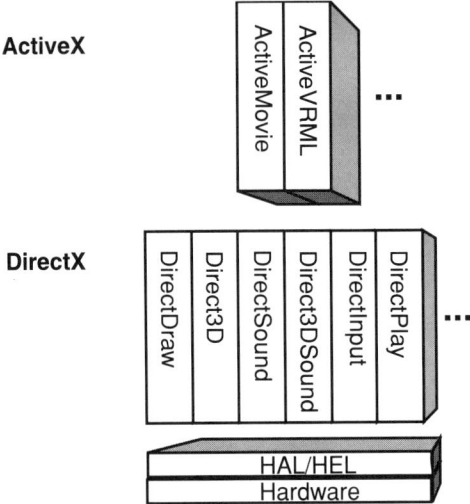

Figure 3-1. The big picture of DirectX and ActiveX.

DirectX: Interface to Graphics Hardware

Figure 3-2 shows how DirectX is an interface to graphics hardware. This view of DirectX shows the layered relationship between an application and the higher- and lower-level interfaces. The application writes to GDI, D3D retained mode, OpenGL, or ActiveMovie as the highest application level. Drop down one level, and you can program directly to DirectDraw and Direct3D immediate mode. However, you are working conceptually one layer closer to the hardware. HAL and the Windows DDI represent the lowest-level interface above the graphics hardware.

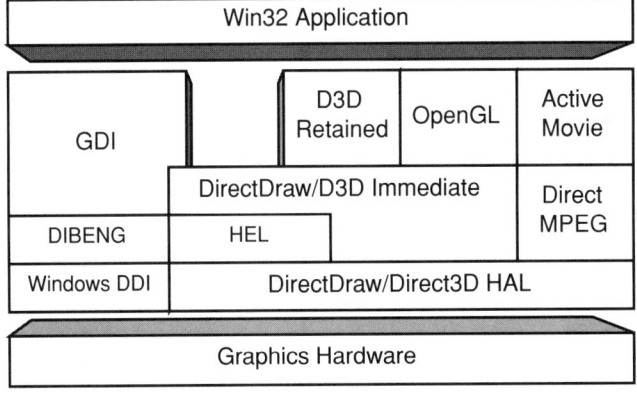

Figure 3-2. The DirectX as an interface to graphics hardware.

Note two interesting things about this view. First, OpenGL is sitting on top of Direct3D. As of this writing, this is not the case (on NT, OpenGL sits on top of a version of 3D-DDI or its own client driver). But the chart shows an intent to make Direct3D the core interface to 3D hardware on the Windows platform. Second, notice how DirectDraw and D3D immediate mode are starting to creep underneath GDI. This is a signal that perhaps over time, GDI will tend to use DirectX as a low-level interface.

DirectX: Where Media Types Collide

From an application development point of view, the DirectX family of technologies presents a more complex and integrated environment than that shown in Figure 3-2. Figure 3-3 probably corresponds more closely to how an application developer would conceptualize and use DirectX than the previous two figures do.

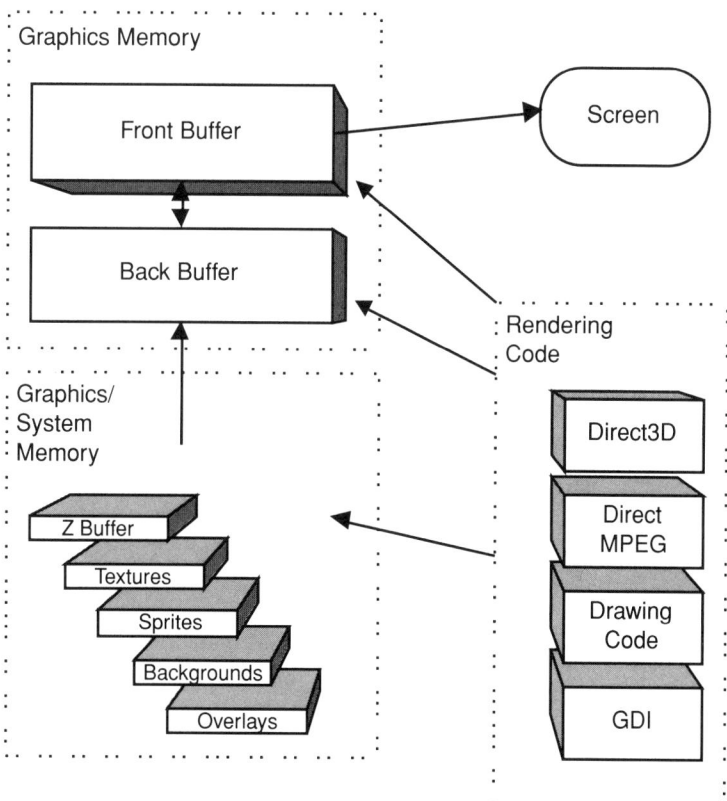

Figure 3-3. Application development view of DirectX.

The front buffer corresponds to what you see on the screen. The back buffer is generally where you compose your image using a combination of techniques and tools, although you can write to the front buffer if you want. When your back buffer is complete, you flip it so that it becomes the new front buffer. The old front buffer is now the back buffer. A pool of associated graphics memory surfaces (some may actually be located in system memory) plays various support and composition roles. The key to DirectX is how you put all these pieces together into a composition engine.

Compare DirectX to the traditional multimedia world view. In the traditional multimedia view, different media types tend to stay in their own boxes—video goes in one region on the screen, text in another, UI in another, and so on. Mixing tends to be mostly of the overlay variety, like text on top of an image.

DirectX, however, mixes and intermingles media types in almost any way the application developer finds interesting. Video could be a texture for 3D rendering; 2D images could have a z-buffer; sprites and overlays could be the target of 3D rendering. It is up to the application developer to define the use of graphics memory and combine the various functions that can be applied to memory. In the PC world, game developers have been among the first to recognize and exploit this intermingling nature of 3D, frame buffers, and the DirectX architecture. This brings up the historical background to DirectX, which starts with games.

Phase 1: The Game SDK

So where did all this DirectX stuff come from and where is it heading? The DirectX family burst onto the public scene in spring 1995 as the GDK, the Game Developers' Kit or Game SDK. The Game SDK was actually the DirectX technologies, packaged for game developers. In this incarnation, DirectX had three key public goals:

1. Conquer games. Games have been one of the last commercially viable bastions of DOS. Game developers historically have avoided Windows in favor of DOS for to-the-metal graphics development, partly because of *constitutional* distrust of Microsoft and partly because of practical limitations of Windows GDI and WinG for game development. DirectX (nee Game SDK) had a simple goal: Offer game developers a compelling reason to migrate from DOS to Windows95.

2. Kill DOS. Wooing game developers to Windows 95 is a diplomatic way of saying that making DOS irrelevant to new software development has long been a Microsoft agenda.

3. **Cut a "New Deal" with hardware.** Through HAL and HEL, a key goal of the Game SDK was to catalyze a new industry dynamic of hardware innovation and competition. I discuss this DirectX philosophy of HAL and HEL in the upcoming section "HAL and HEL."

Overall, DirectX was enormously successful in achieving these goals.

Phase 2: DirectX as a Direct OS

There is an old saying that in business, you never really win—you just get a chance to play in a bigger league. This is an apt description for what has happened to DirectX after its early success. DirectX was solving problems that were broader than simply games, so two new goals became clear (or original goals lurking behind the Game SDK came into focus).

1. **Become a Direct OS.** In the classic sense, DirectX has moved into an operating system role. It is the code between the worlds of software and hardware.

2. **Provide Internet solutions.** In case you haven't noticed, Microsoft has gotten Internet religion with a vengeance. DirectX, like every other division within Microsoft, has been tasked to take on the Internet. Although the full consequences of this new task are not fully clear as of this writing, you can expect that new features and functionality in the DirectX family will one way or another be aimed at or repurposed for the Internet. For example, DirectPlay is one DirectX effort with clear implications for the Internet. DirectPlay has a strong overlap with Direct3D in the area of multiuser 3D (online games, shared spaces, and so on).

Phase 3: UI?

If the DirectX family continues to evolve successfully, what will be next? It is easy to assume that other Direct technology candidates wait in the wings, as do future versions of the current DirectX family members. But a big task that could remain for DirectX is greater integration into the user interface itself. This kind of integration likely would involve a good deal of time and planning and may well be beyond realistic planning horizons.

HAL and HEL

HAL and HEL are the underpinnings of the DirectX "philosophy." Both are intended to provide a consistent software interface to hardware, thereby emulating in software the missing hardware functionality. The generic DirectX HAL/HEL architecture is shown in Figure 3-4.

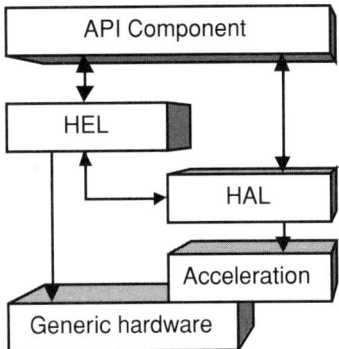

Figure 3-4. The generic DirectX HAL/HEL architecture.

Several tenets derive from the HAL/HEL philosophy. DirectX components are supposed to tell the application which functions are available in hardware and which are available only in software. To further this, HAL drivers are supposed to implement specific functionality, not validate parameters, and just perform the operation requested. Hardware drivers are not supposed to emulate software features that are not accelerated by the hardware. Context information is supposed to be maintained and provided by the API component, not by the HAL.

HAL and HEL are wonderfully elegant concepts that cope with the need to have a consistent interface to hardware while at the same time encouraging innovation and performance competition on the hardware side. By and large, they have worked remarkably well. However, there are inherent limitations and contradictions that you should be aware of, as described below.

First, it is important to recognize that consistency, differentiation, and innovation are incompatible goals. Nevertheless, the HAL/HEL concept involves simultaneously pursuing these three objectives.

1. **Consistency.** An API needs consistency to be viable.
2. **Differentiation.** Hardware makers need to differentiate their products in order to keep their heads above commodity pricing.
3. **Innovation.** Everyone needs innovation to continue.

It is not surprising that these conflicting needs create rough spots in DirectX. Two in particular will affect you as a 3D application developer:

1. **Hardware peeks through.** 3D hardware has a way of peeking through the HAL/HEL layer. For example, when you take a look at some of the hardware capabilities that you can query for in D3D immediate mode, you may start to wonder how you can take advantage of these capabilities without making the distinction of whether or not they are hardware-accelerated.

2. **Not all features are scaleable.** A fundamental premise of the HAL/HEL philosophy is that a software-only implementation is adequate if a feature is not hardware-accelerated. Unfortunately, this is not necessarily the case. For example, say you want antialiased, mipmapped, textured 3D in 24-bit color with alpha-blended overlays. These are hardware-acceleration features that are likely to be supported sooner or later on some 3D boards. Try this in software only, however, and your system is likely to grind to a halt. This is because hardware often can handle multiple features without speed degradation, whereas each additional feature you add in software adds additional overhead on the CPU. So you will have to make your application scaleable if you want it to run on a wide range of hardware. Ideally, you'll give users the option of turning features off and on until they find the level of performance that works for them. You'll have to avoid making your application dependent on a particular hardware-accelerated feature. However, you may find this difficult, since last year's cool demo of an optional feature has a way of quickly becoming a required feature.

Overview of DirectDraw

Although this book is not about DirectDraw, a little DirectDraw background may be helpful. A DirectDraw object represents the display device. You spawn DirectDrawSurface objects off of the DirectDraw object. Each DirectDrawSurface object represents a linear block of display memory that you can modify. The primary surface is what is visible on screen. Your nonvisible surfaces (back buffers) are typically located in graphics memory, although in some cases they could be in system memory. Palettes and Clipper objects are attached to DirectDraw surfaces. A simple overview of DirectDraw is shown in Figure 3-5.

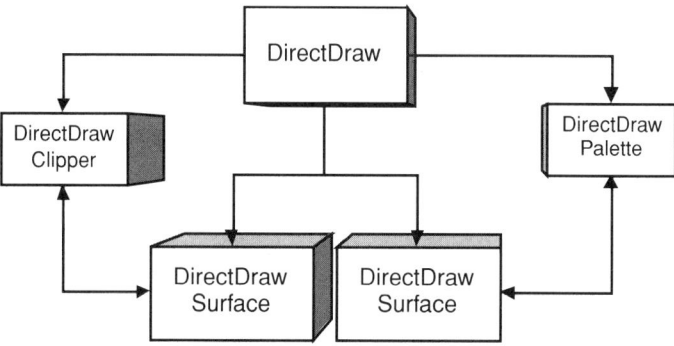

Figure 3-5. DirectDraw overview.

There are several kinds of DirectDraw surfaces that are of particular interest in the context of Direct3D. An **overlay** (same as a sprite) is a surface that when displayed does not alter the pixels of other surfaces behind it. A **texture map** is a surface that Direct3D uses to wrap on 3D objects. A z-buffer is used to represent depth. Each pixel has a 16- or 32-bit value you use to represent depth from the surface of the screen.

Direct3D and the British 3D Invasion

You may associate realtime 3D with super-powerful graphics workstations and assume that Direct3D is some sort of inevitable downward migration of workstation 3D. Actually, Direct3D and the other major PC 3D engines (Renderware and BRender) trace their inspirational origins to a much humbler venue: the English video game scene of the early 80s.

And for all the talk in this book of super-multimedia, hardware-accelerated computers of the future, it is perhaps interesting to note the most humbly inspirational 3D game of all: Elite. A game of wireframe ships and missiles with filled-in circles for suns, Elite inspired a generation of young English hackers to admire and emulate it. Written by David Braben and Ian Bell, it was the must-have 3D game of its day. The original version ran on a BBC Micro, powered by 2 MHz 6502. Yes, 2 megahertz, which overall delivered graphics processing well less than one hundredth of today's almost-ready-for-cool-3D Pentiums. But the BBC Micro had an in-line assembler built into its Basic interpreter and no sprite engine, so wireframe 3D was the way to go.

One member of the Elite-inspired generation was Servan Keondjian, one of the authors of RenderMorphics' Reality Lab along with Doug Rabson. (RenderMorphics was acquired by Microsoft to become Direct3D.) At 14, Servan got a BBC and fell in love with 3D. After college (Imperial College London, Physics) and a stint in a game company (Magnetic Scrolls), Servan played piano in a band at night and programmed his 3D engine by day.

In 1993, Servan, Kate Seekings (St. Hughes College, Oxford University, English Literature, one-time TV sitcom producer), and Doug Rabson (Bristol University, Mathematics and Computer Science) launched RenderMorphics with their savings, encouraged in part by Osman Kent of 3Dlabs, another British-grown 3D company. Seekings subsequently upped her credentials with a quick masters in computer graphics at Middlesex University. It's interesting to note that her 3D rendering library, developed with input from Keondjian and Rabson, was submitted as a school project and was flunked for not following the assigned specs closely enough. Let that be a lesson to professors everywhere!

A whirlwind followed: A stateside trip in late '93 netted a Kaleida license and Virgin as the first game licensee. At the first trade show they attended (SIGGRAPH '94) they were spotted by Microsoft, and the company was acquired in February 1995. Seekings was 28; Keondjian, 25; Rabson, 27.

Direct3D Overview

After the acquisition of RenderMorphics, Microsoft went about integrating Reality Lab into Microsoft's DirectX family of APIs. Along the way, there were some twists and turns. The immediate mode component of Reality Lab absorbed the solution then current for hardware acceleration, 3D-DDI, which was architected by graphics and optimization guru Michael Abrash. (3D-DDI actually lives on, on the NT platform, although it is slated for eventual replacement by an NT version of Direct3D.) The API was migrated to a COM (Component Object Model) architecture and generally nudged, morphed, and evolved.

The final Direct3D architecture ended up as shown in Figure 3-6: The retained mode sits on the immediate mode, which in turn sits on the HAL. The execute buffer (a list of geometry data and commands) is acted upon by transform, lighting, and rasterization modules and is eventually written out to a DirectDraw surface.

The COM Model

COM, the Component Object Model, is Microsoft's standardized calling convention for software components and is used as the calling interface for the Direct3D family. If you have not worked with the COM interface, your initial reaction may be that COM is an unnecessarily complex way of connecting to a set of services. It conjures up images of Microsoft's OLE, of which COM is a small architectural element. And you may have concerns that adding the COM overhead may be counterproductive to the implementation of a high-performance graphics API. As you will see, however, the designers of the retained mode API put a good deal of effort into extracting the benefits of the COM model while avoiding potential overhead side effects. From the retained mode programming view, COM is really just a software component interface and management system.

In COM terms, a software component is simply a chunk of code that provides services through "interfaces." An **interface** is a group of related functions (functions are called *methods* in COM's object-oriented terminology). A COM component is a lot like a C++ object, although you can access only a COM component's methods, never its data. (To get data out of a COM

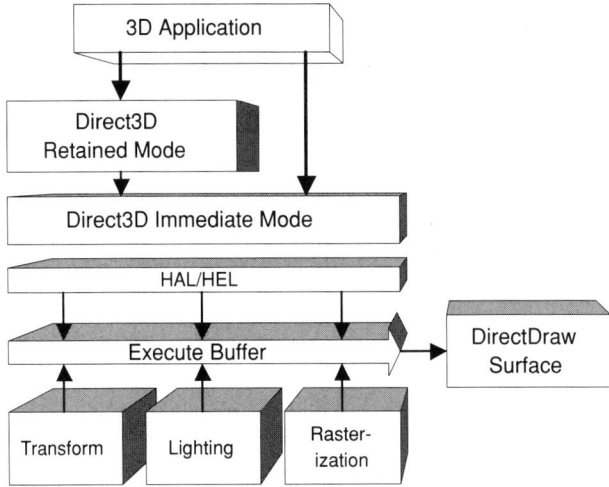

Figure 3-6. Direct3D architecture.

component, you have to call a function that returns data. This is good object-oriented design anyway.)

When you call a method in a COM component, you do not actually call the method directly. Instead, you use double indirection through a virtual function table, also called the v-table or just VTBL. V-tables are the architectural method through which COM achieves numerous design goals, such as managing multiple instances and providing a binary-standard, language-independent calling interface for a given platform (hardware and operating system combination). But from a programming viewpoint, you need to know only that you get a pointer to a function table, which itself contains the pointers to the actual functions.

Standard Interfaces

A COM object can have multiple interfaces. Every COM component is required to have a standard set of methods, called the **IUnknown** base interface. The Release, AddRef, and QueryInterface are the most relevant IUnknown methods for the retained mode; the Initialize method is also implemented but does not actually do anything. Every retained mode component also supports the retained mode common object interface. This interface is a set of functions for things like naming objects and attaching additional application-specific data to them. The COM interface to retained mode components is summarized in Figure 3-7.

Chapter 3 The DirectX Architecture

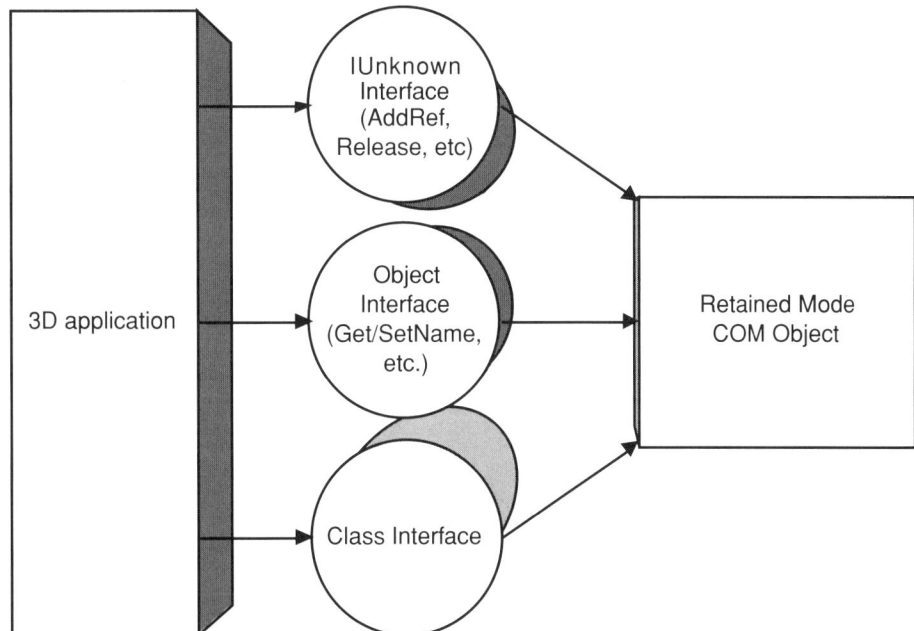

Figure 3-7. The COM interface to retained mode components.

With the Object interface, every retained mode component can have a name and 32 bits of user-defined data attached to it. You get and set the object's name with GetName and SetName, respectively, and get and set the user-specific bits with GetAppData and SetAppData, respectively. Note that these user-specific bits are not interpreted or changed by the API itself, so you could use them for something like storing a pointer to additional data attached to a retained mode component. (But also note that to extract this pointer, you must already have a pointer to the object itself!)

To round out the object-oriented facilities, you can get the name of the class of the component with GetClassName and add a destructor-like function with AddDestroyCallback (and remove the previously added destructor with RemoveDestroyCallback). The destructor function is called when the component's COM reference count drops to 0 and its memory is deleted, so you should not call the methods of the component itself in your destructor function. This means you should not call the GetAppData method in your destroy function to get an object-specific pointer that you have stored with SetAppData. Instead, pass the pointer to your object-specific data as an argument to your destroy function when you call the AddDestroyCallback method. The methods are summarized in Table 3-1.

Table 3-1. Standard methods available for all retained mode components through the IUnknown and Object interfaces

Method	Description
IUnknown Interface	
QueryInterface	The COM method to determine if the object supports a particular interface.
Initialize	The startup initialization of the object (not used by retained mode; objects are initialized automatically when created).
AddRef	The increment reference count (attaches another instance use of the object).
Release	The decrement reference count (when the count goes to 0, the object destroys itself).
Object Interface	
Get/SetName	Gets/sets an identifying name for the object.
GetClassName	Gets the name of the type of the object.
Get/SetAppData	Sets/gets user-defined 32 bits of data attached to the object.
Copy	Creates a copy of a mesh or frame object.
Add/RemoveDestroyCallback	Registers/removes a destructor-like function called after an object is destroyed.

COM and Performance Programming

Does the COM model, with its components, double-indirection virtual tables, and get/set methods, undermine the overall goal of high performance that a 3D API like Direct3D's retained mode must strive for? No. But some hoop-jumping is required. You will also find some resulting awkward constructs, particularly in the area of manipulating blocks of data.

One performance issue concerns component calling overhead. Although this may not be immediately obvious, the component calling overhead, even with double indirection, has an absolutely insignificant effect on overall performance. This is because far more processing cycles are required to render the objects of a scene than are required to traverse the scene graph of objects. It is important to recognize that rendering demands a huge amount of processing. The comparison here is between a handful of cycles per frame (perhaps hundreds for a lot of components) versus the millions of cycles it takes to render the scene.

Two other performance issues worth considering are raised by the retained mode API: the overhead of creating and destroying objects and the overhead of reading data into and out of COM objects. Because you cannot access data directly in a COM component, a block of data (such as the list of vertices) has to be read out of the object, modified, and then passed back in.

Every COM class (not every COM object created from the class) has a unique identifier, called its GUID (globally unique identifier, pronounced goo-id). This GUID is used by the operating system to find the class description in order to create an object instance, which requires checking the system registry and other high overhead events.

Chapter 4

Fundamentals of Realtime Rendering

Earlier in this book, I described the PC industry as a predator. However, when it comes to the adoption of technology, sometimes it seems more like a scavenger, picking over technologies that other industries have already mastered, seeking juicy, easy-to-digest morsels to satisfy its own appetite. Such is the case with adapting the techniques and technologies of realtime 3D to the PC environment of Direct3D.

The fundamental concept of realtime 3D is simple: Mathematically transform the points of a triangle from 3D space to screen coordinates, apply some lighting values, and then draw the triangle on screen. The key issues in doing this, however, center around how to achieve the highest overall image quality and speed within a given set of cost and processing constraints.

It is in this area of seeking techniques to improve the image quality of realtime 3D rendering that PC scavenging most comes into play. Techniques have already been developed for existing 3D environments such as flight simulators. These techniques include level-of-detail, mipmapping, and filtering. But technologies always have a way of being application-specific in their implementation, and when a technology is adapted to new environments, even slight differences can get magnified. So this chapter is in essence about how PCs generally and Direct3D specifically are adapting and using traditional realtime 3D technologies and techniques, particularly these:

- Execute buffers and frame trees
- The 3D pipeline

- Level of detail
- Texturing and filtering
- Mipmaps

Finally, I look at the concept of progressive meshing, which may be the PC era's first substantive contribution to realtime 3D.

Key Concepts

Here are some key starting concepts you need in order to understand realtime 3D rendering:

- **Rendering means drawing. Rendering** is the process of drawing 3D data to an output device. For realtime rendering, this output device is a block of memory that will be subsequently displayed on screen. The basic technique is to build a complete image for each frame as a separate buffer and then flip (or blit) that frame to the screen.

- **Rendering is a pipeline.** Rendering is a multistep process, generally referred to as a *pipeline,* that is, several processing steps are needed to render 3D data. Graphics accelerators (chips other than the CPU) can speed one or more steps. The key stages of the rendering pipeline are geometry transform (converting *x,y,z* points in 3D space into their corresponding 2D *x,y* screen coordinates), lighting (calculating color on surfaces based on lights in the scene), and rasterization (drawing triangles into graphics memory). Each stage can be broken down further, but this should give you a basic conceptual framework.

- **Rendering is triangle-based.** In Direct3D, what gets rendered are triangles, points, and lines. Whatever kind of 3D data you want to display, such as curved surfaces, multisided data, or voxel data, gets decomposed to these primitives in the rendering pipeline. There is one big "out" in that you can write whatever you want directly to the frame buffer, using whatever 3D or 2D techniques to create the effect you are seeking.

- **Execute buffer = low-level render data.** Also known as the *display list,* the **execute buffer** is a block of memory that contains a low-level description of 3D data and what commands to do to it. The execute buffer is what the renderer "renders."

- **Frame tree = high-level render data.** Also known as the *scene graph,* the **frame tree** is a hierarchical organization of 3D data before it is reduced to an execute buffer.

- **Lighting is not shading; shading is not lighting.** Lighting is the calculation of color at a particular point on 3D geometry. For practical purposes, this means calculating light at each vertex. Shading is the rasterization technique that interpolates color value across the face of a triangle as it is drawn. In other words, shading is filling in the triangles when they are drawn on the screen. The distinction between lighting and shading is subtle and arbitrary and has nothing to do with how light works in the real world. It is simply the result of how the 3D pipeline gets organized.

The Frame Tree

The frame tree, also called a scene graph, is the most common organizational structure for 3D scene data. What is in the frame tree and how you use it are also fundamental issues of 3D application design. A question you will face as you address this issue is whether you should think of your application as mixed into, or sitting on top of, the frame tree. I talk further about this in Chapter 9. For now, focus on the implication of the frame tree for the rendering side of things. You can think of a frame tree in a couple of ways, as shown in Figure 4-1.

What makes the frame tree so fundamental? Even if you are using an immediate mode, the concept of a frame tree is still very important. This is because child nodes inherit their location in 3D space from their parents. This means renderers are "state based"—the state of the renderer, at least the 3D coordinates, is based on what part of the tree has already been traversed.

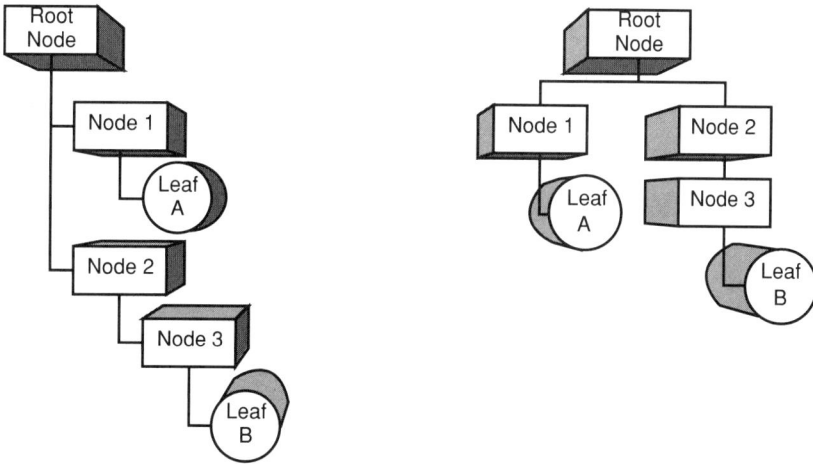

Figure 4-1. Two ways to conceptualize a frame tree structure.

The Rendering Pipeline

Figure 4-2 shows the basic elements of a 3D pipeline. I cover this pipeline more in depth later in the book, particularly in Chapter 8, where I discuss Direct3D's immediate mode. The broad view, however, is that triangles are first transformed, then lit, and then rasterized.

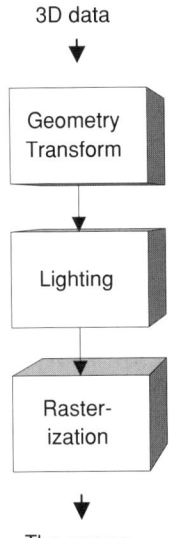

Figure 4-2. The 3D pipeline.

The three-step 3D pipeline shown in the figure may seem a gross oversimplification, but it is actually quite a good description to keep in mind. Making this three-step pipeline work well (or getting control of one of the three steps) is at the heart of much of what goes on in building the 3D infrastructure.

Z-buffering

If triangles are simply drawn to a memory buffer, then how does the renderer know which triangle should be on top if there are several triangles covering the same pixel on screen? There is no good way, but there are two adequate ways that offer competing trade-offs: z-buffering and z-sorting. Both are brute force algorithms, but they work quickly enough to handle the enormous volume of 3D data that must go through the 3D pipeline.

Z-sorting, also known as the painters algorithm, takes the approach that the rasterization module should not have to care about triangle visibility. The triangles are simply passed through the pipeline sorted in reverse-z order (back-to-front as you look at the screen). The closer triangles are drawn on top of the ones that are farther away.

Z-sorting works fine for many cases. The retained mode code handles sorting the triangles of each mesh and must re-sort each time the camera or object moves. Z-sorting breaks down, however, when meshes collide in space. Now the triangles of both meshes must be z-sorted together or things will not look right. Direct3D's retained mode punts on this, so you have to keep your meshes apart if you use z-sorting. Moreover, there are cases in which a triangle can be both in front of and behind another triangle at the same time. Think of a little triangle floating next to a big triangle that is slanted away from you—part of the big triangle is in front of the little triangle, and part of it is behind. Which one gets drawn first? The same problem exists if two triangles intersect in 3D space.

Direct3D also supports z-buffering. Z-buffering is a fast, brute force method of throwing a lot of memory at solving the which-triangle-on-top problem. Z-buffering is shown in Figure 4-3.

The idea of z-buffering is simply to have the rasterization code check for each pixel it writes to see whether a closer pixel has already been written. If so, the rasterizer stops further processing on the pixel that is farther away.

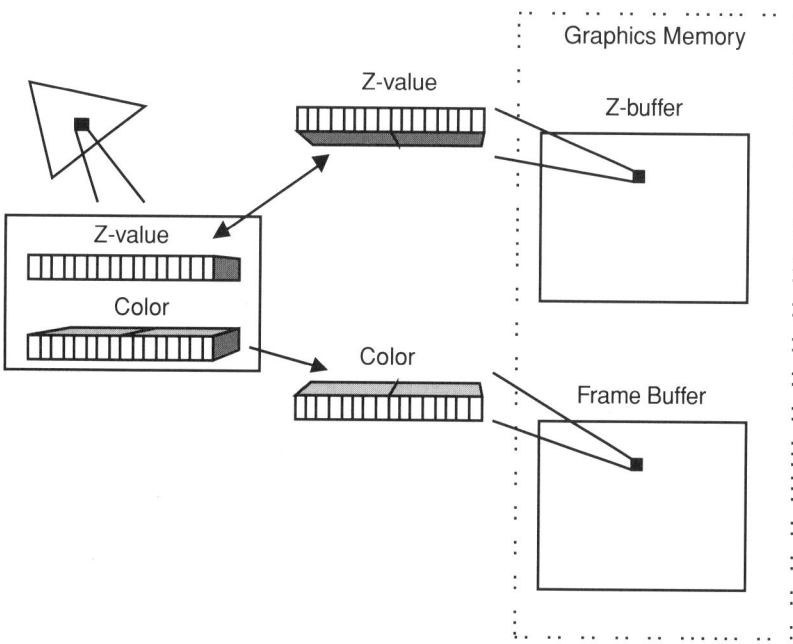

Figure 4-3. Z-buffering.

Z-buffering requires keeping a depth value for each pixel on the screen. (A depth value of 16 bits is the norm on PCs, but some workstations use 24 or 32 bits.) The block of memory that contains this per-pixel z depth information is called the z-buffer.

The benefit of z-buffering is that all pixels are drawn correctly all the time, with little preprocessing. It still makes sense to sort the individual triangles, though, but this time in front-to-back order, the opposite of z-sorting. It is faster to have pixels fail the z test than pass because you eliminate further processing steps, and it is faster to read and compare with the z-buffer than to read, compare, and write a z-buffer value.

Lights

Lights change the color of vertices. The lighting module takes the *normal vector* of a vertex and, based on its angle with a light source, determines how much color and intensity from the light source to apply to that vertex.

So what is the normal vector of a vertex? Figure 4-4 shows the idea. Each triangle faces a certain direction. Draw a line facing out perpendicular to the face of the triangle; this is the **normal vector,** or just the **normal,** to the triangle's face. Average the normals of each triangle adjacent to a vertex (i.e., use that vertex as one of its three corners), and you obtain the normal for the vertex. In Figure 4-4, the small solid arrows are the normals of each triangle face. The dotted arrow is the normal of the faces (i.e., it is the average direction of all the solid arrows).

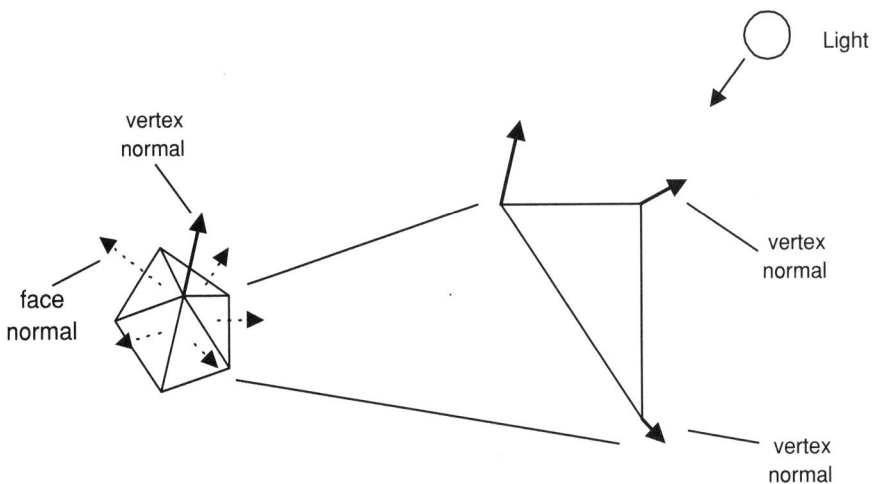

Figure 4-4. Light calculation.

The math involved in this is not something the 3D application developer has to do; the lighting code does it. However, the basic concepts of vectors, normals, and their relationships comprise a general technique that has application to a wide range of 3D application development.

Shading

Shading is filling in the inside of a polygon when it is drawn to the screen. There are several levels of shading quality, starting with wireframe and progressing to flat, then Gouraud, and then Phong.

- **Wireframe.** Displays only the lines between vertices.
- **Flat shading.** Also called faceted shading. Colors each triangle with a single, constant color.
- **Gouraud shading.** Also called intensity interpolation shading or color interpolation shading. Gouraud shading is shown in Figure 4-5. The color at point S on the triangle is set to an interpolated value between Color A and Color B. If S is halfway across the triangle in the x-direction, it is halfway between Colors A and B. In turn, Color A is interpolated in the y-direction between Colors 1 and 2 and likewise for Color B (between Colors 1 and 3).

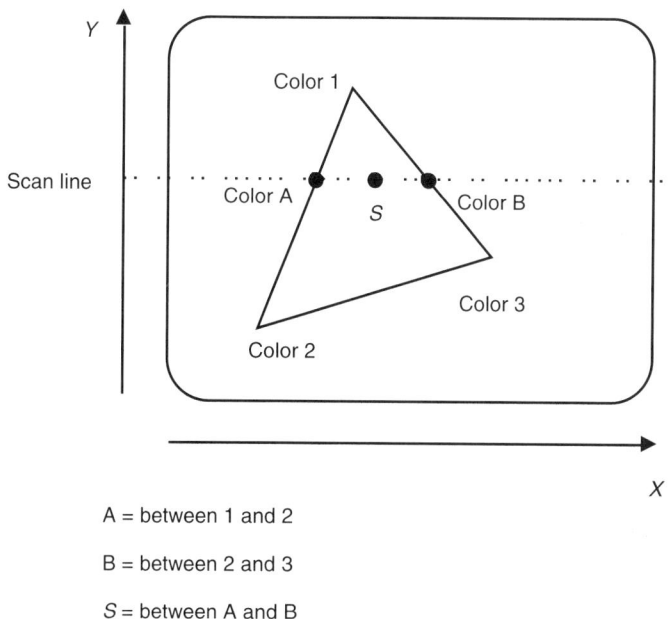

A = between 1 and 2

B = between 2 and 3

S = between A and B

Figure 4-5. Gouraud shading.

- **Phong shading.** Takes Gouraud shading one step further. Instead of the color values at the vertices being interpolated, the normal vectors are interpolated as shown in Figure 4-6. The difference may seem subtle; after all, the vertices are normals used to calculate the colors at the vertices in the first place. The difference, however, is that with Phong shading you can include lighting calculations at the per-pixel level that provide better-looking specular highlights. Phong shading was scheduled to be in Direct3D but was dropped late in the beta cycle. Flags are included in data structures referencing Phong shading, but for now you can ignore them. Microsoft has stated that Phong shading will be supported in a future version of Direct3D.

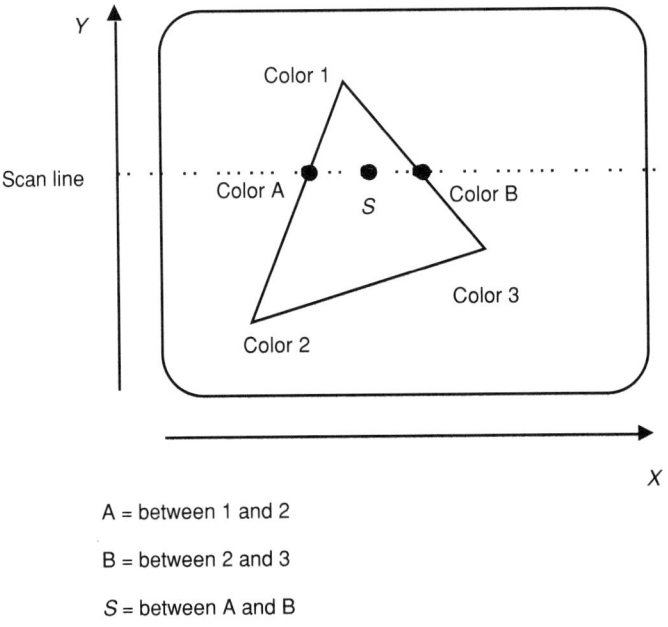

Figure 4-6. Phong shading.

Meshes

A **mesh** is a collection of triangles. In 3D they are the main thing you actually see. Direct3D uses the common convention of breaking meshes into two parts: a vertex table and a face table, as shown in Figure 4-7.

Vertices describe the *x*, *y*, and *z* points and the color of points in 3D space (they also have normal vectors attached to them for shading purposes). The face table simply points into the vertex table by index to define a triangle.

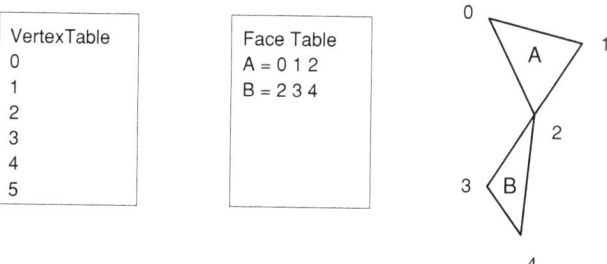

Figure 4-7. Meshes.

This structure has the advantage of making it easy to organize the reuse of a vertex by several triangles. Each triangle can simply use an index pointer to the same vertex.

LOD

LOD means level of detail. It is a major technique used in workstation 3D simulations to improve image quality while conserving polygon budgets. The idea is very simple: When an object is far from the camera, a version of the object with fewer polygons is displayed. This means that someone has to build multiple versions of the object in a modeling package, some of which support this feature with built-in polygon reduction.

LOD increases the overall size of the 3D data because you need multiple versions of an object. This adds additional memory demand and slows transmission over the Internet. Still, by using LOD for effective polygon budget management you can dramatically improve the complexity of the scene.

Direct3D does not support LOD directly, although some other retained mode 3D APIs do. You can implement LOD yourself by switching manually between different versions of mesh objects.

Color Models

There are two ways of representing colors: RGB and ramp, as shown in Figure 4-8. RGB color is what you want; ramp color is what you may get stuck with. RGB color is a lot easier to handle in pixel processing. The one exception is texture compression, which converts an RGB texture into a paletized (ramp) color model to save graphics memory. However, RGB color requires at least 16 bits per pixel, so it is slower to render. But the trend is toward favoring RGB over ramp color. On the plus side, 3D chips seem to provide RGB color at the speed of ramp color, and graphics memory prices continue to drop.

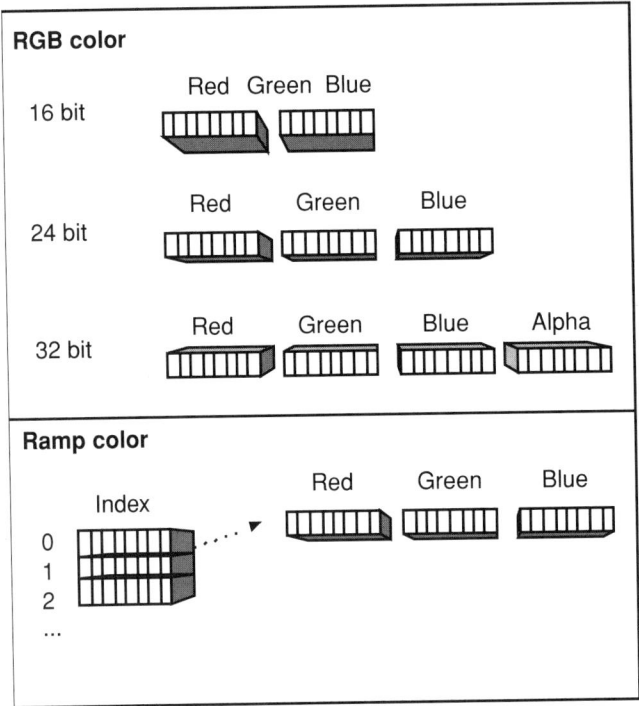

Figure 4-8. RGB and ramp color models.

Texture Mapping

Texture mapping substitutes pixels for polygons. The renderer simply wraps a texture image around a mesh in the rasterization phase of the 3D pipeline. In theory, this simply means that, for each pixel on the screen, the renderer figures out the corresponding texel in the texture map. Think of a texel as a pixel in a texture map.

The theory is that there is much less overhead in displaying a set of pixels than in processing a polygon. But even more important, the artistic quality of the rendered image can be dramatically improved by the artistic quality of the texture map you use. However, the processing and system resources involved in having a renderer do a good job of displaying a texture map can be surprisingly high. The degree of texture rendering quality is defined by how much memory, processing, and bandwidth you are willing to allocate to the texture filtering task.

The entry level of decent quality texture mapping is perspective correction. Some early boards did not do perspective corrections, and the results were dreadful. The only fix is to break polygons into small enough sizes so that the bad effect is reduced. Perspective correction requires a per-pixel divide operation. This is computationally intense and only the beginning of the process of improving texture image quality.

Texture Filtering Techniques

In filtering techniques, textures start to come into their own as an image-quality enhancing rendering technique. The most common filtering techniques are summarized in Table 4-1.

Table 4-1. Texture filtering techniques

Technique	What It Does
Point sampling (nearest neighbor)	Chooses the nearest texel in the texture map.
Linear (bilinear filtering)	Interpolates (takes the average of) the 4 nearest texels.
Mipmapping nearest (mipmapping)	Point sample (nearest texel) in one mipmap.
Linear mip	Takes 1 pixel from each of two mipmaps; averages the two.
Linear mip nearest	Bilinear filter (4 texels) on one mipmap.
Trilinear mipmapping	Bilinear filter on two mipmaps (4 texels each), average 2 resulting texels.

Point Sampling

Point sampling is the simplest method of using a texture. The rendering software simply calculates the single pixel in the texture map that is closest to the location to be displayed on screen. Point sampling produces the lowest quality image. As objects move on screen, they tend to sparkle and textures appear to crawl.

Linear (Bilinear Filtering)

In bilinear filtering, four adjacent texture pixels are sampled and the weighted average of their values taken. Bilinear filtering is the entry level of filtering. Bilinear filtering softens a texture and makes its edges look less jagged.

Bilinear filtering works best for objects that are close to midway, like terrains and walls. It makes textures look fuzzy instead of chunky when you look at them close up. It also makes small textures (textures made of a small number of pixels) look reasonably good.

This type of filtering requires nothing of the 3D application programmer—think of it as something you simply turn on or off. It happens when the rasterization code gets the data it needs from the texture map. There is a performance hit in software-only rendering, but any hardware accelerator should be able to provide bilinear filtering with little system overhead.

Mipmapping

Mipmapping is really level-of-detail management for textures. Mip stands for *multum in parvo,* that is, many things in a small place. A **mipmap** is a sequence of textures representing the same image, each of which is a progressively lower resolution, prefiltered representation of the image. Each lower resolution version of the original image is one quarter the size of the previous one. If you add up all of them, the memory overhead is one third more than a regular texture map.

Mipmapping makes distant objects look better. This is because if your texture has far more texels than corresponding rendered pixels on the screen (the case when your object is far away), the renderer cannot find a single texel (or block of four texels, in the case of bilinear filtering) that will accurately correspond to the pixel to be displayed on the screen. The four mipmap levels shown in Table 4-1 provide a more appropriate texel representation of your texture map for these object-in-the distance situations. Mipmapping is a big deal on traditional military flight simulators. If you pay a bizillion dollars for a superfancy flight simulator, you can bet everyone will expect those planes to look good in the distance and not show image artifacting as they move closer.

For straight, unfiltered mipmapping (mip nearest), the renderer simply chooses which mipmap to use. But the image quality of mipmapping improves if additional filtering is applied, as summarized in Table 4-1. Trilinear mipmapping is considered the top-level texture filtering. (Although some people talk of a next generation of anisotropic filtering or other techniques, none have appeared in volume as of this writing.) Trilinear mipmapping, however, taxes the PC architecture because it requires so many memory read and write operations per pixel actually drawn.

The traditional organization of a mipmap is shown in Figure 4-9.

Mipmaps in Direct3D

You can create and manipulate a mipmap as a DirectDraw surface for use with Direct3D. However, its organization differs somewhat from the traditional mipmap and is worth taking time to examine. The primary reason for this difference is the need to fit mipmaps into DirectDraw's basic structure

Chapter 4 Fundamentals of Realtime Rendering

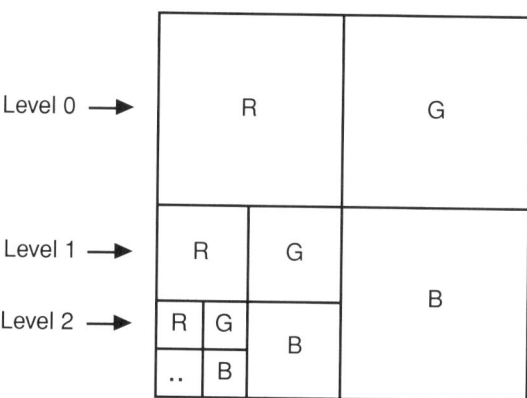

Figure 4-9. Traditional organization of a mipmap.

for textures, rather than adding a special DirectDraw mipmap data structure. The actual data is identical; it's just laid out differently.

DirectDraw mipmaps are a chain of attached texture surfaces, with each mipmap level represented by a different surface. The highest resolution texture is at the head of the chain. Each surface has the next level down of mipmap surface attached to it, down to the lowest resolution level of the mipmap. Each level in the mipmap chain is a power of two smaller than the previous level. In other words, it is a quarter of the size of the next largest, just as with a regular mipmap. But the DirectDraw mipmap chain is not broken into its RGB components; it is just a standard DirectDraw format.

Recall that the DirectDraw concept is to build a back buffer that is flipped to the front, viewable buffer when drawing is complete. This idea has been carried over to DirectDraw mipmaps, thereby allowing you to have animatable mipmaps, with each level having its own back buffer. I am sure there is probably also some other clever use for DirectDraw's animatable, back-buffered mipmap textures chains beyond 3D rendering, but I haven't thought of what it might be. DirectDraw's organization of mipmap surfaces is shown in Figure 4-10.

To create a single level of a mipmap texture surface, you would simply use DirectDraw's IDirectDraw::CreateSurface method and specify the DDSCAPS_MIPMAP surface capability. You would also need to specify DDSCAPS_TEXTURE because DirectDraw expects mipmaps to be textures. You can build an entire chain of mipmaps with a single call to IDirectDraw::CreateSurface. Or you can build a chain manually by multiple calls to the IDirectDrawSurface::AddAttachedSurface method.

The following code example shows how you could build a chain of five mipmap levels of sizes 256 × 256, 128 × 128, 64 × 64, 32 × 32, and 16 × 16:

```
DDSURFACEDESC ddsd;
LPDIRECTDRAWSURFACE lpDDMipMap;
ZeroMemory (&ddsd, sizeof(ddsd));
ddsd.dwSize = sizeof(ddsd);
ddsd.dwFlags = DDSD_CAPS | DDSD_MIPMAPCOUNT;
ddsd.dwMipMapCount = 5;
ddsd.ddsCaps.dwCaps = DDSCAPS_TEXTURE |
DDSCAPS_MIPMAP | DDSCAPS_COMPLEX;
ddsd.dwWidth = 256UL;
ddsd.dwHeight = 256UL;
ddres = lpDD->CreateSurface(&ddsd, &lpDDMipMap);
```

If you omit the number of mipmap levels, the IDirectDraw::CreateSurface method will create a chain of surfaces, each a power of two smaller than the previous one, down to the smallest possible size. If you omit the width and height, IDirectDraw::CreateSurface will create the number of levels you specify, with sizes going up from 1 × 1.

To make your mipmap chain flippable (i.e., to have a front and back buffer for each level), you have to do it manually. Either you can build a mipmap chain and manually attach back buffers with the IDirectDrawSurface::AddAttachedSurface method, or you can create a sequence of flippable front/back buffer-attached surface pairs and then build the mipmap with IDirectDrawSurface::AddAttachedSurface.

Once you have your chain of mipmap surfaces, you can walk through the chain using IDirectDrawSurface::GetAttachedSurface method, specifying the DDSCAPS_MIPMAP and DDSCAPS_TEXTURE capability flags.

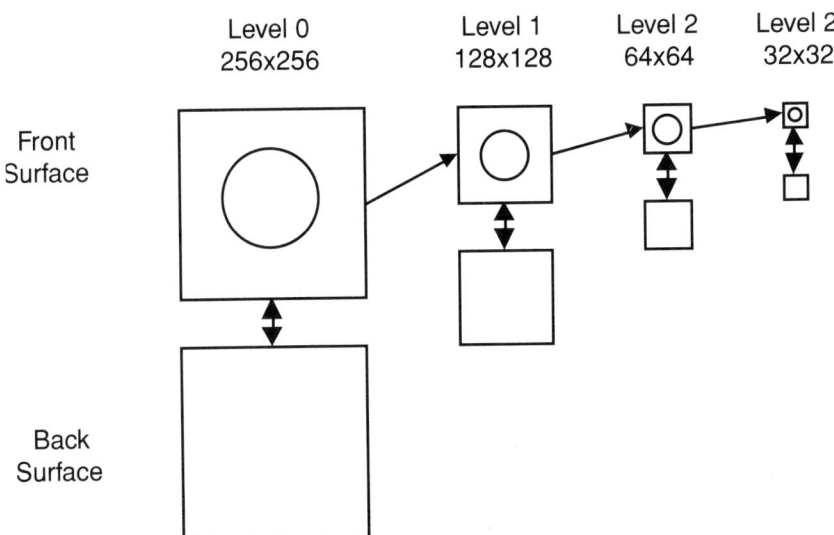

Figure 4-10. **DirectDraw organization of mipmap surfaces.**

Other Rendering Features

Rounding out the standard quality-improving rendering features are alpha blending, antialiasing, and fog and depth cueing.

- **Alpha blending.** Alpha blending is the blending of two colors based on a transparency value. Think of the transparency value as an opacity value—it is simply the opposite way of saying the same thing. Alpha values are stored either for an entire block of memory or on a per-pixel basis.

- **Antialiasing.** Antialiasing is a technique to remove the stair-step jaggies on the edges of pixel images. The key antialiasing technique is oversampling. The renderer keeps track of things at the subpixel level and then filters up to the pixel level upon display.

- **Fog and depth cueing.** Fog and depth cueing are really the same thing: A color is blended in based on z depth. In fact, on some rasterizing chips you can do one or the other, but not both at the same time. For fog, you would probably blend in more white with z depth. With depth cueing, you would darken objects with z depth to make them seem to fade away.

The Next Step: Progressive Transmission?

The demands of the Internet, online gaming, and quality-hungry 3D application design are pushing for even more sophisticated, integrated, and versatile concepts of level of detail than have been traditionally delivered by flight and military simulation applications. Traditional level of detail and mipmapping work well for fixed objects like airplanes as they move from the horizon to firing range. But what if you want a super-realistic virtual human to be viewed on your Web page? Is there a different set of patterns, assumptions, and basic requirements at work?

As a 3D application developer, you should be aware that numerous efforts are underway to deliver a new generation of LOD-related functionality in a progressive transmission framework. Many developers would like 3D models to be as progressively transmissable as progressive GIF files, which appear to come into focus with each transmission pass as you load a Web page. Progressive transmission restirs the traditional pot of level of detail and mipmapping. If you just send successive levels of geometric detail, you end up sending multiple versions of the same object, hardly an efficient approach in the bandwidth-constrained Internet era. Mipmaps contain less overhead (one third less than a full-size texture) but offer little in the way of progressive transmission (or compression) of large textures.

I won't hesitate to guess what will come of the desire to add progressive transmission as a core quality feature in the design of realtime 3D rendering systems. You will find actively debated surface techniques, from traditional bezier patches to exotic and little-known subdivision surfaces, wavelet compression for textures and geometry, and a host of other possible techniques. Although sophisticated new techniques often take years to mature, the Web-speed Internet era has contributed to the rushing of many new technologies to market.

Chapter 5

3D Hardware

Nowhere have the ideas of realtime 3D, DirectX, and the potential of a desktop supercomputer had greater impact than on the design architecture of PCs themselves. In this chapter, I examine the hardware implications of realtime 3D on PCs.

Why You Should Care About Hardware

The technical computer world is made of two kinds of people: software and hardware people. And except for "system software" people who design hardware/software interfaces like drivers and operating systems, the two kinds often don't have a lot to talk about with each other. Most software people spend their time working at the level of APIs, protocols, operating system calls, authoring tools, and languages and algorithms. Their level of familiarity with hardware is usually limited to some specific information about how CPUs work. They may also have some familiarity with programming hardware registers as memory locations that are read to and written from to make a piece of hardware go (although the registers are usually not hardware at all, but a software driver's idea of an interface to hardware).

But 3D changes the dynamics of the traditional conversation between software and hardware people. If you are interested in 3D application programming, becoming familiar with hardware is essential. Doing so will help you understand not only what kind of features 3D acceleration can and cannot offer, but also the performance limitations of software-only 3D rendering. A greater understanding of 3D acceleration will help you understand where computers are heading and what you should plan for.

The PCI Bus

On PCs, graphics has always been treated as a peripheral. In the super-multimedia era, this just will not cut it. The question is, what will eventually be done about it. This problem is likely to continue to dog the design of PCs for some time, as a new generation of video peripherals (i.e., TV) will bring even more bandwidth demands to the PCI bus. Figure 5-1 shows the layout of a PCI system.

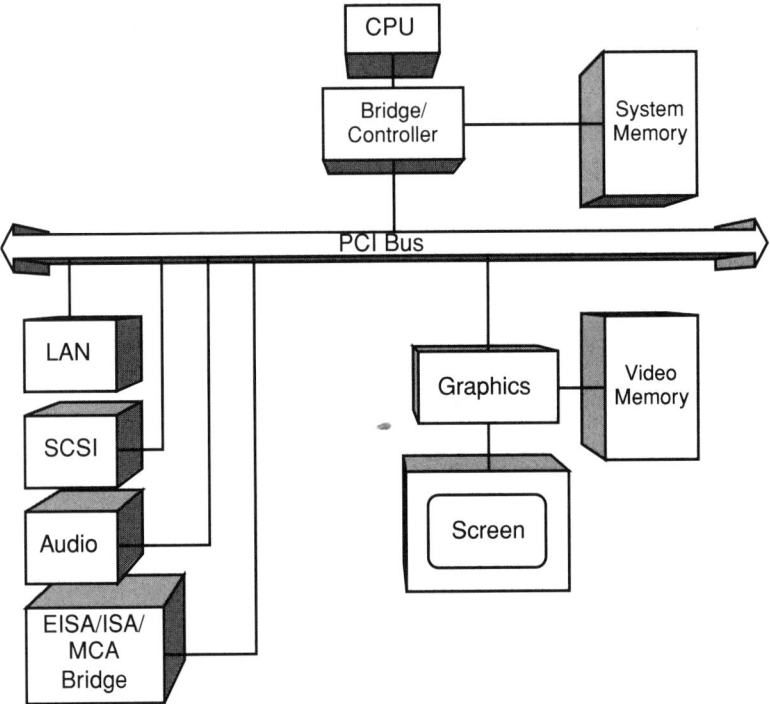

Figure 5-1. Layout of a PCI system.

Bandwidth is perhaps the key issue facing the advancement of 3D graphics performance on PCs. The theoretical maximum data transfer rate for the ISA bus was 8.33 MB/sec (4.165 million transfers per second over a 16-bit data path). EISA brought out a 32-bit data bit, thus expanding the theoretical maximum transfer rate to 33 MB/sec. Microchannel supports some 40 MB/sec.

When PCI offered 132 MB/sec, many people felt this would be plenty for years. It wasn't. It failed to take into account that graphics chips can access local graphics memory at rates of 100 to 1,000 MB/sec. With 3D, these chips need this kind of speed.

3D Thumbnail Calculations

To understand the demand of 3D rendering on bus bandwidth, first consider the general relationship between 3D rendering and graphics memory, as shown in Figure 5-2.

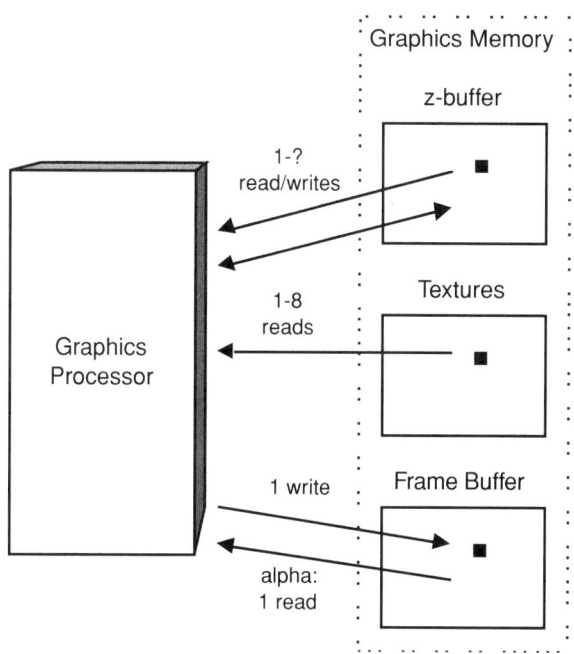

Figure 5-2. Graphics memory access by graphics processor.

Simply updating the graphics memory 30 frames/sec requires some 18 million bytes per second of bandwidth:

$$640 \times 480 = 307{,}200 \text{ pixels/frame} \times 16 \text{ bits/pixel}$$
$$= 614{,}400 \text{ bytes/frame} \times 30 \text{ frames/sec}$$
$$= 18.432 \text{ million bytes/sec}$$

But when you add the texturing, filtering, and alpha processing functions, the amount can balloon to well beyond what PCI can handle:

18.432 million bytes/sec
　× (1 frame buffer write
　+ 2 z-buffer read-writes
　+ 8 MIP texture read-writes
　+ 1 alpha read)
　= 221.118 million read-writes/sec

And we haven't added PCI bus traffic for sound, streaming video data from a CD, and the overhead of transferring vertex data across the PCI bus. Further, remember that the maximum PCI numbers are theoretical maximums; systems actually function at a much lower rate. Finally, remember that other peripherals such as hard disks and CDs share the PCI bus.

Here is the kicker: PCI can't handle individual read-writes at anything like these speeds! The PCI bus is designed for burst transfer of blocks of data, not for many individual read-writes of data. There is a 60-ns wait between each transfer operation. This latency is trivial if you are transferring large blocks of data, but it kills this kind of use of the PCI bus. And not all graphics data fits in 32-bit blocks; z-buffers are 16 bits, while colors are 16, 24, or 32 bits.

Add to this equation the balancing of geometry calculations that typically happen on the CPU and the small amount of texture memory that is actually available on a typical graphics board and, inside your PC, you have virtual bandwidth gridlock as it tries to handle 3D graphics.

Accelerated Graphics Port

Something has to give. Many companies have proposed different systems that would allow graphics chips to have direct access to main memory in order to offload potential graphics.

Intel has proposed at least a partial solution to the bus bandwidth bottleneck with AGP, Accelerated Graphics Port. The layout of an AGP system is shown in Figure 5-3.

AGP is a special-purpose graphics port that is supposed to supplement the PCI bus by offloading graphics-related bus traffic to a special point-to-point connector. It is scheduled to appear on PCs in early 1997, with volume shipments in the second half of that year. The AGP port is physically separate from the PCI bus and uses a separate connector. There would still be a frame buffer (i.e., dedicated graphics memory) because, unlike under some unified memory architecture proposals, the entire frame buffer is not moved into system memory.

In theory, the AGP port could allow z-buffering, alpha blending, and texturing operations to happen in system memory. It also could allow system

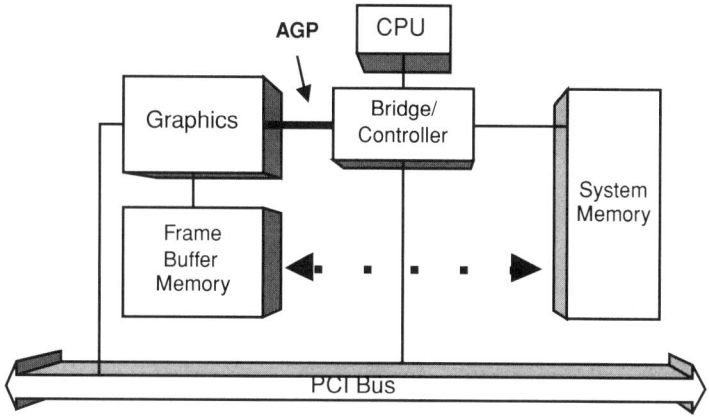

Figure 5-3. Layout of an AGP system.

memory to be dynamically reallocated for graphics purposes. More likely, however, the AGP port will end up supporting texture memory swapping functions between system and graphics memory and will handle the transmission of vertex data from the CPU to the graphics processor.

So that you can get a better sense of what all this is about, I'll examine a single 3D chip in more depth. I'll use 3Dlabs' Permedia 3D chip, a successful consumer 3D chip that is used by Creative Labs and others, and its geometry-helper chip, the Delta.

The Permedia 3D Chip in Depth

The Permedia family of chips is a useful reference chip because it is intended as both a 3D game chip and a general-purpose ("pervasive") 3D solution. Also, since 3Dlabs also produces the GLINT 3D chip, which was originally designed to accelerate OpenGL, the Permedia chip has some OpenGL concepts.

There are two standard layouts for a Permedia-based board, as shown in Figures 5-4 and 5-5. The standard layout in Figure 5-4 is aimed at low-cost, high-volume game and multimedia uses. It is based on a Permedia chip, no Delta chip, and 2 to 4 MB of SGRAM memory (Synchronous Graphics RAM, which costs less than VRAM and is available from numerous RAM producers).

The Delta Chip

I start with the professional layer. This layer uses an additional chip, called the Delta chip, as an intermediate processing chip between the CPU. Starting with the Delta chip will help lead you into the rasterization phase because the

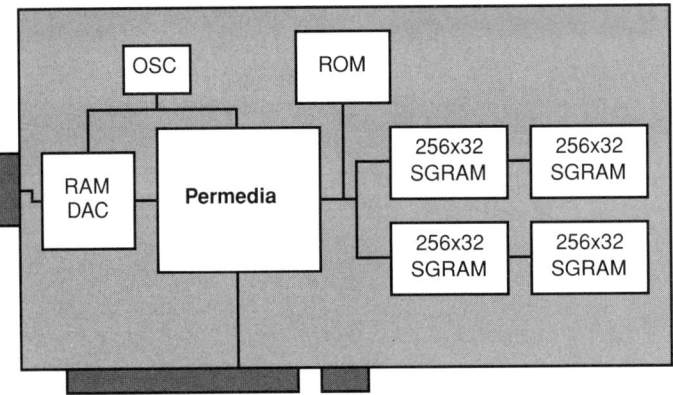

Figure 5-4. Standard Permedia board layout: 2–4 MB SGRAM, no Delta chip.

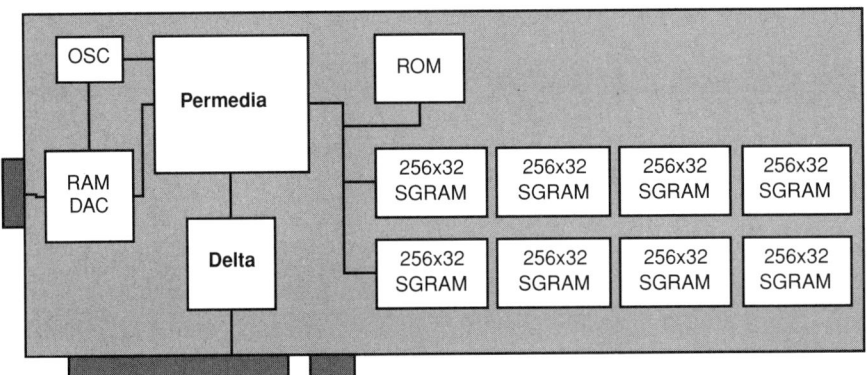

Figure 5-5. Power Permedia board layout: 4–8 MB SGRAM plus Delta chip.

functions of the Delta chip are a little easier to understand at first than the hard-core rasterization functions.

The Delta chip is intended to break a bottleneck in 3D geometry processing on the CPU by offloading from the CPU some time-consuming set-up operations such as slope calculations and conversion between floating-point and fixed-point number formats. In essence, the Delta is a "rasterization preprocessor"; it simply sets up data into a format that the Permedia chip requires. Without a Delta chip, the CPU would perform these set-up functions.

Figure 5-6 gives a programmer's view of the purpose of the Delta chip. From this view, the Delta chip is a "front end" to the Permedia rasterization. (Actually, it also can be a front end to 3Dlabs' higher-end, OpenGL-oriented GLINT chip.) There is one inaccuracy in this illustration. The Delta chip actually communicates with the Permedia chip through the PCI bus. I'll leave it to you to draw an illustration that illustrates this!

Chapter 5 3D Hardware

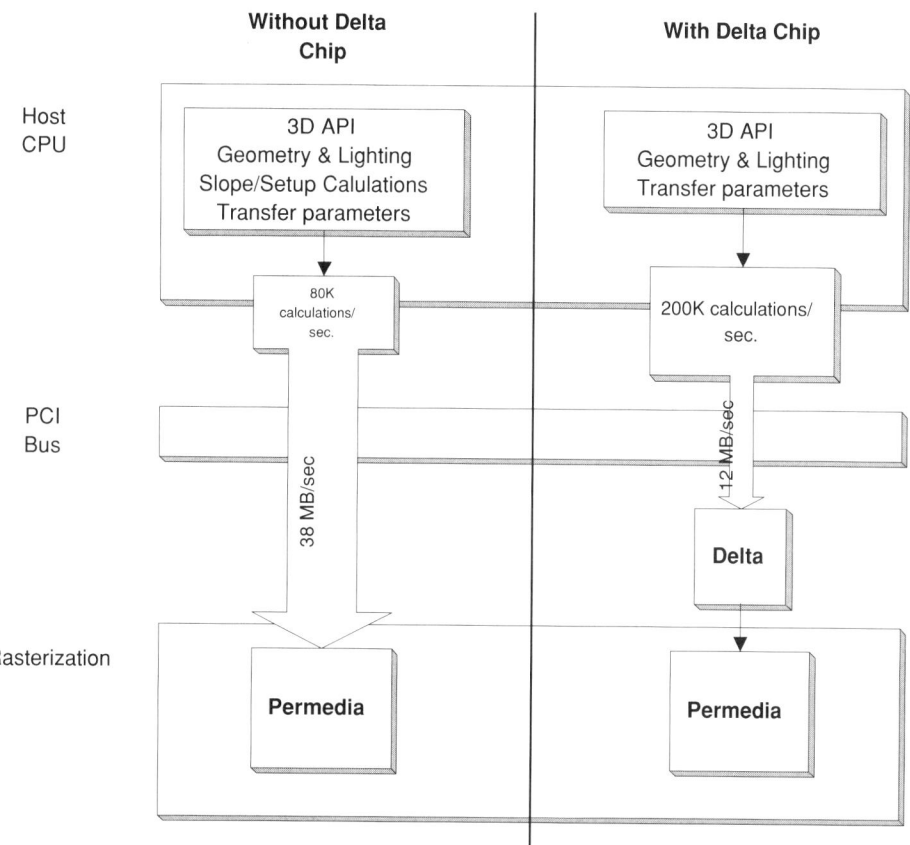

Figure 5-6. PCI bus and the Delta chip.

In essence, the Delta chip accepts data on one triangle at a time, specifically the coordinates of the vertices plus color, depth, fog, and texture parameters. It can accept numbers in either floating-point or fixed-point format, but does its internal calculations in floating-point format. It then outputs results in fixed-point format (which is the format that the Permedia chip needs; I cover that format shortly). Finally the Delta chip passes on set-up information. I cover this set-up information soon as well.

Delta Programming Model

To the programmer, the Delta chip looks like a set of registers (41 32-bit-wide memory locations). You fill in the registers to make things happen.

The first set of registers (13 32-bit values) are three blocks called the *vertex stores*. There is one vertex store for each of the three vertices of a triangle (you guessed it; the Delta chip is a triangle processor!). You fill in the values for each of the three vertices of the triangle you want to display and then tell the chip to process the vertices and pass information on to the Permedia chip.

Table 5-1 shows the register block that represents a single vertex of a triangle. Each register offset represents a 32-bit parameter, and each 32-bit parameter value can be in either fixed-point or floating-point format. Starting from the bottom, the coordinate values are the x-, y-, and z-values of the vertex as it is to appear on the screen. The z-value is a scaled value from 0 (closest) to 1 (farthest away). Color values are the red, green, blue, and alpha (amount of transparency) values for the triangle at that vertex, each scaled from 0 to 1. For textures, s and t are the corresponding locations in the texture map for the triangle at the vertex (the letters u and v are sometimes used when referring to texture map coordinates). Ks is the amount of specular (reflective) light at the vertex; Kd is the amount of diffuse (ambient) light.

Table 5-1. The vertex store register group of the Delta chip

Category	Register Offset	Parameter
Texture	0	s
	1	t
	2	q
	3	Ks
	4	Kd
Color	5	red
	6	green
	7	blue
	8	alpha
Fog	9	f
Coordinate	10	x
	11	y
	12	z

Once you fill in the vertex values for three vertices (plus some other general values in the Permedia chip registers, which I get to in a moment), you fill in another register with a DrawTriangle command. Then, voila! Instant triangle image in your frame buffer!

If you want to display a chain or mesh of triangles, then for each subsequent triangle you replace one of the three vertex store register blocks to define an adjacent triangle. Figure 5-7 shows the approach. T1, T2, and T3 are adjacent triangles in a mesh. To display the first triangle, you put information on its three vertices in the three vertex stores (V1, V2, and V3). To display the second triangle, you replace one vertex store (V1) with vertex

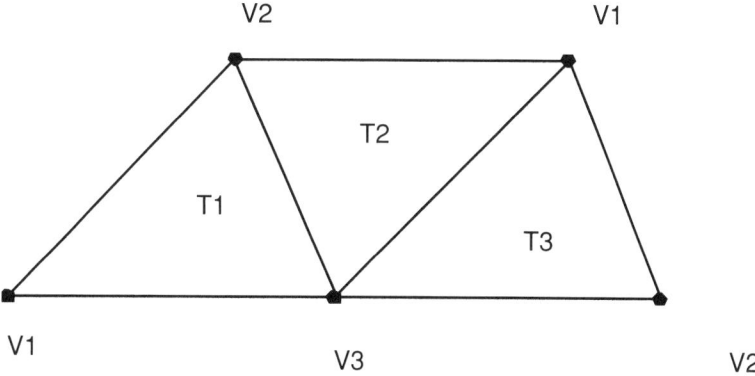

Figure 5-7. Displaying a chain of triangles with the Delta chip's three vertex stores.

information about the nonadjacent vertex of triangle 2 (T2). Follow a similar round-robin replacement for triangle 3, replacing the V2, and so on. This way, each new triangle requires setting up only one new vertex.

Sounds pretty easy so far, doesn't it? Well, as you may have guessed, nothing in 3D is ever that easy. So let's move on to the hard part: What the heck *is* rasterization, anyway?

The Permedia Rasterization

The Permedia's rasterization pipeline is summarized in Figure 5-8. I'll walk through it a step at a time.

Think of the Permedia chip as a box with three interfaces:

1. the PCI bus (PCI I/F),
2. graphics memory, and
3. the video output.

The CPU and programmer use the PCI interface to communicate with the rasterization pipeline, both to input data and to get "host out" information about rasterization status. They also use it to reach the VGA chip, graphics memory, and the video out port.

The FIFO Pipeline

As with the Delta chip, you "see" a set of registers. You fill in the registers, send a command to a command register, and away goes the chip. When you fill in the registers, you are really sending commands that are queued in a FIFO (first in/first out) pipeline that holds 32 32-bit commands. The

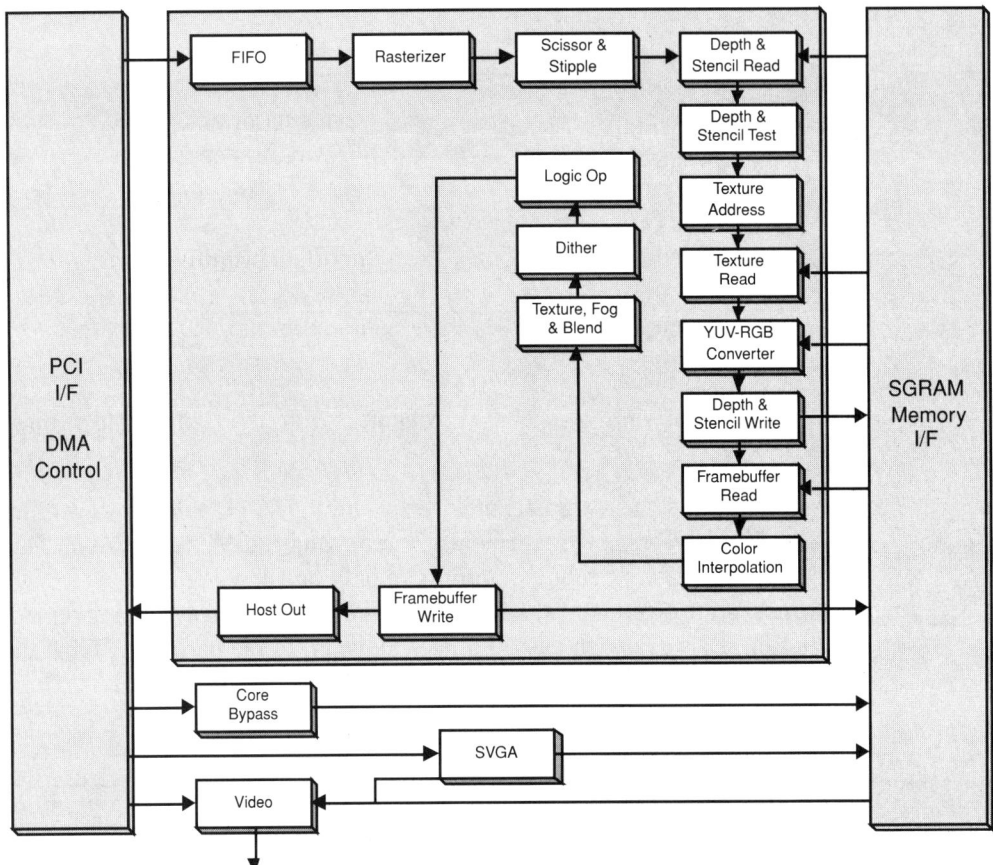

Figure 5-8. Schematic of the Permedia rasterization pipeline.

commands are processed one at a time. So that the CPU doesn't have to wait around, a DMA (direct memory access) mechanism buffers a big block of data that is waiting to enter the pipeline.

The Rasterization Pipeline

Data and commands leave the FIFO pipeline and enter the rasterization pipeline. The **rasterization pipeline** is a series of processing steps on the way to putting pixels on the screen. Follow the arrows on the illustration to see the order in which data goes through the pipeline.

Note, you can bypass the rasterization pipeline through the core bypass and write directly to the frame buffer memory. Likewise, you can write directly to the SVGA chip or to video out.

Rasterizer

The rasterizer converts triangle data into a series of fragments. Fragments are the fundamental graphics primitives that Permedia draws. They are pixel-wide lines, single-pixel points, and screen-aligned trapezoids. These are all that Permedia can draw. Everything else must be decomposed into these basic primitives.

Screen-aligned trapezoids are the most important primitive. A trapezoid is a quadrilateral (four-sided polygon) with two sides that are parallel. *Screen-aligned* means that the parallel sides are parallel to the *x*-axis of the screen. In other words, the top and bottom of the trapezoid are horizontal, like for a table. If your shape is not a screen-aligned trapezoid, you must break it into smaller parts until you have a screen-aligned trapezoid. (A triangle counts a trapezoid with one of the parallel sides on zero width.) See Figure 5-9.

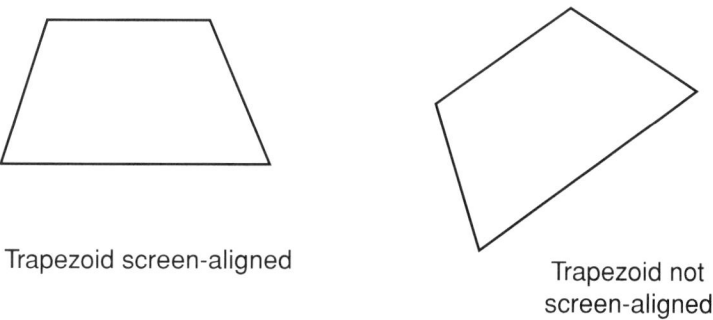

Figure 5-9. Two trapezoids. The one on the left is screen-aligned.

For example, if you want to display a triangle, as shown in Figure 5-10, you must break it into two screen-aligned trapezoids (in this case, screen-aligned triangles).

But you're not done! A trapezoid needs to be screen-aligned so that it can then be drawn as a series of screen scan lines of constantly changing widths. Each of these scan line segments is called a *span*. To determine the size of the span at each scan line, you need to calculate the delta (the amount of change in width and starting *x*) between each scan line and enter these values into the appropriate registers. There are a few further complications, such as ensuring there is no double-drawing of edge pixels of adjacent trapezoids. You also need to figure out the "dominant edges" of triangles, that is, the sides over which the *y*-value changes the most.

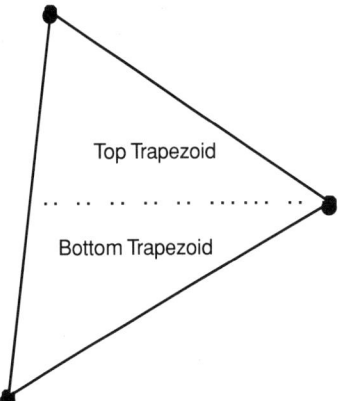

Figure 5-10. Breaking a triangle into two screen-aligned trapezoids (actually, screen-aligned triangles).

Recall from the previous section where I talked about the Delta chip that the chip passes on set-up information. All of these precalculations of polygons into screen-aligned triangles, deltas, and dominant edges are that set-up information. If you don't have a Delta chip, then all of this set-up is done by the CPU; this can be time-consuming. Also, sending all the set-up data can be taxing on the PCI bus. Remember, this set-up is only a small part of the geometry pipeline. You are going to want thousands of triangles to be displayed in each frame and as many frames per second as you can get!

Scissor and Stipple

Each segment is run through a scissor test. This test determines if the segment is actually on the screen and within a user-defined screen region. Segments that are out of screen range are discarded, segments that are partially in range are cut to the part that is visible, and segments that are visible are passed.

The stipple test compares the segment to an 8×8 pixel (user-defined) grid pattern of on/off bits. Bits of the segment that are on are passed to the next step; bits that are off are discarded. Stippling can be a computationally cheap way of creating a "screen-door" transparency effect. This is sometimes called "cheesy transparency." OpenGL includes it as a method to get some translucency effects on hardware that does not support blending (I talk about blending soon). You can even use stippling to create a "fade-into-the-background" effect by using a series of stipple patterns with an increasing number of bits turned on. You could also use stippling to create dashed lines and to create shadow effects.

Depth and Stencil Read and Test

The stencil and depth tests both involve examining the appropriate memory buffers stored in the frame buffer memory. First, the frame buffer is read to get the appropriate stencil and depth buffer values at a particular screen location. Next, the fragment is tested against a stencil buffer and either is accepted or is rejected from further processing. A stencil is a bit mask that is placed over the screen. It indicates areas in which there should be no rendering. Imagine rendering a view through a car windshield. The shape of the edge of the windshield is probably slanted and would cover part of the screen. This covered-up area could be represented by the stencil buffer.

The depth test compares each pixel against the z-buffer to determine if something is already being displayed at that pixel location that is closer to the viewpoint.

Texture Address and Texture Read

The texture address step calculates the address of the texel (the pixel in the texture map) that corresponds to the current fragment. Perspective correction may be used to make this calculation, based on a specified Q value (Q is a value calculated by the Permedia chip). The perspective correction can be done faster by division by Q or, more accurately, by an interpolated Q.

YUV-RGB Converter

The YUV-RGB step converts YUV color values to RGB format and applies a chroma test. Check the glossary for a definition of the YUV format. The chroma test specifies a range of color values (inside or outside specified minimum and maximum values). If the fragment passes this test, it continues on; otherwise it is discarded. Think of the chroma test as a blue-screen test. For example, any part of an image that is within a certain range of blue is never written to the screen so that the rest of the image will seem to sit on top of a background.

Depth and Stencil Write

The depth buffer (the z-buffer) and the stencil buffers are updated if appropriate.

Framebuffer Read

The actual pixel value that is already in the framebuffer is read. This value may be used in subsequent stages.

Color Interpolation

The actual color at the current pixel location is calculated. At this stage, Gouraud or flat shading is applied to the pixel.

Texture, Fog, and Blend

Texture, fog, and blend values are mixed with the fragment's color to determine the final color to be displayed. Textures can be applied to a pixel in three ways: copy, decal, or modulate. In copy mode, the texture color replaces the current pixel color. In decal mode, the texture color is blended with the current pixel color using the texture alpha value. In modulate mode, the pixel's current color and the texture color are multiplied together.

Next, fog (or depth cueing, which is the same thing) is applied to the pixel. A current color is faded to a constant color based on the depth value in the z-buffer. Finally, the current color is blended with the color currently in the frame buffer.

Dither

The color can be dithered to reduce the internal color format to an 8-bit-per-pixel color.

Logic Op

A logical operation can be performed with the pixel color already in the frame buffer, such as an XOR operation.

Framebuffer Write

Whew! You're finally ready to write the pixel to the frame buffer.

Host Out

Finally, the Permedia chip updates some register values in the programming interface to alert the CPU that the operation is complete.

So there you go. You've walked through a rasterization pipeline and lived! Sit back, relax, and ponder how many hundreds of thousand of fragments must travel through the rasterization pipeline per second before your brain starts to notice a decent moving image.

Part II

Programming in Three Dimensions

Chapter 6

Retained Mode Architecture

The Direct3D retained mode API is a collection of interrelated COM objects. To understand how to program the retained mode, you first need to understand three things:

1. How to build a 3D scene graph out of retained mode components
2. What the COM model is and how COM components work
3. What the different retained mode COM components do and how they interrelate

In this chapter, I discuss the retained mode components and the COM model and show you how to build a retained mode scene graph. Consider that this chapter gives you the technical background to begin actually programming with the retained mode API, which you will start to do in the next chapter.

The Retained Mode Scene Graph

Your goal in using the retained mode API is to build a 3D scene graph out of retained mode components. You then change the scene by changing the scene graph layout and by changing the appearance and location of the components in the scene. A simple retained mode scene graph could be organized something like that shown in Figure 6-1.

Frames are the key organizing component of a retained mode scene graph. A frame is like an empty, invisible point in 3D space to which you attach

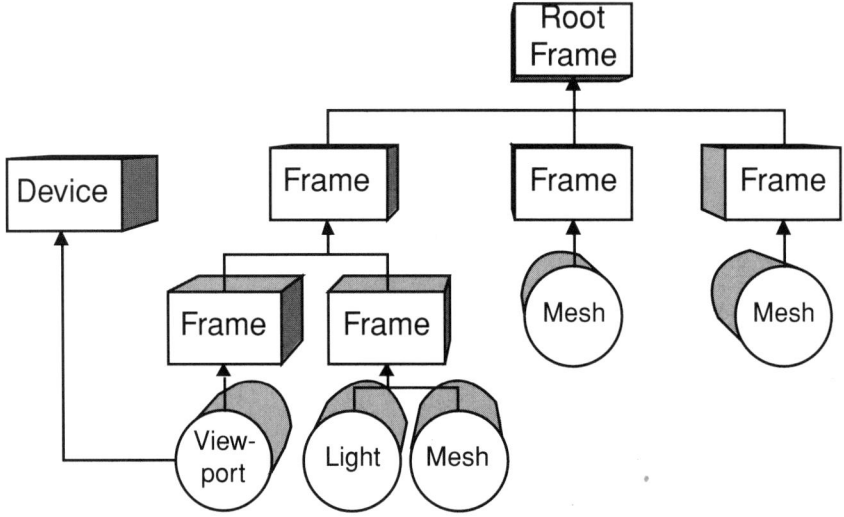

Figure 6-1. A simple retained mode scene graph.

meshes of polygons, lights, and cameras (called viewports). Move a frame, and the objects attached to it move with the frame. Frames can have other frames attached to them as children. When you move a parent frame, the child frames move also, as well as any objects attached to those child frames. The top-level parent of a 3D scene is the root frame, much like a root directory on a hard disk. The retained mode API uses a left-handed coordinate system ($+x$ to left, $+y$ up, and $+z$ into the screen).

Scenes are rendered to a display device, called simply a device. A viewport component connects a scene to a device. A viewport is attached to a frame. When you move the frame, the view of the scene as seen through the viewport also moves.

Retained Mode Components

Unfortunately, retained mode programming is not quite as simple as is implied by the scene graph in Figure 6-1. The seemingly simple relationships between the various retained mode components are actually fairly complex. When you include all of the different types of retained mode components, a more complete overview looks like Figure 6-2.

I spend the rest of this chapter describing this figure. Expect to refer to it repeatedly as you digest the following material. Here's a nutshell description. You link a core set of retained mode functions and macros into your 3D application. One function, Direct3DRMCreate, creates a COM component

Chapter 6 Retained Mode Architecture

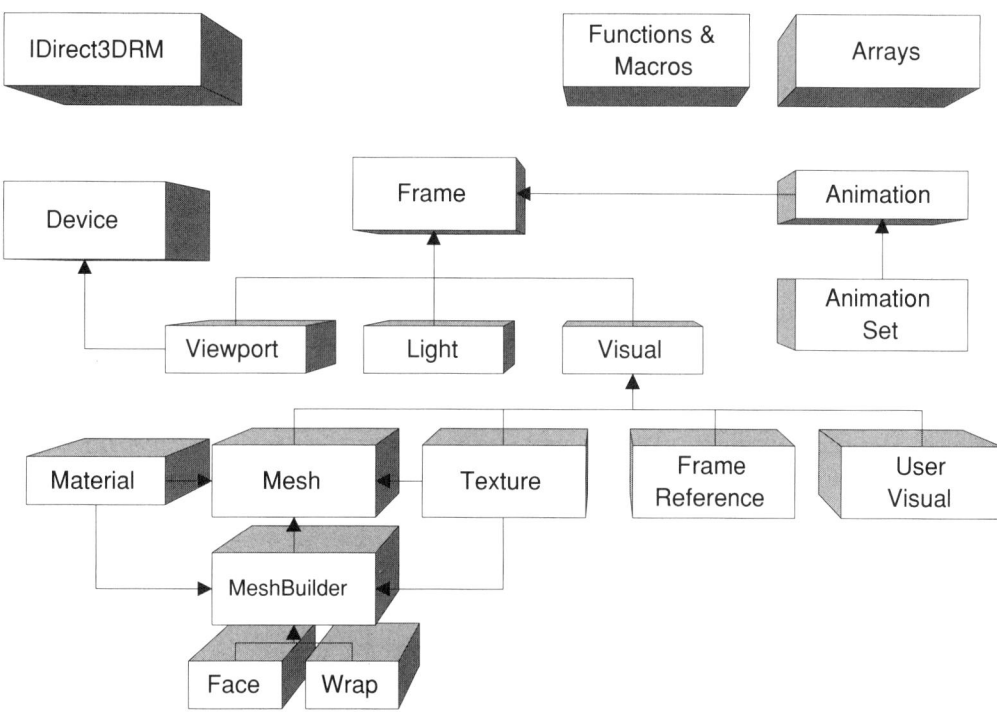

Figure 6-2. Overview of D3D retained mode component interrelations.

called IDirect3DRM. You use this object as the main API manager and to create further COM components out of which you build your 3D scene.

Scenes are organized around frames and displayed to devices as described in the previous section. The key geometry primitive is the mesh component. The appearance of a mesh is affected by material components. A material component describes the reflective properties of a mesh's surface. A mesh's appearance also is affected by textures, which are wrapped onto meshes (the type of wrapping is defined in a wrap component). You can also attach lights and textures to frames. (Textures are called *decals* when they are attached directly to a frame rather than wrapped around a mesh.)

MeshBuilder is a component for building mesh components. You can also build a new mesh with methods of the mesh component itself. The distinction between the two is important. A MeshBuilder object is used to create Mesh objects. MeshBuilder takes as input geometric data as well as material, texture, and face components (a face is a single polygon). It provides an additional, and somewhat different, set of capabilities for building and modifying a mesh compared to the mesh component itself. MeshBuilder gives you direct access to individual faces and texture wrapping coordinates. Mesh builds meshes out of sets of faces called groups.

To round things out, the retained mode API includes a few macros and functions that would not make sense to implement as separate components. These include basic math functions, as well as a set of array components for organizing groups of like components.

Table 6-1 summarizes the components of the retained mode API. Note that all the objects' names begin with "IDirect3DRM." For example, the Device object is actually called "IDirect3DRMDevice." (The preface IDirect3DRM has been left off in this table and the rest of this chapter to make things a little easier to understand.)

Table 6-1. Summary of retained mode components

Component Name	Description
Application Management	
IDirect3DRM	The retained mode manager object; creates other objects.
Device	The rendering target (where the image goes); either the graphics memory or window.
Object	An interface (set of methods) available on all types of retained mode objects.
Scene Viewing	
Viewport	The camera view of the 3D scene.
Picked	Identifies a visual object that corresponds to a given 2D point (such as a mouse pointer screen coordinate).
3D Scene	
Frame	The nodes of the 3D scene graph or tree. Each frame has a position and orientation, and lights and meshes are attached to a frame.
Visual	Not a separate type of object, but the types of objects that can be seen in a 3D scene when attached to a frame; meshes and decals (floating textures) that are attached to a frame.
UserVisual	An object that you render yourself by dropping down to the immediate mode.
Light	One of five types of lights that can illuminate a 3D scene.
Meshes	
Mesh	A set of polygon faces.
MeshBuilder	An object that creates and modifies a mesh.

Table 6-1. Summary of retained mode components *(continued)*

Component Name	Description
Face	A single polygon in a mesh.
Material	The color and reflectivity characteristics of a mesh or face surface.

Textures

Texture	Specifies that a rectangular image is wrapped on a mesh or face or displayed unattached to a mesh or face.
Wrap	Specifies how a texture is wrapped onto a face or mesh.

Animation

Animation	An engine that interpolates (i.e., calculates changing values for) position, orientation, and scaling over time.
AnimationSet	A set of Animation components.

Several retained mode components can be grouped into arrays, thereby making it simpler to apply wholescale operations to the entire group. The available array components are given in Table 6-2.

Each array component supports the GetSize and GetElement methods. GetSize returns the count of components in the array; GetElement returns a pointer to a particular component in the array.

There are a few quirks and curious anomalies, as you would expect in any sophisticated API. For example, a Visual is not actually a component; it is an interface with no methods that is always with certain other interfaces. However, you can have an array of Visuals (a VisualArray). Viewports are like cameras, although a frame is called a camera. Settings that affect an entire scene can be accessed through any frame of the scene, not just the root frame (there is no "scene" object per se). And a frame can be attached to another frame both as a child and as a Visual. The two are not same thing (a frame can be the child of only one other frame).

Table 6-2. Array components

DeviceArray
FrameArray
LightArray
ViewportArray
VisualArray
PickedArray

To bring all this into focus, you'll need to understand what exactly is a component or object in retained mode terms, which brings us to the COM model.

Standard Retained Mode Interfaces

As discussed earlier in the chapter, a COM object can have multiple interfaces, or groups of functions, and every COM component must have a standard set of methods, called the IUknown base interface. The Release, AddRef, and QueryInterface are the most relevant IUnknown methods for the retained mode; the Initialize method is also implemented but does not actually do anything. Every retained mode component also supports the retained mode common object interface, which is a set of functions for things like naming objects and attaching additional application-specific data to them. The COM interface to retained mode components is summarized in Figure 6-3, and the methods are listed in Table 6-3.

With the Object interface, every retained mode component can have a name and 32 bits of user-defined data attached to it. You get and set the object's name with GetName and SetName, respectively, and get and set the

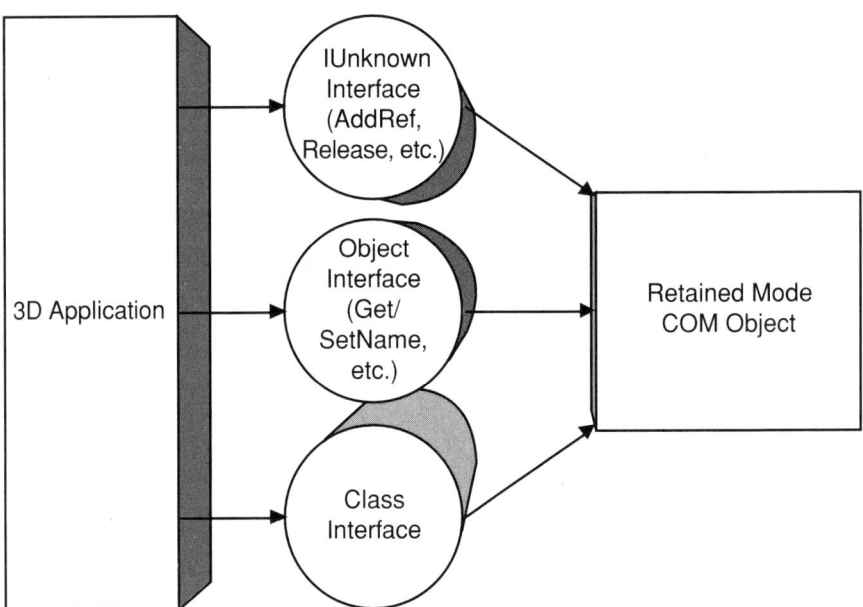

Figure 6-3. The COM interface to retained mode components.

Table 6-3. Standard methods available for all retained mode components through the IUnknown and Object interfaces

Method	Description
IUnknown Interface	
QueryInterface	COM method to determine if object supports a particular interface.
Initialize	Startup initialization of an object (not used by retained mode; objects are initialized automatically when created).
AddRef	Increment reference count (attaches another instance use of an object).
Release	Decrement reference count (when count goes to 0, the object destroys itself).
Object Interface	
Get/SetName	Gets/sets an identifying name for the object.
GetClassName	Gets the name of the type of the object.
Get/SetAppData	Gets/sets user-defined 32 bits of data attached to an object.
Clone	Creates a copy of a mesh or frame object.
Add/RemoveDestroyCallback	Registers/removes a destructor-like function called after an object is destroyed.

user-specific bits with GetAppData and SetAppData, respectively. Note that these user-specific bits are not interpreted or changed by the API itself, so you can use them for something like storing a pointer to additional data attached to a retained mode component. (But note that to extract this pointer, you must already have a pointer to the object itself!)

Rounding out the object-oriented facilities, GetClassName fetches the name of the class of the component, AddDestroyCallback adds a destructor-like function, and RemoveDestroyCallback removes the previously added destructor. The destructor function is called when the component's COM reference count drops to 0 and its memory is deleted, so you should not call the methods of the component itself in your destructor function. This means that you should not call the GetAppData method in your destroy function to get an object-specific pointer that you have stored with SetAppData. Instead, pass the pointer to your object-specific data as an argument to your destroy function when you call the AddDestroyCallback method.

COM and Performance Programming

Does the COM model, with its components, double-indirection virtual tables, and get/set methods, undermine the overall goal of high performance that a 3D API like Direct3D's retained mode must strive for? No, but some hoop-jumping is required. You also will find some resulting awkward constructs, particularly in the area of manipulating blocks of data.

The component calling overhead, even with double indirection, has an absolutely insignificant effect on overall performance, although this may not be immediately obvious. This is because of the amount of processing cycles it takes to render a scene. The comparison here is between a handful of cycles per frame (perhaps hundreds for a lot of components) versus the millions of cycles it takes to render the scene.

Two other performance issues are raised by the retained mode API that are worth considering: the overhead of creating and destroying objects and the overhead of reading in and out data. Every COM class (not every COM object created from the class) has a unique identifier, called its GUID (globally unique identifier, pronounced goo-id). In standard OLE environments, this GUID is used by the operating system to find the class description in order to create an object instance (creating an object instance normally requires checking the system registry and other high overhead events). For the traditional view of a COM object as a semipermanent thing embedded in a word processing document or spreadsheet, the performance hit of going out to the registry is not that significant. In the area of performance graphics, however, this overhead is unacceptable.

There is a very simple workaround to all this OLE overhead: Avoid it completely. The three required methods of the IUnknown interface—QueryInterface, AddRef, and Release—are trivially simple to code. QueryInterface simply returns a pointer to a v-table, which itself is just a data structure. AddRef increments some internally maintained variable. Release decrements the variable and destroys the object if the count reaches 0.

This workaround is the approach the retained mode takes. The IDirect3DRM object is a mini-COM object factory, spawning these simplified COM objects without ever actually invoking OLE. In some sense, you could consider DirectX's use of COM to be OLE with an enormous overhead and infrastructure removed.

The second issue is the overhead of reading in and out data from COM objects. Because you cannot access data directly in a COM component, a block of data (such as the list of vertices) has to be read out of the object, modified, and then passed back in. In general, this is not a problem in the retained mode, except for meshes. If you want to morph a mesh (make the shape of the mesh change over time), you have to get the vertices out of the object and then write them back in. This can be a cumbersome overhead, since the mesh object itself has no built-in morphing mechanism. However, since the output of the retained mode is data that fills in an execute buffer, there are times when it would be helpful to be able to get that execute buffer data or read into the retained mode execute buffer data.

The IDirect3DRM Object

IDirect3DRM is the manager object for the retained mode. You create the IDirect3DRM object with a call to the Direct3DRM Create function and then use the IDirect3DRM object to create other retained mode objects. Table 6-4 shows the IDirect3DRM objects.

Table 6-4. IDirect3DRM methods

Method	Description
Render Management	
Tick	Updates the movement of frames, renders to a device, and calls callback functions.
Device Creation	
CreateDeviceFromClipper	Creates a device from a DirectDraw Clipper object.
CreateDeviceFromD3D	Creates a retained mode device from immediate mode D3D objects.
CreateDeviceFromSurface	Creates a device from a DirectDraw surface.
Object Management	
CreateXXX	A set of methods that creates retained mode objects.
GetNamedObject	Finds an object by name.
EnumerateObjects	Calls a specified function for all objects.
GetDevices	Gets a list of all devices.
File Management	
Get/Set/AddSearchPath	Gets, sets, adds file search paths.
Load	Loads objects from a .x file.
Texture Management	
SetDefaultTextureColors	Sets the default number of colors assigned to a texture.

Table 6-4. **IDirect3DRM methods** *(continued)*

Method	Description
SetDefaultTextureShades	Sets the default number of colors assigned to a material color.
LoadTexture	Loads a .bmp or PPM (portable Pixmap) file as a texture.
LoadTextureFromResource	Loads a texture from a resource.

Devices

A device is the visual display destination for rendering. Think of a device as the block of graphics memory into which you render your scene. In fact, this graphics memory is always a DirectDraw surface, which you will either flip to the front to become visible or use as a texture for another retained mode device. You can have more than one device at a time and can organize them with a DeviceArray. Note that in a Windows environment, you will need to handle WM_Paint and WM_Activate messages. You do this with the IDirect3DRMWinDevice interface of a device object.

You cannot resize a device once it is created, although you can resize your viewport into the device. This means that the window on the screen may be smaller than your device and show only a portion of the device's area. Also, the actual size of your device may differ from the size you specified at creation (you should check the actual size with the GetWidth and GetHeight methods). You can set the maximum rendering quality supported by a device, from wireframe to Phong shading. (Although DirectX II does not support Phong shading, a future version may.)

Devices support one of two color models: RGB or ramp. The RGB model represents colors by their red, green, and blue components. If the display depth of the device is fewer than 24 bits, then the RGB color is reduced down to the appropriate color depth.

For internal color representation, the ramp mode uses a palette of colors instead of 24-bit RGB colors. Ramp mode is an indexed color mode, for each color is an index into a color table. Ramp mode can use 8-bit or 16-bit indices to define the ramp of colors. The renderer doesn't know what the color pointed to actually is; it just makes assumptions based on what you tell it. For example, for each color you specify the number of shades. Colored lights are treated as white lights in the ramp mode. This is why sometimes the ramp mode is called the monochromatic mode.

Chapter 6 Retained Mode Architecture

Which color model is preferable depends on the target hardware. Ramp color mode is faster in software only, but hardware rasterizing chips prefer RGB color. In ramp mode, you specify how many shades (adjacent colors in the palette) are used for each basic color. Over time, ramp mode is likely to continue to play a role in 16-bit color, MMX environments. Its main disadvantage, which may be minor, is that it does not support colored lights.

The Device object methods are summarized in Table 6-5.

Table 6-5. Device methods

Method	Description
Update Functions	
Update	Copies the image in the device to the screen.
Add/RemoveUpdateCallback	A user-defined callback function called when Update is performed.
Device Settings	
Get/SetColorModel	Gets/sets the color model (ramp or RGB).
Get/SetDither	Gets/sets the dither. True = dither is on.
Get/SetGamma	Gets/sets the gamma value.
Get/SetPalette	Gets/sets the palette functions for an 8-bit color model.
Get/SetQuality	Gets/sets the maximum render quality for a device.
Get/SetShades	Gets/sets the number of colors used for rendering a material color in the ramp color model.
Get/SetTextureQuality	Gets/sets the texture quality. Applies to the RGB color model only.
Get/SetWireframeOptions	Gets/sets wireframe options. Wireframes can be rendered with backfaces and hidden lines shown.
Sync	Locks vertical sync (seldom needed).
Device Info	
GetHeight/Width	Gets the height and/or width of a device.
GetImageFormat	Gets the preferred image format for the device.
GetPolygonsDrawn	Gets the total number of polygons rendered to the device (includes backfaces, but not polygons outside the viewing frustum).
Windows Devices	
HandleActivate	Responds to a Windows WM_PAINT message.
HandlePaint	Responds to a Windows WM_ACTIVATE message.

Viewports

A viewport is a camera that uses a frame object as its locational reference point in the 3D scene. A viewport is not actually an object in the scene. Rather it references a frame in the scene in order to get its position and orientation. The camera reference frame is a parameter that you specify when the viewport is created (CreateViewport). Later, you can change the camera reference frame of an existing viewport by using the SetCamera method.

This camera frame defines both which scene is to be rendered (the one the frame is attached to, which is really just the root frame for a particular scene) and the viewing position and direction. The viewport renders only what is visible when looking along the positive z-axis of the camera frame, with the up direction taken from the positive y-axis of the camera frame.

You can do several things with a viewport:

- Render a scene to the device.
- Configure the camera.
- Pick objects in the scene.

I discuss the first two here and the third in the next section.

You render a scene to a device (a DirectDraw surface) with Viewport::Clear (clears the DirectDraw surface to the background color) and Viewport::Render. To actually display what you have rendered, you must call the Device:Update method.

An important use of the viewport is to configure what part of the scene you can actually see from the vantage point of a particular frame. What you can see is called the *viewing frustum*, the visible 3D volume in a scene positioned relative to the viewport's camera. A viewing frustum is shown in Figure 6-4. For perspective viewing, the frustum is a truncated pyramid with the point of the pyramid at the camera and the camera's z-axis going from the point of the pyramid to the middle of its base. The front clipping plane, D, and back clipping plane, F (set by using the Viewport::SetFront and Viewport::SetBack methods), define the top and bottom of the truncated pyramid laying on its side. The height of the front clipping plane is $2h$ and defines the field of view (h can be set using Viewport::SetField).

The angle of view is defined by the following equation, which can be used to calculate a value for h when a particular camera angle is desired:

$$2 \tan^{-1} \frac{h}{D}$$

The methods of the Viewport object are summarized in Table 6-6.

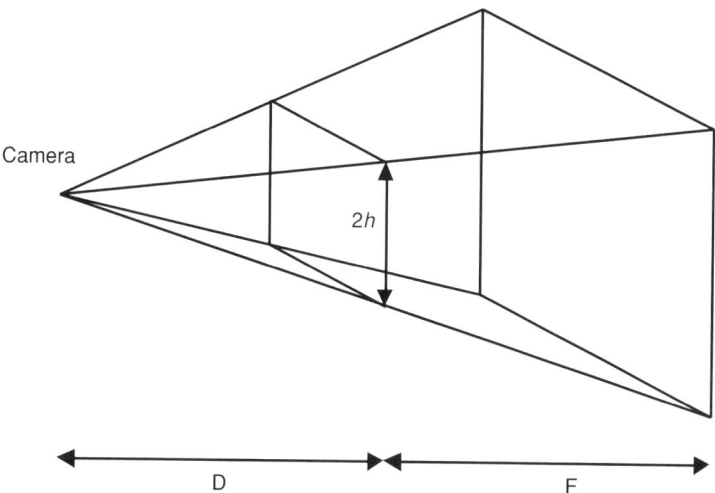

Figure 6-4. A viewing frustum.

Table 6-6. Viewport methods

Method	Description
Rendering	
Clear	Clears the viewport to the background color.
Render	Renders a scene to the device.
ForceUpdate	Forces a region to be updated (copied to screen on the next call to Device::Update).
Configuration	
Get/SetBack	Gets/sets back the clipping plane.
Get/SetCamera	Gets/sets the frame that the viewport uses as a camera into 3D scene.
Get/SetField	Gets/sets the field of view.
Get/SetFront	Gets/sets the front clipping plane.
Get/SetPlane	Gets/sets the front clipping plane (left, right, bottom, top).
Get/SetProjection	Gets/sets the projection type (perspective or orthographic).
Get/SetUniformScaling	Gets/sets the uniform scaling. True if the viewport scales uniformly.
GetX/Y/Width/Height	Gets the viewport's current offsets into a device.
Transforming	
Transform	Converts a point from world coordinates to screen coordinates.
InverseTransform	Converts a point from screen coordinates to world coordinates.

Picking and Transforming

The retained mode API implements two concepts to help you convert back and forth between 2D screen coordinates: picking and transforming. Picking allows you to find what items in your 3D scene intersect with a given screen location. Transforming converts a point back and forth between screen coordinates and world coordinates.

You pick objects through the viewport interface. You pass the Viewport::Pick() method the x and y screen coordinates. If that screen location hits any objects, the method returns a depth-sorted list of them (a PickedArray). You then use IDirect3DRMPickedArray::GetPick to get further information about what objects and faces were actually picked. The Pick methods are summarized in Table 6-7.

Table 6-7. Pick methods

Method	Description
Picking	
Viewport::Pick	Finds objects at a given screen location.
PickedArray::GetPicked	Returns faces at a given screen location.

The Transform method converts a point from world coordinates to screen coordinates, and InverseTransform converts a point from screen coordinates to world coordinates. To understand how these methods work, you need to understand homogeneous coordinates as used by these methods. Homogeneous coordinates have a w value in addition to x-, y-, and z-values. To convert a homogeneous coordinate to a regular x-, y-, or z-value, divide by w. Transform uses this four-element homogeneous form to avoid scaling by an infinite amount for points near the camera.

Frames

The frame object is the workhorse of the retained mode API. You use frames to organize your scene and determine how to make things move. The frame object has a large number of methods, but breaking them down into categories is fairly straightforward, as shown in Figure 6-5.

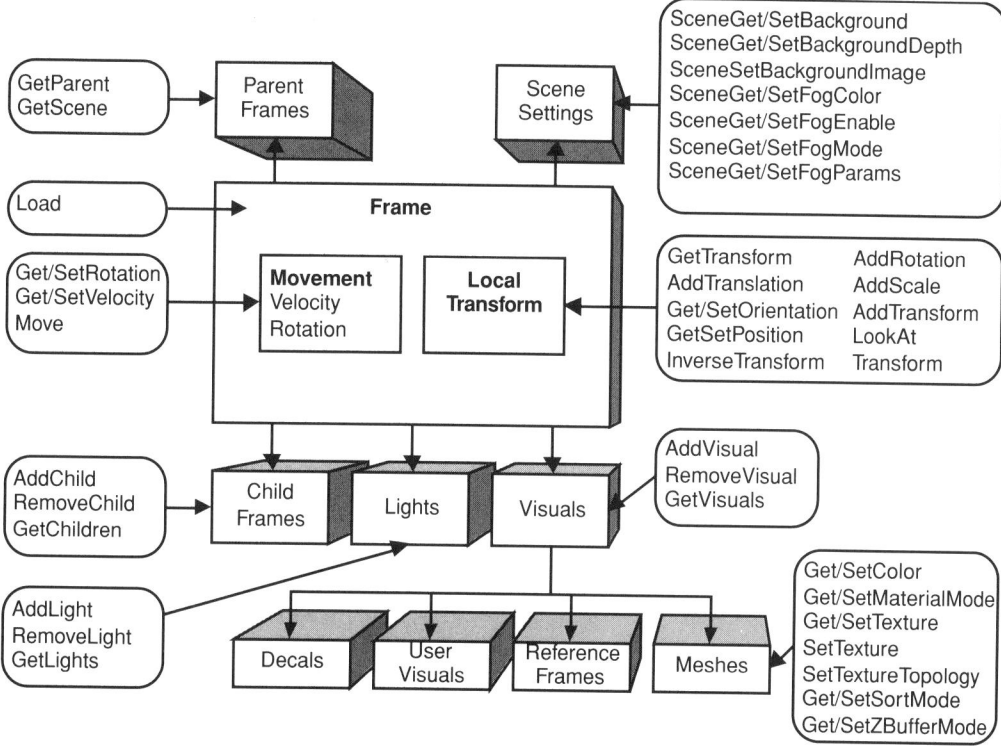

Figure 6-5. A frame and its methods.

The Scene Graph

Frames are organized into scenes. A frame with a parent of NULL is the root of the scene (like the root directory on your hard drive). A scene is a graph of frames, with parents, children, and siblings. You attach a child frame with AddChild, remove it with DeleteChild, and get an array of child frames attached to the frame with GetChildren. Be careful when you delete a child. When you use DeleteChild, the child and all the objects in its hierarchy (attached lights, child frames, meshes, and so on) have their COM reference counts decremented (i.e., ::Release is called on them). If a COM object's reference count reaches 0, it is automatically destroyed. If you do not want all of these objects automatically destroyed, you must increment their reference counts with ::AddRef before using DeleteChild.

You can get the root frame of the scene for any frame with GetScene, which simply returns the root frame. You can detach a frame from one parent and attach it to another parent by using AddChild to add it to the other parent.

When you do this, the frame will have the same location in world space, but its position relative to its parent frame (its local transform) will be reset in relation to the new parent.

The Local Transform

The location and orientation of the frame are described by its local transform, a 4 × 4 matrix stored in the frame object. If you are fuzzy on what a matrix is, for purposes of this discussion all you really need to understand is that a matrix is a set of numbers that represents a formula. When you apply this formula to a point in 3D space (a point that has an x-, y-, and z-coordinate), you get the corresponding 2D coordinates (x and y) on the screen.

Points expressed in terms of a particular frame are called *local*, or *model, coordinates*. Think of an apple. A spot on the top of the apple might be two inches above the center of the apple. You can think of this spot at this same location (two inches above the center) no matter where the apple is in the world and which way it is facing. The expression "two inches above the center of the apple" in this sense would refer to local coordinates.

Actually, the local transform simply describes the location and orientation of a frame in relation to its parent frame. If you have a chain of children and grandchildren and so on descending from a root frame, the position in world space of the lowest frame in the hierarchy will be based on a combination of the frame's own local transform and all the local transforms of all the parents up the chain. Think of an apple on a plate on a table in a moving train. The apple's location in the world can be defined by its relationship to the plate, whose location can be defined in terms of the table, whose location can be defined in terms of the train (and yes the world is in the solar system and so on . . .).

Transforming Coordinates

To convert a point (called a vector by the retained mode) expressed in the local transform (for example, a worm one inch from the center of the aforementioned apple) into the coordinates of the parent frame (the same worm's location in relation to the center of the plate the apple is sitting on), you use the following matrix multiplication formula:

> Point in parent coordinates = point in child frame coordinates
>   * child frame transformation matrix

For convenience sake, the frame has several methods that help you to perform these kinds of calculations. These methods—Get/SetPosition, Get/SetRotation, Get/SetVelocity, and LookAt—allow you to perform frame operations using another frame as a reference. In the apple/plate example, you would use GetPosition on the worm frame using the plate frame as the reference frame to get the worm's location in "plate space." To orient a frame in reference to world coordinates, you use the root frame of the scene as the reference frame.

You also can convert a point from frame coordinates to world coordinates and vice versa by using the Transform and InverseTransform methods. Transform converts a point in frame coordinates into world coordinates. This returns the same result as GetPosition using the root frame of the scene as the reference frame. InverseTransform transforms a point in world coordinates into frame coordinates.

Visuals

A frame is just an invisible point in 3D space with a location and orientation expressed by a local transform matrix. To see something, you have to attach it to the frame. The "something" you attach is called a *Visual*. A Visual is not a retained mode object. Rather it is several types of retained mode objects:

- A mesh object.
- A texture object. A texture object is called a *decal* when it is attached to a frame as a visual.
- A UserVisual object that you render yourself.
- A frame.

The main Visual you will use is the mesh object.

You also can attach a frame as a Visual to another frame. Called a **reference,** this Visual allows you to reuse the same set of frames more than once in a scene. This process differs from attaching the frame as a child. A referenced frame will be returned by the method GetVisuals, and a child frame will be returned by the method GetChildren. A frame can be the child of only one parent at a time. If you use AddChild, specifying a frame that is already the child of another frame, that child will be detached from its old parent before being attached as a child to its new parent. Be careful with referenced frames. Do not attach a parent frame as a Visual to one of its children; you'll create an endless loop!

Moving a Frame

There are four basic ways to make a frame move:

1. Change the local transform.
2. Apply a default velocity and rotation.

3. Attach a move callback.
4. Attach an animation.

Each approach is described next.

Change the Local Transform

You can change the location and orientation of a frame by changing the values in its local transform matrix using such methods as AddTransform, AddScale, AddRotation, and AddTranslation. With AddTransform, you can replace the existing transform or premultiply or postmultiply with the existing transform. You can change the local transform in a way that may be easier to conceptualize by using the methods SetPosition, SetOrientation, and LookAt. These methods also set the local transform. They allow you to express the result you want in terms of location and orientation instead of the more abstract concept of a transform matrix.

Apply a Default Velocity and Rotation

Each frame has an intrinsic velocity and rotation that are applied each time a scene is rendered. These values are both 0 by default. You set them with the SetRotation and SetVelocity methods. SetRotation is very different from the similar-sounding AddRotation method. AddRotation causes a one-time rotation by changing the local transform matrix. SetRotation sets an amount of rotation that is applied to the local transform each time the scene is rendered.

The frame's default velocity and rotation are applied each time the scene is rendered. However, you also can force a move by calling Frame::Move. The Move method applies the velocity and rotation values without rendering the scene. You can scale the amount of rotation and velocity applied on a particular move via the delta parameter of the Move method. If you call Move with a delta parameter value of 1, the full amount of rotation and velocity is applied to the frame. If you specify a delta of 2, then twice these values will be applied. The delta parameter allows you to apply a constant rotation and velocity over time. You keep track of how much time has passed since the last time the frame was moved and scale the delta parameter value appropriately. Probably the easiest way to do this is to set the default velocity and rotation to the total amount you want the frame to move in one second. Then pass as the delta parameter value the number of seconds since the last move.

All of this requires you to keep track of both the time and the last time the frame moved. You may wonder then how useful the frame's default velocity and rotation really are as an application feature. The answer is, probably not much. It makes for a great demo of twirling objects, but as an application feature, it is deficient. It requires so much tracking of data by the application itself that you could just as easily set the frame's position and orientation directly.

Attach a Move Callback

A more sophisticated way to move a frame is to define your own move callback function using the AddMoveCallback method. The callback function is passed the same delta parameter value that is used to scale the application of the frame's default velocity and rotation.

Attach an Animation

Another way to move a frame is to attach an animation object to it. The Animation and AnimationSets methods are discussed later in this chapter.

Z-buffer and Sort Modes

Two sets of methods are available that affect low-level rendering: Get/SetSortMode and Get/SetZBufferMode. The usefulness of these methods may not be immediately obvious. They potentially open a path to the evolution of the retained mode into a more powerful, performance-oriented retained mode API. They give you at least one tool to optimize the performance of the immediate mode that runs underneath the retained mode, while allowing you to stay at the conceptually higher-level retained mode API.

The key point to understand is this: If z-buffering is on, polygons should be rendered (sorted) in front-to-back order; if z-buffering is off, polygons should be rendered in back-to-front order. Sort order means the order in which the polygons appear in the execute buffer of rendering commands that are passed by the retained mode API to the immediate mode API at render time. If z-buffering is off, then the immediate mode renderer simply draws the polygons in the order they appear in the buffer. So you want the polygons closer to be drawn on top of the ones farther away. When z-buffering is on, having the polygons sorted in the execute buffer from front to back speeds the rendering process. This is because more pixels will fail the z test, since a closer polygon has already been drawn and the z test will reject the pixel from further processing. Failing the z test is faster than passing the z test because doing a read/compare cycle is faster than doing a read/compare/write cycle. This may seem like a trivial point, but the order of the read/compare cycle can have a very significant impact on the overall rendering speed.

These two sets of methods are only the beginning of the kind of optimizing that would make sense to implement in or on top of a retained mode API. There are all sorts of high-level techniques at the retained mode that would optimize the results achievable at the immediate mode API. Common areas of optimization include

- high-level culling (identifying a block of polygons that is not visible because it is behind other polygons),
- state sorting (organizing like kinds of polygons, such as all red polygons, so that they are rendered as a block),
- frame collapsing (converting a chain of frames into a single frame and eliminating levels of matrix calculations at render time), and
- caching (flagging things that you don't want to change, such as lighting calculations on a particular mesh, so that they don't have to be recalculated for each render).

But alas, though such features are built into the current version of Direct3D's retained mode, the application developer has no access to how they work. If you want to have direct control over these kinds of features, you will have to either implement them on top of the retained mode or write your own retained mode API.

The methods associated with Frame are summarized in Table 6-8.

Table 6-8. **Frame object methods**

Method	Description
Frame Hierarchy	
GetParent	Gets the parent frame.
Add/RemoveChild	Adds/removes a child frame.
GetChildren	Gets an array of child frames.
GetScene	Gets the root scene frame of a frame.
Attached Components	
Add/RemoveLight	Adds/removes light.
Add/RemoveVisual	Adds/removes a Visual (a mesh or decal).
GetLights	Gets an array of lights attached to the frame.
GetVisuals	Gets an array of Visuals attached to the frame.
Movement	
SetRotation	Sets the rotation for the frame each time ::Tick or ::Move is called.

Table 6-8. Frame object methods *(continued)*

Method	Description
SetVelocity	Sets the distance the frame moves each time ::Tick or ::Move is called.
Move	Applies rotations and velocities to all frames in the scene.
Add/RemoveMoveCallback	Adds/removes a function to be called each time the frame is touched by a move traversal (i.e., its velocity and rotation are applied).
Meshes	
BuildMesh	Combines meshes attached to the frame (and frame's children) into single attached mesh.
Get/SetColor	Gets/sets the default color for the frame's meshes.
SetColorRGB	Gets/sets the default color for the frame's meshes.
Get/SetMaterialMode	Gets/sets the material mode for the frame's meshes (whether the mesh color and texture are inherited from the frame or the frame's parent).
Texture	
Get/SetTexture	Gets/sets the default texture for the frame's meshes.
SetTextureTopology	Gets/sets the default texture topology for the frame's meshes.
Local Transform	
GetTransform	Gets the local transform of the frame.
AddRotation	Adds rotation to the frame's local transform.
AddScale	Scales the local transform.
AddTransform	Transforms the local coordinates by matrix.
AddTranslation	Adds translation to the local coordinates.
Position	
Get/SetOrientation	Gets/sets the orientation relative to another frame.
Get/SetPosition	Gets/sets the position relative to another frame.
Transform	Converts a vector from frame coordinates to world coordinates.
InverseTransform	Converts a vector from world coordinates to frame coordinates.
LookAt	Points the frame toward another frame.

Table 6-8. **Frame object methods** *(continued)*

Method	Description
Scene	
SceneGet/SetBackground	Gets/sets the scene background color.
SceneSetBackgroundRGB	Sets the scene background color (RGB).
SceneGet/SetBackgroundDepth	Gets/sets the scene background depth buffer.
SceneSetBackgroundImage	Sets the scene background image.
SceneGet/SetFogColor	Gets/sets the scene fog color.
SceneGet/SetFogEnable	Gets/sets fog enabling. True = scene fog is enabled.
SceneGetFogMode	Gets the scene fog mode.
SceneGetFogParams	Gets the scene fog parameters.
Render Management	
Get/SetSortMode	Sorts polygons front to back or back to front.
Get/SetZBufferMode	Turns z-buffering on/off.

Lights

Direct3D retained mode supports five types of lights:

1. Ambient
2. Directional
3. Parallel point
4. Point
5. Spotlight

Lights are attached to frames much like Visuals are. The location and orientation of the light in the scene are defined by the location and orientation of the frame to which they are attached. However, lights are not Visuals. You don't see them; they help you see things. Also, although lights have color, in the ramp color mode this color is ignored and lights are treated as monochromatic (i.e., white).

Ambient light. Ambient light illuminates everything in the scene equally, regardless of the orientation, position, and surface characteristics of the objects in the scene. It does not matter to which frame in a scene an ambient light is attached or the position and orientation of the frame to which it is attached. The effect of the ambient light on all objects in the scene will be the same. If you have several ambient lights in a scene, they combine to increase the total ambient light. Hence if you have a frame hierarchy representing an object that you plan to add to and delete from the scene, you should not attach an ambient light to the object. This is because when you add that object to the scene you will change the ambient light for the entire scene. Ambient light is the fastest light to render.

Directional light. A directional light source has orientation but no position. It simulates distant light sources, such as the sun. A directional light takes its orientation from the frame to which it is attached. It is the fastest light to render after ambient light.

Parallel point light. A parallel point light has both orientation and position. The light goes out in both directions. Two meshes on either side of a parallel point light source are lit on the side that faces the position of the light. The parallel point light has similar rendering speed to a directional light.

Point light. A point light has position but no orientation. It sends out light equally in all directions from its position. A point light has a slower rendering time but better quality than directional and parallel point lights. It is slower because the direction vector of the light must be recalculated for each face within range (in flat-shaded mode) or every vertex in range (in Gouraud-shaded mode). Directional and point parallel lights have their direction vector calculated only once and then apply the same direction vector to every face or vertex in range.

Spotlight. A spotlight emits a cone of light with a bright central core called the *umbra* surrounded by a more dimly lit *penumbra*, as shown in Figure 6-6. You set the angles of a spotlight's penumbra and umbra with SetPenumbra and SetUmbra.

The methods of the Light object are summarized in Table 6-9.

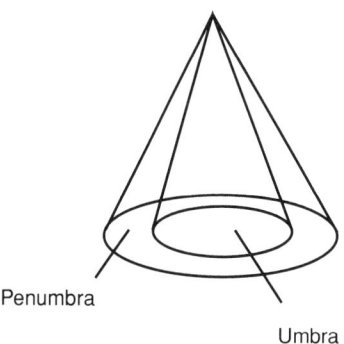

Figure 6-6. A spotlight's umbra and penumbra.

Table 6-9. Light methods

Method	Description
Get/SetColor	Gets/sets the color.
Get/SetConstantAttenuation	Gets/sets the constant attenuation factor.
Get/SetLinearAttenuation	Gets/sets the linear attenuation factor.
Get/SetPenumbra	Gets/sets the penumbra angle.
GetSetQuadraticAttenuation	Gets/sets the quadratic attenuation factor.
Get/SetRange	Gets/sets the range.
Get/SetType	Gets/sets the light type.
Get/SetUmbra	Gets/sets the umbra angle.

The Mesh Component

A mesh is a set of polygon faces. It is the main visual object of a 3D scene. A Mesh object is therefore one of the cornerstones of the retained mode API. It reflects the good and bad of COM-based object-oriented API design. The good side is that Mesh objects provide you with a high-level, encapsulated API into 3D data that eventually gets sent to the immediate mode as a messy, complicated execute buffer of triangles, states settings, and so on. The bad side is that sometimes you will find this abstraction to be too high-level or off-point from what you might actually want to do with a mesh. Partially, this is because the retained mode was intended to be a high-level API that was supposed to isolate you from messy performance and other details. The reality is that one application's messy detail has a way of being another application's essential differentiating feature.

There is an escape hatch: the UserVisual object. UserVisual allows you to build your own mesh data in any way you want because it expects you to drop down to the immediate mode at render time and build your own execute buffer. But as you can imagine, this can be a significant amount of work. Also, you lose such benefits as the ability to load your 3D data with a standard API call. So the UserVisual can be a convenient marketing answer to shortcomings in the Mesh object. However, before you leap into creating your own UserVisuals, make sure you cannot make the standard Mesh object work for you. Hopefully, you can make the Mesh object work for you and you can simply load in a Mesh object with textures and colors already applied (using the Frame::Load method).

There are actually two mesh-related objects: Mesh and MeshBuilder. The Mesh object is what is attached to a frame and is rendered. MeshBuilder is a tool to build Mesh objects. However, you also can build a mesh with the Mesh object itself. The relationship between Mesh and MeshBuilder is somewhat awkward. They overlap each other in some ways and not in others. The Mesh object methods are summarized in Table 6-10.

For a Mesh object to be rendered, it first must be added to a frame using Frame::AddVisual. One mesh can be added to multiple frames to create multiple references to that Mesh object. A texture can be wrapped around a mesh, using the Texture and Wrap objects.

Groups

The key organizing principle of a mesh is the *group*. A **group** is a collection of polygons in a mesh that can have its own material, color, and texture. Each face of a polygon is in turn defined by a set of vertices (corner points) and normals (vectors, like arrows that show the direction that a vertex is facing

Table 6-10. Mesh methods

Method	Description
GetBox	Retrieves the bounding box (the minimum and maximum *x*, *y*, and *z*).
Group Management	
AddGroup	Groups a set of faces in a mesh and gives them an identifier.
GetGroup	Retrieves face and vertex data about a group.
Get/SetGroupColor	Gets/sets a color for a group.
SetGroupColorRGB	Sets a color for a group.
GetGroupCount	Retrieves a number of groups in the Mesh object.
Get/SetGroupMapping	Gets/sets texture mapping settings (wrap u, wrap v, and perspective correction).
GetGroupMaterial	Gets the material for a group.
Get/SetGroupQuality	Gets/sets the render quality for a group.
Get/SetGroupTexture	Gets/sets the texture for a group.
Get/SetVertices	Gets/sets the vertex positions for a group.
General	
Save	Saves the mesh to the file.
Scale	Resizes the mesh.
Translate	Moves vertices in mesh.

for lighting calculations). Vertices and normals can be shared by multiple faces in a mesh. Groups have no names and are not retained mode objects. As a result, you cannot create, say, a spaceship mesh with a group identified as "cockpit_cover." You will need to use different meshes.

Why have groups instead of separate meshes attached to one or more frames? For some kinds of meshes, groups make a lot of sense, particularly an object with nonmoving parts or different-colored faces. Another reason may concern performance. It is unclear exactly what the retained mode API does with groups of polygons. However, it would be fair to assume that it may do some kind of state management on the groups of a mesh. For example, it may put all the red triangles together in a block so that the immediate mode renderer does not have to change internal state variables more often than necessary. However, this kind of state sorting might conflict with the sorting of meshes front to back and back to front as described previously in the section on frames.

Using Groups

Figure 6-7 gives an overview of the internal structure of a Mesh object and the methods you can perform on it. If you have a prebuilt model that you can load with Frame::Load, you may not need to actually use the methods of the

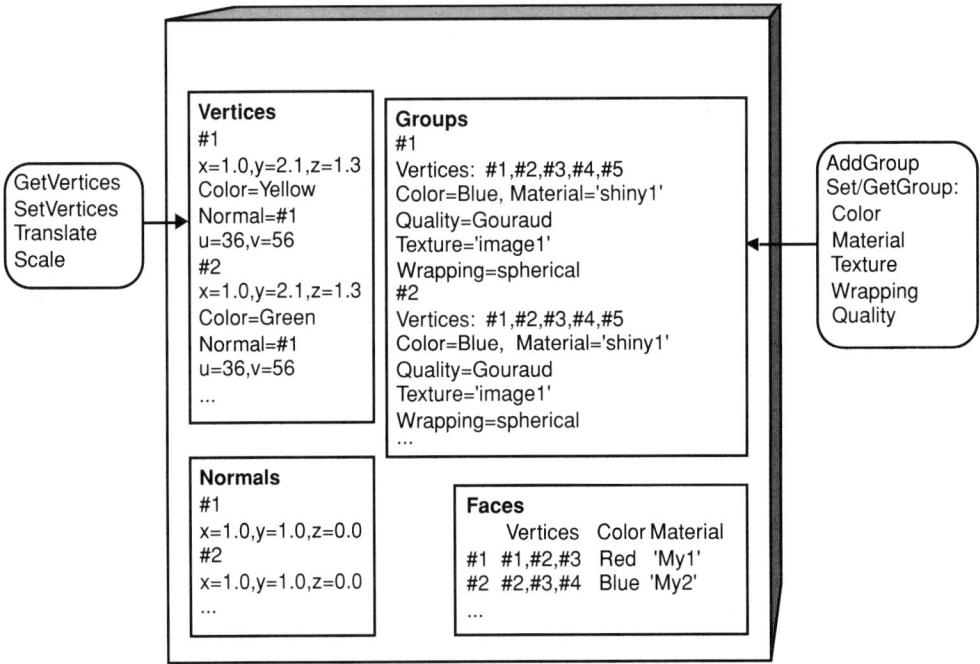

Figure 6-7. Methods and internal data structures of the mesh component.

Mesh object. Also, you can create a Mesh object from a MeshBuilder object, as discussed next.

But if you want to build or modify a mesh through the API, here is what you do:

1. Use AddGroup to add a group of faces to the mesh. When you use AddGroup, you specify the number of vertices and faces, and the method returns an identifier number to access the group on subsequent calls. The added group is uninitialized. That is, the color is white; there is no texture or material, and each vertex's position, normal, and color are set to 0.
2. Then set the locations of the vertices with SetVertices. Set the overall texture, material, and color settings for the group with such methods as SetGroupColor, SetGroupMaterial, SetGroupTexture, SetGroup-Wrapping, and SetGroupQuality. Note that both a vertex and a group have a color. The color of the group overrides the color of the vertex.

If you want to morph your mesh (cause the individual vertices of the mesh to move), you use multiple calls to SetVertices. There are no built-in vertex-level interpolation functions in the retained mode, so you will have to build your own vertex-level functionality similar to that of the frame-level Animation object.

MeshBuilder Component

The MeshBuilder object is a tool to build Mesh objects. It does not support the group concept of the Mesh object, but because it operates in terms of vertices and faces, you may find it easier to use. A MeshBuilder object cannot be rendered directly. It first must be converted into a Mesh object and attached to a Frame. Also, because the created meshes have no groups, you cannot access the individual vertices with Mesh::GetVertices. A Mesh object can be converted into a MeshBuilder object, but the group organization will be lost and the mesh will be converted into a collection of faces and vertices. You can load and save meshes with the MeshBuilder object. The organization of a MeshBuilder object is shown in Figure 6-8. Table 6-11 gives its methods.

You can set the color of all the faces in a MeshBuilder object with Set-Color. However, there is no corresponding MeshBuilder::GetColor because not all faces in a MeshBuilder component need to have the same color. This is because new faces you add (with MeshBuilder::AddFace) can be of a different color. Note that both vertices and faces may have colors. If a face has a color, the face color overrides the vertex color, which is then ignored.

The vertex normals are used when lighting calculations. The vertex normal is a vector, like an arrow that points in the direction that the vertex

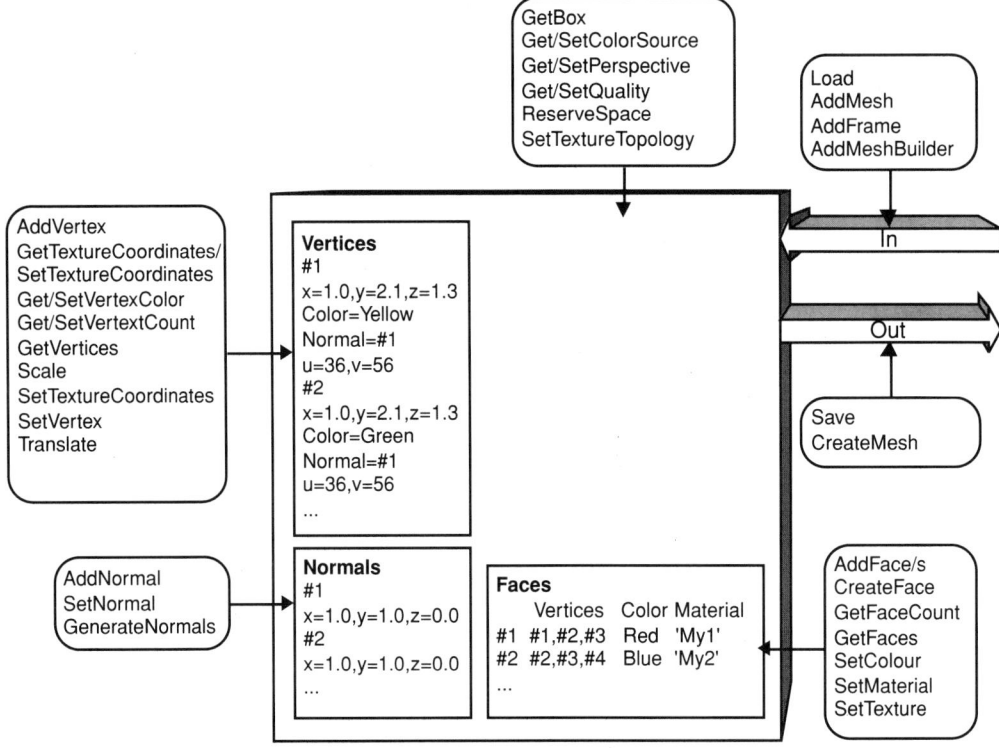

Figure 6-8. The MeshBuilder component, its internal data, and its methods.

Table 6-11. MeshBuilder methods

Method	Description
Input/Output	
Load	Loads a mesh from a file.
Save	Saves a mesh to file.
CreateMesh	Creates a Mesh object from a MeshBuilder object.
AddMesh	Loads a mesh into a MeshBuilder object.
AddFrame	Loads the meshes of a frame into a MeshBuilder object.
AddMeshBuilder	Loads one MeshBuilder object into another.
Vertices	
AddVertex	Adds a vertex.
AddNormal	Adds a normal.

Table 6-11. MeshBuilder methods *(continued)*

Method	Description
GetVertices	Gets the vertices already added to a MeshBuilder object.
SetVertex	Sets the *x, y, z* position of a specified vertex.
Get/SetVertexColor	Gets/sets the color of a specified vertex.
SetVertexColorRGB	Sets the color of the specified vertex (RGB).
GetVertexCount	Gets the number of vertices.
Translate	Moves all vertex positions by a specified amount.
Scale	Resizes a mesh.
SetNormal	Sets the normal vector of a specified vertex.
Faces	
GetFaceCount	Gets the number of faces already added to the MeshBuilder object.
GetFaces	Gets the faces of the MeshBuilder object.
AddFace	Adds a face.
AddFaces	Adds a set of faces.
CreateFace	Adds a new face that has no vertices.
SetColor	Sets the color of all faces.
SetColorRGB	Sets the color of all faces (RGB).
SetMaterial	Sets the material for all faces.
GenerateNormals	Generates the average vertex normals from adjoining faces.
Texture	
SetTexture	Sets the texture for all faces.
SetTextureTopology	Sets the texture topology.
Get/SetTextureCoordinates	Gets/sets the texture coordinates of a specified vertex.
Get/SetPerspective	Gets/sets the perspective. True if perspective correction on.
General Management	
GetBox	Gets the bounding box.
Get/SetColorSource	Gets/sets the color source.
Get/SetQuality	Gets/sets the render quality.
ReserveSpace	Reserves space for adding vertices, normals, or faces.

faces. Now, a corner of a polygon does not naturally point in a certain direction. So you can either set normals manually (which should be unit vectors) or force them to be calculated automatically by using MeshBuilder::GenerateNormals, which averages the face normals of surrounding faces.

You can add a MeshBuilder object directly to a frame, in which case a Mesh object is created automatically. However, if you do it this way and you later want to find the Mesh object, you will have to query the frame to find out what meshes are attached to it.

Face

A face is a polygon—a multisided figure—with each corner a vertex. In the retained mode API, face components are intimately connected with MeshBuilder components. Once a MeshBuilder object is converted into a Mesh object, you can no longer retrieve the individual faces (this is apparently for performance reasons in the design to the Mesh object, which performs internal optimizations).

You can create a face component with the IDirect3DRM::CreateFace method. This method creates a "free floating" face unconnected with a mesh that is "empty" (i.e., has no vertices). You add vertices to the face object, then add the face to a MeshBuilder with the MeshBuilder::AddFace or MeshBuilder::AddFaces methods. However, once you add the face it is no longer "free floating" and cannot be added to another mesh. Alternatively, you can create an empty face that is already attached to a particular MeshBuilder object by using the MeshBuilder::CreateMesh method.

To get a face out of a MeshBuilder object, use the MeshBuilder::GetFace method. For a face already attached to a MeshBuilder object, you can add vertices by their index in the MeshBuilder object with the Face::AddVertexAndNormalIndexed method.

The methods of the Face object are summarized in Table 6-12.

Table 6-12. Face methods

Method	Description
Vertex	
AddVertex	Adds a vertex to a face.
AddVertexAndNormalIndexed	Adds a vertex to a face, using the vertex index into MeshBuilder.
GetVertex	Gets the position and normal of a vertex.
GetVertexCount	Gets the count of vertices.

Chapter 6 Retained Mode Architecture

Table 6-12. **Face methods** *(continued)*

Method	Description
GetVertexIndex	Gets the index in the MeshBuilder object of a vertex.
GetVertices	Gets the position and normal of each vertex in a face.
GetNormal	Gets the normal of a face.
Appearance	
Get/SetColor	Gets/sets the color for a face.
SetColorRGB	Sets the color RGB for a face.
Get/SetMaterial	Gets/sets the material for a face.
Texture	
Get/SetTexture	Gets/sets the texture for a face.
GetTextureCoordinateIndex	Gets the texture coordinate index in MeshBuilder.
Get/SetTextureCoordinates	Gets/sets the texture coordinates.
Get/SetTextureTopology	Gets/sets the wrapping method for a face.

Material

A material object describes how a surface reflects light, that is, the reflective properties of a surface, not its color (color is set for each vertex, face, or group of faces). A material has two parts: emissive—whether a surface emits light—and specular—how reflective of light a surface is. The sharpness of a surface's specular property is further defined by the specular power: a value of 5 looks metallic while higher values look more and more plastic.

There are several ways to apply a material to an object. On a Mesh object, you use IDirect3DRMMesh::SetGroupMaterial; on a MeshBuilder, you use IDirect3DRMMeshBuilder::SetMaterial; and on a face, you use IDirect3DRMFace::SetMaterial. Note that a mesh's material setting can be overridden by its frame setting with IDirect3DRMFrame::SetMaterialMode. This method forces the material for a mesh to be inherited from the frame's material setting or the parent frame's material setting.

The methods of the Material object are summarized in Table 6-13.

Shadow

A **shadow** is a projection onto a plane of a Visual (a mesh) and a light. The shadow object is a Visual that you then add to the frame that contains the Visual that casts the shadow. To create a shadow, you call

Table 6-13. Material methods

Method	Description
Get/SetEmissive	Gets/sets the emissive component.
Get/SetPower	Gets/sets the specular exponent.
Get/SetSpecular	Gets/sets the power used for the specular exponent.

IDirect3DRM::CreateShadow, specifying a mesh, a light, and a plane onto which to project the shadow of the mesh from the light. Then, to make the shadow visible, you attach to a frame the shadow object that is created.

Texture

A **texture** is a rectangular array of pixels. In RGB color mode, a texture can be 8-, 24-, or 32-bit color; in the ramp color model, it must be 8-bit color. A texture doesn't have to be square, although the renderer will probably process it more efficiently if it is. Also, the renderer will probably prefer that it be a power of two (32×32, 64×64, 128×128, and so on).

You can create a retained mode texture in one of four ways:

1. Create a texture from a DirectDraw surface with IDirect3DRM::CreateTextureFromSurface.
2. Create a texture from a memory block using IDirect3DRM::CreateTexture, which uses a D3DRMIMAGE structure as its input.
3. Load a texture from a file with IDirect3DRM::LoadTexture method, which allows your application to load a texture from a file. The texture should be in Windows bitmap (.bmp) or Portable Pixmap (.ppm) format. The Portable Pixmap format is a holdover from Reality Lab's pre-Microsoft days. It probably makes sense to stick with the Microsoft-supported .bmp file format for your textures.
4. Create your own texture-loading callback function that is called by a Load method. You would use this callback to define your own way to load a texture file that is not in a .bmp or .ppm format (in which case you can simply use IDirect3DRM::LoadTexture). In the future, textures likely will be embeddable in an .x file.

Decals

Textures not only can be wrapped around meshes; they also can be rendered directly as floating images in the scene. In this case, the texture is called a **decal.** A decal is viewport-aligned, meaning it faces toward the screen

Chapter 6 Retained Mode Architecture

Table 6-14. Texture methods

Method	Description
Texture	
Changed	Tells the renderer that the texture has changed.
Get/SetColors	Gets/sets the maximum number of colors used in the texture.
GetImage	Gets the texture's image.
Get/SetOpacity	Gets/sets the texture's opacity map.
Get/SetShades	Gets/sets the number of shades used for rendering each color in the texture.
Decal	
Get/SetDecalDepth	Gets/sets the depth sorting properties of decal.
Get/SetDecalOrigin	Gets/sets the decal origin.
Get/SetDecalScale	Gets/sets the decal scale.
Get/SetDecalSize	Gets/sets the decal size.
GetDecalTransparency	Gets the decal transparency.
SetDecalTransparentColor	Sets the decal transparent color.

at the location in the 3D scene of the frame to which the decal is attached as a visual.

The Texture object methods are summarized in Table 6-14.

Wrap

You use the Wrap object to calculate texture coordinates to apply to a mesh. There are four kinds of wrapping available:

1. Flat
2. Cylindrical
3. Spherical
4. Chrome

Except for chrome wrapping, you are likely to find wrapping a cumbersome way of calculating texture mapping. This is because texture wrapping is a universal tool of 3D modeling tools. When you export your original 3D mesh from a modeling package, you should be able to export a texture map anyway. (However, beware that some import/export facilities may handle only geometry, not textures.)

So you may wonder why you should approach texture mapping as a 3D application programming issue through API calls when there are superior tools that already do the same thing. Perhaps you may want to create a simple object through API calls rather than loading it from a file. Direct3D does not have built-in primitive mesh types (spheres, tori, and so on), so you may have a need to do this. In this case, the wrapping functions may be of use. However, even for primitives you may find it simpler to create them and apply a texture in a modeling tool and export the result than write a routine in D3D. Also, you may want to animate the placement of a texture on a mesh.

The Wrap methods are summarized in Table 6-15.

Table 6-15. Wrap methods

Method	Description
Apply	Applies a wrap to a mesh or face.
ApplyRelative	Applies a wrap to a mesh or face relative to a world transform.

UserVisual

A UserVisual object is the escape hatch that allows you to extend the rendering functionality of the retained mode. A UserVisual object has no methods. You simply specify, when you create the object, a callback function that will be called by the renderer during the render traversal.

The renderer calls your UserVisual callback on two occasions. First the renderer calls to find out if the UserVisual is visible on the screen. So when is it visible? That is up to you. The UserVisual has no bounding box of its own, so you just have to come up with your own technique of deciding when your UserVisual is visible. If you tell the renderer that the UserVisual is visible, your callback will be called a second time later in the render traversal when it is told to actually render itself. At this point, your application is expected to drop down to the immediate mode, figure out what is going on, build an execute buffer, and render it. It would be nice if you could simply pass back an execute buffer and tell the renderer to render it appropriately, but this kind of functionality is not supported in the UserVisual mechanism.

Animation and AnimationSets

Animation and AnimationSets are a key vehicle for adding behavior to 3D scenes created with Direct3D. The Animation and AnimationSet components describe how a transform will be modified over time, often in reference to an RLFrame object. You use an Animation component to animate the position,

Chapter 6 Retained Mode Architecture

Table 6-16. Animation and AnimationSet methods

Method	Description
Animation	
AddPosition/Rotate/ScaleKey	Adds the position of/rotates/scales the key to the Animation object at a specified time.
GetSetOptions	Gets/sets animation options.
Get/SetType	Types are open (stops playing when the end of the data is reached) and closed (loops back to the beginning) animation types.
SetFrame	Sets the frame for this animation.
SetPositionsInterpolation	Sets the type of position interpolation (linear or cubic spline).
SetTime	Sets the current time for an Animation object.
AnimationSet	
Add/RemoveAnimation	Adds/removes an Animation object to the set.
SetTime	Sets the current time for the AnimationSet.

orientation, and scaling of Visuals, lights, and viewports. AnimationSet is simply an object that groups together a set of Animation objects. Table 6-16 gives the methods for Animation and AnimationSet.

Rotation keys in an Animation object are represented in **quaternions.** A quaternion is a mathematical technique that is used to represent an orientation in 3D space as a combination of a direction vector and a rotation angle around that vector. I discuss quaternions more fully in the 3D math section (Chapter 14). For now, rest assured that the retained mode provides essential functions that will eliminate your having to become a math wizard in order to use quaternions. (These functions are RMQuaternionFromMatrix, RMMatrixFromQuaternion, RMQuaternionFromRotation, RMQuaternionMultiply, and RMQuaternionSlerp.)

Chapter 7

A Simple 3D Scene

Starting and loading a simple scene is both easy and hard in Direct3D. Which it is depends on your perspective. The steps to starting a Direct3D session are fairly straightforward, although you might have trouble realizing this from some of the meandering sample code that is provided with the Direct3D SDK. In essence, you simply want to build a skeleton consisting of a retained mode Device and a Viewport object, a root frame for your scene, and a camera frame. To this skeleton, you add or load frames, hierarchies, meshes, and lights. Then, your application code will manipulate the Direct3D scene graph so that something interesting happens. This chapter is about the first part—getting your scene set up. Chapters 9 through 11 address the concepts and techniques for actually getting something interesting to happen in the basic scene graph.

Getting Started

The sample code with Direct3D is, well, meandering. It has been a sore spot for many beta developers who have wanted to get started with Direct3D only to find themselves wading through file after file looking for the answer to a simple question: Hey, how do I turn this Direct3D thing on?

The sample code problem is compounded by Direct3D's documentation. It sometimes tries to make things easier by trying to explain what the sample code is doing. An SDK worth its salt needs to include some code that is actually good enough to use as a starting point to do something. This is particularly true with setting up a 3D scene. This is something that everyone needs to do. Most people starting out simply want a chunk of code they can call with a command that says: Make me a 3D window and make it this big.

So will this chapter "fix" the meandering code problem of D3D's SDK? Well, yes and no. Yes, in terms of identifying the basic concepts of initializing a 3D session with Direct3D. These are actually very straightforward. But no in the sense of providing you with a comprehensive framework that adds enough features to Direct3D to make it an out-of-the-box application framework.

So let's begin. Note that the code in this chapter does not have error checking. Here, the key goal is to describe the actual method calls you need to make. Error-checking code simply makes things look a little more complicated than they really are. If a particular D3D method fails, you will of course need to trap the error. So examples of error-checking code can be found in the D3D sample code. In this chapter, the rval parameter is a return code from the method call. You need to verify that the method did not fail before proceeding.

Also note that your code will need to release retained mode objects when you are done with them. This involves a call to the Release method. Remember that a QueryInterface call increases the internal reference count of a COM object and therefore requires a corresponding call to Release.

Initializing D3D

The first step in using Direct3D is to initialize the system. You do this with a call to DirectDrawCreate. This is a routine you link into your application. You then get a Direct3D interface off of this object:

```
LPDIRECTDRAW lpDD;
LPDIRECT3D lpD3D;
rval=DirectDrawCreate(NULL, &lpDD, NULL);
rval=lpDD->QueryInterface(IID_IDirect3D, (void**) &lpD3D);
```

Creating the Device

Your next job is to create the retained mode device object. You have two options here, one complicated and one simple.

The complicated way is to query the system to determine which Direct3D drivers are actually installed on your system. To do this, use the device enumeration calls. The methods allow you to find a device based on a particular attribute or name.

You need to do this kind of checking for the device because there are several separate devices. Ramp mode is a separate device, as is the RGB mode device. A hardware device can install multiple drivers also.

The much simpler way, and the way recommended by Microsoft for most applications, is to use a default device. This is because there are likely to be multiple devices installed on your system, at a minimum a ramp device and an RGB device for software rendering.

To create a default device, call IDirect3DRM::CreateDeviceFromClipper with a NULL for the requested device (the lpGUID parameter). This call will search the system for a device that meets the criteria specified in Table 7-1. It first will look for a hardware-accelerated device. If it finds none that meets the default criteria, it next will search for a software-only device, and subsequently will choose the ramp version. The software-only version of the renderer meets these criteria, so there will always be at least a software renderer found when you call CreateDeviceFromClipper in this way. If an application has special needs that are not met by this list of default settings, it needs only to enumerate devices instead of specifying NULL for lpGUID.

Table 7-1. Device capabilities of the default retained mode device

D3DPCMPCAPS_LESSEQUAL
D3DPMISCCAPS_CULLCCW
D3DPRASTERCAPS_FOGVERTEX
D3DPSHADECAPS_ALPHAFLATSTIPPLED
D3DPTADDRESSCAPS_WRAP
D3DPTBLENDCAPS_COPY | D3DPTBLENDCAPS_MODULATE
D3DPTEXTURECAPS_PERSPECTIVE | D3DPTEXTURECAPS_TRANSPARENCY
D3DPTFILTERCAPS_NEAREST

The parameters for the CreateDeviceFromClipper call are described as follows:

```
HRESULT CreateDeviceFromClipper(LPDIRECTDRAWCLIPPER
    lpDDClipper, LPGUID lpGUID, int width, int height,
    LPDIRECT3DRMDEVICE * lplpD3DRMDevice);
```

A call to CreateDeviceFromClipper would look like:

```
rval=lpD3DRM->CreateDeviceFromClipper(lpDDClipper, NULL,
    width, height, &rmdevice);
```

- The parameter lpDDClipper is the address of a DirectDrawClipper object.
- The parameter lpGUID is the GUID of the device you seek to use and is what should normally be set to NULL.
- Width and height are the size of the device, which is the maximum size of a window on the screen.
- lplpD3DRMDevice is an address that will be filled with a pointer to an IDirect3DRMDevice interface if the call succeeds.

Setting Render Quality

Now that you have a device, you may want to configure the generic rendering quality settings. You do this with three methods:

1. IDirect3DRMDevice::SetQuality, which sets the rendering quality
2. IDirect3DRMDevice::SetDither, which sets the dithering flag
3. IDirect3DRMDevice::SetTextureQuality, which sets the texture quality

You call these methods as follows:

```
rval=rmdevice->SetQuality(renderqualityflag);
rval=rmdevice->SetDither(TRUE);
rval=rmdevice->SetTextureQuality(TRUE);
```

You also can configure two other rendering parameters. IDirect3DRM Device::SetShades sets the number of shades in a ramp of colors used for shading. IDirect3DRM::SetDefaultTextureShades sets the default number of shades for textures.

The following code sets to 4 the number of shades of color for a particular color. It also sets the number of color shades for textures to 4.

```
rval=rmdevice->SetShades(4)))
rval=rmdevice->SetDefaultTextureShades(4)))
```

If your screen is in 16- or 24-bit mode, you will want to set these values much higher, say to 256.

Creating a Camera Frame and Viewport

The process of creating a camera can be a little confusing. A Viewport object is not the camera, and the camera frame is not the camera. It is the two together that is the camera. You need the frame first because the Viewport needs to have a frame object as a parameter for the call to CreateViewport.

To create a scene frame, call CreateFrame with a NULL pointer for the parent:

```
LPDIRECT3DRMFRAME scene=NULL;
rval=rmdevice->CreateFrame(NULL, &scene)))
```

To create a camera frame, create a frame attached to the root frame of the scene:

```
LPDIRECT3DRMFRAME camera = NULL;
rval=rmdevice->CreateFrame(scene, &camera)))
```

Then use the CreateViewport method both to create the Viewport and to attach it to the camera frame at the same time:

```
rval=rmdevice->CreateViewport(camera, 0, 0, width, height,
    &view);
```

You can then configure the Viewport. For example, to set the back plane of the Viewport, you would use a call like this:

```
rval=view->SetBack(D3DVAL(5000.0));
```

Once you have a frame object, you can move it and manipulate it with the many frame methods described in Chapter 6. For example, to set the position, orientation, and rotation of your camera frame, your code would look like this:

```
rval=camera->SetPosition( camera, scene, D3DVAL(0),
    -D3DVAL(0), -D3DVAL(10));
rval=camera->SetOrientation(camera, scene, D3DVAL(0),
    D3DVAL(0), D3DVAL(1), D3DVAL(0),D3DVAL(1), D3DVAL(0))
```

Setting Up Lights

Setting up lights involves creating a light object and then attaching the light object to a frame in your scene. You can add an ambient light to any frame in the scene; it will affect the whole scene. It is easiest to simply add the ambient light to the root frame, as shown in the following code fragment (which assumes that the scene is in fact the root frame of the scene):

```
rval=lpD3DRM->CreateLightRGB( D3DRMLIGHT_AMBIENT, D3DVAL(0.1),
    D3DVAL(0.1), D3DVAL(0.1), &light2))
```

If you wanted to add a directional light to a scene, you may want to attach it to its own frame, as follows:

```
LPDIRECT3DRMFRAME lightframe = NULL;
LPDIRECT3DRMLIGHT lightobject = NULL;
rval=lpD3DRM->CreateFrame(scene, &lightframe);
rval=lightframe->SetPosition(scene, D3DVAL(5),D3DVAL(5),
    -D3DVAL(1));
rval=lpD3DRM->CreateLightRGB(D3DRMLIGHT_DIRECTIONAL,
    D3DVAL(0.9),D3DVAL(0.8), D3DVAL(0.7), &lightobject))
rval=lightframe->AddLight(lightframe, lightobject)))
```

Loading a Mesh

The last step in building a simple scene is to load a mesh. In this case, you will simply load an existing mesh, rather than build one. In reality, meshes are almost always modeled in a modeling package rather than created by writing code that defines the vertices and faces of the mesh and so on. Even if you want a simple box, you will find it quicker and easier to draw it in a modeling package, export it or convert it into .x, and then load it.

In this case, you will load a mesh called mymesh.x into a Meshbuilder and then attach the Meshbuilder object to a frame with the AddVisual method:

```
LPDIRECT3DRMMESHBUILDER mymeshbuilder = NULL;
rval=lpD3DRM->CreateMeshBuilder(lpD3DRM, &mymeshbuilder);
rval=mymeshbuilder->Load("mymesh.x", NULL, D3DRMLOAD_FROMFILE,
    NULL, NULL);
```

You then create a frame and attach the mesh to the frame:

```
rval=lpD3DRM->CreateFrame(scene, &meshframe);
meshframe->AddVisual(egg, (LPDIRECT3DRMVISUAL)
mymeshbuilder));
```

Note the casting of the `mymeshbuilder` into an `LPDIRECT3DRM VISUAL` type. Meshes, not Meshbuilders, are what are actually attached to a frame. The Meshbuilder gets converted into a Mesh object, and that is what is attached to the frame. The Meshbuilder object still exists separately from the Mesh attached to the frame.

Summing Up

This chapter may give you an uneasy feeling: Is 3D application programming really as simple as this? In some ways, yes. You build a scene graph and manipulate the objects in the scene graph. You can try to make this concept seem more complex, but this is really the basic metaphor for 3D application programming.

And in another sense, 3D application programming is even easier than this. All of the programming in this chapter (and almost all of the sample code in the Direct3D SDK for that matter) should not really need to be programmed at all. A reasonably complete file format with a basic Direct3D viewer ought to be able to easily handle these kinds of initialize and load issues as file format and file content, rather than as programming issues.

But in another way, of course, 3D application programming is not that simple. Once you have loaded a scene, you want something interesting to happen. And as you will see, accomplishing this moves you well beyond the basics of API calls on scene graph objects.

Chapter 8

Immediate Mode

The splitting of Direct3D into the retained and immediate modes presents developers with three choices. You can develop your application for the retained mode, for the immediate mode, or for a combination of both by using the retained mode's UserVisual object.

In this chapter, I present an overview of Direct3D's immediate mode to help you understand these choices. But be forewarned: The immediate mode offers pitfalls that may go beyond its initial appeal as a to-the-metal performance alternative to the retained mode.

Writing a complete 3D application in the immediate mode requires that you, in essence, write your own retained mode API. You can avoid the headache of doing this by using the retained mode's UserVisual to set up and configure the immediate mode for you. However, in this case you will not be able to save your 3D data to the .x file.

Use Immediate Mode or Retained Mode?

Many 3D application developers are likely to prefer working with Direct3D's retained mode. However, the reality is that the immediate mode is where a lot of the action is. Early adopters of Direct3D have tended to be existing 3D game and tool companies whose main interest has been to have an industry-standard interface to 3D hardware acceleration. They have been less interested in dropping their existing 3D engines and technologies and adopting the retained mode in order to get 3D hardware acceleration, so the easiest path has been to adopt Direct3D's low-level immediate mode as an alternative back end to whatever they are currently doing. In this sense, Direct3D's immediate mode serves as a porting target platform for existing 3D engines.

The result of this is that Direct3D is being adopted bottom-up in many quarters starting with the immediate mode, rather than top-down with developers first getting their feet wet with the retained mode and working their way down. This early widespread adoption and knowledge of the immediate mode is likely to impact the future direction of the retained mode, as developers will in the future not want to drop their immediate mode code to use the retained mode. This is not to say that no one uses the retained mode. In general, however, you will probably find that companies with existing 3D engines, which they believe will give them a continuing proprietary advantage, tend toward the immediate mode in order to get access to 3D hardware acceleration.

Does this mean that the only way to develop a commercial-quality application is to use the immediate mode? Some developers think so. Some chip companies have even promoted the idea of dropping down closer to the chip, either by programming directly to a particular chip or chip-specific proprietary API from the chip vendor.

But before you leap into the immediate mode, be forewarned: Immediate mode programming is very complex, even more complex than it appears. The immediate mode is in essence device-dependent, not device-independent, requiring an application to be very aware of many of the individual capabilities of the particular hardware or software driver being used. In fact, the only way you may be sure that an immediate mode application will run on a particular hardware configuration may be to actually run it on that hardware. Also, you should recognize that the Direct3D retained mode sits on top of the immediate mode (i.e., it creates immediate mode execute buffers). Finally, it is unclear whether, if you delve into immediate mode programming, you will end up with code that is better optimized than Direct3D's retained mode.

Overview of Immediate Mode

For a 3D polygon to be displayed on the screen, it must be transformed, lit, and rasterized. These three steps are the job of the Direct3D immediate mode, as illustrated in Figure 8-1.

The key mechanism of the immediate mode is the **execute buffer,** a memory buffer that you fill with a set of 3D vertices followed by a set of instructions that describe what to do with those vertices. The execute buffer is processed in turn by the transform, lighting, and rasterization modules. The transform module converts vertices from world space (3D coordinates) to 2D

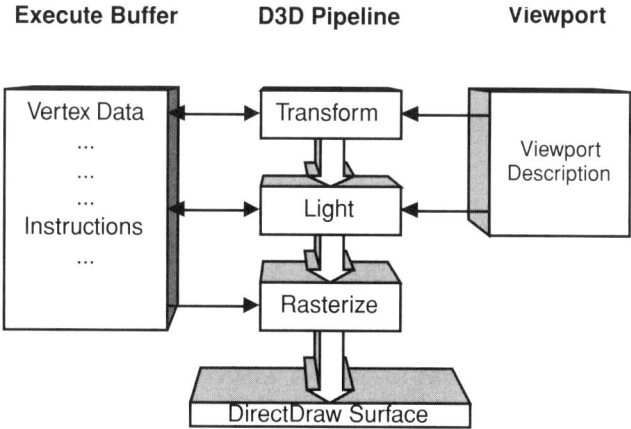

Figure 8-1. Immediate mode overview: the three steps for displaying a 3D polygon.

screen coordinates. The lighting module calculates the color values at each vertex, based on a stack of lights. The rasterization module draws the objects (triangles, lines, and points) to the frame buffer.

The immediate mode rendering pipeline is triggered by a call to the IDirect3DDevice::Execute method. The renderer first examines the vertex list at the beginning of the execute buffer to see if the vertices need to be transformed or transformed and lit (the structure you use for the vertex data tells the renderer what to do). If the vertices do need to be transformed and/or lit, the transform and lighting modules are invoked to process the vertex data. After these operations are completed, the instruction list is parsed and rendered.

The main reason for breaking the immediate mode into the three modules of transform, lighting, and rasterization is the way hardware acceleration works. Normally, only the rasterization module will be supported by a 3D acceleration chip, with the transform and lighting modules being software drivers that run on the host CPU. But it is possible for all three modules to be accelerated. So the architecture was designed to allow multiple possibilities. Also, there are actually different software versions of the modules. There are two different lighting modules and two rasterization modules. You can even switch between modules between frames, thereby allowing for special effects.

The Immediate Mode and COM

Like the retained mode API, the immediate mode API uses the COM model, so you should review the discussion of COM in the retained mode chapter (Chapter 3) before you read the rest of this chapter. As noted there, the COM model is not a significant performance issue for the retained mode because each COM component will be touched, at most, only a handful of times each time a scene is rendered.

It is a different story with immediate mode. Recall that in the COM model, only methods are exposed, never the data itself. But if your data is hundreds, or thousands, of vertices with their associated colors, textures, and normals and each must be passed through several stages of a pipeline, the overhead of v-tables and the sloshing of data in and out of COM objects would easily swamp a performance renderer. So don't look for COM components for the transform, lighting, and rasterization modules as you might expect: They don't exist!

So a different approach than a methods-only COM model is required for the immediate mode. You will find that the meat of the immediate mode is in data structures that reside outside of COM modules. When the immediate mode starts to rumba, the COM model gets out of the way!

What Is an Execute Buffer?

The execute buffer is the driving data structure of Direct3D's immediate mode. It is simply a block of memory that you allocate and fill with raw 3D data—vertices, colors, etc.—that describes triangles, lines, and points.

The execute buffer has two parts: a list of vertices, followed by a set of instructions that reference the vertices. The instructions tell the immediate mode modules what to do with the vertices, for example, "Draw a triangle using vertices 1, 2, and 3." The data of an execute buffer looks like Figure 8-2. An example of a common instruction is a triangle list (D3DOP_TRIANGLE), which is simply a list of triangle primitives that reference vertices in the vertex list.

The execute buffer supports several different data types that describe vertices in the data list. The immediate mode will process the vertices differently depending on the data type you use for the vertices.

The maximum allowable size of an execute buffer depends on the specific 3D acceleration hardware you are using. You can determine this size by calling the IDirect3DDevice::GetCaps method and examining the dwMaxBufferSize member of the D3DDEVICEDESC structure. If you are using the Direct3D's software-only rendering code instead of hardware acceleration, Microsoft recommends an execute buffer size of 64K. When your application can take advantage of hardware acceleration, however, Microsoft recommends you use a smaller execute buffer. Why? Apparently secondary memory caches are set up this way. However, it would be nice if a greater effort had been made to make the execute buffer work the same in both situations.

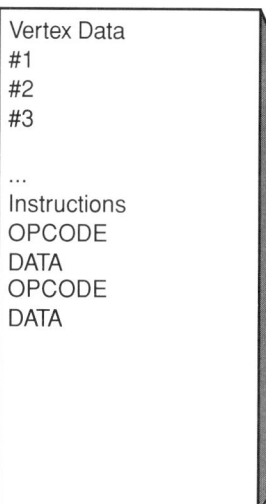

Figure 8-2. Immediate mode execute buffer.

Note that instructions in an execute buffer can reference only vertices in the same execute buffer, not another execute buffer. This offers an advantage to the renderer. If the transform module determines that all the vertices in an execute buffer fall outside view (i.e., are outside the viewing frustum), the entire execute buffer can be rejected from further processing by the lighting and rasterization buffer. You may find this an inconvenience, since you may want to think of the vertices as a separate block that you want different sets of instructions to reference. Direct3D just won't let you do this. So if this is important to you, you will just have to live without it. Also, you may have to break your execute buffer into several buffers to fit the maximum size of a particular hardware accelerator.

Transform Module

The first stop in the 3D pipeline for the execute buffer is the transform module. Actually, the execute buffer does not really go anywhere; a pointer to it is simply passed to the transform module. The results of the processing of the execute buffer by the transform module are stored back into the execute buffer. While the execute buffer is being processed, it cannot be accessed by your application.

The transform module handles the transformation of geometry from 3D coordinates into screen coordinates. If none of the vertices are in view, then the entire buffer can be rejected from further processing.

The module uses three 4 × 4 matrices, one each for the view, world, and projection transformations. This means that, in effect, the transform module has four user-modifiable state registers: viewport matrix, viewing matrix, world matrix, and projection matrix. These matrices can describe arbitrary projection matrices, thereby allowing perspective and orthographic views. The transform module combines these matrices internally into a transform matrix. This matrix represents the complete transformation that converts 3D points from their model space coordinates into 2D screen coordinates. When you change the viewing, world, or projection matrix, the transform matrix maintained by the transform module is updated. (You may set the transform matrix directly, but this is discouraged because it would circumvent internal optimizations.)

There are actually two ways to access the transform module. The normal way is the standard 3D pipeline, which passes a pointer to an execute buffer to the transform module. You also can call the transform module directly. You would call the transform module directly to do a bounding box test on an object to see if any of it is visible before you send the whole object (and all its vertices) into the pipeline through the execute buffer. Also, if you had a set of vectors that you wanted to transform for an application-specific operation, you would call the transform module directly, using the D3DTRANSFORMDATA structure.

Lighting Module

After the vertices in the execute buffer have been converted to screen coordinates, the next stop is the lighting module. As with the transform module, the execute buffer stays in place; only a pointer is passed to the lighting module. The results of the lighting module processing are stored back into the execute buffer.

The job of the lighting module is to process each of the vertices in the execute buffer in order to add color. Color for each vertex is calculated from data about the lights, shading model, etc., that the lighting module keeps. The module maintains a stack of current lights (directional, point lights, and spotlight sources), the level for ambient light, and a material. As with the transform module, you can call the lighting module directly. Do so by using the D3DLIGHTINGELEMENT structure.

Rasterization Module

Once the vertices in your execute buffer are transformed and lit, you send the execute buffer to the rasterization buffer. Unlike the other two modules, you call the rasterization module only through the execute buffer, not directly.

The job of the rasterization module is to draw the triangles, lines, and points described in the execute buffer.

Immediate Mode COM Components

Now you should have a basic sense of the 3D pipeline of Direct3D's immediate mode. Next, I examine the COM components that the immediate mode uses as an API to the 3D pipeline. Remember: The transform, lighting, and rasterization modules are not the COM object organization of the immediate mode. This may be confusing, but if you understand this you will find it easier to understand the immediate mode API.

The COM components of the immediate mode are described in Table 8-1.

Table 8-1. Immediate mode COM components

Component Name	Description
IDirect3D	The immediate mode manager object.
Device	The hardware device.
Viewport	The screen region to which to draw.
ExecuteBuffer	A list of vertex data and rendering instructions.
Light	A light source.
Material	The surface properties, such as color and texture.
Texture	An image to wrap on a model or display as a background.

The Big Picture

Figure 8-3 presents the big picture of the immediate mode.

IDirect3D

The IDirect3D is actually an interface (a set of methods) available on a DirectDraw surface COM object. To get a pointer to the IDirect3D interface on a DirectDraw object, you call the QueryInterface method:

```
lpDirectDraw->QueryInterface(
    IID_IDirect3D, // IDirect3D interface ID
    lpD3D);        // Address of a Direct3D object
```

You can use the methods of the IDirect3D interface to create other immediate mode objects (viewports, lights, and materials) or to find Direct3D devices. Once you have a pointer to this interface, you can think of it as an object that contains a list of viewports, lights, materials, and devices. The

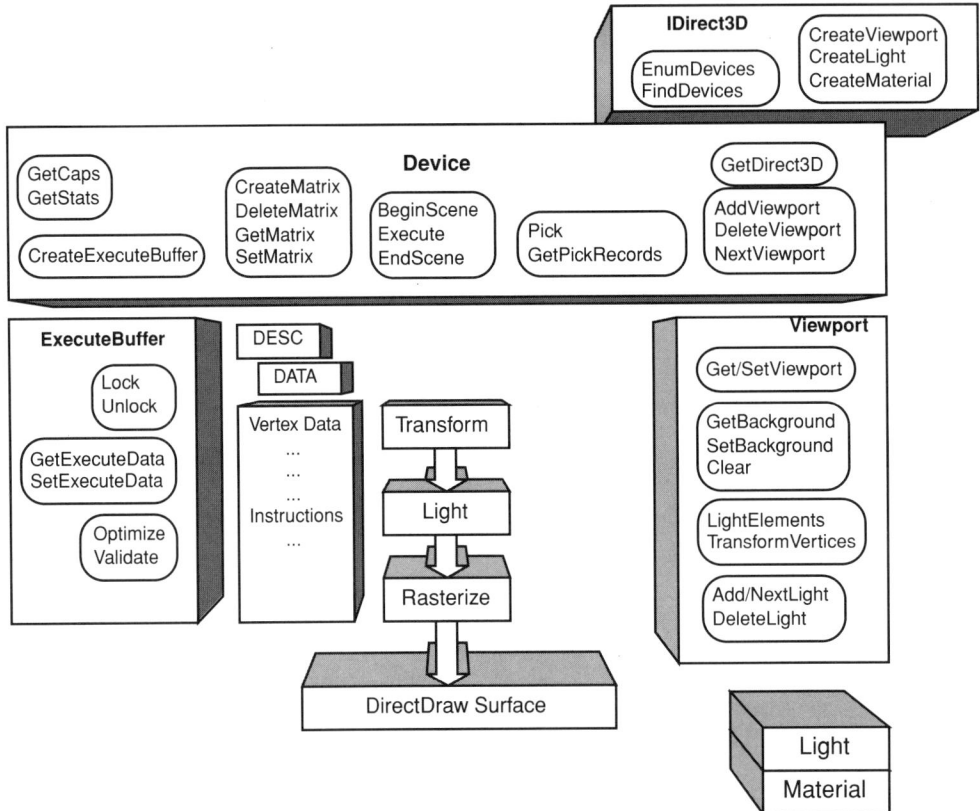

Figure 8-3. Immediate mode organization, components, and methods.

IDirect3D itself does not do much, but it is the starting place for the immediate mode API. One way to conceptualize the IDirect3D interface is shown in Figure 8-4.

Device

The immediate mode device is the main workhorse object. Its methods and relationship to other objects are shown in Figure 8-5.

You can create a Direct3D device object by calling the IDirectDraw-Surface::QueryInterface method for a back-buffer surface. The following example calls the IDirectDraw::CreateSurface method and then the IDirectDrawSurface::GetAttachedSurface method to retrieve the back-buffer surface:

Chapter 8   Immediate Mode

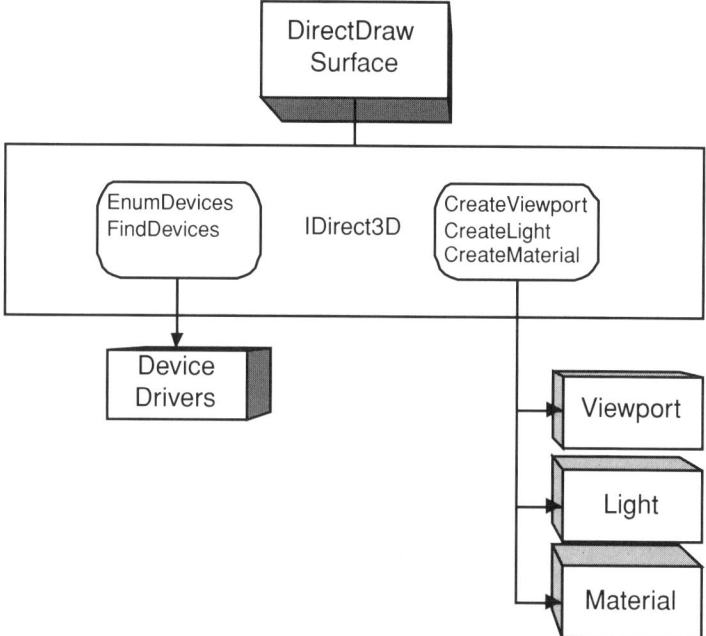

Figure 8-4. IDirect3D object.

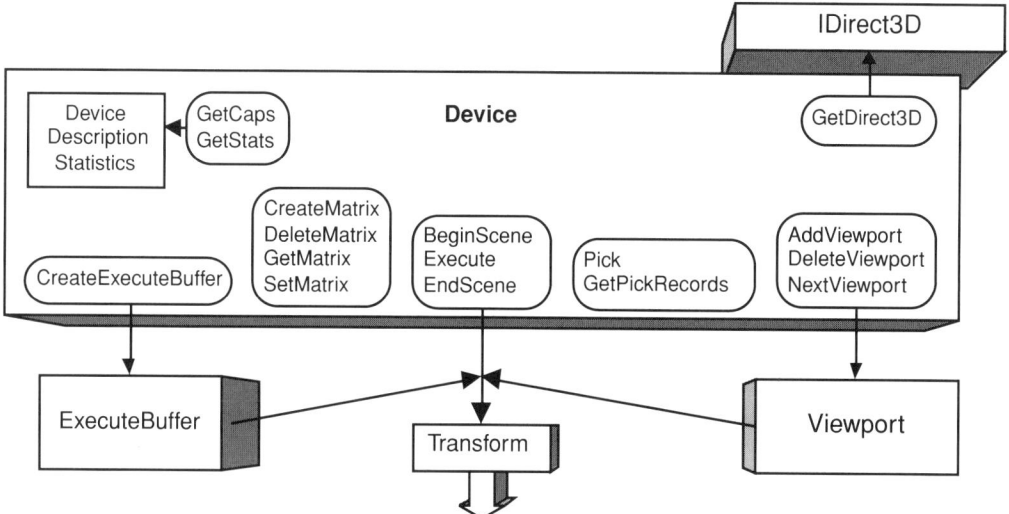

Figure 8-5. Direct3D device object.

```
lpDirectDraw->CreateSurface(
    lpDDSurfDesc,      // address of DDSURFACEDESC structure
    lpFrontBuffer,     // address of DIRECTDRAWSURFACE structure
    pUnkOuter);        // NULL
lpFrontBuffer->GetAttachedSurface(
    &ddscaps,          // address of DDSCAPS structure
    &lpBackBuffer);    // address of DIRECTDRAWSURFACE structure
lpBackBuffer->QueryInterface(
    GUIDforID3DDevice, // ID for IDirect3DDevice interface
    lpD3DDevice);      // address of DIRECT3DDEVICE object
```

The first parameter of the call to the IDirectDrawSurface::QueryInterface method for the back buffer is the GUID for the IDirect3DDevice interface. You can retrieve this GUID by calling the IDirect3D::EnumDevices method. The system supplies the GUID when it calls the EnumDevicesCallback function you give in the call to IDirect3D::EnumDevices.

A Direct3D device object resides on (or "is owned by") the interface list and has its own list of execute buffers and viewports. It also has a list of textures and materials, each of which points to the next texture or material in the list and also points back to the device.

The methods of the IDirect3DDevice interface report hardware capabilities, maintain a list of viewports, manipulate matrix objects, and execute execute buffer objects. To start the whole rasterization process, you call IDirect3DDevice::Execute. Direct3D then examines the vertexType member to determine whether the vertex needs to be transformed or lit.

The 3DDEVICEDESC Structure

In spite of a lot of discussion you may have heard about the hardware abstraction layer (HAL) and hardware emulation layer (HEL), it is important to recognize that at its core, the immediate mode is a quite device-dependent architecture. You are expected to query the device for a good deal of specific information, so your execute buffers are likely to end up device-dependent.

So where do you start to identify the device-dependent elements of the immediate mode that you will need to deal with? They are contained primarily in the 3DDEVICEDESC structure, which is illustrated in Figure 8-6.

Of course your question will be, which of these capabilities matters? Unfortunately, there is no clear answer. This structure seems to abstract and anticipate a range of chip designs and features. Probably your best bet in this area is to try to find a generic approach and then call the individual chip makers for advice on what they recommend you should look for in the 3DDEVICEDESC structure for your particular application.

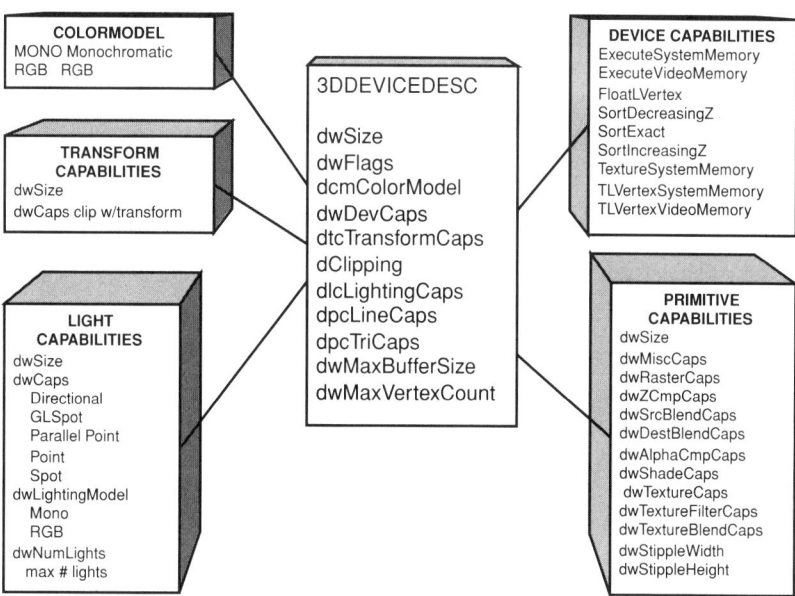

Figure 8-6. The 3DDEVICEDESC structure.

ExecuteBuffer Object

An execute buffer is a complex beast. To understand it, you must distinguish among the following:

- The ExecuteBuffer object
- The data structures that describe an execute buffer
- The execute buffer itself

The ExecuteBuffer object is a COM object that you create with IDirect3D Device::CreateExecuteBuffer. Each execute buffer is self-contained, that is, its instructions can reference only vertices in that execute buffer. Note that only one vertex type can be used in a particular execute buffer. The execute buffer may be in graphics memory. The methods you can perform on an ExecuteBuffer object are described in Table 8-2.

You can create a Direct3D ExecuteBuffer object by calling the IDirect3DDevice::CreateExecuteBuffer method, as follows:

```
lpD3DDevice->CreateExecuteBuffer(
    lpDesc,                     // address of DIRECT3DEXECUTEBUFFERDESC
                                   structure
    lplpDirect3DExecuteBuffer,  // address to contain a pointer to the
                                // Direct3DExecuteBuffer object
    pUnkOuter);                 // NULL
```

Table 8-2. Execute buffer methods

Category	Method
Execute data	GetExecuteData
	SetExecuteData
Lock and unlock	Lock
	Unlock
Miscellaneous	Optimize
	Validate

Execute buffer objects reside on a device list. You can use the IDirect3DDevice::CreateExecuteBuffer method to allocate space for the actual buffer, which may be on the hardware device.

Filling the Execute Buffer

The buffer is filled with two contiguous arrays of vertices and opcodes by using the following calls to the IDirect3DExecuteBuffer::Lock, IDirect3DExecuteBuffer::Unlock, and IDirect3DExecuteBuffer::SetExecuteData methods:

```
lpD3DExBuf->Lock(
lpDesc);. // address of DIRECT3DEXECUTEBUFFERDESC structure
lpD3DExBuf->Unlock();
lpD3DExBuf->SetExecuteData(
lpData);   // address of D3DEXECUTEDATA structure
```

The last call in the preceding example is to the IDirect3DExecuteBuffer::SetExecuteData method. This method notifies Direct3D, where the two parts of the buffer reside relative to the address that was returned by the call to the IDirect3DExecuteBuffer::Lock method.

ExecuteBuffer Data Structures

Figure 8-7 shows more clearly the dynamics among the ExecuteBuffer object, the D3DEXECUTEBUFFERDESC and D3DEXECUTEDATA structures, and the data in the execute buffer itself.

Vertex Structure

An execute buffer has two parts: an array of vertices (each typically with position, normal vector, and texture coordinates) and an array of opcode/operand groups. When an application calls the IDirect3DDevice::

Chapter 8   Immediate Mode

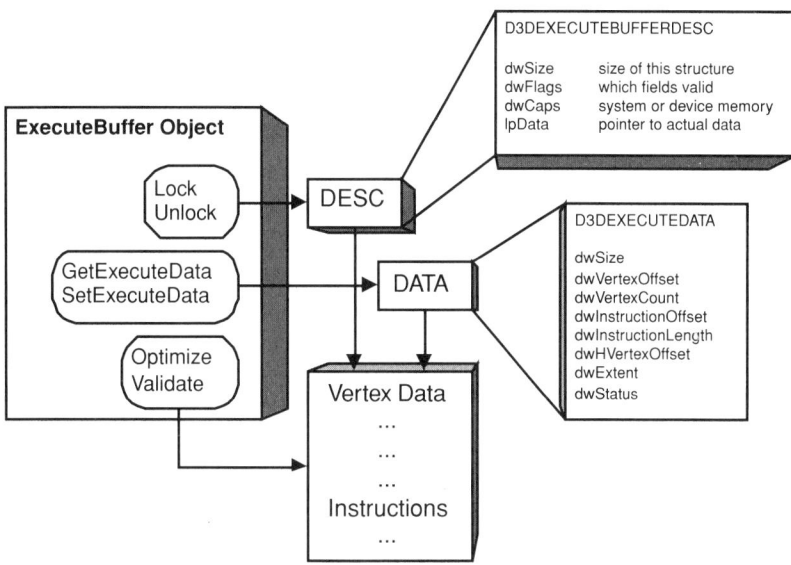

Figure 8-7. Relationship of ExecuteBuffer objects and structure.

Execute method, the system examines the vertexType member of the D3DEXECUTEDATA buffer to determine whether the vertex list needs to be transformed or transformed and lit. The different types of vertex data structures are shown in Figure 8-8.

A display list can contain four different vertex types. For rasterization-only hardware, the application should use the D3DTLVERTEX structure, which is a transformed and lit vertex. It contains screen coordinates and colors. If the hardware handles the transformations, the application should use a D3DLVERTEX structure. This structure contains only data and a color that would be filled by software lighting. If the hardware supports lighting, the application simply uses a vertex because this can be both transformed and lighted.

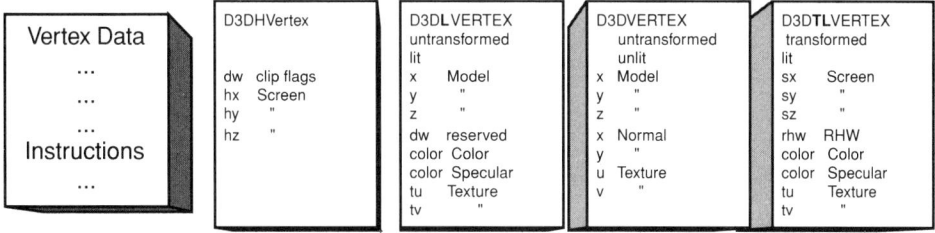

Figure 8-8. Vertex data structures.

Execute Buffer Instructions

The instructions in the execute buffer are organized into opcode/operand pairs. The opcode specifies the instructions; the operand is the data that is used for the instructions. Each opcode has its own type of operand data types and structures, depending on the kind of data opcode needs. You need to know the operand data structure for the opcode you want to use; the opcode itself does not tell you. One opcode can have several operands following it; the system simply performs the relevant operation on each operand. Opcodes and their operands are described with the D3DOPCODE enumerated type.

The execute buffer opcodes are described in Table 8-3.

Table 8-3. Execute buffer opcodes

OPCODE	DESCRIPTION	OPERAND
Point	Displays a point.	The index of a point.
Line	Displays a line.	The vertices of the segments of the line.
TriangleList	Displays a triangle.	Three vertices plus edge flags.
MatrixLoad	Loads a matrix.	The handles to the destination and source matrices.
MatrixMultiply	Multiplies two matrices.	The handles to the result matrix, the first source matrix, and the second source matrix.
StateTransform	Sets a state variable in the transform module.	The variable identifier and new value.
StateLight	Sets a state variable in the lighting module.	D3DRENDERSTATETYPE data structure.
StateRender	Sets a state variable in the rasterization module.	D3DRENDERSTATETYPE data structure.
ProcessVertices	Processes the light and transform vertices.	D3DPROCESSVERTICES structure.
TextureLoad	Loads a texture.	The handles to the destination and source texture.
Exit	Indicates the end of the opcode list.	No operand.
BranchForward	Forces a branch (a jump forward in the opcode list).	D3DBRANCH data structure.
Span	Defines a span (a list of points—and colors—with the same *y*-value).	The D3DSPAN structure—count of spans, index to first vertex, each new span starts with a new *y*-value.

An overview of the opcode/operand relationships is shown in Figure 8-9. Each instruction in the execute buffer is a D3DINSTRUCTION structure. This structure contains the opcode, the size of the data for each operand, and the number of operands (data units) that follow. You could make the size value for an operand larger than is required by the operand itself (operand structures themselves are of a fixed size), so you could embed additional data in the operand structure that would not be processed by Direct3D. Figure 8-9 groups the opcodes by conceptual category and then shows the operand data structure for each operand type.

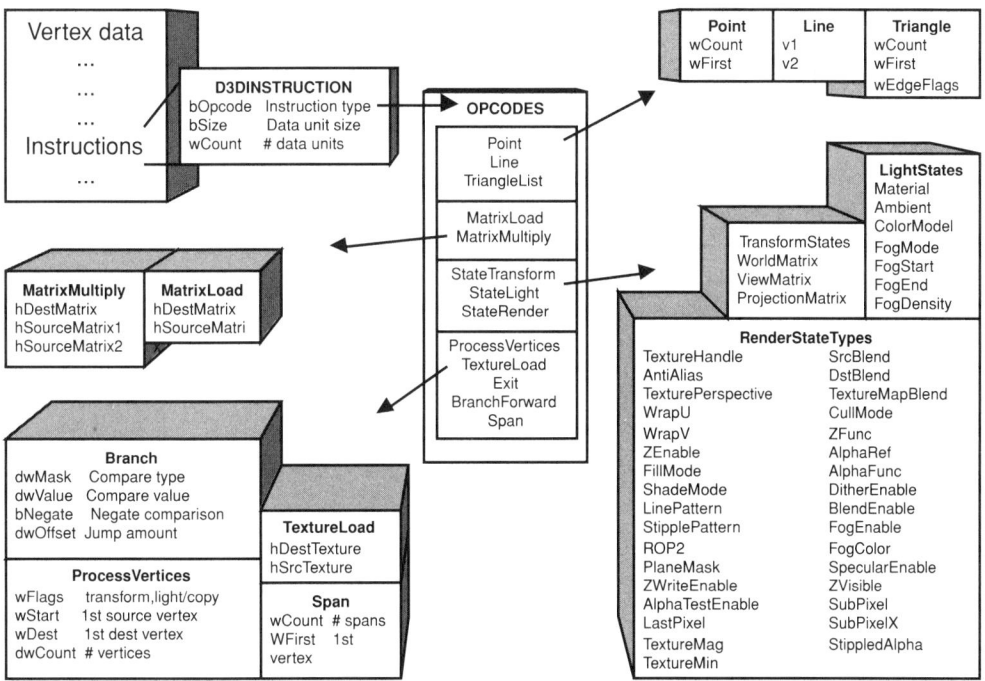

Figure 8-9. Overview of the execute buffer opcode/operand relationship.

From the figure you should get a sense of the ways to go about using an execute buffer and the extent to which the COM model gets out of the way when the renderer gets going. To configure the internal states of the rendering system, you put state codes in the execute buffer. To draw lines and polygons, you put the opcodes in the execute buffer. You use the opcodes to set textures, matrices, and materials. In other words, the execute buffer is like a language that describes the operations that the renderer is to perform.

The Rendering Loop

The code for launching a rendering of an execute buffer is very short:

```
lpIMdevice->BeginScene();
lpIMdevice->Execute(lpExecuteBuffer,
  lpIMviewport, D3DEXECUTE_UNCLIPPED);
lpIMdevice->EndScene();
```

UserVisuals and the Immediate Mode

The retained mode's UserVisual provides a potential lower-effort entry point into the arcane domain of the immediate mode. The UserVisual allows you to attach a callback function to a particular frame that is called at render time. This callback function is passed a pointer to the retained mode device and Viewport objects, which you then use to access the underlying immediate mode device and Viewport object. You can then render an execute buffer to the immediate mode device.

The advantage of using the UserVisual approach is that you can still get the application-level benefits of the retained mode. The disadvantage is that UserVisual does not do quite enough for you.

To use a UserVisual, you first define a callback function using the parameters specified for a UserVisual callback. The following code fragment shows the basic idea of a UserVisual callback:

```
int AUserVisualCallback(
LPDIRECT3DRMUSERVISUAL lpD3DRMUV,
LPVOID lparg,
D3DRMUSERVISUALREASON lpD3DRMUVreason,
LPDIRECT3DRMDEVICE lpD3DRMDev,
LPDIRECT3DRMVIEWPORT lpD3DRMview)
{
    LPDIRECT3DDEVICE lpIMdevice = NULL;
    LPDIRECT3DVIEWPORT lpIMviewport = NULL;
    if (reason == D3DRMUSERVISUAL_CANSEE)
     return TRUE;
    if (reason == D3DRMUSERVISUAL_RENDER)
    {
    lpD3DRMDev->GetDirect3DDevice(&lpIMdevice);
        lpD3DRMview->GetDirect3DViewport(&lpIMviewport);
    lpExecuteBuffer->Lock(&desc);
    <update execute buffer>
    lpExecuteBuffer->Unlock(&desc);
```

```
        lpIMDevice->Execute(Executebuffer,lpIMviewport,
        D3DEXECUTE_CLIPPED)
    return D3D_OK;
    }
}
```

The UserVisual callback is called two times during the rendering process. First, it is called with the parameter "reason" set to D3DRMUSER-VISUAL_CANSEE. The callback is supposed to determine if the UserVisual is currently in view and, if so, return the value of TRUE. To determine whether the UserVisual is in view, you use the retained mode Viewport that is passed as a parameter (lpD3DRMview) to the callback. It would be nice if you could specify a bounding box or bounding sphere as the size and location of the UserVisual within the frame to which it is attached. Alas, the UserVisual mechanism is not that sophisticated.

The second time the callback is called is with the flag D3DRMUSER-VISUAL_RENDER. It is on this call that you render your 3D data. The immediate mode is already set up for you when you use this approach; that is, the matrices are set up and so on.

From the point of view of a retained mode user, probably the single largest drawback to using the UserVisual is that there is no way to save and reload the execute buffers that you would want to attach.

Chapter 9

World Management 101

Now that you know the basics of Direct3D and how it works, how can you use Direct3D to build a 3D application? In this chapter, I explore making the conceptual and practical leap from spinning teapots and simplistic object viewer demos into the realm of interesting 3D applications. Often, this boils down to a deceptively simple question: How do you get from a scene graph to an application?

But first, a warning: This subject can be a mind-bender. 3D introduces concepts of spatiality, time, and interactivity into application development, kind of like taking a user interface with nonmodal and modal elements and stoking it into hyperspace. This is an area of active research, development, and debate in many 3D-related fields. Is there such a thing as a viable, generalized 3D application-authoring environment, like a 3D Macromedia Director? What role do standards such as VRML play? Is this a programming, authoring, or modeling issue, or all three?

Don't count on a quick, universal solution to 3D application design. Debates have raged for years about what is the best approach or tool set for putting together database, multimedia, and other applications. For 3D application development, it is easy to imagine the same will occur. Even if you are eager to get on with coding for what you think is a relatively simple application, you'll need to put in some conceptualizing design effort. You'll have to build some code on top of Direct3D for pretty much anything but the most trivial demo.

3D application design does raise some recurring common themes, including traversal, actors, events, godforces, and the user. In this chapter, I examine these as well as some specific strategies using Direct3D to address them. In essence, every 3D application needs some kind of application framework. Further, since few are available to buy at this stage of the industry, you will probably have to write your own. Also, the issue of networked 3D has a powerful design implication, which I examine in Chapter 11. Think of this as a food-for-thought chapter as you start to design your 3D application.

The 3D Application Framework

As of this writing, the field of general-purpose 3D application frameworks is evolving. In essence, though, the concepts that seem to be involved fall into three basic categories: worlds, things, and behaviors.

A **world** is a region of 3D space larger than a single scene graph. A **thing** is an abstraction of objects and entities that exist in a world. In this chapter, I call things "actors." A **behavior** means change, either over time (interpolation and animation) or as a result of events (messages, causality, and interactions between people and things).

Why Not an MFC Wrapper?

One tempting but overly simplistic approach to building a 3D application framework is to write a set of MFC wrappers around each of Direct3D's COM objects. Although this approach offers certain benefits, it does not address the core issues of world management.

One benefit is that it puts an MFC face around the less familiar performance COM approaches that Direct3D uses. An MFC is more familiar to many programmers. Also, MFC wrapper objects can be extended much more easily than Direct3D's COM objects, which currently do not support the concepts of aggregation, containment, attachment, and inheritance.

If a future .x file format parser were to evolve in a way sophisticated enough to load both MFC objects and COM objects, you might be able to integrate MFC object persistence with the .x file format. However, now there are no tools that support this kind of functionality. In essence, a simplistic wrapper approach would end up putting an MFC object face on a COM object. That is, you would have a COM object inside an MFC object, with no way to save both in the same place.

The core functionality you need to implement to achieve world management is at a higher level of abstraction. This is not to say that MFC could not be useful for Direct3D application development. Far from it. First, MFC would be a very useful vehicle for encapsulating windows and device management, just as it is for managing Windows programming. The retained mode's Device and IDirect3DRM objects, for example, would be an ideal candidate for MFC encapsulation. But the key to world management is in a higher-level set of concepts; this is where an MFC approach could come into its own. But you first must aim at a higher level of abstraction that includes worlds, things, and behaviors. And efforts to address these kinds of issues in such areas as military simulations, CAD/CAM, and VRML indicate that these issues go far deeper than which language wrapper you use. In this chapter, I start to address the underlying issues involved.

What About a World "on Top of" a Scene Graph?

Another appealing approach is simply to ignore the particular underlying 3D retained mode API and build a generic, API-independent application framework. Such an approach could have a lot of merit and involve a lot of work, but it may in the long run be the winning design approach to 3D world management.

The idea is to draw a design line between the retained mode and the application framework. If the application framework in essence drives the scene graph "from above," then you could think of 3D application programming in a generic, abstract environment, independent of a particular API like Direct3D.

The strength of this approach is that it isolates 3D application design from many implementation details. In fact, a well-designed application framework could conceivably ignore the retained mode altogether and write directly to the immediate mode. Note, however, that this does not mean the functions of the retained mode (scene-graph level data management and execute buffer optimization) can be ignored. In this case, these would simply be incorporated into a higher-level application framework.

The weakness of this approach is that many features—such as traversal, picking, and interpolation—end up being duplicated at two levels. Moreover, the strengths of a particular API may get missed if you implement a generic world database model.

To clarify these issues, I next define and discuss certain basic concepts. First, some key definitions:

Traversal: A walk through the scene tree that can generate callbacks (calls to user-defined functions attached to particular frames).

Actor: A shape that has properties and intelligence.

Event: A methodology that actors use to interact and communicate with each other that "something has happened."

Godforce: A thing that influences or controls the scene and actors.

The user: The person or persons using the 3D application. Sometimes the user plays the role of an actor, a godforce, or merely a bystander in the application.

Your 3D application may or may not address these concepts. However, they tend to show up often in a wide range of 3D applications.

A generic 3D application design scenario could look something like the following. Your application will have "things"—actors—positioned in a 3D scene—a world. These actors will do things and interact with each other in some way—objects will collide, robots will chase each other, machine parts will be connected, etc. Some godlike forces will influence and control the whole scene—introduce or remove actors, update the scene, tell the actors to do something, etc. The user will either watch as a bystander, participate in the scene as an actor, or act as a godforce that changes and directs things.

I use this basic 3D scenario as a generic reference design for this chapter. Although this design likely will not match your own needs or preferences, my goal is to give you a reasonably clear reference point against which to develop your own design ideas. Figure 9-1 shows a schematic overview of a generic 3D application design.

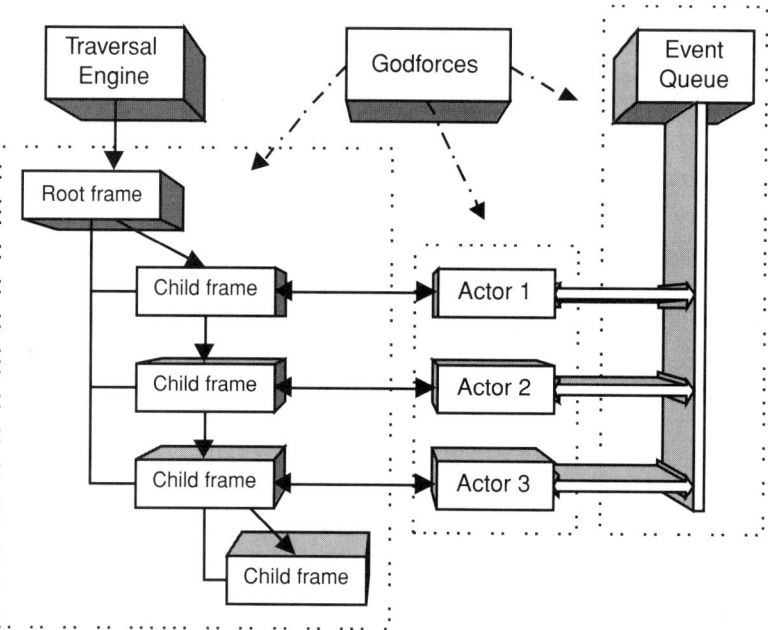

Figure 9-1. Schematic overview of a generic 3D application design.

Traversal Engine

Traversal is the cost-free design engine of 3D applications built on retained mode APIs. In this context, it means the systematic visiting of each node in the scene's frame tree structure. Think of a traversal as a single pass that touches each of the frames in your scene. It starts with the root frame of the scene, does something with it and then in turn visits each of the frame's children (if it has any) and does something with each. Next, it visits the frame's siblings.

The traversal path for a simple set of frames is shown by the solid arrows in Figure 9-2. Think of your hierarchical organization as an outline; traversal means simply going down the outline, stopping at every entry. If you think of a hierarchical organization like a corporation's organizational chart (CEO at the top, VP's below, etc.), then traversal goes down from left to right.

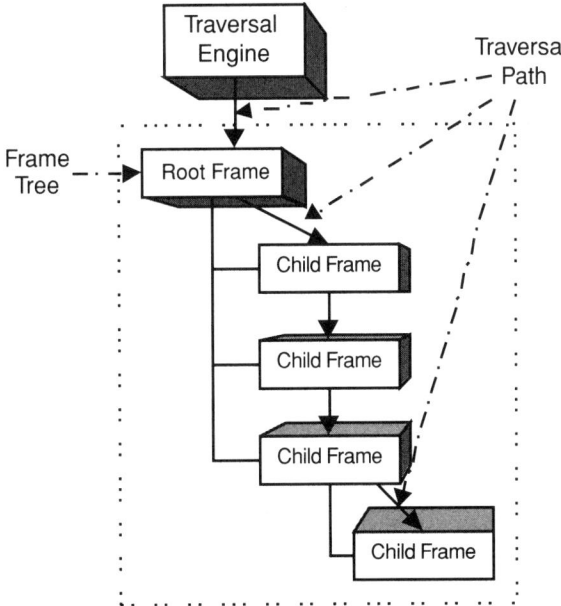

Figure 9-2. The traversal path through a frame tree.

Notice that the rendering code of a retained mode API has to traverse the frame tree in order to display it. This is how the rendering code determines the location of each shape (through the chain of transformation matrices up to the root). This also is how it finds any inherited state information. The default color of a mesh, for example, might be inherited from its parent frame, which may have inherited its default color from its parent, and so on. So since a retained mode API has the basic traversal code built in, it is a short step to let the application developer use this traversal mechanism as part of an application design. Otherwise, you could just write your own traversal code that would examine the frame tree each time the scene is rendered to the frame buffer so as to determine what has changed. The typical method to make traversal available to the developer is to provide special-purpose callbacks, user-supplied functions that are called when a frame is visited on traversal.

Some APIs get fancy with the kinds of traversal and callbacks they support. Some have different special-purpose traversals, such as collision detection, user-defined traversals, and culling (eliminating whole chunks of the frame tree from further processing because they are out of view). SGI's Performer API even allows for multiple simultaneous traversals supported by multiple processors, primarily for culling traversal.

Direct3D Traversal

Direct3D supports two kinds of traversals to which you can attach callbacks: a move traversal (to which you attach move callbacks) and a render traversal (to which you attach user visuals). The key point is that in your callback function, you can change the frame in some way in your callback code. You can make the frame (or its children) move in some way, modify the frame's mesh in some way (say, make traffic light change color), and so on.

You attach a move traversal callback function to a particular frame with IDirect3DRMFrame::AddMoveCallback and remove it with IDirect3DRMFrame::RemoveMoveCallback. You can attach more than one callback to a frame; on traversal they are called in the order they were created.

The move traversal is initiated either by a call to IDirect3DRMFrame::Move or to IDirect3DRM::Tick. The Move method launches a traversal for the frame on which you call the method and the frame hierarchy attached to it. For each frame in the given hierarchy, the default rotations and velocities are applied (the values you set with IDirect3DRMFrame::SetRotation and IDirect3DRMFrame::SetVelocity), the move callbacks are called, and attached animations are queried. If you call the Move method on the root frame of the scene, the entire scene is traversed.

The Tick method performs the retained mode heartbeat and applies to the whole scene. Tick performs a move traversal just like the Move method, but it also renders the scene to the current device. Control is returned when the rendering cycle is complete.

Both Tick and Move allow you to specify a relative tick value. This value both scales the default frame rotations and velocities and gets passed on to the move callbacks. It is a roundabout way of compensating for the passage of time. The default rotation and velocity for a frame are multiplied by the tick value before they are applied to the frame's actual location. If the tick value is 1, the full amount is applied; if it is 2, twice the value is applied; and so on.

In essence, you can attach callbacks to frames. Think of the move traversal path as making a detour through the callback before going on to the next frame. The solid arrows in Figure 9-3 show this extended traversal path when move callbacks are added.

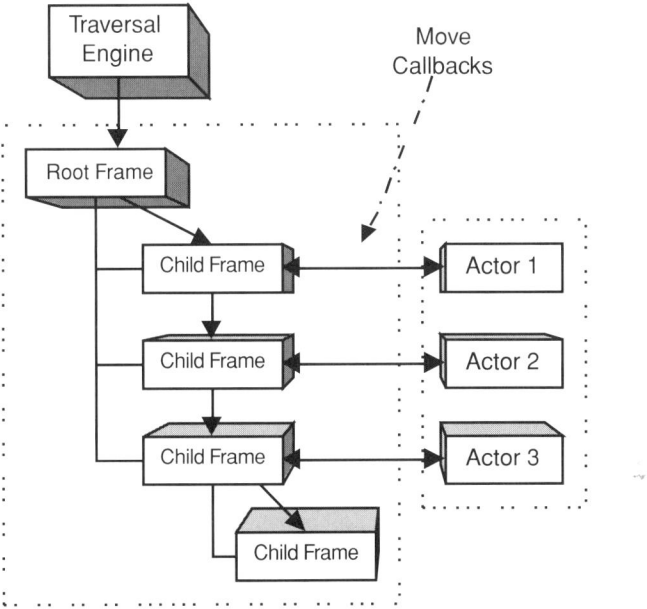

Figure 9-3. Move traversal with callbacks.

You also can think of user visuals as traversal callbacks, except they happen on the render traversal, not the move traversal. Since in the user visual callback you render your own data to the immediate mode, you can of course modify what you display from frame to frame.

Limits of Traversal

There are limits to what you can do to a frame tree during the move callback. The callback passes the address of the current frame to the move callback so that the callback code will know what frame it is attached to (you could attach the same callback code to different frames). But don't delete the current frame—you'll confuse the heck out of the traversal code! Also, if you change a frame that is located previously in the hierarchy, remember that the move traversal has already visited it. And if you change a frame that is later in the hierarchy, it will be visited later in the course of the traversal.

Actors as Things

So what should this function do that gets called during traversal, and how does it know what to do to the frame tree? This brings us to the next general design concept that shows up in 3D applications: things, or as I call them, actors.

Look around you. If you are in a room, you might see a table, some books, a chair, a picture on the wall. If you are outside (you lucky dog, reading a book like this outside!), you may see a tree, some rocks, the sky, the ground. And wherever you are, you may see some people. These are the "things" of our visual world. Pretty obvious, eh?

When you build a 3D scene, you are likely going to want "things" in it. Sometimes your simulated "things" might be imitations of things in the real world—such as a virtual room you can walk around in; sometimes they might be more abstract—such as a box whose height represents a value in a bar chart. Some of these "things" are pretty dumb; they just sit there. Some are like walls; they don't do anything themselves, but other things can run into them. Sometimes they are quite intelligent, containing an algorithmic ability to interact with the scene around them or change and move over time. And sometimes they are simply a proxy representation for a user in the 3D scene.

I refer to this general concept of "things" as actors, for lack of a better term. The term "things" seems a little too silly, while "objects" is too confusing when you also are talking about object-oriented objects. Another possible term is "entities," but this seems a little too abstract. "Actor" may be a little bit of overkill for a concept that describes a chair or rock, but it conveys a sense of action and potential that has a nice ring to it. The term fits well when you get into more sophisticated 3D realms, like programming virtual people.

So what exactly is an actor? Here is a stab at a definition (or if you prefer to think of an actor as an object-oriented way, here is an abstraction): An actor is a shape with properties and intelligence. The concept of actors as an abstract encapsulation of things with intelligence and properties is a recurring theme in many areas of 3D. The state of the art is actually more a yearning: People would like to make things and put them in their own worlds and have them just behave in ways appropriate for the scene they are in. In the 3D modeling field, people speak of "smart models"—modeled shapes that can have properties and data like animation attached to them. In the CAD field, there is the concept of intelligent shapes or components. Games designers have "nonplayer characters"—characters that appear in your game and are not real people but that act based on some sort of artificial intelligence algorithm. DIS has entities (the basic building block) or computer-generated forces (the war-game equivalent of nonplayer characters). In virtual spaces, people speak of "avatars," visual representations of people in virtual spaces.

By now, I hope you are putting the concepts of traversal and actors together: You use traversal to trigger the intelligence and behavior of actors in your scene.

Building Actors in Direct3D

So how do you use Direct3D to implement your concept of an actor. Here are some potential approaches.

- **Frame/mesh pairs as actors**

Probably the simplest concept of an actor in Direct3D is either a mesh or a frame with a mesh attached. You'll probably want to opt for at least a frame and a mesh as your abstraction of the simplest actor. By including the frame, you can move and rotate your actor, give it default rotation and velocity, and attach a callback to it (move callbacks attach to frames, not meshes).

- **Actors with moving parts**

Next up the ladder of increasing complexity are actors with moving parts, such as a door with a doorknob or a window that opens. The easiest way to implement such an actor is to have a top-level frame represent the actor as a whole and have child frames represent the parts. You could implement a separate move callback to make each part of the actor move, but it might be simpler to implement a single callback attached to the actor's top-level frame and have it handle manipulating the parts.

- **Frame reference as actor**

Recall that you can attach a frame to a frame as a reference instead of a child. In this case, you could have multiple actors based on the same frame hierarchy. However, all of these actors would behave in the same way, which may not be what you want.

- **Animated actors**

AnimationSets are an obvious choice to add animation sequences to an actor in Direct3D. Basically, the general direction of movement and the moving parts of your actor are driven by an AnimationSet attached to the appropriate frames.

- **Skinned characters as actors**

  Using animations has limits when you want to create human-like characters. Animations apply to frames, not to the individual polygons of a mesh. So joints are where two different meshes attached to two different frames meet. You will not have a cleanly skinned joint. This is because the vertices belong to different meshes, so the renderer cannot shade between them.

- **Self-LODing actors**

  Direct3D does not support LOD to the degree that many retained mode APIs do. However, you could implement LOD with Add/RemoveChild commands during the move traversal. Note that the same concept of switching between different versions of the same model can be used to create simple animation cycles.

- **Actors attached to actors**

  Sometimes you may want to have an actor attached to another actor. For example, think of a robot picking up a cup and putting it on a table. You will likely want to think of the robot, cup, and table as separate actors. So somehow you need to distinguish in the frame hierarchy between, for example, a child frame that is an arm (and part of a thing) and a child frame that is a cup (and therefore a separate thing). If you allow actors to be attached to actors, you need to check for attached actors before you delete an actor.

- **COM objects as actors**

  If you buy into the Direct3D performance COM religion, you may eventually want to use COM objects to represent actors. You may want to think of things like "in-scene activation" as the 3D equivalent of OLE's in-place activation. COM actor objects could be attached to frames in the scene graph, COM wrapper objects could encapsulate chunks of frame graph hierarchy, and so on. Although there is no support in Direct3D for COM extensions of this sort, you could implement actor objects independent of Direct3D.

Making Actors Persistent

You'll see in Chapter 13 that some help is evolving in the DirectX file format for making at least the properties of objects persistent.

Events as Things

In your 3D application, you will likely need to use events: Something will happen that will cause something else to happen. You may want the user to click a 3D file folder and have it open. You may want the robot to fall down when it gets shot. You may want a door to open when the avatar or actor gets near it. In any event (excuse the expression), you are likely to want to include the causality of events in your 3D scene.

Event management in software design is at once a trivially simple and an enormously complicated issue. At one level, you can look at event management as a core function of Windows itself, since Windows routes all sorts of messages to the various windows on the screen for processing. But you certainly do not want to write an entire Windows message management system just to get a 3D application up and running! To bring the concept of events into focus, take a look at Figure 9-4. The idea of events as messages plays a large role in multiuser 3D, as I explain in Chapter 11.

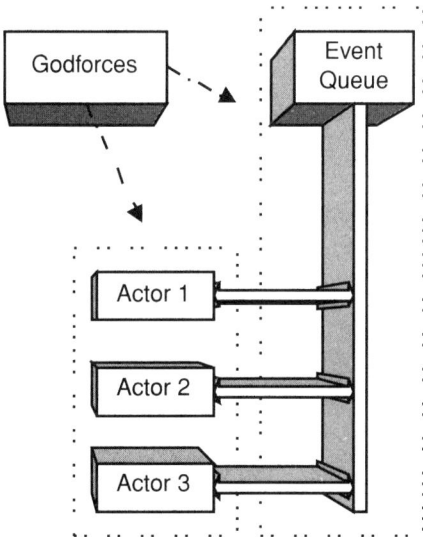

Figure 9-4. An event queue.

Godforces as Things

One seductive aspect of 3D is the feeling that you can play god. You can create a world that looks enough like the real world to be interesting and then break with impunity whatever laws of physics, logic, or civilization you'd like. Universal concepts you will need to deal with include life and death, big worlds, forces of nature, and orchestration of events.

Gravity, wind, magnetism, explosions—you may find that creating these kinds of forces in a 3D scene has irresistible appeal.

In a reasonably sophisticated 3D scene, things will have a life span. From a mundane technical point of view, objects will be added to and removed from the scene graph and will be created and destroyed in the normal create-and-destroy cycle of object-oriented, COM objects. But from an application level, actors will be born, have a lifetime, and then die—avatars will join and leave the 3D scene, objects will drop from visibility as the viewpoint changes, and so on.

One problem with move callbacks, and traversal engines in general, is that they assume the actors already exist. Also, during a traversal is usually a bad time for something to delete itself (although you could certainly implement a traversal algorithm that had nodes die in the course of the traversal). Often, however, you may find it easier to think of some pre-traversal "force" that adds or deletes actors before the traversal.

There is a good chance that the 3D scene you want to display is bigger than a single field of view or bigger than makes sense to implement as a single scene graph. For example, a multiroom 3D scene may make sense to implement as more than one scene graph. A set of 3D graphs or data visualizations may likewise make more sense as multiple scene graphs than as a single one. An earth-based simulation may want to break a terrain into separate tiled areas. In these cases, it may make sense to implement a scene graph of scene graphs. The top-level scene graph could be a skeleton that holds sub-scene graphs. The sub-scene graphs could be added or deleted from the top-level scene graph as needed.

Orchestration

The concept of actors sometimes gets pretty stretched, particularly when you want to bring about a particular scenario. Think of this example: Suppose you have a driving simulation and you want someone to run a red light just as the user's car nears the intersection. How does the errant car know how to be in the right place at the right time? You don't want to have the car just pop up at the last second—that would look pretty unconvincing. And what if the user was driving slowly? How would the other car know what speed to go to arrive at the intersection at the right time?

One way to conceptualize this kind of situation is what I call *orchestration*. Orchestration means you have code independent of any particular actor in your scene that looks around and coordinates things so that things happen in a certain way. In the driving simulation example, an orchestrator routine could monitor the speed of the user's car and tell the other car to speed up or slow down so that they would arrive at the intersection at the appropriate time. Other examples of orchestrated behavior: having a group of monsters chase you if you shoot one of them and flocking behaviors, such as a herd of buffalo running by.

The User: Bystander, Godforce, or Actor?

Before you get too involved in traversal, godforces, and actors, it is important to remember that there has to be a place for the user in all this. But where? This will depend on what kind of application you are building. Here are some options.

The User as Bystander

The most superficial role for the user to play in a 3D scene is that of a mere bystander. The user just watches what is going on, perhaps walking around to check things out. Examples of this bystander role include a walkthrough viewer (like a walkthrough of an architectural model) and a godview (not to be confused with a godforce), that is, an observer role in a military simulation. Although the bystander role may at first sound trivial, it can actually get interesting when you start thinking of different locations from which you can watch a simulation. Also, event-driven simulations sometimes have the option to save and replay the event stream, thereby allowing for later playback from various angles. For a bystander role to be interesting, however, something interesting must be going on in the scene—either interesting data or an interesting happening. Imagine a hockey game in which the user is in essence a camera attached to the puck.

Implementing a basic user-as-bystander in Direct3D is relatively straightforward. Simply define one or more cameras (viewports attached to the scene through a frame) and allow the user some ways to move the camera. However, it is important to note that there are no 3D navigation user interface conventions that are widespread enough for users to intuitively just start using. The user will likely feel awkward and frustrated. A quick solution for this is to set up some default "scenic vistas" in your scene that your user can hop to without navigation. Another solution is to define some interesting walkways for the user to follow. One convenient way to do this is to use Animations and attach them to the Viewport frame. Then give the user a simple way to slide along the interpolated path. If you want to get fancy, attach a camera frame to a spline-path interpolated frame and constrain the movement of the camera frame in some way. In this way, you can build a wide path, like a street, so that the user has a basic direction in which to go but can wander and look around a bit.

The User as Godforce

On the other end of the spectrum from user-as-bystander is having the user be a godforce or perhaps *the* godforce. Think of a 3D construction set, like Lincoln Logs or Legos, or a 3D modeling package. In this situation, the user controls all, picking up and moving things and generally arranging the world.

Perhaps the most extreme user-as-godforce example is a modeling package. In a modeling package, the user manipulates directly and manually each element of the frame tree, meshes, etc. But this level of power may not be as appealing as it might first seem. Modeling and constructing at the mesh and frame level to get interesting and beautiful results is an artistic endeavor. If you are expecting users of your 3D application to be casual users, they are probably going to be frustrated if you give them too much power. They probably will want to move around actors, not frames and meshes.

The User as Actor

Depending on the type of conceptual immersion you want your user to have in your 3D scene, you may want to think of your user as just another actor. In this case, the user is hooked up to one of the actors in your scene and programmatically communicates with other actors through an event queue. In other words, the user is the algorithm that drives a particular actor. Avatars and role-playing games are examples of this user-as-actor conceptual role. And of course race games and flight simulations use the user-as-actor concept. However, you will find this metaphor to have a wider application. Many people, for example, imagine a 3D desktop metaphor for the basic user interface to the computer—your application is arranged on a desk, files are in file folders (or some kind of 3D "tree space"), and so on.

Variations on a Theme

Now that we have a basic application framework, let's take a few shots at it to round out this chapter. I am sure that you have your own ideas. Application design has a way of begetting application environments, which beget authoring tools. Here are a few variations that come to mind.

Roll-your-own traversal. There is no law that says you have to use Direct3D's move traversal to walk through the frame tree. You could ignore it completely and write code to traverse your actors directly. You could implement this in any number of ways, such as simply having a "NextActor" pointer as a property on each of a collection of actor objects.

No event queue. Instead of an event queue, you could have each actor be intelligent enough to tell the other actors what to do directly. For example, if your avatar actor runs into the door actor, it could simply call the door's "OpenMe" method. You should note, however, that you may still need the concept of traversal, or at least multithreading, for your actors to be triggered.

Actors as godforces. Perhaps you would rather think of things I have called godforces as properties of the object in your scene. For example, you could think of gravity not as a force that affects an actor but as a property inherent in the behavior of an actor.

So What's the Right Way?

You should have enough food for thought for one chapter, although you may still be thinking, so what's the right way to put the pieces together? I feel that, over time, you will see application environments that take different slants on implementing in different ways the concepts discussed in this chapter. You can be sure that there are people who are working hard on implementing what may someday indeed be the Direct3D equivalent of a Macromedia Director, a general-purpose 3D multimedia authoring tool that will get you up and running in no time with a robust and rich 3D application. Even assuming so, however, performance and optimization issues may require such a product still to give the developer direct access to Direct3D, rather than simply laying a layer on top of Direct3D that isolates the developer from it. Perhaps the concept of 3D application frameworks may take years to gel into viable products. Or maybe this will never happen.

Chapter 10

The Zen of 3D Performance

Achieving good performance is the central challenge of realtime 3D. If you've got enough performance, you can do anything you want; if you don't, you won't be able to do anything well enough to bother. But once you go down the realtime 3D application path, get ready for a sobering dose of reality: You'll never get enough 3D performance. And it doesn't matter whether you're the world's best loop-unrolling assembly language optimization guru or the most casual VRML Web home page builder. Everyone is in the same boat. Realtime 3D, the "unbounded problem space" of multimedia, is an absolutely insatiable MIP sucker. When a twenty-first century equivalent of a handheld Game Boy delivers realtime *Toy Story*–quality rendering (which took over a hundred present-day workstation-months to render), I guarantee that some manager will come into some poor programmer's office and say, "It still looks a little plastic. Can't you speed it up?"

Tips, Tricks, and Pitfalls

In this chapter, you'll finally face this performance beast that haunts the halls of the 3D infrastructure when I discuss the techniques, maxims, issues, and pitfalls surrounding maximizing 3D performance with Direct3D. The overall goal is straightforward: Manage your total system resources to maximize the aspects of 3D performance most important to your application, while reserving enough system resources to handle the rest of your application. But be forewarned: 3D performance is a beast of almost mythic proportions, inspiring tales of terror and woe, conflicting approaches, and finger pointing. The bottom line is that the optimizing tools and functions you need simply are not yet available, in Direct3D specifically or in the PC environment generally. You will have to find ways to deal with this. Following are my suggestions for overcoming this limitation.

Beware the Blame Game

The 3D performance issue starts with unrealistic expectations fueled not only by hype but by people's innate desire for more visually rich experiences from their computers. When performance falls short of expectation, blame is on the way. And beware, dear 3D application developer, for the hot potato game of blame will end with you. Chip makers will say you did not optimize for their chip. API vendors will say you did not learn the performance tricks. CPU vendors will say you did not use the instruction set well enough. Bus designers will say you failed to create an application that balances system bandwidth. Your competitors will say that they have better 3D gurus and piles of proprietary code.

You have two lines of defense: Learn the tricks and have great content.

Get Humble

Before you start to gloat that the 3D performance beast means a full-employment act for self-styled 3D optimization gurus for years to come, take a sobering look at Figure 10-1. No matter how much optimizing you think you can do, you will not achieve the orders of magnitude of performance that are likely to be in store in the coming years or that are expected by consumers as good enough.

Note the film textures on this figure. TV broadcast quality today is something like 525 lines refreshed at 30 frames/sec (60 fields), although you see only about 480 lines. The rough computer equivalent is 640 × 480 resolution at 24-bit color (although some would say 32-bit color is necessary to get real broadcast-quality look). As an uncompressed video stream, this is 307,200 pixels/sec (921,000 bytes/sec at 24-bit color). Of course, compression techniques like MPEG reduce the data stream, but the pixels will have to be uncompressed and processed to get into the frame buffer. Film quality is somewhere around 3,000 lines by 1,000 pixels per line at a minimum of 36-bit color, 24 frames/sec. That brings a film-quality texture in at a pixel fill rate of 72 million pixels/sec with a 12MB frame buffer. Of course, this range of performance will bring all sorts of compression, memory management, bandwidth, and filtering issues, but you get the basic idea.

Chapter 10 The Zen of 3D Performance

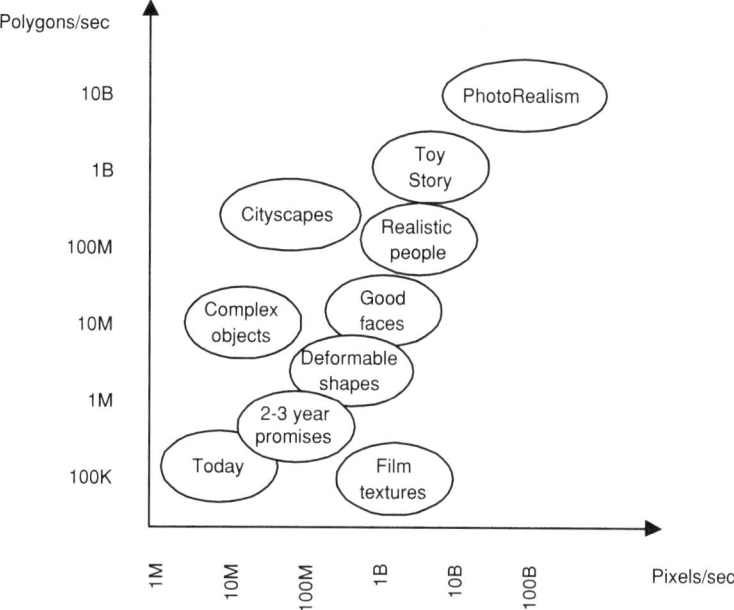

Figure 10-1. **3D performance requirements.**

Understand the Scalable Base

Never have developers had to face such a wide range of performance in the installed hardware base as they are likely to face with 3D. Combine the range of CPUs, 3D graphics boards and their competing architectures, and rendering quality techniques (from flat-shaded to trilinear mipmapping and beyond). My estimate is that overall 3D performance is likely to increase something like tenfold in the next three to five years. This will happen partly because graphics performance on PCs has tended to lag for years, and there is an unimplemented catch-up capability in the 3D infrastructure and technology that is likely to be put to use in the next few years.

To describe overall 3D performance as it may evolve over the next three to five years, I have made up an imaginary benchmark that I call *polypixels* (hmm—better trademark that name), as shown in Figure 10-2. This is an amalgam of the two basic ways by which people tend to measure 3D performance: polygons per second, which emphasizes geometry, and pixel fill rate, which emphasizes rasterization.

I would say that as a general rule of thumb, it becomes very difficult to design a single performance application that scales well across a fourfold or more performance range. It is very difficult to find a scalable feature set that will make good use of the top performance while being acceptable at the low end.

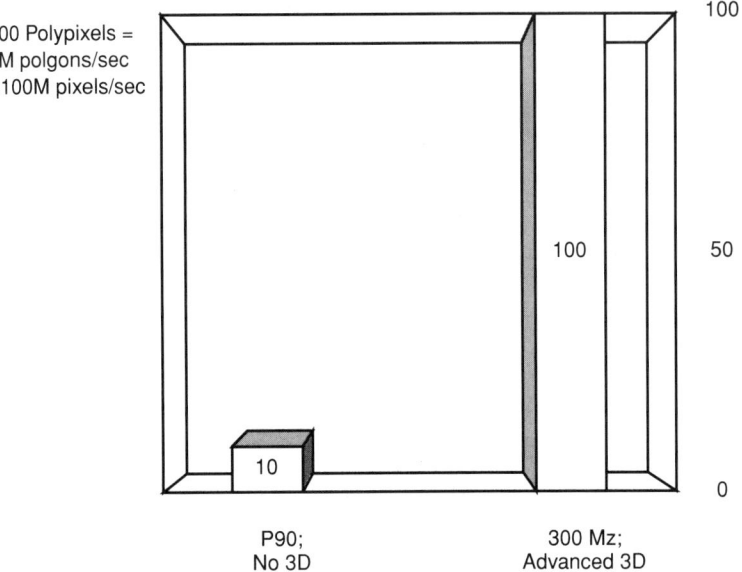

Figure 10-2. Polypixels.

Beware of Moore's Law

Reasonably sophisticated commercial applications often take one to two years from concept to ship. This time frame is likely to hold true for 3D applications. So if Moore's law—that computing power will double every 18 months—and the predictions in the previous sections hold true, very likely the 3D application you start today will enter a market that has significantly more powerful PCs than exist today.

Is this guaranteed? Definitely not. Moore's law is not a law; it's simply an observation. No pundit (let alone Moore) will go to jail if computing power fails to follow the curve. And it is important to note that with 3D, the issue is not just the speed of the CPU, but also the speed of bandwidth, the cost of memory, the design of 3D chips, and a host of other factors.

So how can you gauge what your target platform will be for a project under development? You can't. No one can. If you want to get into this field, you will have to be very careful. Underestimate the performance curve, and you may have a product that has an anemic feature set compared to a competitor that bet on a steeper curve. Overestimate the performance curve, and you may have a product that won't run on enough computers.

To add more pressure in this picture, I suggest that you recognize that hardware companies and OS companies make their money by selling the newest, shiniest, and most powerful stuff. As for the old stuff—well, your installed base for software sales is their last year's model. Their view of what is an appropriate installed base for you to target a title may be different from your's. It is counterintuitive to a big part of the history of software development on PCs to purposely target your application to only a small part of the installed base. But this is exactly what hardware companies are eager for you to do. With some 60 million computers per year being shipped, maybe they have a point, that worrying about the existing installed base is passe. But maybe they don't.

One final factor you should take into account: Moore's law is sometimes enforced through bribes. In the 3D application field, it is not uncommon for 3D chip companies to pay developers to port their titles to a particular chip. In fact, some estimates are that a significant portion of PC 3D application sales in 1996 and 1997 will be from porting and bundling fees from chip makers who want to attract the short supply of compelling 3D titles to their chips.

Scale Image Quality

The easiest optimization available to you in 3D is simply to provide the user the option of turning off or on rendering features, such as Gouraud shading, dithering, and bilinear filtering. The next step above this would be to have your application automatically turn off these features depending on the speed and power of the computer. This technique is sometimes used in modeling tools; when you move your model, the model temporarily reverts to wireframe. However, Direct3D provides little direct support for this kind of feature toggling. You can of course turn rendering features on and off, but you will have to program all this yourself.

Use High-Level Culling

Probably the single most effective technique you can use to improve your 3D performance is the implementation of high-level culling. The fastest polygon is the one you don't render. This means identifying blocks of polygons that do not actually need to go down the rendering pipeline because they won't actually be seen in the end. Direct3D's retained mode does some of this, but it is impossible to know just what the mode exactly does.

Scale Frame Rate

The second easiest method for scaling your application is to drop frames. If the computer can handle only 10 frames/sec, then scale your movement and animations to correspond to this frame rate. Direct3D provides some basic techniques for scaling your frame rate in this way. For example, you can pass a value to the move update that will scale the speed and rotation values. This value is also passed to any custom move traversal callbacks you have attached to your frame.

You will need to generalize this concept to any ongoing movements that you want to implement. For example, if you use AnimationSets, you will need to keep track of the current time. (Unfortunately, the retained mode does not do this for you, which would seem to be a logical enough thing for it to do.) You then will need to adjust the interpolation scaling value you pass to the AnimationSet.

Scale Texture Quality

Render speed is a function of render quality, unless you have a powerful graphics chip that incurs no speed penalty for turning on features like bilinear filtering. Your application should always provide the set of standard texture filtering options in the particular system and allow the user to turn these features off if they choose. This is such a basic idea, you would think that Direct3D would provide a mechanism for you to provide this feature automatically (or at least almost automatically) so that you could routinely pass it along to the user, but it does not do so, at least not directly.

Forgo Mipmapping

Mipmapping raises a troubling set of issues. Most cards do not yet support it in hardware, so you are likely to take a severe performance hit if you turn it on. Also, you cannot store mipmaps in the .x file format, at least not yet in a way that you could load them. Some APIs have built-in mipmap generation, but Direct3D does not. Unless you have a large budget and are willing to tinker with your content a lot, you may want to pass on mipmapping until there is more transparent support of it in both Direct3D and in graphics chips.

Beware of to-the-Metal Myths

There is a persistent myth in 3D application programming circles on PCs: If you really want performance, you need to program directly to the immediate mode. This is not true in general, although it may be the case with Direct3D, and not for reasons of getting faster performance by programming closer to the metal.

On graphics workstations, there is a much greater emphasis on the responsibility of scene graph APIs like Performer to perform optimization work for the application developer. The idea that you can speed up your performance by organizing your execute buffer better than the scene graph can simply says that the scene graph API is not taking into account the hardware for which it is building execute buffers.

But there is another aspect to the to-the-metal myth. Many established 3D game companies already have their own 3D engines that are quite fast and well done. These companies have no real interest in switching to Direct3D, and their 3D engine programmers pride themselves on beating the speed of anything Microsoft does. Are they closer to the metal? No, they are just better. They don't get better performance by writing to the immediate mode, but by looking at the immediate mode as a porting target for finished code.

Understand Traditional Optimization

The core axiom of optimization techniques is that you should assume nothing and test everything. Classic books like Michael Abrash's *Zen of Optimization* have clearly articulated this premise. Largely it boils down to either fine-grained timing of short sections of code or an analysis of overall algorithms to produce a better way.

Unfortunately, neither of these is supported directly by Direct3D. There is no way to know exactly what is going on in the pipeline, so you have no practical way to know where the actual bottleneck is. You can guess, and you may be right, but there is no way to actually prove it. This is true at both the retained mode and the immediate mode. Once you send an execute buffer to the renderer, there is no practical way to know anything other than how long the whole rendering pipeline took to complete. And at the retained mode, the execute buffer is not exposed, so you have no way to analyze the high-level optimization algorithms or implement your own. In essence, you fly blind. The message is that if you want performance, just go write your own engine and hook it up to the immediate mode. So Direct3D presents a stark contrast on the optimization front to the programmer: Do it our way and trust us, or do it your way and we will provide little help. Perhaps over time, this all-or-nothing optimization proposition of Direct3D will disappear.

Manage Your Resources

Another way to look at optimization is to consider that there probably are more things you want your computer to do at the same time than simply render the 3D scene. You will also want, for example, sound, IO interaction, and application logic. If you think of your total system resources (CPU, memory, bandwidth, etc.), you may want to think of global allocation of resources along the lines shown in Figure 10-3.

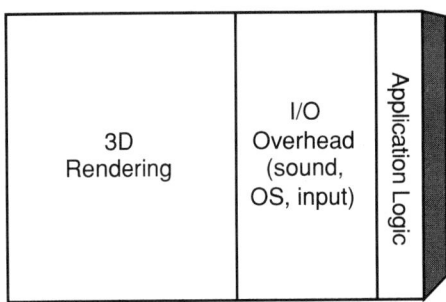

Figure 10-3. An example of allocation of system resources.

3D rendering is likely to take up the single largest block of your system resources, but there still have to be some resources left over for something else. Unfortunately, Direct3D doesn't do anything to help you manage your system resources or even identify how they are being used. You are just going to have to imagine what is going on and make your best guess.

Balance Your Pipeline

One way to view resource management is as a balancing of a pipeline. The 3D is a pipeline in the sense that rendering is a multiple-step process. The pipeline is only as fast as its slowest point. The slowest step in the pipeline will define the final speed. So you need to be aware of where you are choking the pipeline.

The moral of this is, don't play leapfrog in a pipeline. If your bottleneck is rasterization, it does not matter how many polygons can get processed; they still will have to wait to be drawn. The concept of balancing the pipeline is shown in Figure 10-4.

Pipeline balancing makes the most sense when you have a real, rather than a conceptual, 3D pipeline. If you are working in a software-only environment, you are simply allocating CPU time and system resources. Unfortunately, Direct3D, as with system resources, does little to help you, in this case by identifying where the bottleneck is. You are just going to have to make an educated guess.

Understand the Resource Big Picture

Let's take a look at the big picture of resource management, as shown in Figure 10-5. It will help you get a sense of the overall complexity of the optimization task. As you have probably figured out, optimization goes far beyond optimizing a single code loop or algorithm. In essence, there are trade-offs to be made. Following are some of them.

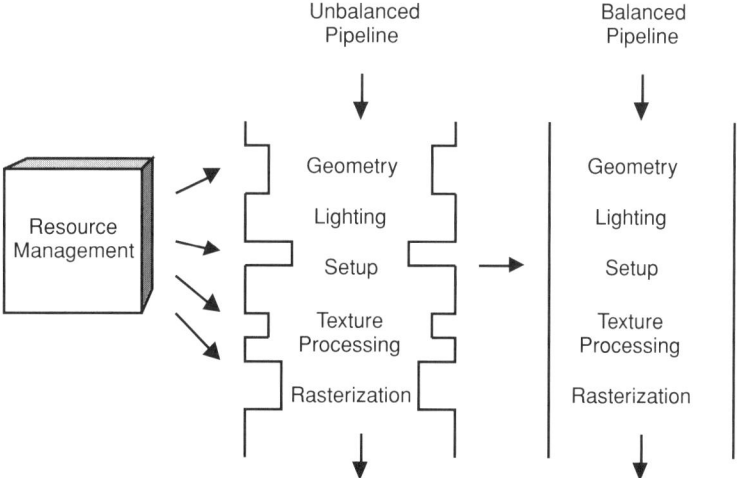

Figure 10-4. Balancing the pipeline.

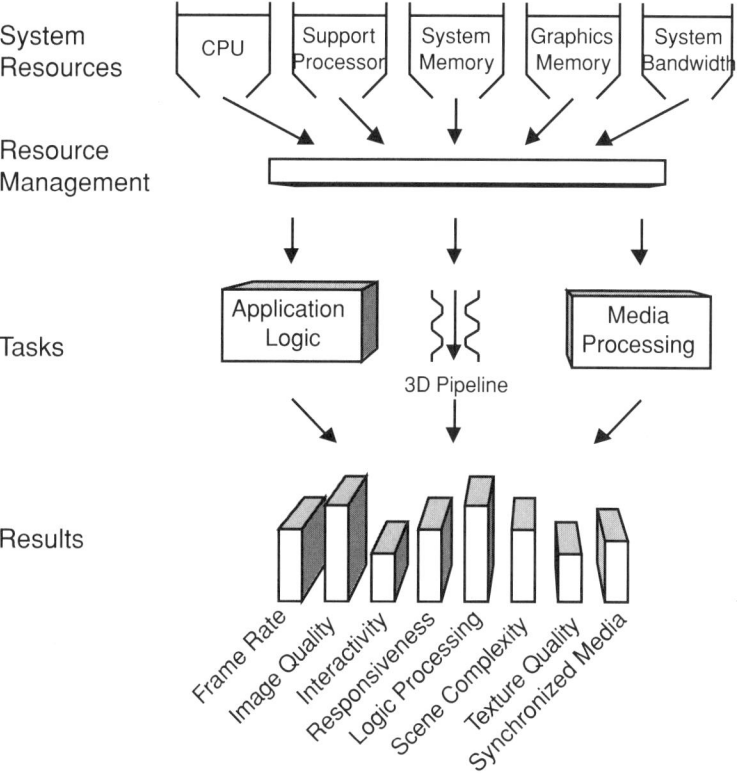

Figure 10-5. The resource big picture.

- **Image quality versus speed.** This is not a direct trade-off. Depending on the system, image quality may or may not have a performance penalty. A well-designed 3D chip should at least offer greater image quality with no overall speed degradation. Whether this actually happens on a particular board or chip is just something that will have to be tested.
- **Content costs versus programming costs.** It is important to note that for many 3D applications, 3D content creation is typically a larger part of the budget than is 3D programming. Using the immediate mode will raise your content creation costs. So will supporting multiple versions of the same content, such as 8- and 16-bit palettes or mipmaps and regular texture maps. You probably should think about how much optimization you can afford, particularly how it may affect the cost of creating your content.
- **Memory versus bandwidth.** Memory and bandwidth have a way of trading off with each other, depending in particular on what you want to do with graphics memory. Put your textures in the graphics frame buffer, and the chip can access them quickly. However, your application will have to cross the PCI bus to change them.
- **Frame rate versus latency.** You may think that high frame rates (the number of times a scene is rendered per second) and low latency (the amount of time it takes to respond to user interaction) are essentially the same thing. They aren't. This is because different techniques are used to achieve them, and these techniques can be mutually exclusive. The less that is changeable in your scene, the faster you can make it go. However, it is unclear how much this matters to Direct3D's retained mode, since it is impossible to tell exactly how data is organized inside the COM objects.

Real Programmers Use the Immediate Mode!

There is a common belief that if you want to achieve real performance, you will have to "drop down" to the immediate mode. There is truth in this, but not exactly the truth you might think. Actually, it is possible to write a better retained mode API that is better than Direct3D's API. That is really what you are doing when you "drop down" to the immediate mode.

Recall for a moment what a retained mode API actually does. It creates output (data, commands, execute buffers) that are passed on to the immediate mode API. In essence, then, a retained mode is an optimization program for running an immediate mode API efficiently. So can someone write a retained mode API that is better at optimizing the data flow to Direct3D's immediate mode than Direct3D's own retained mode? Sure. Here are some basic techniques:

1. Do a better job at the higher-level abstraction optimization. This is not exactly "dropping down."
2. Do a better job at optimizing the data sent to the immediate mode. This is hard.
3. Focus on a special-purpose need.
4. Go around the immediate mode.

In fact, Microsoft has pretty much made it clear that the immediate mode is there for anyone who wants a hardware-accelerated back end for their own retained mode API. The whole point of DirectX is to give you flexibility in how you go about doing things. If you already have your own API, and it maps well to the immediate mode, it may very well make sense to use it.

Probably the area in which Microsoft will have you beat, however, is in drivers that interface to the immediate mode renderers. You may very well be able to beat Microsoft at its own game—selling operating systems, working with hardware companies to get hardware to support OS's—and do it at pennies on the dollar compared to Microsoft's costs. However, I suggest that you may want to think twice before you embark on such a venture.

Can You Trust the Retained Mode?

If you are planning to use Direct3D's retained mode API, the previous section may have invoked some pretty scary thoughts. What if Direct3D's retained mode just isn't as good as proprietary APIs? There are some signs that this may be a problem for users of the retained mode, although it is hard to tell. The retained mode does not expose a lot of information about what it is doing exactly, what kinds of execute buffers it is building, how it is managing textures for you, and so on. So there is an element of faith in using the retained mode; you have to trust that it is actually doing the right thing for you in a given circumstance.

One way to protect yourself may be to use the UserVisual, which provides an easy route to the immediate mode in the retained mode. This may give you a relatively less painful way to optimize parts of your 3D application.

Another way to protect yourself may simply be to speak up and tell Microsoft and other API vendors what features and optimizations you would like. The strongest voices and most defined constituencies in the building of the PC 3D infrastructure were clearly the chip makers and existing 3D game companies that wanted a new generation of 3D acceleration of PCs. Neither of these groups particularly cared about how well the retained mode worked. The retained mode was not something the chip makers accelerated directly, so it was out of their line of sight. Existing 3D game companies tended to already have their own 3D APIs, and some viewed the retained mode as something of a threat to their business.

Use Fog

Using fog is a cheesy performance technique, but it can hide a lot of performance issues. Many chips support fogging, so you simply put your problem stuff enough away in the z direction so that the fog will obscure it.

To Z or Not to Z

Z-buffering is an easy, simple rendering technique. In theory, the renderer does not have to think about the depth order of polygons; it just checks to see whether each pixel already has a pixel with a smaller z depth.

In practice, however, this brute force approach to rendering leaves a lot to be desired. First, the z-buffer takes up a lot of memory—16 bits per pixel on the screen. Assuming that 2MB graphics boards will be the standard new graphics board over the next two years, then this is a large chunk of graphics memory that you could use for textures.

Note that the AGP system could change the equation here. By moving textures into system memory, AGP could open up more graphics memory for the z-buffer (or higher-resolution graphics modes). But still, memory—particularly graphics memory—is a fixed, scarce resource, so a chunk that big needs to be put to best use.

There are other performance issues involved with a z-buffer. The read/compare/write overhead for each pixel is significant in itself. Just the overhead of clearing that much memory from each frame could be a significant overhead, although graphics blitting is pretty fast.

But perhaps more important, the z-buffer test comes late in the 3D pipeline. This means that 3D data is being unnecessarily processed by the prior steps in the pipeline, like geometry, lighting, and set-up. Why waste processing resources on data that is going to get thrown away? This violates the more fundamental tenet of 3D optimization that the fastest polygon is the one you never have to draw.

Know Thy Depth Complexity

An important formula that will help you budget the amount of complexity you can have in your scene is the **depth complexity formula.** This formula gives you a simple figure that tells you about the complexity of a scene. It goes beyond merely reporting the number of polygons per frame. It describes your maximum scene complexity in terms of total rendered pixels, not polygons.

Say you assume that your rendering engine is capable of 20 megapixels/sec. Suppose also that you want to display in 640 × 480 resolution— a total of 307,200 pixels for each frame. Finally, you want to achieve 30 frames/sec of display. How many times can each pixel on the screen be written to for each frame before you reach the maximum pixel through-put of the renderer? This is what the depth complexity formula tells you. Here's an example of using the formula:

$$\frac{20 \text{ megapixels}}{\text{sec}} \times \frac{\text{frame}}{307{,}000 \text{ pixels}} \times \frac{\text{sec}}{30 \text{ frames}} = 2.17$$

A depth complexity of 2.17 means that on average, your scene cannot be more than 2.17 pixels deep, that is, on average no more than 2.17 surfaces of objects at each pixel on screen. If it is, the renderer will not be able to display at 30 frames/sec. This is just a mathematical fact that you cannot change. If you want more depth complexity, you will need to either get a renderer with a higher pixel fill rate, reduce your resolution, or accept a lower frame rate.

So what exactly does a depth complexity of 2.17 mean? Imagine a piece of paper on a table that is sitting on a floor, as shown in Figure 10-6. Say that in the screen region displaying the piece of paper, the depth complexity is 3. At each screen pixel is a pixel representing the paper, the table, and the floor

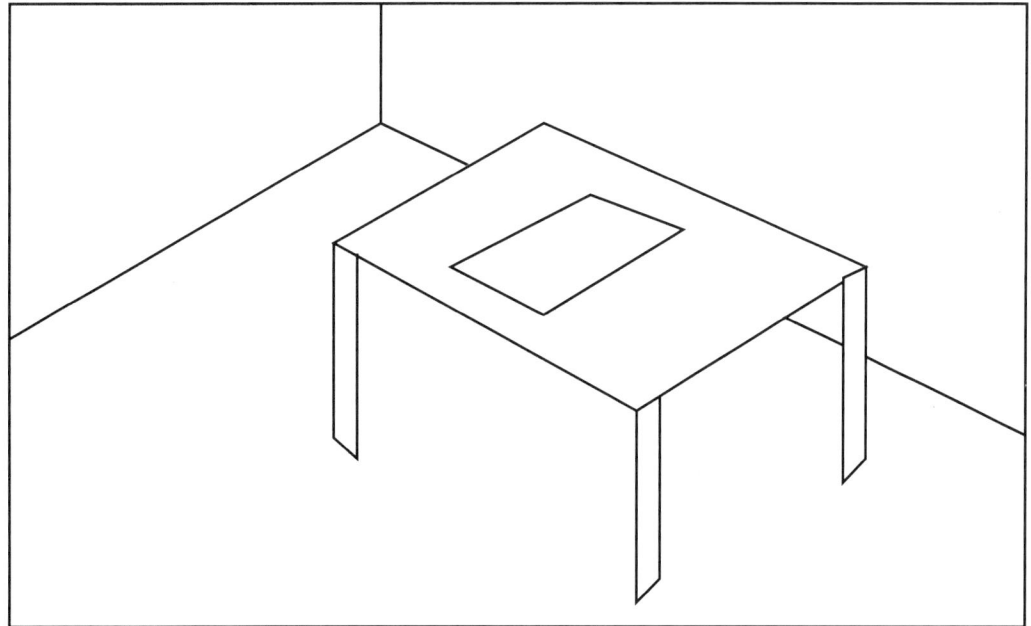

Figure 10-6. Depth complexity.

(at the top of the paper is a pixel for the paper, the table, and the bottom of the wall). Overall, from the angle in the figure, this scene probably has a depth complexity of only a little over 1, because for most of the screen, there is only one object (the floor or wall). So where the paper sits on the table, the depth complexity is 3, while where only the floor or wall shows, the depth complexity is 1.

Avoid State Thrash

Rendering engines are fastest when they do the same thing over and over. Unfortunately, Direct3D gives you very little help in identifying and avoiding state thrash, although in theory, if you work at the immediate mode level, you can set up a mesh that is organized to avoid state thrash. But how do you know what level of state thrash actually makes a difference? You just have to guess.

Microsoft recommends that you make all materials the same (except the texture handle) and allow the textures to specify the coloring. For example, make all the materials white and keep their specular power the same. Many applications do not need more than two materials in a scene: one with a specular power for shiny objects and one without for matte objects. Apparently, switching material is a state thrash that you would do best to avoid, although it is impossible to know exactly how much difference this will make and whether it is worth the trouble. Also, using a single texture per mesh should reduce state thrash.

Use Level of Detail

LOD is a tried-and-true technique taken from flight simulation that both improves image quality and optimizes performance. LOD optimizes performance by reducing the complexity of objects when they are in the distance. Unfortunately, Direct3D does not support LOD (at least not yet), so you are on your own. You have to attach and unattach meshes on the fly. This means there currently is no way to put LOD-type data in the .x format. You have to program the logic of LOD yourself and load and manage the meshes you need on your own.

Optimize Your Meshes

In theory, collapsing a frame hierarchy of meshes into a single mesh should improve performance, because then the same transformation can be applied to all the vertices. Direct3D does allow you to collapse meshes and frames. Doing this, however, can conflict with high-level culling, assuming culling is occurring on a per-mesh basis.

Keep Texel/Pixel Ratio Near 1

Think of the image of a shoe. If it is taking up 10 pixels on the screen, then you are wasting system resources if you have a 256 × 256 texture map wrapped around the image. This may seem obvious, but it means that you may not need textures at all for objects that appear small on the screen.

Use Hardware Stretch

Many chips have a hardware-stretch feature that will scale up an image from a lower resolution on the fly. Sometimes hardware-stretching of a small 3D-rendered image will give you faster performance and image quality comparable to that achieved by rendering at a higher resolution.

Minimize Palettes

If you are using the 8-bit ramp mode, Microsoft recommends several things that you can do to minimize palette overhead. Try to use the same palette for all your textures and keep the number of colors in your palette as few as possible (under 64). Also, use a small material ramp size (16 or less) and use small textures. Further, you can try to put as many small textures as possible in a single 256 × 256 texture. How much difference do these techniques make? It is hard to tell, as many boards are not on the market anyway!

Seek the Fast Path

To close out this chapter, here is a suggestion that may in the long run be your best bet: Find the fast path and get on it. The theory of the fast path is that, over time, a relatively small set of best ways to achieve 3D performance will emerge, just as over time any technology will tend to converge around a relatively small set of best-practice and most-marketable features. This is not a me-too strategy. Fast paths have a way of lying dormant until someone finds them, and they may not be in the place the crowd expects them to be.

As the theory goes, a widely respected benchmark might cause a fast path to develop, as hardware makers always tend to optimize their hardware to look good on the benchmark. Marketing could cause a fast path, if some particular feature or buzzword enters the consumer lexicon and everyone has to have it. ("Dad, we HAVE to have mipmapping! I saw it on TV!") Perhaps a particular game or 3D graphics board will create a de facto benchmark or image quality target. Or a fast path could already exist, and it is just a question of a Darwinian period of experimentation, to identify it.

So how will you find the fast path? Good question. You'll just have to keep a close eye on what people do and how it works.

Part III

Advanced D3D Issues

Chapter 11

Multiuser 3D

Low bandwidth and high latency are the demons of multiuser 3D, and you will have to fight them. You may be thinking, "But I'm working on a single-user 3D app" or "Cable modems (or whatever) will solve the bandwidth problem." Neither of these sidesteps will wash. The demons of bandwidth and latency are unavoidable and ruthless, and there is no quick fix to either. The sooner you start fighting them, the better off you will be.

In this chapter, I explore why the bandwidth and latency issues of multiuser 3D will have such a broad effect on 3D application development in general. This may seem to be an odd journey away from Direct3D, with its stops at network protocols, military simulations, and DirectPlay. But the key point is that multiuser 3D application design raises fundamental issues that are difficult to deal with but that are likely to have an impact on all 3D application development, whether single-user or multiuser.

First, I'll dismiss the standard sidesteps.

- **"My 3D app is single-user."** Wake up and smell the Internet. Realtime 3D and multiuser 3D go hand in hand. Once you have objects interacting in a 3D scene, it is a very short step to imagine different people behind those objects. Online games, avatar chat rooms, collaborative 3D project spaces—everyone has gotten the idea.

Even more important, the design of multiuser 3D applications is likely to be more sophisticated than the design of single-user 3D applications. This means that when multiuser applications are used in a single-user setting, they are likely to be equal to or superior to single-user applications.

- **"(X) will solve the bandwidth problem."** Don't hold your breath. Notwithstanding cable modems, satellite transmission, ISDN, or whatever the bandwidth panacea du jour may be, high bandwidth is not going to be turned on like a switch to every computer in the world. It will be a roll-out, with years of twists and turns.

Don't confuse "a lot of bandwidth" with "infinite bandwidth." And don't forget, your competitors face the same bandwidth constraints. If they do a better job of overcoming them than you do, then you will be hosed. And even if you have all that bandwidth, you still will have to handle it.

Of course, low bandwidth and high latency are fundamental obstacles to multiuser 3D. You can hold your breath for cable modems and other potential solutions, but meanwhile you'll have to make the best of today's 28.8 modems and their built-in latency (10% to 40% of total network latency by some estimates). Value-add connectivity providers offer some hope. In reality, however, the competitive issue is not how much connectivity you have, but how effectively you use it compared to your competitors.

The Big Picture

Figure 11-1 presents a generic overview of what could be called the emerging multiuser 3D infrastructure. Consider this an Internet-era evolution of the 3D infrastructure described in Part I of this book.

The new components are the connectivity interface, the message manager, and the various servers. A connectivity interface is the API that defines the application's connection to the Internet. Think of DirectPlay, sockets, and proprietary network gaming APIs as connectivity interfaces. The message manager defines and manages the actual messages that are sent to the different participants and includes some concept of interpolated dead reckoning. The lobby server is where people meet, the money server manages financial arrangements (if any), and the session server sends and perhaps queues messages between participants.

A (Very) Short Internet Course

Concepts such as reliability and multicasting have a big impact on the design of multiuser 3D, whether you use the Internet, an Intranet, a LAN, or a connectivity provider. Following are brief explanations of some key concepts as shown in Figure 11-2.

Chapter 11 Multiuser 3D

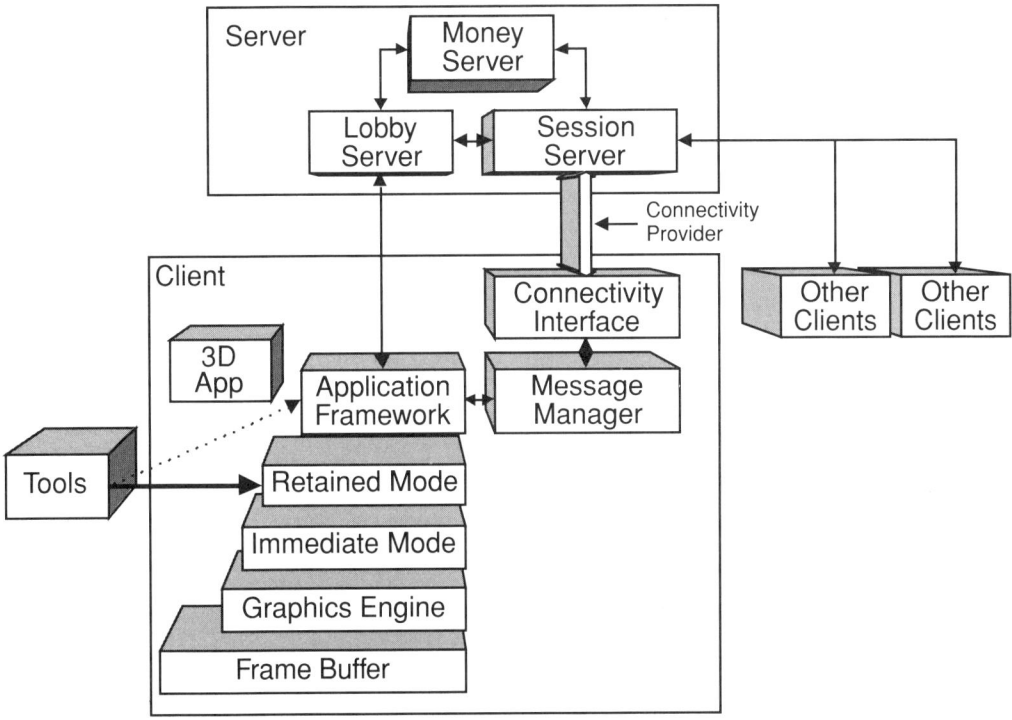

Figure 11-1. The 3D multiuser infrastructure.

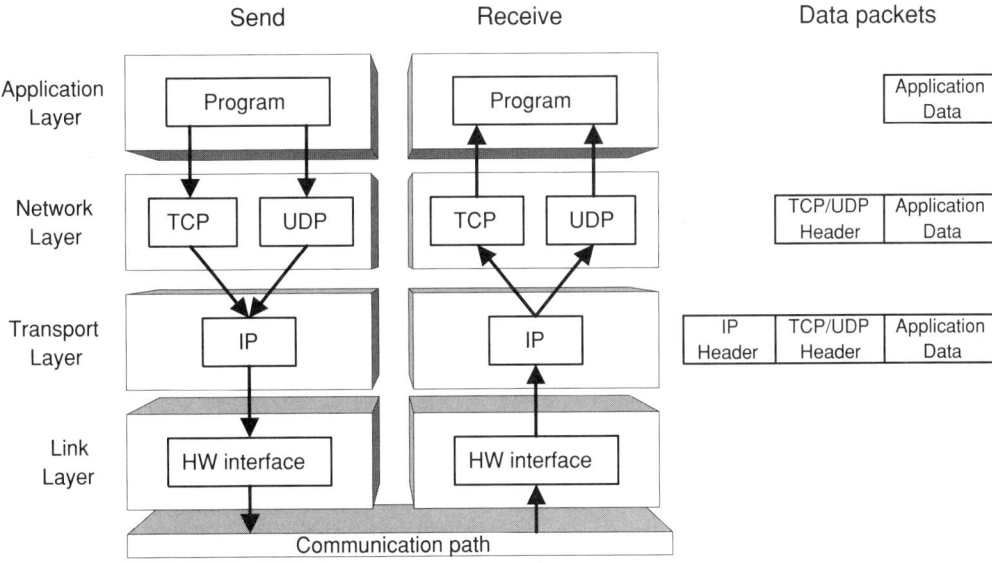

Figure 11-2. Overview of TCP and UDP network layers.

- **Reliability.** Reliability means that delivery of data is guaranteed. Accomplishing this requires a method for acknowledging receipt of the data (i.e., the receiver has to send back a message saying "I got it" or the sender will re-send the message) and validation of the data (typically through checksums). This precise definition of reliability is the critical one (do not rely on the common understanding of reliability as "works well").

- **IP (Internet Protocol).** IP is the network layer protocol. It is unreliable, meaning it does not acknowledge receipt of packets (yes, the Internet really is "unreliable"—it's built that way). A fundamental side effect of this unreliability is that packets might not arrive at the receiver in the order they were sent.

  Why on Earth would the Internet be built on an unreliable protocol? It is just an acknowledgement of reality. There is no way to ever be sure that a packet of data has reached its destination without acknowledgement. So until a packet's receipt is acknowledged, at the lowest level of protocol any network is in this sense unreliable.

- **TCP (Transport Control Protocol).** TCP is a transport layer protocol. It is a reliable protocol built on top of IP. Think of TCP as the protocol that sits on top of IP to make sure that IP packets are actually received.

- **UDP (User Datagram Protocol).** UDP is a lesser-known transport layer protocol compared to TCP. It is unreliable; the chronological order of packets is not guaranteed upon receipt.

- **Unicasting, broadcasting, and multicasting.** Unicasting means sending messages to a single address (host). Broadcasting means sending data to everyone (all hosts on a network). Multicasting means sending to some. A multicast address describes a group of specific hosts, and hosts can join or leave the host group. Multicasting is unreliable, both because it is implemented with UDP and because it is inherently unworkable to have everyone in a multicast group acknowledge receipt of messages.

- **Reliable multicasting.** This doesn't exist. Semireliable multicasting is conceptually possible but tricky. You have to implement your own protocol on top of UDP, probably using the concept of negative acknowledgements (that is, "I'll tell you when I don't receive something I am expecting, rather than every time I receive data").

Distributed Interactive Simulation

If you think of government vision as barely Luddite, think again. The granddaddy of multiuser 3D is Distributed Interactive Simulation, DIS. In some circles, DIS is the prime example of multiuser 3D. For multiuser 3D, DIS is the category-defining architecture that has laid the groundwork and defined the conceptual terrain. A close historical cousin to the Internet, DIS is unlikely to follow it out of the military into civilian use. If the Air Force has flight simulators, why can't the Army have a battle simulator? This may seem to be odd turf indeed.

The histories of DIS and of the Internet are closely linked. Both were designed in essence with parallel design philosophies. Many of the same companies were involved. Following are some key DIS concepts.

- **Entities.** An entity in DIS is a "thing": tank, submarine, missile, bridge, etc.

- **Application autonomy.** This means no central computer controls the whole simulation. No central computer controls the whole world. Autonomous applications (individual computers) control one or more entities in the scene.

- **PDUs (Protocol Data Units).** A PDU is a packet of messages that indicates state change. Dead-reckoning interpolation algorithms fill in between the packets so that movement will appear continuous on different clients without a constant stream of update messages specifying every incremental movement.

- **Ground truth.** Each application communicates the full truth about the current position and directions of the entities it controls. The receiving application determines its own perception of events and entities.

DIS for Nonmilitary Uses

There has long been talk of DIS following the Internet's path out of the military and into civilian use. In fact, the DIS Steering Committee's 1994 road map, "The DIS Vision," asserted that there would likely be an eventual extension of DIS to entertainment, education, and other nonmilitary uses, such as air traffic control systems based from GPS receivers and DIS. Will such a vision ever come about? Certainly not, as DIS is now primarily a military format with military-specific message packets. However, it is possible that down the road things may move in a more generalized direction, as general solutions to multiuser issues emerge.

DirectPlay

DirectPlay is a companion technology to Direct3D, another member of the DirectX family. At first glance, DirectPlay would seem to have little to do with 3D. However, this is not the case. Many online game projects under development are realtime 3D. DirectPlay makes no pretense of providing a direct solution to bandwidth and latency. Instead, it is intended to create a competitive environment in which connectivity providers will vie to provide the best connectivity values.

Think of DirectPlay as a "virtual OS" to communications services, with a strong emphasis on online games. It offers the application developer an abstract and generalized model of communications services. Although DirectPlay was developed primarily for game communication, it could be used for other applications that require communication that is independent of the underlying transport, protocol, or online service.

DirectPlay does not force the game developer to deal with the differences that each of these connectivity solutions represents. Instead, it provides generalized communication capabilities intended to be independent of the network that is used. It shields developers from the underlying complexities of diverse connectivity implementations, thereby freeing them to concentrate on producing a great game.

DirectPlay uses a simple send/receive communication model to implement a connectivity API tailored to the needs of game play. Its architecture is composed of two types of components: DirectPlay itself and the service provider. DirectPlay is provided by Microsoft and presents a common interface to the game. The service provider furnishes medium-specific communication services as requested by DirectPlay. Any organization, including online services, can supply service providers for specialized hardware and communications media. Microsoft includes two service providers with DirectPlay, one for networking and one for modem support.

The DirectPlay interface hides the complexities and unique tasks required to establish an arbitrary communications link inside the DirectPlay service provider implementation. When you design a game for use with DirectPlay, you need concern yourself only with the performance of the communications medium, not with whether that medium is provided by a modem, network, or online service.

The Send/Receive Paradigm

A message can be defined in any way that you require, with the exception of a small number of messages that have been defined by the system. A message should not be excessively large. You can use the IDirectPlay::Send method to send a message to an individual player, to a group, or to all the players in the session. Simply specify as the destination either a player ID, a group ID, or a zero, which sends the message to all players.

To receive a message from the message queue, use the IDirect Play::Receive method. This method allows you to specify whether to retrieve the first message in the queue, only the messages to a particular player, or only those from a particular player. With IDirectPlay::GetMessageCount method, you can retrieve the number of messages waiting for a given player.

3D Design Implications in Creating 3D Multiuser Environments

Several design implications are likely to derive from efforts to create 3D multiuser environments. Although predicting all of them may be premature, I'll venture to discuss a couple of them.

A multiuser scene graph won't work. You need some intermediate abstraction and representation of changes in the 3D scene as it appears on multiple computers. DIS uses the concept of the entity, but perhaps a more object-oriented concept will prevail.

Most important to understanding the impact of multiuser 3D on 3D application design are likely to be the concepts of state update and data packets. In essence, multiple users mean some form of multicasting, which in turn means unreliable protocols. Packets get lost, and arrival order is not guaranteed. This means applications will need to have a self-healing concept of current state. They also must distinguish between messages that must get through and those that can occasionally be missed.

Chapter 12

Motion Capture

"Imitation of real life is not art."—Shamus Culhane

Motion capture is a technique that strikes at the heart of issues of what realtime 3D is as a commercial, communication, and artistic medium. It reopens issues dating back to the early days of rotoscoping over a half-century ago. Will these issues be resolved differently now because of the intervention of the algorithmic power of computers to handle higher and higher levels of abstraction?

Motion capture is the technique of using special physical sensors to record the movement of real human actors on a stage and then playing back the recorded movement data in a 3D scene. It is popular for both high-end animation and for adding movement to 3D games. It is an economical method of getting raw motion into a 3D animation tool compared to the tedious and time-consuming method of 3D keyframing.

In this chapter, I get you started using motion capture in interactive 3D applications and give you the background to understand where motion capture fits into the "big picture" of 3D behavior.

Motion Capture, Rotoscoping, and Art

Motion capture is part of controversy that dates back over a half a century to the early days of movie animation. The issue is, what is the most commercially viable method of creating animation "content": the movement of live actors, the artistic description of movement, computer algorithms, or a combination of all of these?

Turn back the clock for a moment to the late 1930s and early 1940s to explore the importance and place of motion capture technology. The rotoscope was a device invented by Max and Dave Fleischer that made it possible to trace a live-action film frame by frame. The idea was that an animator could use these tracings as the starting point to more quickly, economically, and realistically create cel animations.

However, a different view of the artistic role of animation won out. Animation became more a medium of caricature than realism. That different view was articulated by animator Shamus Culhane: "The best use of animation is when it charicatures [sic], not imitates, real life. . . . [Rotoscoping and animation are] an unhappy marriage of very distinctly different art forms."

So is 3D more like a medium of caricature or more like the realism of human actors? We can hope, dear reader, that your efforts to implement interesting things in 3D will help to answer that question. In favor of the rotoscoping/realism view, it could be said that 3D motion data is much more editable than traditional 2D animation, that human motion is much easier to import, and that the 3D rendering has a distinct inclination toward realism. In favor of the caricature view, it could be said that 3D is in essence simply the art of animation extended into a new dimension, and the traditional winning principles of 2D will therefore ultimately win out in 3D.

Motion Capture Data

To start the examination of the specific issues of using motion capture data, I examine a commonly used ASCII file format for motion capture data, the .bvh file format from BioVision. There are other formats, particularly for high-end animation software, but the BioVision file format has the advantages of being public and in ASCII, so it is easy to understand. Also, canned motion capture files in the .bvh format can be purchased from 3D data suppliers like Viewpoint Datalabs.

I'll start with pieces of a sample .bvh file, shown as follows. Note that the line numbers are not in the file but are for reference in the discussion.

```
1    HIERARCHY
2    ROOT Hips
3    {
4         OFFSET 0.00 0.00 0.00
5         CHANNELS 6 Xposition Yposition Zposition Zrotation Xrotation
              Yrotation
6         JOINT LeftHip
```

```
7                       {
8                               OFFSET 2.66 0.00 0.00
9                               CHANNELS 3 Zrotation Xrotation Yrotation
10                              JOINT LeftKnee
11                              {
12                                      OFFSET 0.00 -17.74 0.00
13                                      CHANNELS 3 Zrotation Xrotation Yrotation
14                                      JOINT LeftAnkle
15                                      {
16                                              OFFSET 0.00 -17.44 0.00
17                                              CHANNELS 3 Zrotation Xrotation
                                                        Yrotation
18                                              End Site
19                                              {
20                                                      OFFSET 0.00 -3.21 0.00
21                                              }
22                                      }
23                              }
24              }
25 . . .
26 }
27 MOTION
28 Frames: 84
29 Frame Time: 0.033333
30 40.68 38.35 -8.10 2.57 11.23 -5.49 . . .
31 . . .
```

Overview of .bvh

First, I overview the different components and then examine the sample file line by line. The .bvh file consists of two parts: the hierarchy part and the motion part. The word "HIERARCHY" in the file starts the hierarchy section.

Hierarchy Section

The hierarchy part describes the skeleton layout of the character to be tracked. Note that different kinds of characters could be tracked: big people, little people, even animals. The .bvh file, however, tracks only the overall movement of the skeleton, such as how the arms and legs move, but it is not fine-grained enough to track something like facial expressions. In essence, you should think of the .bvh file as containing the raw motion data of the larger bones of a skeleton. It is the job of modeling and animation software to put the skin on the skeleton. The components of the hierarchy section are described next.

- **ROOT name**

The name of root node for the character. This is the parent node to which all the other nodes are attached as children (or children of children), in a typical scene graph hierarchy.

- **JOINT name**

The name of a joint attached to the root node or another joint node in the object's hierarchy. Although the .bvh file is organized in terms of joints, you can also think of each joint as the position and rotation of the attached bone, since the two are identical. For example, the LeftAnkle joint defines the position and orientation of the left foot bone in relation to the left shin bone (whose own location and orientation are defined by the LeftKnee joint). The brackets {} contain the definition of a root or joint. Any joint that appears inside the brackets of another joint's definition is a child of that joint.

- **OFFSET x y z**

The at-rest displacement from the parent joint. From this, you can calculate the length of the connecting bone (the distance between the joints).

- **CHANNELS n type type ...**

Specify the type of data channels that are actually tracked in the motion file. The term *n* is the number of channels. The types of channels are xposition, yposition, zposition, xrotation, yrotation, and zrotation. Normally, only the three rotation channels will be tracked. This is because typically you would assume that the distance between the joints is constant, and all you really want to do is monitor how the joints move. Note also that for rotations, the order in the channels line is the order that the rotations should be applied; for example, if zposition is first, it is the first rotation. In theory, this method of channel organization leaves open the possibility of adding additional channels of tracking data. Early versions of the .bvh format, for example, had optional scaling factors that could be used to track changes in the size of a bone attached to a joint. However, in practice, this was not used, so it was dropped.

- **End Site**

Not a particularly useful end appendage of the last joint. No motion data is tracked for it (the joint above it is tacked), so its value remains constant. In the example file, it is used by convention to represent how far off the ground the ankle joint is in the resting position. However, this is a rather backwards way of measuring things. This is because in 3D scenes you usually think of starting with the location of a root (in this case, the hip) as the starting place for calculating locational information of children, not the other way around.

Motion Section

The term "MOTION" starts the motion section. This section contains the actual movement data for the root, joints, and channels defined in the hierarchy section. Each line of data in the motion section has all the channel data for one "frame" (a frame in this context is a sampled instant of time). Each line also contains an entry for each channel defined for the root and each joint, whether or not the value changed from the previous frame. The channel data is in the same order (from left to right) as the channels were defined in the hierarchy section.

- **Frames.** The frames line specifies the number of frames of data stored in the file. Each frame represents the sampling of all the channels at one instant in time.

- **Frame Time.** The frame time is the amount of time, in seconds, between each frame of motion data.

Motion capture systems are generally capable of sampling at a far higher rate (120 to 200 times a second) than a renderer would be capable of playing back (30 times a second or less). Typically, the motion capture service would scale down the data to a manageable rate.

Sample File: Line by Line

Based on the general description given in the previous section, you may find that the sample file makes sense. However, you may find the following comments for selected lines helpful. Note that this sample file is only a fragment. A real file would include all the joints of the characters (the right leg, arms, head, etc.).

Line 1: This identifies the start of the hierarchy definition section.

Line 2: The parent, or root, node of the hierarchy of joints is the hip.

Line 3: The bracket contains the values associated with the root, as well as the children of the root (joints use the same organizing technique).

Line 4: The starting x, y, y location (the offset) of the hip is at 0, 0, 0 in a world coordinate system. Since the x, y, z location is tracked in the motion file (see line 5), then the first frame of motion data (and each subsequent frame) will specify a location for the root node. In practice, you will add your own application-defined initial value to this value (and each frame of offset values for the hip).

Line 5: There are six channels tracked for the hip: three for the x, y, z position and three for the x, y, z rotation. Typically, a motion file will track all six of these values for the root but will track only rotations for the joints. The position of the root defines the location of everything else, given fixed lengths for each bone and specified rotation values at each joint. The rotation angles should be applied in the same order they appear on this line.

Line 6: The left hip joint is connected to the hip bone and is 2.66 inches to the left of the "center" of the hip bone (apologies to anatomy majors).

Line 9: Since only rotation for the left hip is tracked, it is always going to be 2.66 inches away from the center of the hip bone.

Line 12: The left knee in the rest position is exactly 17.74 inches below the left hip. When the hip starts rotating, this will no longer be the case, of course, but it will always be 17.74 inches away.

Line 25: Other joints attached to the hip are not included in this sample.

Line 27: The term MOTION starts the motion data section.

Lines 28 and 29: There are 84 frames of motion data. The time between each frame is 0.033333 seconds.

Line 30: Each line of motion data contains one entry for each channel specified in the hierarchy section, in the order they appear in that section. So the first six values on this line would be the x, y, z position and z, x, y rotation for the root (from line 5), the next three values would be the z, x, y rotation for the left hip (from line 9), and so on. Every value for every channel is specified for every frame, even if the value is 0 or there is no change from the previous frame.

Building Motion Capture Data Structures

The above discussion gives you a sense of what data is in a motion capture file. It likely is fairly clear that you will want to load a motion capture file, store it in some kind of file structure, and then apply it to a 3D object over a time frame that corresponds to the time frame represented by the motion capture file.

In Direct3D, the obvious place to do this is into Direct3D's AnimationSets. Although you can indeed do this, it carries some shortcomings. For example, you cannot edit the motion capture data once it is inside the set and you cannot reduce the number of point samples. Perhaps a third-party developer will fill this hole, or a future version of Direct3D will provide more direct support for playback of motion capture data.

Chapter 13

The DirectX File Format

Sometimes, your second choice turns out to be better than your first choice. This was the case with the Direct3D file format. Originally, the file extension was to be .d3d, which was used in some Direct3D beta versions. However, it was soon discovered that the .d3d file extension was already being used for a file format of another company.

Strike the first choice; enter .x (for DirectX). And as it turns out, .x is a much more appropriate choice, as the file format has turned out to be much more flexible and useful than just another 3D scene file format. In fact, by taking an innovative, generalized approach of representing a 3D scene in a file, the .x format actually offers a very powerful tool for both scene and object data management. Over time, it appears that the DirectX file format is likely to become an extremely significant and useful tool for 3D application development, with ramifications beyond simple scene and geometry description.

The key to understanding the DirectX file format is grasping its simple design premise: Solve the general case, and the special case is easy. The purpose of this chapter is to help you understand the DirectX file format and evaluate its implementation of this "solve the general" approach.

The File Format Failure Syndrome

File formats are often slapped together at the last minute and end up being locked to a particular version of a product. Developers try to hide this last-minute sloppiness by offering API tools that read or write to the file, while hiding the details of the file from the users with some mumbling about the need to reserve the right to make changes and about the proprietary nature of file formats. Marketing folks convince themselves that this inconvenience to users is actually some kind of marketplace advantage because users will get locked to a particular file format and be unable to convert their data to a competing format. Nobody is really fooled by all this, but it is an unhappy fact that rarely do you find a file format that is at once useful, comprehensible, flexible, and accessible. And file formats designed by committee often end up being either too complex, too late, or too undersupported to be a viable alternative.

In the 3D area, the net result of this dynamic is twofold: least-common-denominator file formats tend to win out, and people grow to expect content loss when they convert between file formats. This dynamic is likely to evolve, however, as operating-system-level 3D APIs like Direct3D and Apple's QuickDraw3D include their own file formats.

Fundamentals of 3D Scenes

3D scene file formats present two fundamental problems: how to store the objects that make up the scene and how to store the parent, child, and associative relationships between the objects. Solving these two problems is at the heart of the DirectX file format.

Storing Objects

What is the best way to make objects persistent is one of the classic nagging problems of object-oriented programming. There are two aspects of this problem: saving properties and saving methods. One of the most basic object-oriented concepts is that an object is built of properties and methods. Properties are the data or state variables and methods are the actual code of the functions that are called by the user of the object or used internally by the object.

It is probably fair to say that storing the methods is hard, while storing the properties is relatively easy. However, there is no one, universal way to store an object's properties.

Hierarchical and Associational Relationships

3D scene data requires hierarchical relationships (parent, child, and sibling relationships) and associational relationships (meshes are attached to frames, materials are attached to meshes, and so on). You could call this a hierarchical list or a directed acyclic graph of containers of objects. However, you won't find such a structure as a standard in a library; it is a little too complex.

An Object-Oriented Database?

Put all this together, and you start to have a set of issues that looks something like the issues involved with designing an object-oriented database management system. This is both good and bad. It is good because object-oriented databases (a niche to some, the next big thing in databases to others) are a relatively well-understood discipline (and actually have been particularly meaningful in the related field of CAD). It is bad because you don't want to write one just to be able to load your 3D scene data!

Goals of the .x File Format

So let's see how the .x file designers distilled these general issues of object persistence and hierarchical and associational relationships into some concrete and useful goals that were realistically achievable. It appears that once the commitment was made to take a general approach to a 3D file format, a set of feasible and interesting goals came into focus. They include achieving the following:

- **Application independence.** A key goal of the .x file format is independence from a particular application or domain. Thus you can use the format to store any kind of object data, not just 3d scenes.

- **Extensibility and complex data types.** Application independence requires the ability to define new types of data. As you will see shortly, the .x file format uses templates as its method to support user-defined data types.

- **Hierarchical relationships and optional data.** These two goals are both essential for adequately supporting 3D scenes.

- **Forward/backward compatibility.** In general, a good file format's design should be robust enough to handle forward and backward compatibility (that is, a particular version of an application should be able to read files created with both previous and subsequent versions). In practice, forward and backward compatibility is an oft-cited but hard-to-achieve goal. The DirectX file format proposes two basic tools to handle this goal: GUIDs and data skipping. GUIDS, the unique identifiers that pop up throughout the DirectX design philosophy, provide a convenient method for implementing versioning control. Like COM, a template has a GUID. If the GUID changes, and you don't recognize the new one, then you can avoid version clash. Add to this the idea of skipping data that you don't understand, and you have a basic framework for handling this problem.

182   Part III   Advanced D3D Issues

- **API access.** A file format is not useful if getting data out of it is too difficult. Distributing parsing code is simply not enough to get developers to use a file format. This is a long-term goal for the .x file format.

- **Multiple stream sources.** Gone are the days when a file was a file. A file now could be a local file, a resource, a stream, an Internet document, or a memory file block. As a result, you also need flexible compression and encryption built into the file format, not simply added on as an afterthought.

So can a single file format achieve all of these goals while serving its original purpose of storing 3D scene and geometric data? Actually, it seems it will have to achieve all these goals.

A Simple Example .x File: "Hello_Up"

Next I take a look at a simple .x file. The following is a complete text .x file that describes a vector named "hello_up," which looks straight up in the *y*-direction. Each line is numbered for reference only.

```
1    xof 0301txt 0064                          //header
2    //   A simple .x file                     //comments
3    #    describes a vector named "hello_up"
4    template Vector {                         //template
5    <3D82AB5E-62DA-11cf-AB39-0020AF71E433>    //GUID
6    FLOAT x;                                  //members
7    FLOAT y;
8    FLOAT z;
9    }
10   Vector hello_up{                          //data object
11   0.0;1.0;0.0;                              //the data
12   }
```

Line 1: This is the header. It must be at the beginning of the data stream. It tags the file as an .x file and provides the key parsing information. In this case, "xof" means an .x file type, "0301" means version 3.1, "txt" means a text file (as opposed to a binary or compressed file), and "0064" means a 64-bit size for floating-point numbers.

Lines 2 and 3: These are comments. A comment can begin with either a C++-style double slash (//) or a hash mark (#). Comments can be anywhere in the file (except before the header), may appear on lines with other data, and run to the next new line.

Lines 4–9: This is a template. A template defines the type of data that is expected for a particular kind of data object. A template is made of:

- The term "template" (line 4)
- A template name, in this example "Vector" (line 4)
- A bracketed definition section that starts with { and ends with }, with line ends and whitespace ignored (lines 4 through 9)

Line 5: This is a GUID. Each template has its own (optional) GUID. You can use this GUID later in the file to specify a template, instead of the template's name. (If you are a human rather than a computer program, however, you would probably rather think of the template's name rather than its GUID.)

Lines 6–8: These are member definitions. In this case, the template defines three data members of type float, named *x, y,* and *z*, separated by semicolons.

Lines 10–12: This is a data object. "Vector" indicates that this is a data object of the type "Vector," as defined in the previous template. Its name is "hello_up". Note that there is no forward referencing in an .x file, so the template must come before the data object. In the data member, the end of the member data is indicated by a semicolon. The data members are in the same order as the template definition. In this case, *x* is 0.0, *y* is 1.0, and *z* is 0.0. Since *y* is up, this vector points up!

The File Header

Table 13-1 describes in more detail the different components of the .x file header.

Table 13-1. The .x file header

Type	Size (Bytes)	Required/Optional	Contents	Description
"Magic number"	4	Required	"xof"	The start of an .x stream
Major version	2	Required	03	Major version: 3
Minor version	2	Required	01	Minor version: 1
Format type	4	Required	"txt"	A text file
			"bin"	A binary file
			"com"	A compressed file
Compression type	4	Required if format type is compressed	"lzw" "zip"	Compression types
Float size	4	Optional	0064	64-bit floats
			0032	32-bit floats

The .x file also supports another kind of header: a header template and data object. This is different from the file header and is described in the next two sections.

Header Template

The heart of the .x file format is the template/data object connection. Templates define the type and order of data in data objects; they contain no data. The data objects contain the actual data. Templates are like a structure definition. The general format of a template follows:

```
template <template-name> {
<GUID>
<member1>;
<member2>;
*
<member3>;
[...]
}
```

- The template name is an alphanumeric string, can include an underscore (_), and must not begin with a digit.
- The GUID is required for the template, is formatted in the OSF DCE standard, and is surrounded by angle brackets. GUIDs are nasty creatures to type by hand, but you will probably rarely, if ever, need to do so.
- Template members describe the data elements that data objects based on the template will have. A template must have at least one member. The format of a member is

  ```
  <data-type> <name>;
  ```

  The name is optional, and the data type is either a previously defined template or one of the data primitives listed in Table 13-2.

A template can be open (allows additional data types beyond those in the template), closed (allows only data types in the template), or restricted (allows a normal list of optional data types). Open templates end with [...]; a restricted template includes the optional data types in the ending bracket pair, and a closed template has no ending bracket pair.

Table 13-2. The .x data types

Type	Size
WORD	16 bits
DWORD	32 bits
FLOAT	IEEE float
DOUBLE	64 bits
CHAR	8 bits
UCHAR	8 bits
BYTE	8 bits
STRING	Text surrounded by quotes

You can also define arrays of data with a template. The format for doing this is

```
array <data-type> <name>[dimension-size];
```

The value [dimension-size] can be either an integer or another template member. If it is another template member, then the size of the array will be whatever value is actually assigned to that member in the data object. For example, the following member defines an array of 12 DWORDs that has the name "fixed_list":

```
array DWORD fixed_list[12];
```

The following defines an array of variable length named "variable_list":

```
DWORD arraysize;
array DWORD variable_list[arraysize];
```

Data objects based on the above member will have an array that will be whatever size is specified in the data object for `arraysize`.

There is one special type of template called Header (not the file header, but a template named Header). It is recommended that you use the Header template to define application-specific data such as the version number. However, if you define a dword member of the Header template with the name "flags," then this flags field will have special meaning to the .x file parser. If the value of 0 is encountered in the flags member of a Header data object, then data that follows will be treated as binary. If it is 1, then data that follows will be treated as text. The flags method allows for a technique to combine both text and binary format data in the same file.

Data Objects

Data objects are where you put the actual data in an .x file. The format of a data object is

```
<identifier> [name]{
[GUID]
<member1>;
<member2>;
*
}
```

Typically, the identifier will be the name of a previously defined template. You can also use a primitive like DWORD as an identifier (in which case, the data object would have a single member of that type). Both the name and GUID are optional. If you load an object with the retained mode API and it has no name, the loaded object will have no name.

Members must correspond to the members defined in the template. If there is a series of data members of the same type (integers, floats, or strings), you can organize them in comma-delimited lists like this:

> 1, 2, 3;
>
> 1.0, 3.4, 4.5;
>
> "bird", "dog", "cow";

You can reference a previously defined data object as a data member (by name or GUID). In this case, the value for the member will be the value of the referenced data object.

Following the required member, you can have optional data members in a data object. The meaning and implied syntax of these members will be API-specific and application-specific.

Retained Mode Templates

If you take a look at a DirectX file, you will notice that it has a bunch of templates in the beginning. These are simply the templates that define data objects that match Direct3D's retained mode. These templates must be organized in the file in a particular order; some retained mode templates refer to other retained mode templates, which therefore must appear earlier in the file.

Following is a list of the standard templates used by Direct3D's retained mode:

```
template Header {
  <3D82AB43-62DA-11cf-AB39-0020AF71E433>
  WORD major;
  WORD minor;
  DWORD flags;
}
template Vector {
  <3D82AB5E-62DA-11cf-AB39-0020AF71E433>
  FLOAT x;
  FLOAT y;
  FLOAT z;
}
template Coords2d {
  <F6F23F44-7686-11cf-8F52-0040333594A3>
  FLOAT u;
  FLOAT v;
}
template Matrix4x4 {
  <F6F23F45-7686-11cf-8F52-0040333594A3>
  array FLOAT matrix[16];
}
template ColorRGBA {
  <35FF44E0-6C7C-11cf-8F52-0040333594A3>
  FLOAT red;
  FLOAT green;
  FLOAT blue;
  FLOAT alpha;
}
template ColorRGB {
  <D3E16E81-7835-11cf-8F52-0040333594A3>
  FLOAT red;
  FLOAT green;
  FLOAT blue;
}
template IndexedColor {
  <1630B820-7842-11cf-8F52-0040333594A3>
  DWORD index;
  ColorRGBA indexColor;
}
template Boolean {
  <4885AE61-78E8-11cf-8F52-0040333594A3>
  WORD truefalse;
}
```

```
template Boolean2d {
  <4885AE63-78E8-11cf-8F52-0040333594A3>
  Boolean u;
  Boolean v;
}
template MaterialWrap {
  <4885AE60-78E8-11cf-8F52-0040333594A3>
  Boolean u;
  Boolean v;
}
template TextureFilename {
  <A42790E1-7810-11cf-8F52-0040333594A3>
  STRING filename;
}
template Material {
  <3D82AB4D-62DA-11cf-AB39-0020AF71E433>
  ColorRGBA faceColor;
  FLOAT power;
  ColorRGB specularColor;
  ColorRGB emissiveColor;
  [ . . . ]
}
template MeshFace {
  <3D82AB5F-62DA-11cf-AB39-0020AF71E433>
  DWORD nFaceVertexIndices;
  array DWORD faceVertexIndices[nFaceVertexIndices];
}
template MeshFaceWraps {
  <4885AE62-78E8-11cf-8F52-0040333594A3>
  DWORD nFaceWrapValues;
  Boolean2d faceWrapValues;
}
template MeshTextureCoords {
  <F6F23F40-7686-11cf-8F52-0040333594A3>
  DWORD nTextureCoords;
  array Coords2d textureCoords[nTextureCoords];
}
template MeshMaterialList {
  <F6F23F42-7686-11cf-8F52-0040333594A3>
  DWORD nMaterials;
  DWORD nFaceIndexes;
  array DWORD faceIndexes[nFaceIndexes];
  [Material]
}
```

```
template MeshNormals {
  <F6F23F43-7686-11cf-8F52-0040333594A3>
  DWORD nNormals;
  array Vector normals[nNormals];
  DWORD nFaceNormals;
  array MeshFace faceNormals[nFaceNormals];
}
template MeshVertexColors {
  <1630B821-7842-11cf-8F52-0040333594A3>
  DWORD nVertexColors;
  array IndexedColor vertexColors[nVertexColors];
}
template Mesh {
  <3D82AB44-62DA-11cf-AB39-0020AF71E433>
  DWORD nVertices;
  array Vector vertices[nVertices];
  DWORD nFaces;
  array MeshFace faces[nFaces];
  [ . . . ]
}
template FrameTransformMatrix {
  <F6F23F41-7686-11cf-8F52-0040333594A3>
  Matrix4×4 frameMatrix;
}
template Frame {
  <3D82AB46-62DA-11cf-AB39-0020AF71E433>
  [ . . . ]
}
template FloatKeys {
  <10DD46A9-775B-11cf-8F52-0040333594A3>
  DWORD nValues;
  array FLOAT values[nValues];
}
template TimedFloatKeys {
  <F406B180-7B3B-11cf-8F52-0040333594A3>
  DWORD time;
  FloatKeys tfkeys;
}
template AnimationKey {
  <10DD46A8-775B-11cf-8F52-0040333594A3>
  DWORD keyType;
  DWORD nKeys;
  array TimedFloatKeys keys[nKeys];
}
```

```
template AnimationOptions {
  <E2BF56C0-840F-11cf-8F52-0040333594A3>
  DWORD openclosed;
  DWORD positionquality;
}
template Animation {
  <3D82AB4F-62DA-11cf-AB39-0020AF71E433>
  [ . . . ]
}
template AnimationSet {
  <3D82AB50-62DA-11cf-AB39-0020AF71E433>
  [Animation]
}
```

Retained Mode File-Loading Methods

Now that you have this wonderful, general-purpose file format, how are you going to use it? The retained mode API provides a set of methods that accesses the DirectX file format. These are summarized in Table 13-3.

Table 13-3. Retained mode file-loading methods

Method	Description
IDirect3DRM::Load	A general-purpose object loader.
IDirect3DRMMeshBuilder::Load	Loads a mesh into a Meshbuilder object.
IDirect3DRMAnimationSet::Load	Loads an AnimationSet to an AnimationSet object.
IDirect3DRMFrame::Load	Loads a frame hierarchy to a parent frame.
IDirect3DRMMeshBuilder::Save	Saves a mesh.

The general-purpose Load method takes a big set of parameters: lpFilename, lpvObjName, lplpGUIDs, dwcGUIDs, dwFlags, d3drmLoadProc, lpArgLP, d3drmLoadTextureProc, lpArgLTP, and lpParentFrame. These parameters are described in Part V, but a brief overview here will give you a sense of the range of uses for this method.

To load objects, you first build an array of GUIDS (lplpGUIDs and dwcGUIDs) that identifies the kinds of objects you want to load. For example, you could set up a two-element array containing IID_IDirect3DMeshBuilder and ID_IDirect3DRMAnimationSet to load AnimationSets and MeshBuilder objects.

You can load by object name, position (say, the third object of a specified type), or GUID (the GUID of the data object, not the GUID of the type, which you specify in the lplpGUIDs array). The default setting is to load the top-level object (i.e., the first object of a specified type). You can load from a file, a resource, memory, or a stream.

You also can load by reference or by copying. If you load by reference, the retained mode checks to see whether an object of the specified name already has been loaded, in which case the already-loaded object is used by reference. When you load by copying, the retained mode makes a new copy even if an object of that name has already been loaded. Think of it this way: If you load by reference and load the same file a second time, no new objects will be created. However, if your objects are unnamed in the file, then even if you choose to load by reference you will create unnamed copies.

You also can set up a callback function that will be called when the system reads the specified object. In addition, you can specify the parent frame for loading so that frames can be loaded into an existing scene at a location other than the root frame and AnimationSets can be loaded to a particular frame.

The special-purpose load methods handle frame hierarchies, Mesh-Builders, and AnimationSets. These methods are duplicative of the general-purpose load method, except that you load to an existing object rather than create a new object. Also, you may find these methods a little easier to code, since they have a smaller set of parameters. You cannot set up a general-purpose load callback function with these special-purpose load methods, but the MeshBuilder load does support a specific callback to load textures. The frame loader method loads a hierarchy as a child to the frame object on which you call the load method.

You can save a mesh with IDirect3DRMMeshBuilder::Save.

Future .x File Directions

You may be wondering about a couple of things by now. First, why does the retained mode save only meshes and not things like AnimationSets? And if the DirectX file format is application-independent, where are the support functions to access all this functionality? Do you have to write your own file parser/API to get at any of the data that you could imagine storing in a DirectX file?

In the long run, the answers appear to be that Microsoft intends to expand support for the DirectX file format. A DirectX file format API has been promised, and there has been talk of such things as storing execute buffers in the file format and much more.

My conclusion is that the DirectX file format is a work in progress whose design itself begs for expanded support. I would expect that over time additional functionality would show up, but you'll have to look to Microsoft, not me, for the specifics on this. This is one of those shaky areas, and functionality depends on what your current needs are. You can choose to bet on what functionality will show up—and wait for it—or you can choose to fill the hole yourself and take your chances later.

A More Complex Example File: A Cube

I'll pull this material together by describing a more complex file, in this case, a complete DirectX file that contains an eight-sided cube called "CubeMesh". Examine this file closely, and you should get the hang of how DirectX files are put together. Note that the line numbers are for reference to the discussion and do not appear in an actual file.

```
1    xof 0301txt 0064                         //file header
2    //   A cube named "CubeMesh"             //comment
3                                             //TEMPLATES
4    template Vector {                        //VECTOR
5    <3D82AB5E-62DA-11cf-AB39-0020AF71E433>
6    FLOAT x;                                 //x,y,z
7    FLOAT y;
8    FLOAT z;
9    }
10
11   template MeshFace {                      //MESHFACE
12   <3D82AB5F-62DA-11cf-AB39-0020AF71E433>
13   DWORD nFaceVertexIndices;
14   array DWORD faceVertexIndices[nFaceVertexIndices];
15   }
16
17   template Mesh {                          //MESH
18   <3D82AB44-62DA-11cf-AB39-0020AF71E433>
19   DWORD nVertices;                         //# vertices
20   array Vector vertices[nVertices];        //vertex array
21   DWORD nFaces;                            //# faces
22   array MeshFace faces[nFaces];            //face array
23   }
24
25                                            //DATA OBJECT
26   Mesh CubeMesh {                          //name=CubeMesh
27                                            //VERTEX ARRAY
28   8;                                       //8 vertices
29   1.000000,1.000000,-1.000000,;            //vertex 0
30                                            //x =1, y=1, z=-1
```

```
31     -1.000000,1.000000,-1.000000,;         //vertex 1
32     -1.000000,1.000000,1.000000,;          //and so forth
33     1.000000,1.000000,1.000000,;
34     1.000000,-1.000000,-1.000000,;
35     -1.000000,-1.000000,-1.000000,;
36     -1.000000,-1.000000,1.000000,;
37     1.000000,-1.000000,1.000000,;          //vertex 7
38                                            //FACE ARRAY
39     12;                                    //12 faces
40     3,0,1,2,;                              //face 0 has
41                                            //3 vertices:
42                                            //0,1,2 in
43                                            //Vertex Array
44     3,0,2,3,;                              //face 1
45     3,0,4,5,;                              //face 2
46     3,0,5,1,;
47     3,1,5,6,;
48     3,1,6,2,;
49     3,2,6,7,;
50     3,2,7,3,;
51     3,3,7,4,;
52     3,3,4,0,;
53     3,4,7,6,;
54     3,4,6,5,;;                             //face 11
55     }
```

Line 1: This is the header line.

Lines 2 through 23: These are templates. This file contains three templates: Vector, MeshFace, and Mesh. The main template is Mesh, which defines the data structure for a Mesh data object. Note, however, that a Mesh object is built from two arrays: an array of vertices and an array of faces (see lines 19–22). Vertices and MeshFaces are themselves objects and are defined previously by their own templates. (Remember that Direct3D retained mode uses the term "vector" to mean both the mathematical concept of vector and an x, y, z location in 3D space. In this case, a Vector is used to specify an x, y, z location in space, i.e., the corner points of the faces that build the mesh.)

A Mesh object contains an array of MeshFaces (line 22). MeshFace objects in turn contain an array of indices into the vertex array (line 14). When this all appears as data in the subsequent data object, it means that a Mesh contains an array of variable-length arrays (i.e., an array of faces, each face being a variable-length array of indices into the vertex array).

Lines 26–55: This is the Mesh data object. A Mesh is made of a vertex array and a face array. The vertex array (lines 28–37) contains eight vertices (vectors). The face array (lines 39–54) contains 12 faces. Each face contains three vertices, so it is of course a triangle. Each of the six sides of the cube is made of two triangles. The first face (face 0 on line 40) is made of indices 0, 1, and 2 into the vertex array. This means simply that the first triangle of the cube uses as its corners the first, second, and third points (vectors) in the previous vertex array.

Adding a Material

Now I look at a fragment of an .x file that describes a material that could be attached to the cube just examined:

```
1    template ColorRGBA {
2    <35FF44E0-6C7C-11cf-8F52-0040333594A3>
3    FLOAT red;
4    FLOAT green;
5    FLOAT blue;
6    FLOAT alpha;
7    }
8    template ColorRGB {
9    <D3E16E81-7835-11cf-8F52-0040333594A3>
10   FLOAT red;
11   FLOAT green;
12   FLOAT blue;
13   }
14   template Material {
15   <3D82AB4D-62DA-11cf-AB39-0020AF71E433>
16   ColorRGBA ambientColor;
17   FLOAT power;
18   ColorRGB specularColor;
19   ColorRGB emissiveColor;
20   }
21   Material RedMaterial{
22   1.000000,1.000000,1.000000,1.000000,;       //ambient
23   0.000000,;                                   /power
24   0.000000,0.000000,0.000000,;                 //specular
25   0.000000,0.000000,0.000000;;                 //emissive
26   }
```

Notice that this fragment contains three templates: Material, ColorRGBA, and ColorRGB. The Material template uses a ColorRGBA template, a float, and two ColorRGB's to define its data structure. So does this mean the material corresponds to the retained modes material object? Not exactly. The retained mode API supports IDirect3DRMMaterial::SetEmissive, IDirect3DRMMaterial::SetPower, and IDirect3DRMMaterial::SetSpecular but no ambient color. Ambient colors are set on meshes through methods on MeshBuilder and Mesh.

Representing Hierarchy

Hierarchical relations in an .x file are inferred from the positioning of data objects. To make one data object a child of another data object, you put it inside the parent object's brackets, after the parent's required data members.

The following .x file describes a hierarchy of four nodes (objects of type TreeNode), each of which has an arbitrary DWORD value. The root node is named "Root," which has two children: "Child1" and "Child2." "Child2" has a child named "GrandChild1."

```
1    template TreeNode {
2        DWORD NodeValue
3    }
4    TreeNode Root {
5        5
6        TreeNode Child1 {4}
7        TreeNode Child2 {
8            3
9            TreeNode GrandChild1 {8}
10       }
11   }
```

Lines 1 through 3 define a TreeNode template, which includes a single DWORD data member named NodeValue. Lines 4 and 5 are the root data object (the bracket ends on line 11), which has a NodeValue of 5. Line 6 is Child1 TreeNode. Lines 7 through 10 are Child2 and its child, GrandChild1.

A Frame Hierarchy

To represent a retained mode frame hierarchy in an .x file, you use frame objects and add children to them. The following .x file fragment uses groups to describe a simple robot, with its torso as its root object:

```
group RobotTorso {                                    //ROBOT TORSO
<3D82AB46-62DA-11cf-AB39-0020AF71E433>   //frame GUID
FrameTransformMatrix {..matrix data..}
    group RobotHead {..data..};
    group RobotLeftArm {..data..};
    group RobotRightArm {..data..};
    group RobotLeftLeg {..data..};
    group RobotRightLeg {..data..};
}
```

An AnimationSet

Animations and AnimationSets fit nicely into the .x file structure. An AnimationSet is a collection of Animations, and an Animation contains a set of values, called *keys,* that are interpolated over time—a nice nested hierarchical relationship of contained objects, which is exactly what the .x file format is designed to handle. Here is the basic layout of an AnimationSet:

```
Animation AnAnimationSet {
<GUID-animationset>
    AnAnimation {
    <GUID-animation>
    {frame}
    {AnimationKey}
    }
}
```

The following is an .x file that contains an animation. The AnimationSet applies a path for the robot frame to follow. It is called RobotPath and contains a single animation, called WalkPath. In a more complicated example, you would want more individual animations, such as for the movement of the robot's arms and legs.

The WalkPath animation contains a single Animation key, which consists of three position keys:

```
1 xof 0301txt 0064                              //file header
// A path in a .x file
                                                //TEMPLATES
template FloatKeys {                            //FloatKeys
<10DD46A9-775B-11cf-8F52-0040333594A3>
  DWORD nValues;
  array FLOAT values[nValues];
}
template TimedFloatKeys {                       //TimedFloatKeys
<F406B180-7B3B-11cf-8F52-0040333594A3>
  DWORD time;
  FloatKeys tfkeys;
}
template AnimationKey {                         //AnimationKey
<10DD46A8-775B-11cf-8F52-0040333594A3>
  DWORD keyType;
  DWORD nKeys;
  array TimedFloatKeys keys[nKeys];
}
```

```
group Robot {                                       //ROBOT FRAME OBJECT
<3D82AB46-62DA-11cf-AB39-0020AF71E433>              //frame GUID
FrameTransformMatrix {
1.000000,0.000000,0.000000,0.000000,;
0.000000,1.000000,0.000000,0.000000,;
0.000000,0.000000,1.000000,0.000000,;
0.000000,0.000000,0.000000,1.000000;;
}
AnimationSet RobotPath {                            //ROBOT ANIMATION
<3D82AB5E-62DA-11cf-AB39-0020AF71E433>              //ANIMATIONSET
  Animation WalkPath {
  <3D82AB5E-62DA-11cf-AB39-0020AF71E433>            //ANIMATION
  {Robot}                                           //target frame
  AnimationKey {
    2;                                              //position keys
    3;                                              //3 keys
    10,3,0.000000,0.000000,0.000000,;               //key 1
    20,3,2.000000,3.000000,4.000000,;               //key 2
    30,3,4.000000,6.000000,8.000000,;;              //key 3
    }
  }
}
```

Part IV

3D Resources

Chapter 14

Essential 3D Math

Let's face it: If you do not have a strong math background, you are likely to feel intimidated by 3D math. Pick up any 3D graphics text and you will probably find page after page of academically oriented math material that will certainly overwhelm the uninitiated. But hold off before you conclude that 3D application development will forever be solely the province of an elite core of 3D gurus. Here is the secret: The essential core of 3D math you will need to successfully use Direct3D is smaller than you might think. You can gain a basic understanding without great math talent or academic training.

This is not to say that the field of 3D math is simpler than it appears. Far from it. It is just that the range of topics you need to understand to do API-level development is less than the full breadth of topics that are related to 3D. An analogy would be application programming with a database manager. You do not need to understand every sorting algorithm to write an application with a database manager, although to write a good database manager would certainly require in-depth knowledge of sorting algorithms.

So the goal of this chapter is to help you identify and learn the central concepts that you will actually need to be successful at 3D application programming. But first, I start with what you do not need to know.

What You Do Not Need to Know

To develop a realtime 3D application, you do not need to learn to build your own 3D graphics engine, write a Doom BSP clone, design your own ray tracer or radiosity renderer, or master the intricacies of splines, NURBs surfaces, or wavelets. These are all important, challenging, even critical, areas of 3D graphics research and development. If you pursue mastering one of them, you are likely to develop a base of 3D math knowledge that will transfer to 3D application programming.

In fact, you will find that a huge number of 3D engines, renderers, and Doom clones have been written. There are literally hundreds of hobbyist, near-commercial, and shareware versions of these products. This is partly because commercial versions have been expensive or unavailable on PCs and partly because many people find these projects engrossing. Also, academia has tended to focus on certain topics, such as radiosity rendering, that have markets far smaller today than the likely mass market uses of 3D (although someday, radiosity will likely be a mainstream feature, too!).

The sad fact is that although these versions no doubt have been great learning vehicles for their authors and consumed a huge amount of development time, only a handful have ended up as commercial products. And even more sadly, there is little commercial prospect in the future for these directions beyond a small core of best-of-category implementations. But for a generation of 3D programmers, writing your own seems to have been a rite of passage.

If you are starting out in 3D today, I suggest you consider a different tack. Start by learning to use the tools and products that are already in place. You may someday write a great 3D engine, Doom clone, or renderer, but the fact is that far more people will make their living *using* these kinds of products than *writing* them. So you should recognize the line between systems software development and application software development. Knowing the systems level can certainly help at the application level, but you no longer have to write a 3D system-level component in order to pay your dues and get started in 3D application development. However, much of the existing graphics literature addresses a broader range and depth of math topics than you will need for successful API-level 3D application development.

What You Do Need to Know

Vectors, matrices, quaternions, and planes. These are part of what you do need to know. In this chapter, I help you become familiar with these concepts, with a particular emphasis on how they are used in Direct3D. Here is a preview of these concepts.

- **Vectors.** A vector is a direction and a magnitude. Think of an arrow: The tip points in the direction of a vector, and the length of the arrow is like the magnitude of vector. A vector can represent the speed and direction of a moving object. It also can be used for calculating distances and spatial relations among objects, collision detection, and dynamics.

- **Matrices.** A matrix is a grid of values that is used as a shorthand description of a set of equations. This set of equations (called matrix transforms) is used to convert a point in 3D space from one coordinate system to another. Your computer screen is a 2D coordinate system (x is horizontal, y is vertical); matrix transformations convert objects from 3D coordinates (x, y, and z) into screen coordinates. With inverse transforms, you can go from screen coordinates to 3D coordinates. Matrices also are used to represent movement, scaling, and rotation.

- **Quaternions.** A quaternion (specifically a unit quaternion) describes orientation, which means which way you are facing in 3D space. Think of a quaternion as a vector (which describes the direction an object is facing) plus a rotation around that vector. Direct3D uses quaternions instead of Euler angles (successive rotations around the *x-*, *y-*, and *z-axes*) because quaternions are mathematically convenient for such operations as interpolating between two orientations. Also, in spite of their intimidating name, quaternions are actually easier to conceptualize than Euler angles. Think of an apple, and think of sticking it with an arrow. Rotate the arrow (in your mind, not with your lunch!). A quaternion is the direction of the arrow plus the amount you have rotated the arrow. This value describes the orientation of the apple in space.

- **Planes.** A plane is a flat surface. It can be represented as an equation (*Hint:* You use perpendicular vectors). Plane equations are useful for determining spatial relations between objects.

3D Math Preliminaries

First, I cover some preliminaries, particularly coordinate systems and how Direct3D represents numeric values.

Coordinate Systems

For working with 2D graphics, you should be familiar with the Cartesian coordinate system. This system is the convention of representing the location of a point by its *x-* and *y-*coordinates in relation to an origin. Increasing *x* values move to the left; increasing *y* values move up. Positive *x* values are to the left of the origin. Figure 14-1 shows a 2D Cartesian coordinate system.

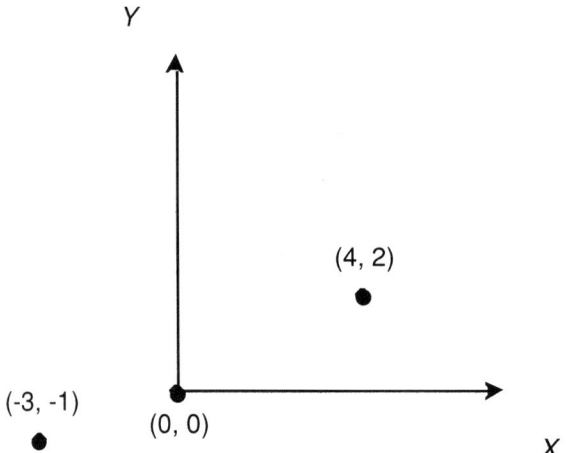

Figure 14-1. The 2D Cartesian coordinate system.

To move to the 3D Cartesian coordinate system, you add a z-coordinate. But which way is the positive z direction? z values coming out of the page could be positive and getting larger or smaller and moving away. Unfortunately, some genius with two hands started the universal and thoroughly confusing convention of referring to these two coordinate systems as right-handed and left-handed. The idea is you hold up your hand and position the fingers in a certain way. In this way, you can represent a right-hand or left-hand system. But there are different conventions for how to hold your hand! The thumb is usually the positive z-axis, but sometimes the arm follows the x-axis and sometimes it follows the y-axis. Figure 14-2 shows a right-handed system.

Here is a technique that you may find less confusing:

3D Cartesian Coordinates: Left- versus Right-Handed Systems
Start with a standard 2D coordinate ($+x$ = left, $+y$ = up).
Right-hand coordinates: z comes *right* out of the screen (z increases as it moves towards you).
Left-hand coordinates: z increases as it moves away from you (z is left in the screen).

Generally, right-handed coordinate systems are more popular in print, because the printed page offers more room to represent all-positive coordinates (x-, y-, and z-coordinates are all positive). Left-handed coordinate systems are usually more popular, but by no means universally used, for computer graphics APIs, perhaps because it might make sense to have larger z values going away from you. Direct3D uses a left-hand coordinate system.

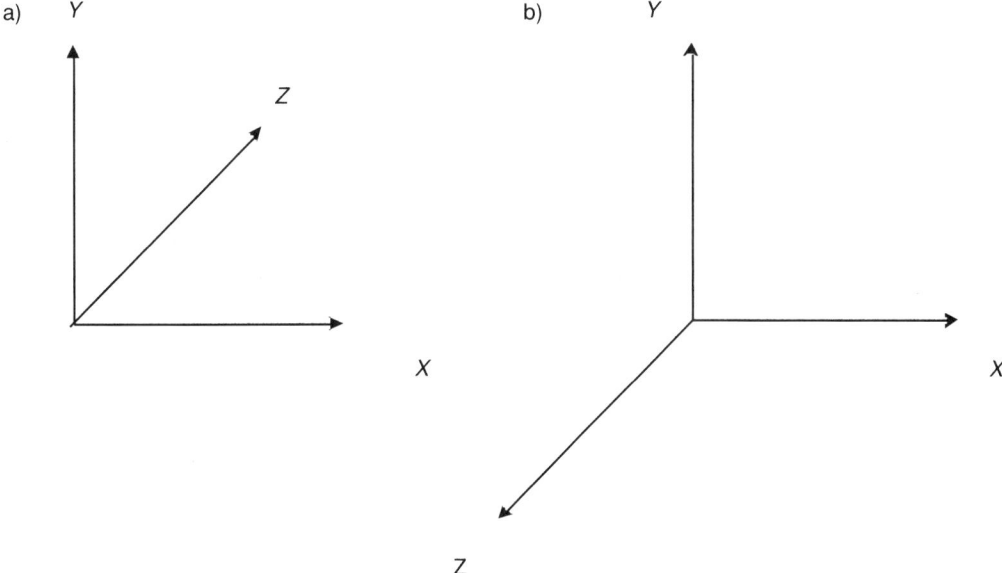

Figure 14-2. Right-handed 3D Cartesian coordinate system. *z* comes "right out" of the page (increases as it moves towards you).

D3DVALUE

To represent numeric values, Direct3D defines a math value type, D3DVALUE, and a math conversion macro, D3DVAL. The D3DVALUE is typedefed as a float, as follows:

```
typedef float D3DVALUE, *LPD3DVALUE;
```

The math conversion macro, D3DVAL, which creates a D3DVALUE, is defined as

```
D3DVAL(val) ((float)val)
```

Good programming practice will require you to use D3DVALUE rather than a float. In the past, the D3DVALUE was a convenient way to hide fixed-point values and floating-point values from the programmer. Although fixed-point numeric values were a popular 3D math type on pre-Pentium and pre-PowerPC computers, it appears that as of this writing floating-point is the numeric type of choice for Direct3D. However, as with any typedefed constant, don't take the risk of assuming that it will remain this way forever.

In support of the D3DVALUE math type, Direct3D provides divide and multiply macros—D3DDivide/Multiply—that divide/multiply one D3DVALUE by another.

Vectors

A vector is not a point, and a point is not a vector, but Direct3D calls both of them vectors. Vectors are one of the most fundamental and useful mathematical concepts you will need to understand to master 3D application programming. Vectors have many uses, from calculating distances and spatial relationships to representing velocity and orientation.

So what is a vector? First of all, a vector is not a point. A point is a location in 3D space, specified by its *x, y,* and *z* values. In geometric terms, a vector is a line segment between two points, like an arrow. The direction of the arrow is the direction of the vector, and length of the arrow is the magnitude of the vector. As shown in Figure 14-3, point *A* is the *initial point* and point *B* is the *terminal point* of the vector. A vector from point *A* to point *B* is sometimes called a **directed line segment** and is written as $\overrightarrow{AB}$. I use the common convention of representing a vector as a lowercase boldface letter, like **v, u,** or **w.**

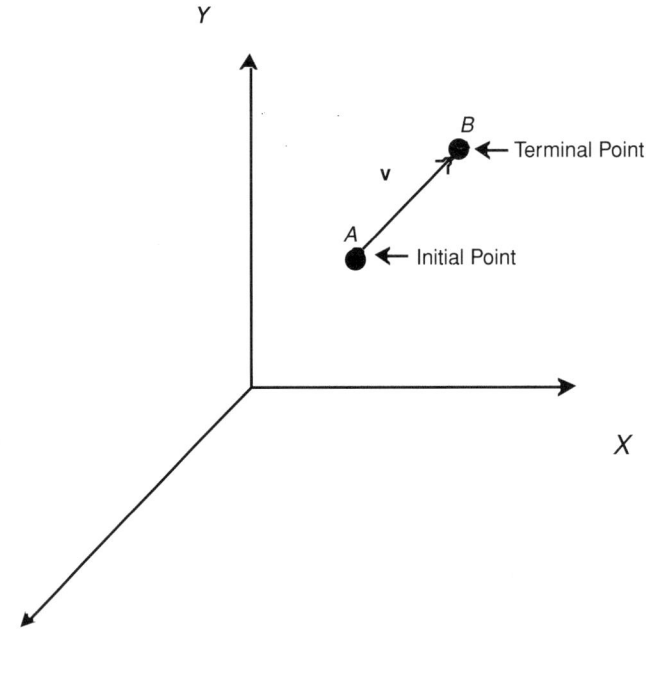

Figure 14-3. A vector from point *A* to point *B*.

Vectors are easily confused with points because both can be described by x, y, and z values. A point is represented by a capital italic, such as A or B. Vectors and points can be represented as a column matrix as

$$\begin{bmatrix} x \\ y \\ z \end{bmatrix}$$

Or a row matrix as

$$[x \ y \ z]$$

I cover matrices in more depth later in the chapter. For now, think of a row or column matrix representing a point or vector as a mathematical unit of three components: x, y, and z.

To be more precise, a vector is a mathematical quantity possessing direction and magnitude. Algebraically, it is the difference between two points. For example, referring to Figure 14-3, we can represent a vector in several ways:

$$\begin{aligned}
\mathbf{v} &= \overline{AB} & \text{A vector is a directed line segment from } A \text{ to } B \\
&= A - B & \text{Which is the difference between points } A \text{ and } B \\
&= \begin{bmatrix} A_x \\ A_y \\ A_z \end{bmatrix} - \begin{bmatrix} B_x \\ B_y \\ B_z \end{bmatrix} & \text{Represented as the difference between two column matrices} \\
&= \begin{bmatrix} \mathbf{v}_x \\ \mathbf{v}_y \\ \mathbf{v}_z \end{bmatrix} & \text{Which is an } x, y, z \text{ triplet of values.}
\end{aligned}$$

One way to think of a vector is as the line segment from the origin (0,0,0) to a point. But remember, the vector itself does not have a location. Here again are the main things to remember about points and vectors:

- A point is a location in space specified by its x, y, and z values.
- A vector is a direction and a length.
- A vector is the difference between two points, so it is expressed as an x, y, and z value.

Retained Mode Vector Support

Direct3D's retained mode provides you a basic set of vector functions, as shown in the Table 14-1.

Table 14-1. Vector functions in retained mode

Vector Functions	Description
D3DVectorAdd/Subtract	Adds/subtracts two vectors.
D3DVectorCrossProduct	Calculates the cross-product of two vectors (i.e., a vector perpendicular to two vectors).
D3DVectorDotProduct	Calculates the dot product of two vectors.
D3DVectorModulus	Calculates the length of a vector.
D3DVectorNormalize	Resizes a vector so that its length is one unit (i.e., a unit vector).
D3DVectorRandom	Creates a unit vector pointing in a random direction.
D3DVectorReflect	Reflects a ray about a given normal.
D3DVectorRotate	Sets the rotation part of a matrix to correspond to a specified rotation around a vector.
D3DVectorScale	Scales a vector.

Finding the Length of a Vector

The length of a vector is shown by the symbol: $\|\mathbf{v}\|$. You can calculate the length using the 3D version of the Pythagorean theorem:

$$\|\mathbf{v}\| = \sqrt{v_x^2 + v_y^2 + v_z^2}$$

A vector with a length of one unit is called a unit, or normalized, vector. To calculate a unit vector, divide the *x*, *y*, and *z* components by the length of the vector. For example, if the vector has a length of 2, then you divide *x*, *y*, and *z* by 2. If the vector has a length of 1—that is, it is *normalized*—then you would divide by 1, which results in the same values.

Figure 14-4 shows the length of a vector.

Vector Multiplication

You can multiply or divide a vector by a value, also called a *scalar*. The result is a longer or shorter vector, pointing in either the same direction or the exact opposite direction (unless you multiply by one, then you of course get the same vector). The result of vector multiplication is sometimes called the **scalar product.**

You simply multiply the *x*, *y*, and *z* components of the vector:

$$k\mathbf{v} = \begin{bmatrix} kv_x & kv_y & kv_z \end{bmatrix}$$

Chapter 14 Essential 3D Math

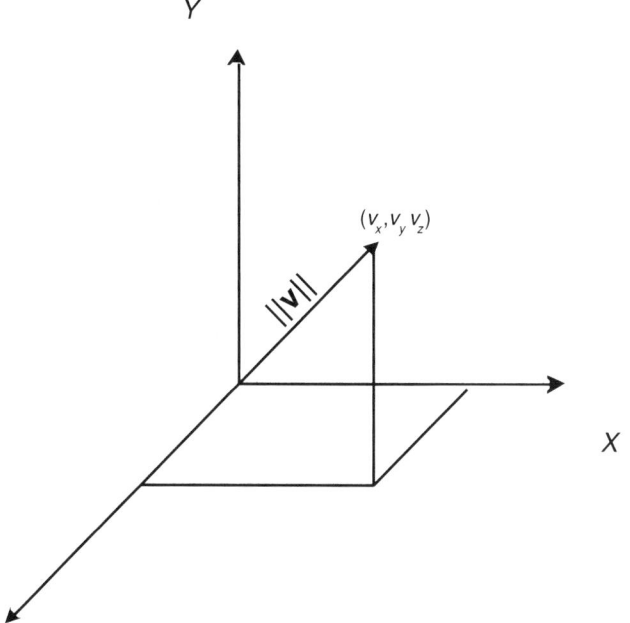

Figure 14-4. Length of a vector.

Vector Addition and Subtraction

Vector addition and subtraction are summarized in Figure 14-5.

If you have a vector **u** of (4, 5, 6) and a vector **v** of (3, 2, 1), then you add them as follows:

$$\mathbf{u} + \mathbf{v} = \begin{bmatrix} (u_x + v_x) & (u_y + v_y) & (u_z + v_z) \end{bmatrix}$$
$$\begin{bmatrix} (4+3) & (5+2) & (6+1) \end{bmatrix}$$
$$\begin{bmatrix} (7) & (7) & (7) \end{bmatrix}$$

Subtracting a vector is like adding the negative of a vector. The negative of a vector is found by multiplying by -1. So using the above values for vectors **u** and **v**, subtraction would be done like this:

$$\mathbf{u} - \mathbf{v} = \begin{bmatrix} (u_x - v_x) & (u_y - v_y) & (u_z - v_z) \end{bmatrix}$$
$$\begin{bmatrix} (4-3) & (5-2) & (6-1) \end{bmatrix}$$
$$\begin{bmatrix} (1) & (3) & (5) \end{bmatrix}$$

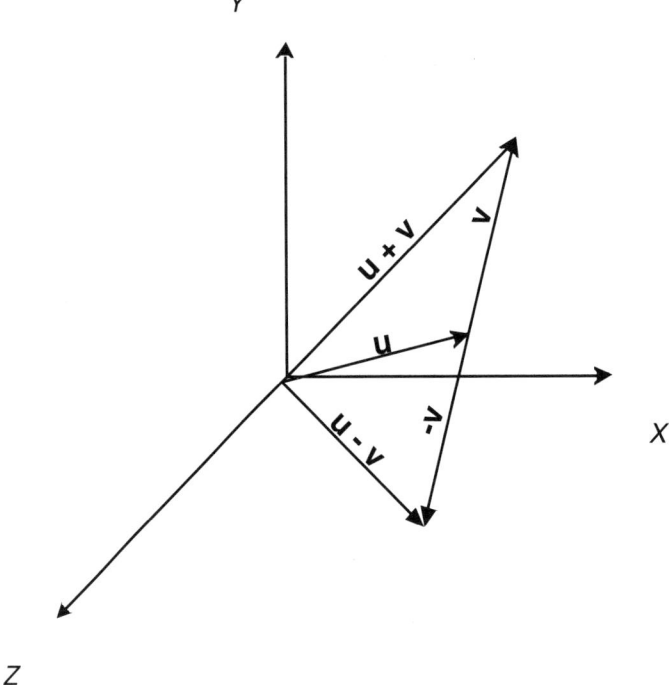

Figure 14-5. Adding and subtracting vectors.

Dot Product

Understanding the dot product is essential to grasping 3D math. I spend a lot of time on it because it can take a while to get a sense of what the dot product really is and why it is so useful.

The dot product has a kind of ubiquitous "Kilroy was here" character in 3D programming: It tends to keep popping up in the most curious places. It is an operation performed on two vectors. The result is a value (not another vector). The value tells you something significant about the relationship between the two vectors. This "something" that the dot product tells you has to do with a combination of the angle between the two vectors and the relative lengths of the vectors. Expect it to take a while for the intuitive feel of the dot product to sink in, just like long ago you probably had to grapple with what the square of a number "feels" like.

The dot product of two vectors **u** and **v** is written as

u · **v**

Don't confuse the little dot for the multiplication symbol; the dot represents only the dot product operation. (The convention for representing matrix multiplication is either no symbol or the x symbol, but never a dot, to avoid confusion.)

Say the x, y, and z components of vectors **u** and **v** are $[u_x \ u_y \ u_z]$ and $[v_x \ v_y \ v_z]$, the dot product of **u** and **v** is

$$\mathbf{u} \cdot \mathbf{v} = u_x v_x + u_y v_y + u_z v_z$$

In plain terms, you multiply the x's together, then add the y's multiplied together, and then add the z's multiplied together.

Here's the calculation of a dot product, based on the two vectors in Figure 14-6. Remember, a vector is not a point; it is the direction and distance between two points! By convention, a single three-part value is used for a vector because the starting point is assumed to be the origin. So vectors don't actually have a location in 3D space; they have only a direction and distance. Hence they could actually start anywhere.

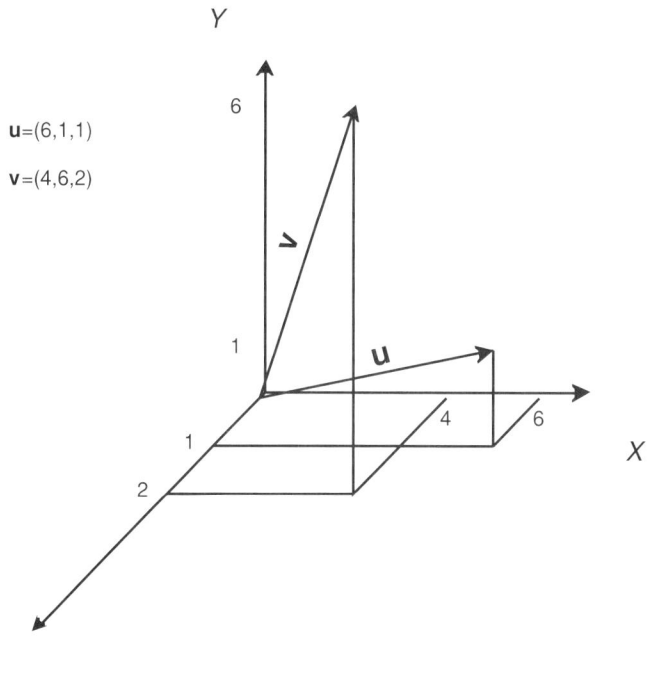

Figure 14-6. Finding the dot product.

In Figure 14-6, vector **u** is (6,1,1) and vector **v** is (4,6,2), so

$$\mathbf{u} \cdot \mathbf{v} = u_x v_x + u_y v_y + u_z v_z$$
$$(6 \times 4) + (1 \times 6) + (1 \times 2)$$
$$24 + 6 + 2$$
$$32$$

In summary, the dot product is a value that expresses a relationship between two vectors. The dot product of two vectors **u** and **v** is

$$\mathbf{u} \cdot \mathbf{v} = u_x v_x + u_y v_y + u_z v_z$$

Think: "x's multiplied plus y's multiplied plus z's multiplied."

Properties of the Dot Product

Some of the properties of the dot product follow:

$\mathbf{u} \cdot \mathbf{0} = \mathbf{0}$
$\mathbf{u} \cdot \mathbf{v} = \mathbf{v} \cdot \mathbf{u}$
$\mathbf{u} \cdot (\mathbf{v} + \mathbf{w}) = (\cdot) + \mathbf{0}$

The dot product can be used to calculate length. Recall from above that the length of a vector is

$$\|\mathbf{v}\| = \sqrt{v_x^2 + v_y^2 + v_z^2}$$

Now imagine two copies of the vector **v** that have the same length and direction. Find the dot product of these two identical vectors (you can think of this as the dot product of a single vector, instead of two vectors) as follows:

$$\mathbf{v} \cdot \mathbf{v} = v_x v_x + v_y v_y + v_z v_z$$
$$= v_x^2 + v_y^2 + v_z^2$$

Notice something? This is the value you take the square root of to get the length of the vector! So the length of a vector can be expressed as

$$\|\mathbf{v}\| = \sqrt{\mathbf{v} \cdot \mathbf{v}}$$

So what, you may say. Why not just use the Pythagorean theorem? Well, in essence you are; you're just expressing it in terms of the dot product.

Converting a Vector to a Unit Vector

A unit vector is a vector of length of one unit. You can convert a vector by a unit vector by dividing each of its components by the length of the vector, that is, by the square root of the dot product.

Chapter 14   Essential 3D Math   213

$$\frac{\mathbf{v}}{\|\mathbf{v}\|} = \frac{\mathbf{v}}{\sqrt{\mathbf{v} \cdot \mathbf{v}}}$$

$$= \frac{\mathbf{v}}{\sqrt{v_x^2 + v_y^2 + v_z^2}}$$

$$= \left[\frac{v_x}{\sqrt{v_x^2 + v_y^2 + v_z^2}} \quad \frac{v_y}{\sqrt{v_x^2 + v_y^2 + v_z^2}} \quad \frac{v_z}{\sqrt{v_x^2 + v_y^2 + v_z^2}} \right]$$

Dot Product of Perpendicular Vectors

The dot product of two perpendicular vectors **u** and **v** is always 0.

Understanding 3D Planes

A plane is the points that lie flat on a surface, right? Not very helpful. Here's a starting point for a mathematical understanding of a plane:

1. A vector that is perpendicular, or orthogonal, to the plane (orthogonal means a **normal vector** perpendicular to the plane).
2. Take any two points on a plane. The vector between them will be perpendicular to a normal vector of the plane.

Watch the wording here, because it is a little loose. Remember, a vector does not have a location in 3D space, only a direction and a magnitude. So every point on a plane has a "perpendicular relationship" with a normal vector to a plane, as shown in Figure 14-7. This perpendicular relationship is the basis for developing a mathematical equation that describes a plane.

Say you know that P_0 is on the plane (as shown in Figure 14-8). How do you know that P is also on the plane? The answer is that the vector from P_0 to P is perpendicular to **n**, a normal vector to the plane.

Recall the discussion of the dot product of two vectors. Two vectors are perpendicular if, and only if, their dot product equals 0. So in this case

$$\mathbf{n} \cdot \mathbf{p} = 0$$

The vector **p** is the difference between point P and point P_0, so replacing the vector **p** with its calculation yields:

$$\mathbf{n} \cdot [(x - x_0) \quad (y - y_0) \quad (z - z_0)] = 0$$

And in this case the vector **n** is (a, b, c). This just means that the vector for **n** could be any values for x, y, and z, so by convention, I use a, b, and c. Substituting the matrix form for **n** gives the following:

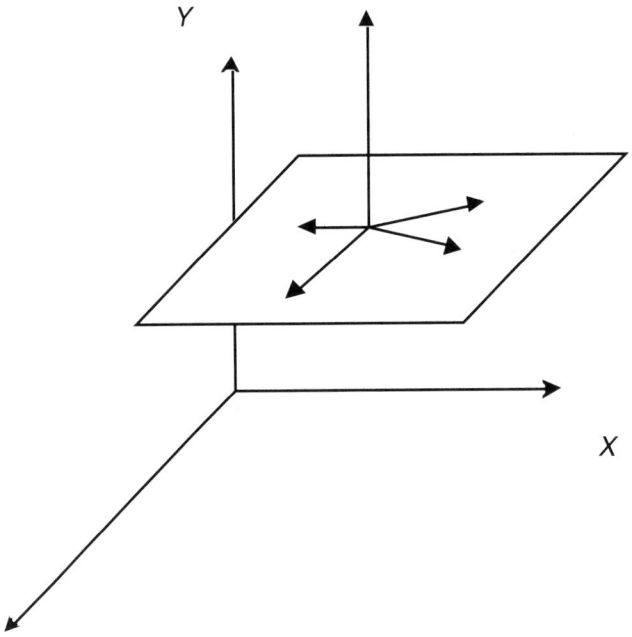

Figure 14-7. Planes.

$$[a \quad b \quad c] \cdot [(x - x_0) \quad (y - y_0) \quad (z - z_0)] = 0$$

Multiplying out the dot product gives what is called the **point-normal form of the equation of a plane:**

$$a(x - x_0) + b(y - y_0) + c(y - y_0) = 0$$

The point-normal form of the equation of a plane means simply that you use the normal to the plane and a point on the plane (actually two points, but who's counting?) to express an equation that is true for all points on the plane.

Multiply out this equation and reorganize this equation, and you will have the **general form of the equation of a plane:**

$$ax + by + cz + d = 0$$

This formula means that for a plane, there is a set of constants, a, b, c, and d such that if you substitute the x, y, and z values of any point on this plane into this formula, you will always get the result 0.

The general form is the generic way of writing the equation of a plane, but it hides a troubling sleight of hand: What is that term d? The term d is actually the scary looking $(-ax_o - by_0 - cy_0)$, which results from reorganizing

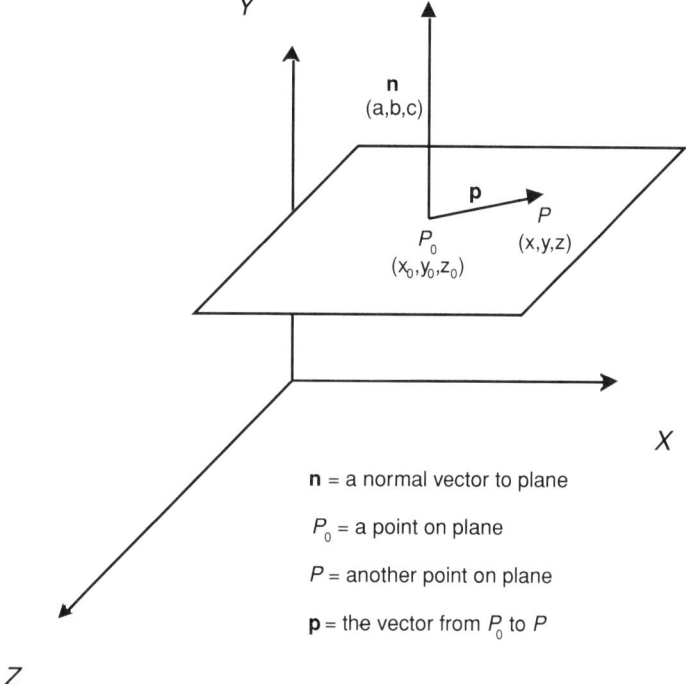

Figure 14-8. Plane normals.

the point-normal form of the plane. However, just as things are starting to get complicated, wouldn't you know that our old friend dot product is back to rescue us? Read on.

The Dot Product and the Equation of a Plane

Recall that the dot product of two vectors is

$\mathbf{u} \cdot \mathbf{v} = u_x v_x + u_y v_y + u_z v_z$

and the general form of the plane equation is

$ax + by + cz + d = 0$

And remember that a, b, and c are the x, y, and z substituted previously, so $\mathbf{n} \cdot \mathbf{p} + d = 0$.

Distance from Point to Plane

Use a unit vector as the normal. The distance from a point to the plane is the distance of a normal vector from the plane to the point, as shown in Figure

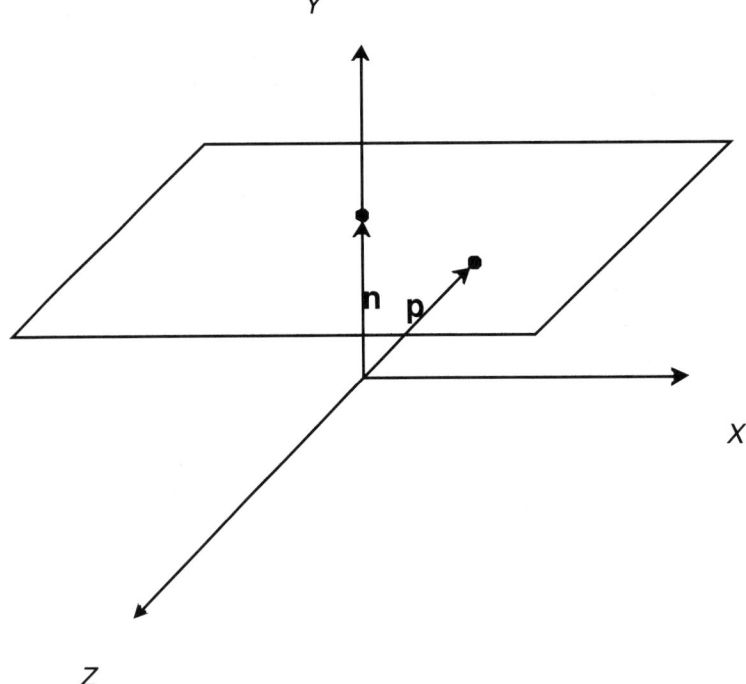

Figure 14-9. Point to plane.

14-9. If you could find this point on the plane that is closest to the *p*, you would then know the vector between them. (A vector is the difference between two points, remember?)

To calculate the distance from a point to a plane, first define the plane equation using a unit normal (a vector of length one unit perpendicular to the plane):

$$\mathbf{n} \cdot \mathbf{p} + d = 0$$
$$\mathbf{p} = \mathbf{q} - d\mathbf{n}$$

Substitute **p** in the equation and solve for *d*:

$$\mathbf{n} \cdot (\mathbf{q} - l\mathbf{n}) + d = 0$$
$$(\mathbf{n} \cdot \mathbf{q}) - l(\mathbf{n} \cdot \mathbf{n}) + d = 0$$
$$(\mathbf{n} \cdot \mathbf{q}) - l + d = 0$$
$$(\mathbf{n} \cdot \mathbf{q}) + d = l$$

Quaternions

A quaternion describes an orientation in 3D space using a vector and a rotation (see Figure 14-10). Take a look at the Direct3D structure for a quaternion:

Chapter 14 Essential 3D Math

```
typedef struct _D3DRMQUATERNION {
    D3DVALUE s;
    D3DVECTOR v;
}D3DRMQUATERNION;
```

From this structure you can see that a quaternion is made of two components, a vector (**v**) and a value (*s*). Think of the vector **v** as the direction you are describing. For example, 0,0,1 would be a vector pointing into the screen (in the direction of the *z*-axis).

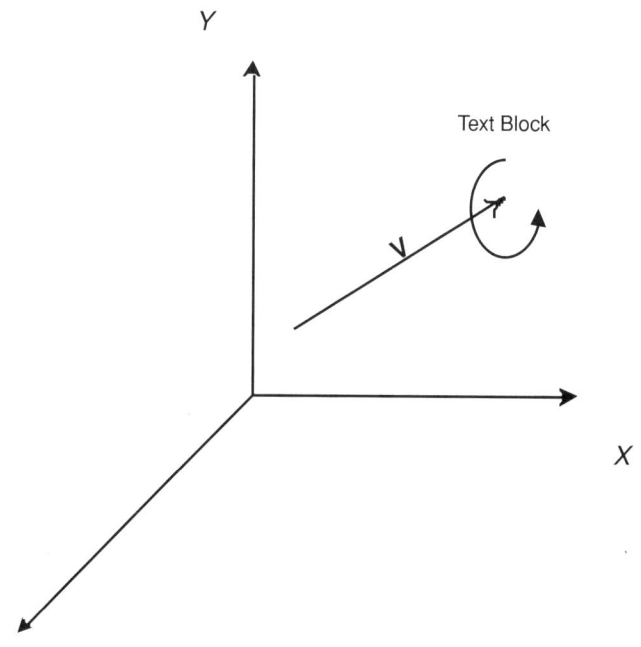

Figure 14-10. Quaternion as a vector and a rotation.

If you multiply a unit quaternion by a unit quaternion, the result is another unit quaternion. Multiplying two quaternions is the same thing as applying two successive rotations.

All possible unit vectors (starting at the origin and pointing in all directions) would look like a sphere with a radius of one. You can think of all unit quaternions as a four-dimensional sphere, representing all possible ways an object could face.

One way to think of a quaternion is as a four-dimensional vector (the first three dimensions are x, y, and z; the fourth dimension is rotation). Pointing up, with no rotation = 0 degrees of rotation around a vector pointing along the z direction.

Recall that in three dimensions, a unit vector is a vector with a length of one unit. You can scale any vector to be a unit vector, in which case you have a vector that points in the same direction as the original vector, but is now of length one unit. Unit vectors are useful because you can perform mathematical calculations with them.

In mathematical notation, a quaternion can be written as:

$q = (s, \mathbf{v})$

To create a unit quaternion, you start with an axis and a rotation:

$(\cos(\theta/2), \mathbf{n}(\sin(\theta - 2)))$

Where θ is the angle:

$\theta = 2\arccos(S)$

$\theta = 2\operatorname{atan}\left(\dfrac{\mathbf{n}\sin(\theta/2)}{\cos(\theta/2)}\right)$

Quaternion Support

The Direct3D retained mode uses quaternions to describe animated and interpolated rotation in IDirect3DRMAnimation::AddRotateKey method.

A quaternion is used to describe the rotation used by IDirect3DRM Animation::AddRotateKey. It is also used in several of Direct3DRM's mathematical functions.

Table 14-2. D3D quaternion functions

Quaternion Functions	Description
D3DRMMatrixFromQuaternion	Converts a unit quaternion into a rotation matrix.
D3DRMQuaternionFromRotation	Calculates a unit quaternion from a vector and a rotation.
D3DRMQuaternionMultiply	Calculates the product of two quaternions.
D3DRMQuaternionSlerp	Interpolates between two quaternions, using spherical linear interpolation.

Chapter 15

Realtime 3D Resources

A wide range of resources on realtime 3D is available, but you will have to search for them. There are no magazines or trade shows directly dedicated to realtime 3D, and much of the literature addresses topics such as computer graphics and virtual reality in general rather than realtime 3D specifically. Furthermore, most 3D tools are targeted for either animation and modeling or CAD uses rather than realtime 3D uses. Still, with some looking you will find a lot of material that you can adapt to 3D application programming.

Information About 3D Accelerators and Boards

An excellent web site, Dimension 3D, tracks 3D accelerator chips and boards:

> http://www.excalibur.net/~3d/

However, the single best source of information on 3D accelerator chips is from the chip makers themselves. Many of these have launched active developer relations programs aimed at educating and wooing developers to their chips. They even occasionally offer 3D boards at reduced or no cost to developers.

There is, however, a fundamental conflict in the attitudes of 3D chip makers. Generally, they are very enthusiastic about Direct3D as a universal 3D acceleration interface for PCs. At the same time, they want and need to differentiate their chips. So expect to find nondisclosure agreements and a few pitches about why you should support a particular feature that is supported in hardware but not in software.

3D chip makers tend to fall into several categories. All of them want to get a large share of the total graphics chip market (some 60 million units a year), but they follow different strategies for doing so. S3 and ATI, traditionally strong VGA suppliers, gained market share quickly by initially offering inexpensive 3D upgrades to existing VGA OEM customers. Venture-funded startups Rendition, 3Dfx, and NVidia tend to aim at the high-end game market on the way to getting a foothold in the OEM market. 3Dlabs tends to pursue both consumer and professional markets.

Here are some of the leading 3D chip makers.

3Dfx Interactive, Inc.
(415) 934-2400
(415) 934-2424
http://www.3dfx.com/

3Dlabs, Inc.
(408) 436-3455
(408) 436-3458 fax
http://www.3dlabs.com/

ATI Technologies, Inc.
(905) 882-2600
http://www.atitech.ca/

Brooktree
(800) 2BT-APPS
http://www.brooktree.com/

Chromatic Research
(408) 752-9100
(408) 752-9101 fax
http://www.chromatic.com

Cirrus Logic
(510) 623-8300
(510) 252-6020 fax
http://www.cirrus.com/

Diamond Multimedia
(408) 325-7000
(408) 325-7070 fax
(800) 468-5846
http://www.diamondmm.com

Matrox Graphics, Inc.
(514) 969-6320
(514) 969-6330 in Quebec
(514) 969-6363 fax
(800) 361-1408
http://www.matrox.com/

NVIDIA Corp.
(408) 720-6100
(408) 720-6111 fax
http://www.nvidia.com/

Oak Technology, USA
(408) 737-0888
(408) 737-3838 fax
http://www.oaktech.com/

Philips Semiconductors
(800) 234-7381
(708) 296-8556 fax
http://www.semiconductors.philips.com/ps/

Real3D (a division of Lockheed Martin)
(800) 393-7730
http://www.real3d.com/

Rendition, Inc.
(415) 335-5900
http://www.rendition.com/

S3
(408) 980-5400
(408) 980-5444 fax
http://www.s3.com/

Samsung
http://www.sec.samsung.co.kr/

SMOS
(408) 922-0200
http://www.smos.com/

Yamaha Systems Technology, Inc.
http://www.yamahayst.com/

Periodicals

Realtime 3D is covered in part by several publications. Modeling and animation magazines (*3D Artist* and *3D Design*) tend to focus on the artistic and production aspects of prerendered 3D stills and animation rather than realtime 3D, although there is some cross-over. The single best academic periodical is the annual Computer Graphics SIGGRAPH conference proceedings. Here are some publications you may find helpful.

ACM Transactions on Graphics
http://www.acm.org/

Computer Graphics Proceedings
SIGGRAPH Annual Conference Series
Published by Addison Wesley Longman, Inc.
http://siggraph.org/

Computer Graphics World
http://www.cgw.com/

Game Developer magazine
(415) 905-3367
(415) 905-4962
http://www.mfi.com/cgdc/

IEEE Computer Graphics and Applications
http://www.computer.org/pubs/cg&a/cg&a.htm

journal of graphics tools
Published by A. K. Peters, Ltd.
http://www.acm.org/jgt/

Ray Tracing News
By Eric Haines
erich@eye.com

3D Artist magazine
(505) 982-3532
(505) 820-6929 fax
http://www.3dartist.com

3D Design magazine
http://www.3d-design.com/

The Wave Report on Digital Media
Fourth Wave, Inc.
http://www.fourthwave.com

Books

Many books cover the academic side of computer graphics, but few cover realtime 3D. You will find many on how to write your own ray tracer or 3D game engine, on virtual reality, or on the math of 3D graphics, but very little on how to write a realtime 3D application. This is because to date the installed base of computers powerful enough to run a realtime 3D application has been small.

One book that every 3D application developer should have is *Computer Graphics: Principles and Practice*. This is a textbook that covers virtually every academic aspect of 3D, although coverage of realtime 3D application development is generally beyond its scope. Still, this is the must-have book. Also useful is the *Graphics Gems* Series. The original *Graphics Gems* may be more accessible and useful for realtime 3D. Subsequent volumes, however, have an occasionally useful article, although generally these volumes are more oriented to research innovations in computer graphics.

Following is publication data on books you may find useful.

Advanced Animation and Rendering Techniques, Alan Watt and Mark Watt, Addison-Wesley 1993, ISBN 0-201-54412-1.

Computer Graphics: Principles and Practice (2nd ed.), J. D. Foley, A. van Dam, S. K. Feinder, J. F. Hughes, Addison-Wesley 1990, ISBN 0-201-12110-7.

Graphics Gems, Andrew Glassner (ed.), Academic Press 1990, ISBN 0-12-286165-5.

3D Computer Animation, John Vince, Addison-Wesley 1992, ISBN 0-201-62756-6.

Conferences and Trade Shows

Other than academic and DIS conferences, there are two conferences that directly address realtime 3D: SIGGRAPH (August, location varies each year) and the Computer Game Developers Conference (April, San Jose, CA).

There are a huge number of academic virtual reality conferences; you may or may not find any useful.

Computer Game Developers' Conference
Computer Game Developers' Association
(415) 948-2432
(415) 948-2744 fax
http://www.cgda.org/
http://www.mfi.com/cgdc/

SIGGRAPH
http://siggraph.org/

VRAIS
IEEE Virtual Reality Annual International Symposium
http://www.eece.unm.edu/eece/conf/vrais/

Newsgroups

Here are some newsgroups that may be useful:

rec.games.programmer
comp.graphics.algorithms
comp.graphics.animation

3D APIs

Hundreds of 3D engines have been released in various forms. The most comprehensive list of these is maintained at the 3D Engines List given below. But the real competitors to Direct3D are RenderWare, BRender, QuickDraw3D, VRML browsers, and proprietary 3D engines owned by established 3D game companies. If you are interested in developing an application that runs on multiple 3D APIs, check out Joey, a 3D API specifically designed to sit on top of a range of 3D back ends and APIs, including Direct3D. You should note, however, that since Direct3D is supported by virtually all 3D chip makers, many other 3D APIs are intended to use Direct3D as their back end. 3DR, a 3D API from Intel, was once a contender, but Intel had trouble lining up hardware drivers. Microsoft has announced that a future version of OpenGL will use some component of Direct3D as its back end.

The following is a list of 3D engine information sources.

BRender
http://www.argonaut.com/

Joey
Crisis in Perspective, Inc.
(503) 227-7826
(503) 223-4453
http://www.joey.com

RenderWare
Criterion Software, Ltd.
44-1483-406200
44-1483-406211 fax
http://www.canon.co.uk/csl/cslhome.html

3D Engines List
http://www.cs.tu-berlin.de/~ki/engines.html

3DR
http://www.intel.com/IAL/3dr/index.htm
http://quickdraw3d.apple.com/

VRML

VRML, the Virtual Reality Modeling Language, is an excellent source of information on developing realtime 3D worlds and applications. As of this writing, a much expanded version 2.0 will add a range of behavior and interactive features. Although version 1.0 failed to live up to the excitement that surrounded its promise of taking the World Wide Web on a fast path to 3D, VRML has become a common reference point for the design of 3D applications. The VRML Internet mailing list is a major discussion forum for VRML design and other 3D-related issues.

Numerous VRML browsers are available from SGI, Netscape, and other companies, and various VRML tools are either available or in the works. Although VRML originally derived from SGI's OpenInventor, some VRML browsers are written on top of Direct3D, so many VRML concepts will be familiar if you know something about Direct3D. Many 3D modeling and animation tools will export VRML files. In fact, VRML is evolving at such a fast pace that any list published in a book is likely to be obsolete by the time it is printed. Here are the best sources for checking out VRML:

The official VRML standards site at http://www.vrml.org/

The San Diego Supercomputer Center VRML repository at http://sdsc.edu/vrml/

Some companies with interesting VRML products include these:

Intervista Software
(415) 648-2749
http://www.intervista.com

OnLive! Technologies
(408) 366-6000
(408) 366-0357 fax
http://www.onlive.com

Template Graphics Software
(619) 457-5359
http://www.tgs.com/

Virtus Corporation
(919) 467-9700

VREAM
(312) 477-0425
http://www.vream.com/

3D Modeling and Animation Tools

There are many 3D modeling and animation packages to choose from. I have included only packages that run on Windows 95 or Windows NT. There also are excellent choices for the Mac and SGI platforms. A good starting point for high-priced, full-featured packages is 3D Studio Max (the volume leader for professional 3D) and Softimage. For mid-range packages, check out Lightwave, and for less expensive packages (under $500), check out trueSpace, Ray Dream, and Trispectives. Here are some to consider.

Amapi
Yonowat, Inc.
(415) 788-1652
(415) 788-1653 fax
http://www.yonowat.com/

Animation Master
Hash, Inc.
(360) 750-0042
(360) 750-0451 fax
http://www.hash.com/

Extreme3D
Macromedia, Inc.
(415) 252-2000
(415) 626-0554 fax
http://www.macromedia.com/

LightWave
Newtek, Inc.
(800) TOASTER
http://www.newtek.com

PhotoModeler
(604) 732-6658
http://www.photomodeler.com/index.htm

Ray Dream
Fractal Design Corporation
(408) 688-8800
(408) 688-8836 fax
http://www.fractal.com/

Real 3D
(519) 676-7414
http://www.realsoftint.com/

Softimage
Microsoft
(800) 576-3846
(818) 365-1359
http://www.microsoft.com/Softimage/

3D Studio Max
Kinetix (Autodesk)
(415) 507-5000
(415) 507-5314 fax
http://www.ktx.com/

Trispectives
3D/EYE, Inc.
(770) 937-9000
(800) WIN95-3D (946-9533)
http://www.eye.com/

Vistapro Landscape Generator
Virtual Reality Labs
(800) 829-VRLI
(805) 545-8515
(805) 781-2259 fax
http://www.callamer.com/vrli/

Visual Reality
Visual Software
(818) 593-3737
http://www.vissoft.com/

Realtime 3D Tools

Realtime 3D tools tend to derive from high-end military simulation tools and carry a high price tag (often $10,000 and up). This may be out of your price range, although some funded game developers use these tools. They are worth a look just to get a sense of feature set. Here are some to consider.

Coryphaeus Software, Inc.
(408) 395-4537
(408) 395-6351 fax
http://www.coryphaeus.com/

FireWalker
Alias|Wavefront
(800) 447-2542
(416) 362-9181
(416) 362-0630 fax

MultiGen, Inc.
(408) 261-4100
(408) 261-4101 fax
http://www.multigen.com/

Nichimen Graphics
(310) 577-0500
(310) 577-0577 fax
http://www.nichimen.com/

OpenGVS
Gemini
(714) 727-1980
(714) 727-3066
http://www.gemtech.com/

3D Models

3D models are the 3D equivalent of clip art. Although in the past 3D models tended to be expensive, prices have been falling quite rapidly. Stock 3D models are becoming very affordable, but expect to pay a higher price for specialty or custom models.

3Name3D
(310) 314-2171
(310) 314-2181
http://www.ywd.com

Acuris, Inc.
(800) OK-ACURIS
(215) 493-4302
http://www.acuris.com/

Humanoid
Crestline Software
(909) 338-1786
http://ourworld.compuserve.com/homepages/crestline/

Mesh Mart
http://cedar.cic.net/~rtilmann/mm/

Plastic Thought, Inc.
(403) 429-5051
(800) 635-5715
(403) 426-0632 fax
http://www.3d-active.com/

Viewpoint DataLabs
(800) DATASET
(801) 229-3000
http://www.viewpoint.com

Zygote Media Group
(800) 267-5170
http://www.zygote.com/

File Converters

The following three companies provide 3D file format conversion tools.

Animetix Technologies, Inc.
http://www.animetix.com/

InterChange, 3D clip art
Syndesis Corporation
(414) 674-5200
(414) 674-6363 fax
http://www.threedee.com/

WorldRender
Mazar Software
(305) 936-0948

Motion Capture

Motion capture–related resources include the following.

BioVision Motion Capture
(415) 292-0333
(800) 866-3463
http://www.bio-vision.com/

Oz Interactive Motion Capture mailing list
http://www.oz.is/motionc/

Web Sites

The following are well-known web sites that focus on 3D-related topics.

GWeb: An Electronic Trade Journal for Computer Animators
http://www.gweb.org/

3D Cafe
http://www.baraboo.com/3dcafe

3DSite
http://www.3dsite.com/3dsite/

ZD3D
http://www.zdnet.com/zdi/vrml/

Research

There is a wealth of research in the field of realtime 3D. Much of it is available, at least in part, on the Internet. This research goes by many names—simulation, computer graphics, virtual reality, virtual humans, and so on. I have listed only a few research sites. In fact, the problem you face is wading through it all to find the most useful information. Note that academic web sites are no different from business web sites in one sense: It is often easier to brag on the Internet than actually describe what you have accomplished!

If you are looking for a place to start, I recommend two sites: Craig Reynolds boids site (*boids* is Reynolds' term for flocking, herd, and schooling behavior, a field in which he has been a key pioneer) and NYU's Media Research Laboratory (very interesting virtual humans).

Brown University
http://www.cs.brown.edu/research/graphics

Center for Human Modeling and Simulation
Department of Computer & Information Science
University of Pennsylvania
http://www.cis.upenn.edu/~hms/index.html

Cornell
http://www.graphics.cornell.edu/

Craig Reynolds' boids
http://reality.sgi.com/employees/craig/

Georgia Tech
http://www.cc.gatech.edu/gvu/animation/Animation.html

Robot Simulators on the Net
http://cswww.essex.ac.uk/Eurobots/simulators.html

Virtual Humans
NYU Media Research Laboratory
(212) 998-3384
(212) 995-4122 fax
http://www.mrl.nyu.edu

Multiuser 3D

Two companies are worth checking out if you are interested in tools to implement multiuser 3D on the Internet—MÄK Technologies and RTIME, Inc.

MÄK Technologies
(617) 876-8085
(617) 876-9208 fax
http://www.mak.com/

RTIME, Inc.
(206) 631-6629
(206) 632-6108 fax
http://www.rtimeinc.com/

DIS

There is a wealth of DIS-related materials on the Internet. The starting point is the Institute for Simulation and Training.

Defense Mapping Agency
http://www.dma.gov/

Institute for Simulation and Training
http://www.ist.ucf.edu/

Modeling & Simulation Resource Repository
http://huachuca-jdbe.army.mil/imsrr/

NPSNET virtual battlefield research group
http://www-npsnet.cs.nps.navy.mil/npsnet/

Terrain Modeling Project Office
http://www.tmpo.dma.gov/

Chapter 16

3DS

The .3ds binary file format is built around "chunks." When you understand how chunks work, you will understand how to examine the data in a .3ds file and extract information from it.

A **chunk** is a piece of data in a .3ds file. Each chunk starts with a chunk header, which consists of 6 bytes. The header is followed by the chunk's data, which may be other chunks. Each chunk header consists of two parts:

1. **ID tag:** An identification tag that is a 16-bit (2-byte) value that identifies what kind of chunk it is
2. **Length value:** A 32-bit (4-byte) value that specifies the total size of the chunk (including the 6-byte header)

A key advantage of using chunks is that you can skip through the file by examining each ID tag until you find some data you want, such as the polygon mesh of an object, a texture, or keyframe animation data. You simply walk through the file, hopping from ID tag to ID tag, each time using the length value to go to the next tag.

But note that the .3ds file is hierarchical in the sense that the data of one chunk may be a set of chunks. So you may have to step inside a chunk and look at the chunks inside it. For example, a texture is not simply one type of chunk, but rather a collection of chunks, some required and some optional, that are organized in a specified order. In fact, there are layers of chunks. A certain chunk may only appear inside of another chunk, which in turn may appear only inside of another chunk. Don't try to make sense of the numbering scheme for the ID tags. It doesn't make sense.

A .3ds file contains a file header chunk:

```
M3DMAGIC  0×4D4D
    M3D_VERSION  0×0002
    MDATA
    KFDATA
```

The chunk hierarchy is organized as follows.

Chunk Hierarchy	Required (R)/ Optional (O)	ID	Length/ Fields	Comments
M3DMAGIC				Starts a .3ds file version.
M3D_Version	R			
			long	
MDATA	R			
KFDATA	O			
MLIBMAGIC				
MAT_ENTRYs				
CMAGIC				
SMAGIC				
LMAGIC				
MDATA				
KFDATA				
MDATA	R			Mesh data section. Required, but only one per file.
-MESH_VERSION	R	3D3E	10	Mesh version. Can appear only once.
			long	.3ds file format revision. R1 = 1, R2 = 2, R3 = 3.
-MAT_ENTRY				Defines materials. See below.
-MASTER_SCALE	R	0100	10	Master scale.
			float	Master scale factor for all geometry coordinates. 1.0 = one unit is 1 in.
-VIEWPORT_LAYOUT				Configuration of the viewport. See below.
-LO_SHADOW_BIAS	O	1400	10	Shadow bias. Can appear only once.
			float	Global shadow low bias.
-HI_SHADOW_BIAS	O	1410	10	High shadow bias (R1 only).
			float	Global shadow high bias.

Chunk Hierarchy	Required (R)/ Optional (O)	ID	Length/ Fields	Comments
-SHADOW_MAP_SIZE	O	1420	8	Shadow size. Can appear only once.
			short	Global shadow map size. Range: 10 to 4,096.
-SHADOW_SAMPLES	O	1430	8	Sample size (R1 only). Can appear only once.
			short	Global shadow sample size.
-SHADOW_RANGE	O	1440	8	Shadow sample range (R1 only).
			short	Global shadow range.
-SHADOW_FILTER	O	1450	10	Shadow filter (R2, R3).
			float	Global shadow filter. Range: 1 (lowest) to 10 (highest).
-RAY_BIAS	O	1460	10	Ray-traced shadow bias (R3).
			float	Global ray-traced shadow bias.
-O_CONSTS	O	1500	18	Construction plane location.
			point	Position of the construction plane in global coordinates.
-AMBIENT_LIGHT	O1	2100	30 or 54	Ambient light setting.
			COLOR_F	Ambient light color, R1 and R2.
			LIN_COLOR_F	Ambient light color, R3.
-BIT_MAP	O1	1100	8 to 19	Bit-mapped background.
			string	Maximum 12 characters plus NULL.
				Bitmap file name, including extension.
-SOLID_BGND	O1	1200	30 or 54	Solid color background.
			COLOR_F	Background color, R1 and R2.
			LIN_COLOR_F	Background color, R3.
-V_GRADIENT	O1	1300	82 or 106	Gradient-colored background.
			float	Midpoint percentage of gradient (0 = top; 1 = bottom).
			COLOR_F	Top color, R1 and R2.
			LIN_COLOR_F	Top color, R3.
			COLOR_F	Middle color, R1 and R2.
			LIN_COLOR_F	Middle color, R3.
			COLOR_F	Bottom color, R1 and R2.
			LIN_COLOR_F	Bottom color, R3.
-USE_BIT_MAP	O1	1101	6	Use bit-mapped background. Can appear only if USE_SOLID_BGND and USE_V_GRADIENT don't appear.

Chunk Hierarchy	Required (R)/ Optional (O)	ID	Length/ Fields	Comments
USE_SOLID_BGND	O1	1201	6	Use solid-colored background. Can appear only if USE_BIT_MAP and USE_V_GRADIENT don't appear.
-USE_V_GRADIENT	O1	1301	6	Use gradient-colored background. Can appear only if USE_SOLID_BGND and USE_BIT_MAP don't appear.
-FOG	O1	2200	22+24+6	Fog definition. Can appear with DISTANCE_CUE and LAYER_FOG, but only one can be active.
			float	Near fogging plane distance. R3 used only if N_CAMERA contains no ranges.
			float	Near fogging plane density. Range: 0.0 (no fog) to 1.0 (maximum fog).
			float	Far fogging plane distance. R3 used only if N_CAMERA contains no ranges.
			float	Far fogging density. Range: 0.0 (no fog) to 1.0 (maximum fog).
			COLOR_F	Fog color.
			FOG_BGND	Flag: When present, fog the background. (ID 2210, length 6 bytes.)
-LAYER_FOG	O1	2302	22+24	Layer fog definition (R3). Can appear with FOG and DISTANCE_CUE, but only one can be active.
			float	Lower z-axis boundary.
			float	Upper x-axis boundary.
			float	Fog density: Range: 0.0 (no fog) to 1.0 (maximum fog).
			unsigned long	Flag: fog options. Bit 20 (0×100000) = background fogging, bit 0 (0×1) = bottom falloff, bit 1 (0×2) = top falloff.
			COLOR_F	Fog color.

Chunk Hierarchy	Required (R)/ Optional (O)	ID	Length/ Fields	Comments
-DISTANCE_CUE	O1	2300	22+6	Distance cue definition. Can appear with FOG, but only one can be used.
			float	Near distance–cue plane distance.
			float	Near distance–cue dimming factor. Range: 0.0 (no dimming) to 1.0 (maximum dimming).
			float	Far distance–cue plane distance.
			float	Far distance–cue dimming factor. Range: 0.0 (no dimming) to 1.0 (maximum dimming).
			DCUE_ BDGND	Distance-cue the background when present (ID 2310, length 6).
-USE_FOG	O1	2201	6	Use fog. Cannot be used if USE_LAYER_FOG or USE_ DISTANCE_CUE has already been used.
-USE_LAYER_FOG	O1	2303	6	Use layer fog. Cannot be used if USE_FOG or USED_ DISTANCE_CUE has already been used.
-USE_DISTANCE_CUE	O1	2301	6	Use distance cue. Cannot be used if USE_FOG or USE_ LAYER_FOG has already been used.
-DEFAULT_VIEW			varies	Defines rendering view.
-NAMED_OBJECT	O	4000	varies	Defines mesh, light, and camera objects. As many of these chunks appear as are needed in a particular file. All names must be unique. A named object contains either an N_TRI_OBJECT, N_DIRECT_LIGHT, or N_CAMERA.
			string	Name of object. 1 to 10 characters + NULL.

Chunk Hierarchy	Required (R)/ Optional (O)	ID	Length/ Fields	Comments
--N_TRI_OBJECT	O1	4100	varies	Meshed object; one per NAMED_OBJECT.
---POINT_ARRAY	R1	4110	8+(9*count)	Vertex list.
			unsigned short	Number of vertices in the list. Range: 1 to 65,535.
			point list	Points, in global coordinates. Must equal the number of vertices.
---POINT_FLAG_ARRAY	O1	4111	8+(2*count)	Vertex flags.
			unsigned short	Number of point flags. Range: 1 to 65,535. Must equal the number of points in POINT_ARRAY.
			short list	List of vertex flags. The meaning is internal to 3DS. Must equal the number of point flags.
---FACE_ARRAY	R1	4120	8+(8*count)+ MSH_MAT_ GROUP+ SMOOTH_ GROUP	Face list.
			unsigned short	Number of faces in the list. Range: 1 to 65,535.
			face list	List of faces. Three vertices per face. Refers to vertices in POINT_ARRAY. No vertex should refer to an index larger than the count in POINT_ARRAY.
---MSH_MAT_GROUP	O	4130	8+(2 to 16) +2*count	Materials list. A list of faces that is assigned the named material. May appear as many times as there are defined materials in the object.
			string	Name of material. 1 to 16 characters + NULL.
			unsigned short	Number of faces assigned to the material. (0 is box-assigned material.)
			unsigned short list	List of face indices, pointing into FACE_ARRAY. No index should be greater than

Chunk Hierarchy	Required (R)/ Optional (O)	ID	Length/ Fields	Comments
				the count of FACE_ARRAY. If the number of faces above is 0, then this list is not present.
---SMOOTH_GROUP	O1	4120	6+(2*(FACE_ ARRAY count))	Smoothing group definitions for all the faces in FACE_ARRAY.
			unsigned long list	Each face can be assigned to a smoothing group by setting one of the bits in the unsigned long. A face can be assigned to only one smoothing group at a time.
---MSH_BOXMAP	O	4190	varies	List of materials used for box mapping. Size depends on the size of strings (R3).
			string	Front-side material. 1 to 16 characters + NULL.
			string	Back-side material. 1 to 16 characters + NULL.
			string	Left-side material. 1 to 16 characters + NULL.
			string	Right-side material. 1 to 16 characters + NULL.
			string	Top-side material. 1 to 16 characters + NULL.
			string	Bottom-side material. 1 to 16 characters + NULL.
---TEX_VERTS	O1	4140	varies	Texture coordinate list.
			unsigned short	Number of texture coordinates (= POINT_ARRAY count).
			texvert list	UV texture map coordinates.
---MESH_MATRIX	O1	4160	54	Transformation matrix (orientation of object).
			float*12	3x4 matrix. Used by Keyframer to determine rotation and center.
---MESH_COLOR	O	4165	7	Mesh editing color (color of wireframe in 3DS user interface). (R3).
			unsigned byte	Color index. Range 0 to 64. Color depends on 3DS editor settings.

Chunk Hierarchy	Required (R)/ Optional (O)	ID	Length/ Fields	Comments
---MESH_TEXTURE_ INFO	R	4170	90	Texture mapping icon information. Contains orientation of mapping icon used to create UV coordinates in 3DS. Not used by the renderer.
			float	*x* tiling repeat value.
			float	*y* tiling repeat value.
			point	Icon position, in global coordinates.
			float	Icon scaling value.
			float*12	3x4 transformation matrix of icon's orientation.
			float	Planar icon width.
			float	Planar icon height.
			float	Cylinder icon height.
---PROC_NAME	O1	4181	19	Procedural name (.axp extension). Can be used only if OBJECT_PROCEDURAL is defined in NAMED_ OBJECT.
			string	12 characters + NULL. Name of animated stand in procedure. (R2, R3).
---PROC_DATA	R	4182	variable	Procedural data.
			variable	A block of data used by the IPAS procedure.
N_DIRECT_LIGHT	O1	4600	varies	Lighting object definition. Can appear only once per NAMED_OBJECT.
			point	Position of light, in global coordinates.
--COLOR_F				Light color.
--DL_OFF	O1	4620	6	Light off switch.
--DL_OUTER_RANGE	O1	465A	10	Light attenuation outer radius. (R3).
			float	Radius size. Range: any non-negative value.
--DL_INNER_RANGE	O1	4659	10	Light attenuation inner radius. (R3).
			float	Radius size. Range: any non-negative value.

Chunk Hierarchy	Required (R)/ Optional (O)	ID	Length/ Fields	Comments
--DL_MULTIPLIER	O1	465B	10	Light intensity multiplier. (R3).
			float	Intensity multiplier. Any positive or negative value, but not 0.
--DL_EXCLUDE	O	4654	7–17	Illumination exclusion. May appear as many times in N_DIRECT_LIGHT as there are objects to exclude. (R3).
			string	1 to 10 characters + NULL. Name of excluded N_TRI_OBJECT.
--DL_ATTENUATE	O1	4625	6	Attenuation flag.
--DL_SPOTLIGHT	O1	4610	varies	Spotlight definition.
			point	Position of spotlight, in global coordinates.
			float	Hotspot cone angle. Range: 1 to 160 degrees.
			float	Falloff cone angle. Range: 1 to 160 degrees.
---DL_SPOT_ROLL	O1	4656	10	Spotlight roll angle. (R3).
			float	Roll angle. Range: −360.0 to 360.0.
---DL_SHADOWED	O1	4630	6	Spotlight shadowed flag.
---DL_LOCAL_ SHADOW2	O1	4641	16	Local shadow casting parameters. (R2, R3).
			float	Local shadow low bias.
			float	Local shadow filter. Range: 1 (lowest) to 10 (highest).
			short	Local shadow map size. Range: 10 to 4,096.
DL_SEE_CONE				
KFDATA	O1	B00A	25	Keyframe data section of .3ds file. Only one per file.
-KFHDR	R1			General keyframe information.
			short	Current revision of keyframe section: R1 = 1, R2 = 2, R3 = 5.
			string	Name of .3ds file, 12 characters + NULL. No longer used.
			long	Animation length in frames. Range: 1 to 32,000.

Chunk Hierarchy	Required (R)/ Optional (O)	ID	Length/ Fields	Comments
-KFSEG	O1	B008	14	Keyframe active segment information. Defines range of frames to be rendered.
			long	First frame of segment.
			long	Last frame of segment.
-KFCURTIME	O1	B009	10	Keyframe current, or active, frame.
			long	Current frame number.

NOTE: The following tags can appear in any order and any number of times.

Chunk Hierarchy	Required (R)/ Optional (O)	ID	Length/ Fields	Comments
-OBJECT_NODE_TAG	O	B002	Variable	Mesh object keyframe data. May appear as many times as needed.
			NODE_ID	Node index control. Optional (R3).
			NODE_HDR	General keyframe object information.
			PIVOT	Rotational pivot and scaling center point.
			INSTANCE_NAME	Name of object instance.
			BOUNDBOX	Mesh object bounding box.
			POS_TRACK_TAG	Mesh position keys.
			ROT_TRACK_TAGSCL_TRACK_TAG	Mesh scaling keys.
			MORPH_TRACK_TAG	Mesh morph keys. Optional.
			HIDE_TRACK_TAG	Mesh hide keys. Optional (R3).
			MORPH_SMOOTH	Morph smoothing angle. Optional.
-CAMERA_NODE_TAG	O	B003	Variable	Camera object keyframe data
			NODE_ID	Node index control. Optional (R3).
			NODE_HDR	Node control information.
			POS_TRACK_TAG	Camera position keys.
			FOV_TRACK_TAG	Camera field of view angle keys.
			ROLL_TRACK_TAG	Camera roll angle keys.

Chunk Hierarchy	Required (R)/ Optional (O)	ID	Length/ Fields	Comments
-TARGET_NODE_TAG	O	B004	variable	Camera target keyframe data.
			NODE_ID	Node index control. Optional (R3).
			NODE_HDR	Node control information.
			POS_TRACK_TAG	Camera target position keys.
-LIGHT_NODE_TAG	O	B005	variable	Omni-light keyframe data.
			NODE_ID	Node index control. Optional (R3).
			NODE_HDR	Node control information.
			POS_TRACK_TAG	Omni light position keys.
			COL_TRACK_TAG	Omni light color keys.
-SPOTLIGHT_NODE_TAG	O	B007	variable	Spotlight keyframe data.
			NODE_ID	Node index control. Optional (R3).
			NODE_HDR	Node control information.
			POS_TRACK_TAG	Spotlight position keys.
			COL_TRACK_TAG	Spotlight color keys.
			HOT_TRACK_TAG	Hotspot angle keys.
			FALL_TRACK_TAG	Falloff angle keys.
			ROLL_TRACK_TAG	Spotlight cone roll keys. Optional (R3).
-L_TARGET_NODE_TAG	O	B006	variable	Spotlight target keyframe data.
			NODE_ID	Node index control. Optional (R3).
			NODE_HDR	Node control information.
			POS_TRACK_TAG	Spotlight target position keys.
-AMBIENT_NODE_TAG	O1			Ambient light keyframe data. (R3).
			NODE_ID	Node index control. Always −1 for AMBIENT_NODE_TAG.
			NODE_HDR	Node control information. Name is always "$AMBIENT$" and parent index is always −1.
			COL_TRACK_TAG	Light color track.

Chunk Hierarchy	Required (R)/ Optional (O)	ID	Length/ Fields	Comments
NODE_ID	O1	B030	8	Node ordering information. Overrides the node order of the KFDATA section (if not present, NODE_ID is assumed to be 65,535). Identifies hierarchical parents in the NODE_HDR chunk (R3).
			unsigned short	Node order ID. Range: 0 to 65,535, but does not need to be sequential or continuous. Identically numbered nodes are sorted by file order. AMBIENT_NODE_TAGs must always be 65,535.
NODE_HDR	R1	B010	16 to 25	General keyframe object information.
			string	Name of the object in the mesh section. 1 to 10 characters + NULL. "$$$DUMMY" creates a special dummy OBJECT_NODE.
			unsigned short	Flag 1. bit 2 = Node render object hide. bit 3 = Light off in keyframer. bit 11 = Hide node in keyframer. bit 12 = Fast draw node in keyframer. bit 14 = Node tag is not an instance.
			unsigned short	Flag 2. bit 1 = Display path. bit 2 = Object node uses autosmoothing. bit 3 = Object node is frozen. bit 5 = Object node uses motion blur. bit 6 = Object node has material morphing. bit 7 = Object node has mesh morphing.
			unsigned short	Parent index. 65,535 = no parent. OBJECT_NODE_TAGs can be parents of any

Chunk Hierarchy	Required (R)/ Optional (O)	ID	Length/ Fields	Comments
				node; CAMERA_NODE_TAGs can be parents of SPOTLIGHT_NODE_TAGs and LIGHT_NODE_TAGS. Index is the order the nodes appear in the file, unless overridden by NODE_ID tags (R3).
PIVOT	R1	B013	18	Rotational pivot and scaling center point.
			point	Offset from center of BOUNDBOX.
INSTANCE_NAME	O1	B011	8 to 17	Instance name of mesh or dummy object.
			string	1 to 10 characters + NULL. Can be the same or different from name in NODE_HDR, but instance names must be unique.
MORPH_SMOOTH	O1	B015	10	Smoothing angle for morphing objects.
			string	Smoothing angle. Range: 0.0 to 180.00.
BOUNDBOX	R1	B014	30	Mesh object bounding box.
			point	Minimum bounding point.
			point	Maximum bounding point.
POS_TRACK_TAG	R1	B020	Varies	Position keys.
			Trackheader	Information common to all key lists.

NOTE: The following fields are repeated as many times as the keys count in trackheader.

Chunk Hierarchy	Required (R)/ Optional (O)	ID	Length/ Fields	Comments
			Keyheader	Key spline values.
			point	Position in global coordinates.
COL_TRACK_TAG	R1	B025	Varies	Light color keys. Can appear only once per LIGHT_NODE or SPOTLIGHT_NODE.
			Trackheader	Information common to all key lists.
			Keyheader	Key spline values.
			float	Red component. Range: 0.0 to 1.0.

Chunk Hierarchy	Required (R)/ Optional (O)	ID	Length/ Fields	Comments
			float	Green component. Range: 0.0 to 1.0.
			float	Blue component. Range: 0.0 to 1.0.
ROT_TRACK_TAG	R1	B021	varies	Mesh object rotation keys.
			trackheader	Information common to all key lists.
			keyheader	Key spline values.
			float	Rotation angle in degrees.
			float	x-component or rotation axis vector.
			float	y-component or rotation axis vector.
			float	z-component or rotation axis vector.
SCL_TRACK_TAG	R1	B022	varies	Mesh object scaling keys.
			trackheader	Information common to all key lists.
			keyheader	Key spline values.
			float	x scaling value.
			float	y scaling value.
			float	z scaling value.
MORPH_TRACK_TAG	O1	B026	varies	Morph object keys.
			trackheader	Information common to all key lists.
			keyheader	Key spline values.
			string	1 to 10 characters + NULL. Name of object to morph to. Target object must have same vertex count as this object instance.
FOV_TRACK_TAG	R1	B023	varies	Camera field of view keys. One per CAMERA_NODE.
			trackheader	Information common to all key lists.
			keyheader	Key spline values.
			float	Field of view angle. Range: 0.00025 to 160 degrees.
ROLL_TRACK_TAG	R1	B024	varies	Camera and spotlight roll angle keys. Required for cameras.
			trackheader	Information common to all key lists.

Chunk Hierarchy	Required (R)/ Optional (O)	ID	Length/ Fields	Comments
			keyheader	Key spline values.
			float	Angle of roll in degrees.
HOT_TRACK_TAG	R1	B027	varies	Hotspot angle keys. Required for SPOTLIGHT_NODE.
			trackheader	Information common to all key lists.
			keyheader	Key spline values.
			float	Angle of hotspot. Range: 1 to 160 degrees.
FALL_TRACK_TAG	R1	B028	varies	Falloff angle keys. Required for SPOTLIGHT_NODE.
			trackheader	Information common to all key lists.
			keyheader	Key spline values.
			float	Angle of falloff. Range: 1 to 160 degrees.
HIDE_TRACK_TAG	O1	B029	varies	Object hide toggle (R3).
			trackheader	Information common to all key lists.
			keyheader	Key spline values.
			trackheader	Data structure that leads every key track. 14 bytes in length.
			unsigned short	Track looping flags.
				bit 0 = duplicate or loop keys.
				bit 1 = smooth last key to first key.
				bit 3 = lock x-axis.
				bit 4 = lock y-axis.
				bit 5 = lock z-axis.
				bit 8 = unlink x-axis.
				bit 9 = unlink y-axis.
				bit 10 = unlink z-axis.
			unsigned long	Unused.
			unsigned long	Unused.
			unsigned long	Number of keys in track.
			keyheader	Data structure common to every key. 26 bytes in length.
			long	Frame number where key occurs.
			short	Spline-related flags:
				bit 0 = use tension.
				bit 1 = use continuity.
				bit 2 = use bias.

Chunk Hierarchy	Required (R)/ Optional (O)	ID	Length/ Fields	Comments
				bit 3 = use ease to.
				bit 4 = use ease from.
				(other bits = 0)
			float	Spline tension. Range: -1.0 to 1.0.
			float	Spline continuity. Range: -1.0 to 1.0.
			float	Spline bias value. Range: -1.0 to 1.0.
			float	Key ease to value. Range: 0.0 to 1.0.
			float	Key ease from value. Range: 0.0 to 1.0.

Chapter 17

.dxf File Format

AutoCAD's .dxf file format (which stands for Drawing Interchange Format) is something like the universal lowest common denominator of 3D file data. With this format Autodesk, publisher of AutoCAD, intended to provide an interchange file format for AutoCAD. .dxf's use for the 3D application programming was happenstance. Autodesk has a native AutoCAD file format, the .dwg file format, which is not documented, and Autodesk discourages using it as an exchange format so that they can change it more easily. The .dxf file format has rudimentary support for 3D applications, primarily 3D faces and polylines.

    Any interchange file format is less than perfect because different applications are always going to have their own features that are not supported in a universal interchange format. But in many ways, the .dxf format is even less perfect than others, which, ironically, may explain its popularity. In general, 3D modeling and authoring tools use .dxf as a crude tool to export 3D faces and polylines, expecting that much "3D content" will be lost in the process. At this low level, .dxf files are easy to deal with, even though their usefulness is limited. But .dxf import/export is a quick and easy way for a 3D modeling package to provide a thin, rickety content bridge to other 3D applications.

    The .dxf file format comes in both ASCII and binary. The ASCII format is more common, so I focus on it. The binary format, however, is conceptually very similar, as I explain shortly.

I will not attempt to provide a complete analysis of the .dxf file format, since much of it is more relevant to the CAD environment. Instead, I focus on the typical use for 3D applications: the exchange of faces and polylines stored in the Entities section of a .dxf file format.

The following information is based on Release 13 of the .dxf format; for the present purpose, however, earlier versions are essentially identical to it.

Overall File Structure of .dxf

The basic idea of .dxf files is *codes* and *associated values*. The codes are called group codes. A group code is simply an ASCII number like 0 or 2 that indicates the type of value (i.e., the type of data variable) that follows. It appears on a line in the file and is followed in the next line by the value associated with that code. Associated values are either integers, floating-point numbers, or text strings. What type of value is associated with a particular group node varies with the number of the group node.

A .dxf file is organized into sections, each identified by a group code and a value. Each section starts with a group code of 0 followed on the next line by the string "SECTION." The next group/value pair is the group code 2 and a string that specifies the name of the section (like "HEADER"). The section is composed of a block of group/value pairs, followed by a end-of-section specifier (group code 0, with a value of "ENDSEC").

There are many kinds of sections that can appear in a .dxf file. In general, you will be interested only in the Entities section, since typically for 3D interchange purposes, the Entities section is the only section used. The other sections, however, are summarized in Table 17.1.

Table 17-1. Group codes

Group Code	Description	If Omitted, Defaults To:
Entity Group Codes		
−1	Application only: Entity name (changes each time the drawing is opened).	Not omitted
0	Entity type.	Not omitted
5	Handle.	Not omitted
6	Linetype name (if not BYLAYER). The special name BYBLOCK indicates a floating linetype. (Optional)	BYLAYER
8	Layer name.	Not omitted
48	Linetype scale. (Optional)	1.0
60	Object visibility: 0 = visible, 1 = invisible. (Optional)	1.0

Table 17-1. Group codes *(continued)*

Group Code	Description	If Omitted, Defaults To:
62	Color number (if not BYLAYER). Zero indicates the BYBLOCK (floating) color. 256 indicates the BYLAYER color. (Optional)	BYLAYER
67	Absent or 0 indicates that the entity is in model space. A 1 indicates that the entity is in paper space. Other values are reserved. (Optional)	0
100	Subclass marker (AcDbEntity).	Not omitted
3D Face Group Codes		
10	.dxf: *x*-value of first corner (in WCS). Application: First corner (in WCS).	
11	.dxf: *x*-value of second corner (in WCS). Application: Second corner (in WCS).	
12	.dxf: *x*-value of third corner (in WCS). Application: Third corner (in WCS).	
13	.dxf: *x*-value of fourth corner. Application: Fourth corner (in WCS) (if only three corners are entered, this is the same as the third corner).	
20, 30	.dxf only: *y*- and *z*-values of first corner (in WCS).	
21, 31	.dxf only: *y*- and *z*-values of second corner (in WCS).	
22, 32	.dxf only: *y*- and *z*-values of third corner (in WCS).	
23, 33	.dxf only: *y*- and *z*-values of fourth corner.	
70	Invisible edge flags. (Default: 0.) (Optional) 1 = First edge is invisible. 2 = Second edge is invisible. 4 = Third edge is invisible. 8 = Fourth edge is invisible.	
100	Subclass marker (AcDbFace).	

A Simple .dxf File

The easiest way to begin understanding the .dxf file format is to examine a small sample such as the following, which contains a single triangle face. It was created with WorldRender 3D from Mazar software and exported in .dxf format.

In the following example, line 1 is a group code of value 0. Line 2 is the value of the group, in this case, a text string "SECTION." This code/value pair indicates the start of a section.

```
1    0
2    SECTION
3    2
4    ENTITIES
5    0
6    3DFACE
7    8
8    WorldAtt0
9    62
10   0
11   10
12   4.000000
13   20
14   96.501809
15   30
16   0.000000
17   11
18   35.200000
19   21
20   71.411339
21   31
22   0.000000
23   12
24   -22.400000
25   22
26   61.761158
27   32
28   0.000000
29   13
30   -22.400000
31   23
32   61.761158
33   33
34   0.000000
35   0
36   ENDSEC
     0
     EOF
```

Sections in a .dxf File

The sections that can appear in a .dxf file are as follows.

Header section. This section holds general information about the drawing. It consists of an AutoCAD database version number and a number of system variables. Each parameter contains a variable name and its associated value.

Classes section. This section holds the information for application-defined classes, whose instances appear in the Blocks, Entities, and Objects sections of the database. A class definition is permanently fixed in class hierarchy.

Tables section. This section contains definitions for the following symbol tables:

- APPID (application identification table)
- DIMSTYLE (dimension style table)
- LAYER (layer table)
- LTYPE (linetype table)
- STYLE (text style table)
- UCS (User Coordinate System table)
- VIEW (view table)
- VPORT (viewport configuration table)
- BLOCK_RECORD

Blocks section. This section contains block definition and drawing entities that make up each block reference in the drawing.

Entities section. This section contains the graphical objects (entities) in the drawing, including block references (insert entities).

Objects section. This section contains the nongraphical objects in the drawing. All objects that are not entities, symbol table records, or symbol tables are stored in this section. Examples of entries in the Objects section are dictionaries that contain styles and groups.

Reading a .dxf File

Some group codes that define an entity always appear; others are optional and appear only if their values differ from the defaults.

As AutoCAD is further enhanced, new group codes will be added to entities to accommodate additional features. Accommodating .dxf files from future releases of AutoCAD will be easier if you write your .dxf processing program in a table-driven way, ignore undefined group codes, and make no assumptions about the order of group codes in an entity.

See Table 17-1 earlier in this chapter for group codes that apply to virtually all entities. Some of the group codes are included with an entity only if the entity has nondefault values for these properties.

Polyline Group Codes

A polyface mesh is represented in .dxf as a variant of a polyline entity. The polyline header is identified as introducing a polyface mesh by the presence of the sixty-fourth bit in the polyline flags (70) group. The 71 group specifies the number of vertices in the mesh, and the 72 group specifies the number of faces. Although these counts are correct for all meshes created with the PFACE command, applications are not required to place correct values in these fields. Following the polyline header is a sequence of vertex entities that specify the vertex coordinates and faces that compose the mesh.

The AutoCAD entity structure imposes a limit on the number of vertices that a given face entity can specify. You can represent more-complex polygons by decomposing them into triangular wedges. Their edges should be made invisible to prevent visible artifacts of this subdivision from being drawn. The PFACE command performs this subdivision automatically, but when applications generate polyface meshes directly, the applications must do this themselves.

The number of vertices per face is the key parameter in this subdivision process. The PFACEVMAX system variable provides an application with the number of vertices per face entity. This value is read-only and is set to 4.

Polyface meshes created with the PFACE command are always generated with all the vertex coordinate entities first, followed by the face definition entities. The code within AutoCAD that processes polyface meshes does not require this ordering. It works even with interleaved vertex coordinates and face definitions as long as no face specifies a vertex with an index that appears after it in the database. Programs that read polyface meshes from .dxf should be tolerant of odd vertex and face ordering. Table 17-2 gives the polyline group codes.

Table 17-2. Polyline group codes

Group Codes	Description
10	.dxf: Always 0. Application: A "dummy" point. The x- and y-coordinates are always 0, and the z-coordinate is the polyline's elevation (in OCS when 2D, WCS when 3D).
20	.dxf only: Always 0.

Table 17-2. Polyline group codes *(continued)*

Group Codes	Description
30	.dxf only: The polyline's elevation (in OCS when 2D, WCS when 3D).
39	Thickness. (Default: 0.) (Optional)
40	Default starting width. (Default: 0.) (Optional)
41	Default ending width. (Default: 0.) (Optional)
66	Vertices-follow flag (always 1 for a polyline).
70	Polyline flag (bit-coded). (Default: 0.) 1 = This is a closed polyline (or a polygon mesh closed in the M direction). 2 = Curve-fit vertices have been added. 4 = Spline-fit vertices have been added. 8 = A 3D polyline. 16 = A 3D polygon mesh. 32 = The polygon mesh is closed in the N direction. 64 = The polyline is a polyface mesh. 128 = The linetype pattern is generated continuously around the vertices of this polyline.
71	Polygon mesh M vertex count. (Default: 0.) (Optional)
72	Polygon mesh N vertex count. (Default: 0.) (Optional)
73	Smooth surface M density. (Default: 0.) (Optional)
74	Smooth surface N density. (Default: 0.) (Optional)
75	Curves and smooth surface type. (Default: 0.) (Optional) Integer codes, not bit-coded. 0 = No smooth surface fitted. 5 = Quadratic B-spline surface. 6 = Cubic B-spline surface. 8 = Bezier surface.
100	Subclass marker (AcDb2dPolyline or AcDb3dPolyline).
210	.dxf: *x*-value of extrusion direction. Application: Extrusion direction. Present only if the entity's extrusion direction is not parallel to the WCS *z*-axis. (Default: 0, 0, 1.) (Optional)
220, 230	.dxf only: *y*- and *z*-values of extrusion direction.

Binary Format .dxf

The ASCII .dxf file format is a complete representation of an AutoCAD drawing in an ASCII text form. It is easily processed by other programs. In addition, AutoCAD can produce or read a binary form of the full .dxf file and accept limited input in another binary file format.

The DXFOUT command provides a binary option that writes binary .dxf files. Such a file contains all of the information present in an ASCII .dxf file but in a more compact form that takes, typically, 25 percent less file space and can be read from and written to more quickly (typically, five times faster) by AutoCAD. Unlike ASCII .dxf files, which entail a trade-off between size and floating-point accuracy, binary .dxf files preserve all of the accuracy in the drawing database. (AutoCAD Release 10 was the first version to support this form of .dxf file; it cannot be read by older versions.)

A binary .dxf file begins with a 22-byte sentinel consisting of the following:

```
AutoCAD Binary .dxf<CR><LF><SUB><NULL>
```

Following the sentinel are group/value pairs as in an ASCII .dxf file but represented in binary form. The group code is a single-byte binary value. The value that follows it is one of the following:

- A 2-byte integer with the least significant byte first and the most significant byte last
- An 8-byte IEEE double-precision floating-point number stored with the least significant byte first and the most significant byte last
- An ASCII string terminated by a 0 (NULL) byte

The type of the datum following a group is determined from the group code by the same rules used in decoding ASCII .dxf files. Translation of angles to degrees and dates to fractional Julian date representation is performed for binary files, as well as for ASCII .dxf files. The comment group, 999, is not used in binary .dxf files.

Extended data group codes are represented in binary .dxf as a single byte with the value 255, followed by a 2-byte integer value containing the actual group code, followed by the actual value.

Extended data long (group code 1071) values occupy 4 bytes of data. Extended data binary chunks (group code 1004) are represented as a single-byte, unsigned integer length, followed by the specified number of bytes of chunk data. For example, to transfer an extended data long group, the following values would appear, occupying 1, 2, and 4 bytes, respectively.

255	Escape group code
1071	True group code
999999	Value for the 1071 group code

Vertex Group

Every vertex that is part of a polyface mesh has its vertex flag 128 bit set. If the entity supplies the coordinate of a vertex of the mesh, its 64 bit is set as well and the 10, 20, 30 groups give the vertex coordinate. The vertex index values are determined by the order in which the vertex entities appear within the polyline, with the first being numbered 1. Vertex group codes are summarized below in Table 17-3.

Table 17-3. Vertex group codes

Group Codes	Description
100	Subclass marker (AcDbVertex).
100	Subclass marker (AcDb2dVertex or AcDb3dPolylineVertex).
10	.dxf: *x*-value of location point (in OCS when 2D and WCS when 3D). Application: Location point (in OCS when 2D and WCS when 3D).
20, 30	.dxf only: *y*- and *z*-values of location point (in OCS when 2D and WCS when 3D).
40	Starting width. (Default: 0.) (Optional)
41	Ending width. (Default: 0.) (Optional)
42	Bulge. (Default: 0.) (Optional) The bulge is the tangent of one fourth the included angle for an arc segment, made negative if the arc goes clockwise from the start point to the endpoint. A bulge of 0 indicates a straight segment, and a bulge of 1 is a semicircle.
70	Vertex flags: 1 = Extra vertex created by curve-fitting. 2 = Curve-fit tangent defined for this vertex. A curve-fit tangent direction of 0 may be omitted from .dxf output but is significant if this bit is set. 4 = Not used. 8 = Spline vertex created by spline-fitting. 16 = Spline frame control point. 32 = 3D polyline vertex. 64 = 3D polygon mesh. 128 = Polyface mesh vertex.

Table 17-3. **Vertex group codes** *(continued)*

Group Codes	Description
50	Curve fit tangent direction.
71	Polyface mesh vertex index. Optional. Present only if nonzero.
72	Polyface mesh vertex index. Optional. Present only if nonzero.
73	Polyface mesh vertex index. Optional. Present only if nonzero.
74	Polyface mesh vertex index. Optional. Present only if nonzero.

If the vertex defines a face of the mesh, its vertex flags group has the 128-bit set but not the 64-bit. In this case, the 10, 20, 30 (location) groups of the face entity are irrelevant and are always written as 0 in a .dxf file. The vertex indexes that define the mesh are given by the 71, 72, 73, and 74 group codes, the values of which specify one of the previously defined vertices by index. If the index is negative, the edge that begins with that vertex is invisible. The first 0 vertex marks the end of the vertices of the face.

```
0
SECTION
2
HEADER
9
$EXTMIN
10
-1.9861111
20
-1.25
9
$EXTMAX
10
1.25
20
1.7083333
0
ENDSEC
0
SECTION
2
TABLES
0
ENDSEC
0
SECTION
```

```
2
ENTITIES
0
POLYLINE
66
1
70
16
62
7
8
LAYER_1
40
0
41
0
71
2
72
2
0
VERTEX
8
LAYER_1
10
-1.9861111
20
1.7083333
30
0
70
64
0
VERTEX
8
LAYER_1
10
-1.9861111
20
0.70833333
30
0
70
64
0
VERTEX
8
LAYER_1
```

```
10
-0.98611111
20
1.7083333
30
0
70
64
0
VERTEX
8
LAYER_1
10
-0.98611111
20
0.70833333
30
0
70
64
0
SEQEND
0
ENDSEC
0
EOF
```

Part V

D3D Reference

Chapter 18

Retained Mode Reference

This section is designed to be a complete reference to the Direct3D retained mode API. The retained mode has over 300 methods and functions, plus data structures, macros, and callback function declarations. As a result, grasping all the relationships can be difficult. However, many of the methods are Get/Set pairs that set or return a value or structure. Likewise, there are a number of Add/Delete pairs. Still, expect that it will take some time for you to digest the entire interface.

Retained Mode COM Objects

Objects v. interfaces	Objects do not have type; they have interfaces. Think of an object as having the "type" of its most significant interface. So a "mesh object" is a COM object created by the retained mode with a mesh interface (set of functions).
Inheritance	All RM objects have interfaces IUnknown and IDirect3DRMObject, so you could think of these as the base class. But you cannot subclass an RM COM object. It is a runtime binary to which you cannot attach a new interface.
What a Visual is	IDirect3DRMVisual is an interface with no (documented) methods. It is always on objects that have certain interfaces and is used by the retained mode as an object-typing mechanism. Only objects with an IDirect3DRMVisual interface can be attached to a frame as a Visual.

	When the retained mode creates a Mesh, Frame, Shadow, or User-Visual object, that object always also has an IDirect3DRMVisual interface.
Interfaces v. callbacks	A callback is a function that the application developer writes and attaches to a COM object through an AddCallback method on the object. A callback is not a COM object, probably because there is no way in D3D to instantiate non-OLE COM objects. Callbacks are called during the processing of the COM object (such as a move traversal).

IDirect3DRM

Description	The retained mode manager object. It creates other retained mode COM objects without having to resort to OLE.
How you create	Call the Direct3DRMCreate function (which is linked into your application).

Table 18.1. IDirect3DRM methods

Category	Methods
Animation	CreateAnimation
	CreateAnimationSet
Devices	CreateDevice
	CreateDeviceFromClipper
	CreateDeviceFromD3D
	CreateDeviceFromSurface
	GetDevices
Enumeration	EnumerateObjects
Faces	CreateFace
Frames	CreateFrame
Lights	CreateLight
	CreateLightRGB
Materials	CreateMaterial
Meshes	CreateMesh
	CreateMeshBuilder
Miscellaneous	CreateObject
	CreateUserVisual
	GetNamedObject
	Load
	Tick

Chapter 18 Retained Mode Reference

Table 18-1. IDirect3DRM methods *(continued)*

Category	Methods
Search Paths	AddSearchPath GetSearchPath SetSearchPath
Shadows	CreateShadow
Textures	CreateTexture CreateTextureFromSurface LoadTexture LoadTextureFromResource SetDefaultTextureColors SetDefaultTextureShades
Viewports	CreateViewport
Wraps	CreateWrap

IDirect3DRMObject

Description	An interface available on all retained mode objects.
How you create	You don't. It's an interface (a set of methods on every RM object).

Table 18-2. IDirect3DRMObject methods

Category	Methods
Application-Specific Data	GetAppData SetAppData
Cloning	Clone
Naming	GetClassName GetName SetName
Notifications	AddDestroyCallback DeleteDestroyCallback

IUnknown

Description	An interface available on all COM objects; therefore it is available on retained mode objects.
How you create	You don't. It's an interface (a set of methods on every RM object).
How you access	Call the method on the object.

Adding interfaces	You cannot directly add an interface to a retained mode COM object. You could use OLE containment or aggregation.
What they do	QueryInterface tells you if an interface (set of methods) is on a particular object. AddRef increases an internal counter. Release decrements an internal counter and destroys the object if the count reaches 0. You can write these functions yourself. If you do, you will have a COM object.

Table 18-3. IUnknown methods implemented on RM objects

Category	Methods
IUnknown	AddRef QueryInterface Release

IDirect3DRMAnimation

Description	Animates position, orientation, and scaling of visuals, lights, and viewports.
How it works	You set keys (specific values for position, orientation, and scaling) at different times. At playback, you set the time for the animation, and it interpolates the value and applies it to the frame.
How you create	Call IDirect3DRM::CreateAnimation. You have to attach the animation object to a frame (IDirect3DRMAnimation::SetFrame) for it to output a result (you cannot directly query the AnimationSet for a value at a particular time).
Time calculation	Time units are arbitrary and start at 0. You decide what each unit means in realtime. A key with a time value of 49 is in the exact middle of an animation whose last time value for a key is 99.
Deleting a key	You have to know its time (you cannot query the object to find out the keys in it).

Table 18-4. IDirect3DRMAnimation methods

Category	Methods
Keys	AddPositionKey AddRotateKey AddScaleKey DeleteKey
Miscellaneous	SetFrame SetTime

Table 18-4. IDirect3DRMAnimation methods *(continued)*

Category	Methods
Options	GetOptions SetOptions

IDirect3DRMAnimationSet

Description	Groups together pieces of complex animations (Direct3DRMAnimation objects) so that you can synchronize the time on all of them with a single call.
What it does	Sets the current time on an AnimationSet with IDirect3DRMAnimationSet::SetTime. The current time for all the attached Animation objects will be set to that time.
How you create	Call IDirect3DRM::CreateAnimationSet.

Table 18-5. IDirect3DRMAnimationSet methods

Category	Methods
Adding, Loading, and Removing	AddAnimation DeleteAnimation Load
Time	SetTime

IDirect3DRMDevice

Description	Encapsulates the display device into a single COM object.
How you create	Call IDirect3DRM::CreateDeviceFromClipper, CreateDeviceFromD3D, and CreateDeviceFromSurface.
Which device	It is recommended that you use the default (NULL) device.
To find devices	IDirect3DRM::GetDevices returns an array of all the devices installed on the computer.
Color models	There are two color models: ramp and RGB. Ramp is 8-bit indexed palettes; RGB is 16-, 24-, or 32-bit true color.
Immediate v. retained mode	Two different devices. From the retained mode, you can get the immediate mode device with IDirect3DRMDevice::GetDirect3DDevice. You would want to do this to display an application-defined UserVisual.
Buffer counts	Two buffers mean you have a front and back buffer, the typical configuration.

Table 18-6. IDirect3DRMDevice methods

Category	Methods
Buffer Counts	GetBufferCount
	SetBufferCount
Color Models	GetColorModel
Dithering	GetDither
	SetDither
Initialization	Init
	InitFromClipper
	InitFromD3D
Miscellaneous	GetDirect3DDevice
	GetHeight
	GetTrianglesDrawn
	GetViewports
	GetWidth
	GetWireframeOptions
	Update
Notifications	AddUpdateCallback
	DeleteUpdateCallback
Rendering Quality	GetQuality
	SetQuality
Shading	GetShades
	SetShades
Texture Quality	GetTextureQuality
	SetTextureQuality

IDirect3DRMFace

Description	Represents a single polygon in a mesh.
Key points	Although you can define polygons, everything gets reduced to triangles.
Used by	MeshBuilder objects.
How you create	Call the IDirect3DRM::CreateFace.

Table 18-7. IDirect3DRMFace methods

Category	Methods
Color	GetColor
	SetColor
	SetColorRGB
Materials	GetMaterial
	SetMaterial
Textures	GetTexture
	GetTextureCoordinateIndex
	GetTextureCoordinates
	GetTextureTopology
	SetTexture
	SetTextureCoordinates
	SetTextureTopology
Vertices and Normals	AddVertex
	AddVertexAndNormalIndexed
	GetNormal
	GetVertex
	GetVertexCount
	GetVertexIndex
	GetVertices

IDirect3DRMFrame

Description	The organizing node of the frame tree (the scene graph structure that organizes your 3D scene into a set of objects).
Key points	Frames are the workhorse organizing tool of your 3D scene.
How you create	Call IDirect3DRM::CreateFrame.
Scenes and frames	A frame created with no parent (specify NULL as the parent) is the root frame of a scene. Also, if you want a free-floating frame unattached to your main scene, create it with a NULL parent and then attach it later to the scene.
Scene settings	There is no separate scene object. You set scene settings on any frame in a scene, and the setting for the whole scene (up to the root frame) will be set.
Visuals	Visuals are things you can see when they are rendered. They include meshes and decals (floating textures). Frames can be attached as

Visuals; this creates a reference, not a copy. You can create your own UserVisual, which you will have to render yourself in the immediate mode.

Table 18-8. IDirect3DRMFrame methods

Category	Methods
Background	GetSceneBackground GetSceneBackgroundDepth SetSceneBackground SetSceneBackgroundDepth SetSceneBackgroundImage SetSceneBackgroundRGB
Color	GetColor SetColor SetColorRGB
Fog	GetSceneFogColor GetSceneFogEnable GetSceneFogMode GetSceneFogParams SetSceneFogColor SetSceneFogEnable SetSceneFogMode SetSceneFogParams
Hierarchies	AddChild DeleteChild GetChildren GetParent GetScene
Lighting	AddLight DeleteLight GetLights
Loading	Load
Material Modes	GetMaterialMode SetMaterialMode
Positioning and Movement	AddMoveCallback AddRotation AddScale AddTranslation DeleteMoveCallback

Chapter 18 Retained Mode Reference

Table 18-8. IDirect3DRMFrame methods *(continued)*

Category	Methods
	GetOrientation
	GetPosition
	GetRotation
	GetVelocity
	LookAt
	Move
	SetOrientation
	SetPosition
	SetRotation
	SetVelocity
Sorting	GetSortMode
	GetZbufferMode
	SetSortMode
	SetZbufferMode
Textures	GetTexture
	GetTextureTopology
	SetTexture
	SetTextureTopology
Transformations	AddTransform
	GetTransform
	InverseTransform
	Transform
Visual Objects	AddVisual
	DeleteVisual
	GetVisuals

IDirect3DRMLight

Description	Provides the lights for your 3D scene.
Key points	Lights are attached to frames.
How you create	Call IDirect3DRM::CreateLight or IDirect3DRM::CreateLightRGB.
Are lights Visuals?	No, not to RM. Light objects have no IDirect3DRMVisual interface on them. You can't pick them or attach them to a frame as a Visual (you attach them as a light with IDirect3DRMFrame::AddLight instead of IDirect3DRMFrame::AddVisual).
Light color	Lights in the ramp color model have no color; they are always monochromatic (that is, they are white lights).

Table 18-9. IDirect3DRMLight methods

Category	Methods
Attenuation	GetConstantAttenuation
	GetLinearAttenuation
	GetQuadraticAttenuation
	SetConstantAttenuation
	SetLinearAttenuation
	SetQuadraticAttenuation
Color	GetColor
	SetColor
	SetColorRGB
Enable Frames	GetEnableFrame
	SetEnableFrame
Light Types	GetType
	SetType
Range	GetRange
	SetRange
Spotlight Options	GetPenumbra
	GetUmbra
	SetPenumbra
	SetUmbra

IDirect3DRMMaterial

Description	Defines the reflectivity properties of the surfaces of meshes.
How you create	Call IDirect3DRM::CreateMaterial.
Materials v. textures	A material is not a texture; a texture is not a material. A texture is an image that is wrapped around a mesh; a material describes how the mesh surface reflects light.
Materials v. colors	A material is not the color of a mesh. Colors are stored separately at the frame, mesh, face, group, or vertex level.
Emissive	Emissive color is actually ambient color. Other objects are not lit by it.

Table 18-10. IDirect3DRMMaterial methods

Category	Methods
Emission	GetEmissive
	SetEmissive

Chapter 18 Retained Mode Reference

Table 18-10. IDirect3DRMMaterial methods *(continued)*

Category	Methods
Power for Specular Exponent	GetPower SetPower
Specular	GetSpecular SetSpecular

IDirect3DRMMesh

Description	The main visual object; that is, a collection of triangles.
How you create	Call IDirect3DRM::CreateMesh.
Groups	A group is a collection of polygons within a Mesh object. Each group can have its own material, color, and texture.
Groups in MeshBuilder	Only Mesh objects, not Meshbuilder objects, support groups.

Table 18-11. IDirect3DRMMesh methods

Category	Methods
Color	GetGroupColor SetGroupColor SetGroupColorRGB
Creation and Information	AddGroup GetBox GetGroup GetGroupCount
Materials	GetGroupMaterial SetGroupMaterial
Miscellaneous	Scale Translate
Rendering Quality	GetGroupQuality SetGroupQuality
Texture Mapping	GetGroupMapping SetGroupMapping
Textures	GetGroupTexture SetGroupTexture
Vertex Positions	GetVertices SetVertices

IDirect3DRMMeshBuilder

Description	A tool for building Mesh objects.
How you create	Call IDirect3DRM::CreateMesh.
MeshBuilder v. Mesh	A MeshBuilder object is a tool to create a Mesh object. Only Mesh objects can be attached to a frame to be rendered. You can convert a MeshBuilder into a Mesh and a Mcsh into a MeshBuilder.
Groups	MeshBuilder does not keep track of Mesh groups, so it is not a superset of Mesh.

Table 18-12. IDirect3DRMMeshBuilder methods

Category	Methods
Color	GetColorSource SetColor SetColorRGB SetColorSource
Creation and Information	GetBox
Faces	AddFaces CreateFace GetFaceCount GetFaces
Loading	Load
Meshes	AddMesh CreateMesh
Miscellaneous	AddFrame AddMeshBuilder ReserveSpace Save Scale SetMaterial Translate
Normals	AddNormal GenerateNormals SetNormal
Perspective	GetPerspective SetPerspective

Chapter 18 Retained Mode Reference

Table 18-12. **IDirect3DRMMeshBuilder methods** *(continued)*

Category	Methods
Rendering Quality	GetQuality SetQuality
Textures	GetTextureCoordinates SetTexture SetTextureCoordinates SetTextureTopology
Vertices	AddVertex GetVertexColor GetVertexCount GetVertices SetVertex SetVertexColor SetVertexColorRGB

IDirect3DRMShadow

Description	Represents a shadow.
How you create	Call IDirect3DRM::CreateShadow.
How it works	The shadow is a projection onto a plane of a Visual (a mesh) and a light. The shadow object is a Visual that you then add to the frame that contains the Visual that casts the shadow.

Table 18-13. **IDirect3DRMShadow methods**

Category	Methods
Initialization	Init

IDirect3DRMTexture

Description	Represents textures (rectangular arrays of pixels that are wrapped around meshes or displayed as decals).
How you create	Call IDirect3DRM::CreateTexture.

Table 18-14. **IDirect3DRMTexture methods**

Category	Methods
Color	GetColors SetColors

Table 18-14. **IDirect3DRMTexture methods** (continued)

Category	Methods
Decals	GetDecalOrigin
	GetDecalScale
	GetDecalSize
	GetDecalTransparency
	GetDecalTransparentColor
	SetDecalOrigin
	SetDecalScale
	SetDecalSize
	SetDecalTransparency
	SetDecalTransparentColor
Images	GetImage
Initialization	InitFromFile
	InitFromResource
	InitFromSurface
Renderer Notification	Changed
Shading	GetShades
	SetShades

IDirect3DRMUserVisual

Description	Initializes IDirect3DRMUserVisual objects.
How you create	Call IDirect3DRM::CreateUserVisual.
Key points	You attach UserVisuals to Frames. You render them yourself by dropping down to the immediate mode.

Table 18-15. **IDirect3DRMUserVisual methods**

Category	Methods
Initialization	Init

IDirect3DRMViewport

Description	A viewport is a camera.
How you create	Call IDirect3DRM::CreateViewport.
Key points	A viewport must be attached to a scene through a frame (called the camera frame). The camera in GetCamera and SetCamera is the frame to which the viewport is attached.

Table 18-16. IDirect3DRMViewport methods

Category	Methods
Camera	GetCamera SetCamera
Clipping Planes	GetBack GetFront GetPlane SetBack SetFront SetPlane
Dimensions	GetHeight GetWidth
Field of View	GetField SetField
Initialization	Init
Miscellaneous	Clear Configure ForceUpdate GetDevice GetDirect3DViewport Pick Render
Offsets	GetX GetY
Projection Types	GetProjection SetProjection
Scaling	GetUniformScaling SetUniformScaling Transformations InverseTransform Transform

IDirect3DRMWinDevice

Description	Handles Windows' Activate and Paint messages.
How you create	You don't. It is an interface on the IDirect3DRMDevice object.
How you access	Call ::QueryInterface on your device, with IID_IDirect3DRMWinDevice on your retained mode device.

Table 18-17. IDirect3DRMWinDevice methods

Category	Methods
Handles	HandleActivate
	HandlePaint

IDirect3DRMWrap

Description	Describes how a texture wraps around an object.
How you create	Call IDirect3DRM::CreateWrap.

Table 18-18. IDirect3DRMWrap methods

Category	Methods
Initialization	Init
Wrap	Apply
	ApplyRelative

IDirect3DRMArray

Description	Represents groups of retained mode objects.
How you create	Even though these arrays are COM objects, you cannot create them directly (with IDirect3DRM::CreateObject). They have no class identifiers (CLSIDs) that you could pass to CreateObject.
Interfaces	Arrays have IUnknown and retained mode Object interfaces, as well as their own interface for getting elements out of the array.
Where they come from	Arrays are objects that are returned by other retained mode operations. You still need to release them using ::Release.
Types of arrays	IDirect3DRMArray
	IDirect3DRMDeviceArray
	IDirect3DRMFaceArray
	IDirect3DRMFrameArray
	IDirect3DRMLightArray
	IDirect3DRMPickedArray
	IDirect3DRMViewportArray
	IDirect3DRMVisualArray
To obtain array objects	
Direct3DRMDeviceArray	Call IDirect3DRM::GetDevices.
Direct3DRMFaceArray	Call IDirect3DRMMeshBuilder::GetFaces.

Direct3DRMFrameArray	Call IDirect3DRMPickedArray::GetPick or IDirect3DRMFrame::GetChildren.
Direct3DRMLightArray	Call Direct3DRMFrame::GetLights.
Direct3DRMPickedArray	Call IDirect3DRMViewport::Pick.
Direct3DRMViewport-Array	Call IDirect3DRMDevice::GetViewports.
Direct3DRMVisualArray	Call IDirect3DRMFrame::GetVisuals.

Table 18-19. Array methods

Category	Methods
Information	GetElement GetPick (IDirect3DRMPickedArray) GetSize

All RM Objects

Object::Method	**::AddRef**
Example	`ULONG AddRef();`
Description	Increases the reference count of the object by 1 and returns the object's new reference count. An object's reference count is 1 when it is created. An object's reference count is increased every time you obtain an interface on an object (call QueryInterface to get an interface and the call succeeds). Use the Release method to decrease the reference count of the object by 1.
Object::Method	**::QueryInterface**
Example	`HRESULT QueryInterface(REFIID riid, LPVOID* obp);`
Description	Determines if the object supports a particular COM interface. If it does, the system increases the reference count for the object and returns a pointer to that object interface. You will need to decrement the reference count by calling the method, even if you never actually call any of the interface's methods. The method allows objects to be extended by Microsoft and third parties without interfering with each other's existing or future functionality.
`riid`	Reference identifier of the interface being requested.
`obp`	Address of a pointer that will be filled with the interface pointer if the query is successful.

Object::Method	**::Release**
Example	`ULONG Release();`
Description	Decreases the reference count of the object by 1 and returns the new reference count of the object. A COM object deallocates itself when its reference count reaches 0. Use the AddRef method to increase the reference count of the object by 1.

IDirect3DRMObject

Object::Method	**IDirect3DRMObject::AddDestroyCallback**
Example	`HRESULT AddDestroyCallback(D3DRMOBJECTCALLBACK lpCallback, LPVOID lpArg);`
Description	Registers a function to be called when an object is destroyed.
`lpCallback`	User-defined callback function that will be called when the object is destroyed.
`lpArg`	Address of application-defined data passed to the callback function. Because this function is called after the object has been destroyed, you should not call this function with the object as an argument.
Object::Method	**IDirect3DRMObject::Clone**
Example	`HRESULT Clone(LPUNKNOWN pUnkOuter, REFIID riid, LPVOID *ppvObj);`
Description	Creates a copy of an object.
`pUnkOuter`	Allows COM aggregation features.
`riid`	Identifier of the object being copied.
`ppvObj`	Address that will be set to the copy of the object.
Object::Method	**IDirect3DRMObject::DeleteDestroyCallback**
Example	`HRESULT DeleteDestroyCallback(D3DRMOBJECTCALL-BACK d3drmObjProc, LPVOID lpArg);`
Description	Removes a function previously registered with the IDirect3DRM-Object::AddDestroyCallback method.
`d3drmObjProc`	User-defined D3DRMOBJECTCALLBACK callback function that will be called when the object is destroyed.
`lpArg`	Address of application-defined data passed to the callback function.
Object::Method	**IDirect3DRMObject::GetAppData**
Example	`DWORD GetAppData();`

Chapter 18 Retained Mode Reference

Description	Returns the 32 bits of application-specific data in the object. Default is 0 (if you haven't set it to something else).
Object::Method	**IDirect3DRMObject::GetClassName**
Example	`HRESULT GetClassName(LPDWORD lpdwSize, LPSTR lpName);`
Description	Returns the name of the object's class.
`lpdwSize`	Address of a variable containing the size, in bytes, of the buffer pointed to by the lpName parameter.
`lpName`	Address of a variable that will be set to a NULL-terminated string identifying the class name. If this parameter is NULL, the lpdwSize parameter will be set to the required size for the string.
Object::Method	**IDirect3DRMObject::GetName**
Example	`HRESULT GetName(LPDWORD lpdwSize, LPSTR lpName);`
Description	Returns the object's name. By default, retained mode objects have no name (this call returns NULL). You have to assign one with IDirect3DRMObject::SetName, or the name may be loaded with the object from a file.
`lpdwSize`	Address of a variable containing the size, in bytes, of the buffer pointed to by the lpName parameter.
`lpName`	Address of a variable that will be set to a NULL-terminated string identifying the object's name. If this parameter is NULL, the lpdwSize parameter will be set to the required size for the string.
Object::Method	**IDirect3DRMObject::SetAppData**
Example	`HRESULT SetAppData(DWORD ulData);`
Description	Sets the 32 bits of application-specific data in the object.
`ulData`	User-defined data to be stored with the object.
Object::Method	**IDirect3DRMObject::SetName**
Example	`HRESULT SetName(const char * lpName);`
Description	Sets the object's name.
`lpName`	Name for the object.

IDirect3DRM

Object::Method	**IDirect3DRM::AddSearchPath**
Example	`HRESULT AddSearchPath(LPCSTR lpPath);`

Description	Adds a list of directories to the end of the current file's search path. Directories in the list are separated by semicolons (;).
`lpPath`	Address of a NULL-terminated string specifying the path to add to the current search path.
Object::Method	**IDirect3DRM::CreateAnimation**
Example	`HRESULT CreateAnimation(LPDIRECT3DRMANIMATION * lplpD3DRMAnimation);`
Description	Creates an empty Direct3DRMAnimation object.
`lplpD3DRM-Animation`	Address to be filled with a pointer to an IDirect3DRMAnimation interface if the call succeeds.
Object::Method	**IDirect3DRM::CreateAnimationSet**
Example	`HRESULT CreateAnimationSet (LPDIRECT3DRM-ANIMATIONSET * lplpD3DRMAnimationSet);`
Description	Creates an empty Direct3DRMAnimationSet object.
`lplpD3DRM-AnimationSet`	Address to be filled with a pointer to an IDirect3DRMAnimationSet interface if the call succeeds.
Object::Method	**IDirect3DRM::CreateDevice**
Example	`HRESULT CreateDevice(DWORD dwWidth, DWORD dwHeight, LPDIRECT3DRMDEVICE* lplpD3DRM-Device);`
Note	Not implemented on the Windows platform.
Object::Method	**IDirect3DRM::CreateDeviceFromClipper**
Example	`HRESULT CreateDeviceFromClipper(LPDIRECTDRAW-CLIPPER lpDDClipper, LPGUID lpGUID, int width, int height, LPDIRECT3DRMDEVICE * lplpD3DRMDevice);`
Description	Creates a Direct3DRM Windows device by using a specified DirectDrawClipper object. If the lpGUID parameter is NULL, the system searches for a device with a default set of device capabilities. This is the recommended way to create a retained mode device because it always works, even if the user installs new hardware. If a hardware device is not found, the ramp software-only driver is loaded. If you want to use a device other than the default, you must first determine what devices are available on the system by using IDirect3DRM::GetDevices. The default device is sought based on the following D3DPRIMCAPS flags:

Chapter 18 Retained Mode Reference

	D3DPCMPCAPS_LESSEQUAL
	D3DPMISCCAPS_CULLCCW
	D3DPRASTERCAPS_FOGVERTEX
	D3DPSHADECAPS_ALPHAFLATSTIPPLED
	D3DPTADDRESSCAPS_WRAP
	D3DPTBLENDCAPS_COPY
	  | D3DPTBLENDCAPS_MODULATE
	D3DPTEXTURECAPS_PERSPECTIVE
	  | D3DPTEXTURECAPS_TRANSPARENCY
	D3DPTFILTERCAPS_NEAREST

`lpDDClipper`	Address of a DirectDrawClipper object.
`lpGUID`	Address of a GUID. This parameter can be NULL.
`width` and `height`	Width and height of the device to be created.
`lplpD3DRMDevice`	Address to be filled with a pointer to an IDirect3DRMDevice interface if the call succeeds.
Object::Method	**IDirect3DRM::CreateDeviceFromD3D**
Example	`HRESULT CreateDeviceFromD3D(LPDIRECT3D lpD3D, LPDIRECT3DDEVICE lpD3DDev, LPDIRECT3DRMDEVICE * lplpD3DRMDevice);`
Description	Creates a retained mode device object from already-created immediate mode objects.
`lpD3D`	Address of an instance of Direct3D immediate mode.
`lpD3Ddev`	Address of an immediate mode Direct3D device object.
`lplpD3DRMDevice`	Address to be filled with a pointer to an IDirect3DRMDevice interface if the call succeeds.
Object::Method	**IDirect3DRM::CreateDeviceFromSurface**
Example	`HRESULT CreateDeviceFromSurface(LPGUID lpGUID, LPDIRECTDRAW lpDD, LPDIRECTDRAWSURFACE lpDDSBack, LPDIRECT3DRMDEVICE * lplpD3DRMDevice);`
Description	Creates a Windows device for rendering from the specified DirectDraw surfaces.
`lpGUID`	Address of the GUID that identifies the requested device driver. If you specify NULL, the default device driver is used.
`lpDD`	Address of the DirectDraw object that is the source of the DirectDraw surface.
`lpDDSBack`	Address of the DirectDrawSurface object that represents the back buffer.

`lplpD3DRMDevice`	Address to be filled with a pointer to an IDirect3DRMDevice interface if the call succeeds.
Object::Method	**IDirect3DRM::CreateFace**
Example	`HRESULT CreateFace(LPDIRECT3DRMFACE * lplpd3drmFace);`
Description	Creates a face object.
`lplpd3drmFace`	Address to be filled with a pointer to an IDirect3DRMFace interface if the call succeeds.
Object::Method	**IDirect3DRM::CreateFrame**
Example	`HRESULT CreateFrame(LPDIRECT3DRMFRAME lpD3DRMFrame, LPDIRECT3DRMFRAME* lplpD3DRMFrame);`
Description	Creates a new frame. Specify NULL as the parent to create the root frame of a new scene. You can later attach one scene hierarchy to another by using the IDirect3DRMFrame::AddChild method.
`lpD3DRMFrame`	Address of a frame that is to be the parent of the new frame.
`lplpD3DRMFrame`	Address to be filled with a pointer to an IDirect3DRMFrame interface if the call succeeds.
Object::Method	**IDirect3DRM::CreateLight**
Example	`HRESULT CreateLight(D3DRMLIGHTTYPE d3drmltLightType, D3DCOLOR cColor, LPDIRECT3DRMLIGHT* lplpD3DRMLight);`
Description	Creates a new light source with the given type and color.
`d3drmltLightType`	One of the D3DRMLIGHTTYPE types.
`cColor`	Color of the light.
`lplpD3DRMLight`	Address to be filled with a pointer to an IDirect3DRMLight interface if the call succeeds.
Object::Method	**IDirect3DRM::CreateLightRGB**
Example	`HRESULT CreateLightRGB(D3DRMLIGHTTYPE ltLightType, D3DVALUE vRed, D3DVALUE vGreen, D3DVALUE vBlue, LPDIRECT3DRMLIGHT* lplpD3DRMLight);`
Description	Creates a new light source with the given type and color.
`ltLightType`	One of the D3DRMLIGHTTYPE types.
`vRed, vGreen, and vBlue`	Color of the light.
`lplpD3DRMLight`	Address to be filled with a pointer to an IDirect3DRMLight interface if the call succeeds.

Object::Method	**IDirect3DRM::CreateMaterial**
Example	`HRESULT CreateMaterial(D3DVALUE vPower, LPDIRECT3DRMMATERIAL * lplpD3DRMMaterial);`
Description	Creates a material with the given specular properties.
`vPower`	Sharpness of reflected highlights. A value of 5 produces a metallic look; higher values look more plastic.
`lplpD3DRMMaterial`	Address to be filled with a pointer to an IDirect3DRMMaterial interface if the call succeeds.
Object::Method	**IDirect3DRM::CreateMesh**
Example	`HRESULT CreateMesh(LPDIRECT3DRMMESH* lplpD3DRMMesh);`
Description	Creates a new Mesh object with no faces. You have to attach a mesh to a frame with IDirect3DRMFrame::AddVisual before it will be rendered.
`lplpD3DRMMesh`	Address to be filled with a pointer to an IDirect3DRMMesh interface if the call succeeds.
Object::Method	**IDirect3DRM::CreateMeshBuilder**
Example	`HRESULT CreateMeshBuilder(LPDIRECT3DRMMESHBUILDER* lplpD3DRMMeshBuilder);`
Description	Creates a new MeshBuilder object.
`lplpD3DRMMeshBuilder`	Address to be filled with a pointer to an IDirect3DRMMeshBuilder interface if the call succeeds.
Object::Method	**IDirect3DRM::CreateObject**
Example	`HRESULT CreateObject(REFCLSID rclsid, LPUNKNOWN pUnkOuter, REFIID riid, LPVOID FAR* ppv);`
Description	Creates a new, uninitialized object. To initialize the object, call the object's Init method. You should call the Init method only one time, and you should not call it at all on objects created with the other IDirect3DRM create methods. Applications can use this method to implement OLE aggregation in Direct3DRM objects, but aggregation is not supported directly in Direct3D.
`rclsid`	Class identifier for the new object.
`pUnkOuter`	Allows COM aggregation features.
`riid`	Interface identifier of the object to be created.
`ppv`	Address of a pointer to the object.

Object::Method	**IDirect3DRM::CreateShadow**
Example	`HRESULT CreateShadow(LPDIRECT3DRMVISUAL lpVisual,LPDIRECT3DRMLIGHT lpLight, D3DVALUE px, D3DVALUE py, D3DVALUE pz, D3DVALUE nx, D3DVALUE ny, D3DVALUE nz,LPDIRECT3DRMVISUAL * lplpShadow);`
Description	Creates a shadow object. The shadow is a projection onto a plane of a Visual (a mesh) and a light. The shadow object is a Visual that you then add to the frame that contains the Visual that casts the shadow.
`lpVisual`	Address of the Direct3DRMVisual object that is casting the shadow.
`lpLight`	Address of the IDirect3DRMLight interface that is the light source.
`px, py, and pz`	Plane on which the shadow is to be projected.
`nx, ny, and nz`	Normal to the plane on which the shadow is to be projected.
`lplpShadow`	Address of a pointer to be initialized with a valid pointer to the shadow Visual if the call succeeds.
Object::Method	**IDirect3DRM::CreateTexture**
Example	`HRESULT CreateTexture(LPD3DRMIMAGE lpImage, LPDIRECT3DRMTEXTURE* lplpD3DRMTexture);`
Description	Creates a texture from an image in memory. The image memory is used as the texture rather than a copy of the image being made. When you change the image, the change is rendered the next time the image is rendered. This means you can use a texture as both a rendering target and as a texture.
`lpImage`	Address of a D3DRMIMAGE structure describing the source for the texture.
`lplpD3DRMTexture`	Address to be filled with a pointer to an IDirect3DRMTexture interface if the call succeeds.
Object::Method	**IDirect3DRM::CreateTextureFromSurface**
Example	`HRESULT CreateTextureFromSurface (LPDIRECTDRAWSURFACE lpDDS, LPDIRECT3DRMTEXTURE * lplpD3DRMTexture);`
Description	Creates a texture from a DirectDraw surface.
`lpDDS`	Address of the DirectDrawSurface object containing the texture.
`lplpD3DRMTexture`	Address to be filled with a pointer to an IDirect3DRMTexture interface if the call succeeds.

Chapter 18 Retained Mode Reference

Object::Method	**IDirect3DRM::CreateUserVisual**
Example	HRESULT CreateUserVisual(D3DRMUSERVISUALCALL-BACK fn, LPVOID lpArg, LPDIRECT3DRMUSERVISUAL * lplpD3DRMUV);
Description	Creates an application-defined Visual object, which can then be added to a scene and rendered by using an application-defined handler.
fn	Application-defined D3DRMUSERVISUALCALLBACK callback function.
lpArg	Address of application-defined data passed to the callback function.
lplpD3DRMUV	Address to be filled with a pointer to an IDirect3DRMUserVisual interface if the call succeeds.
Object::Method	**IDirect3DRM::CreateViewport**
Example	HRESULT CreateViewport(LPDIRECT3DRMDEVICE lpDev, LPDIRECT3DRMFRAME lpCamera, DWORD dwXPos, DWORD dwYPos, DWORD dwWidth, DWORD dwHeight, LPDIRECT3DRMVIEWPORT* lplpD3DRMViewport);
Description	Creates a viewport on a device with device coordinates (dwXPos, dwYPos) to (dwXPos + dwWidth, dwYPos + dwHeight). A viewport is your camera into the scene. It takes its position and orientation from the frame to which it is attached.
lpDev	Device on which the viewport is to be created.
lpCamera	Frame that describes the position and direction of the viewport.
dwXPos, dwYPos, dwWidth, and dwHeight	Position and size of the viewport, in device coordinates.
lplpD3DRMViewport	Address to be filled with a pointer to an IDirect3DRMViewport interface if the call succeeds.
Object::Method	**IDirect3DRM::CreateWrap**
Example	HRESULT CreateWrap(D3DRMWRAPTYPE type, LPDIRECT3DRMFRAME lpRef, D3DVALUE ox, D3DVALUE oy, D3DVALUE oz, D3DVALUE dx, D3DVALUE dy, D3DVALUE dz, D3DVALUE ux, D3DVALUE uy, D3DVALUE uz, D3DVALUE ou, D3DVALUE ov, D3DVALUE su, D3DVALUE sv, LPDIRECT3DRMWRAP* lplpD3DRMWrap);

Description	Creates a wrapping function that can be used to assign texture coordinates to faces and meshes. The vector [*ox oy oz*] gives the origin of the wrap, [*dx dy dz*] gives its *z*-axis, and [*ux uy uz*] gives its *y*-axis. The 2D vectors [*ou ov*] and [*su sv*] give an origin and scale factor in the texture applied to the result of the wrapping function.
type	A D3DRMWRAPTYPE flag.
lpRef	Reference frame for the wrap.
ox, oy, and oz	Origin of the wrap.
dx, dy, and dz	The *z*-axis of the wrap.
ux, uy, and uz	The *y*-axis of the wrap.
ou and ov	Origin in the texture.
su and sv	Scale factor in the texture.
lplpD3DRMWrap	Address to be filled with a pointer to an IDirect3DRMWrap interface if the call succeeds.
Object::Method	**IDirect3DRM::EnumerateObjects**
Example	HRESULT EnumerateObjects(D3DRMOBJECTCALLBACK func, LPVOID lpArg);
Description	Calls the callback function specified by the func parameter for each Direct3DRM object.
func	Application-defined D3DRMOBJECTCALLBACK callback function to be called with each Direct3DRMObject object and the application-defined argument.
lpArg	Address of application-defined data passed to the callback function.
Object::Method	**IDirect3DRM::GetDevices**
Example	HRESULT GetDevices(LPDIRECT3DRMDEVICEARRAY* lplpDevArray);
Description	Returns all the Direct3DRM devices that have been created in the system.
lplpDevArray	Address of a pointer that will be filled with the resulting array of Direct3DRM devices. For information about the Direct3DRM-DeviceArray object, see the information in this part on the IDirect3DRMDeviceArray interface.
Object::Method	**IDirect3DRM::GetNamedObject**
Example	HRESULT GetNamedObject(const char * lpName, LPDIRECT3DRMOBJECT* lplpD3DRMObject);
Description	Finds a Direct3DRMObject by name.

Chapter 18 Retained Mode Reference

`lpName`	Name of the object to be searched for.
`lplpD3DRMObject`	Address of a pointer to be initialized with a valid Direct3DRM Object pointer if the call succeeds.
Object::Method	**IDirect3DRM::GetSearchPath**
Example	`HRESULT GetSearchPath(DWORD * lpdwSize, LPSTR lpszPath);`
Description	Returns the current file search path.
`lpdwSize`	Address of the number of returned path elements. This parameter cannot be NULL.
`lpszPath`	Address of a NULL-terminated string specifying the search path. If this parameter is NULL, the method returns the size of the required string in the location pointed to by the lpdwSize parameter.
Object::Method	**IDirect3DRM::Load**
Example	`HRESULT Load(LPVOID lpvObjSource, LPVOID lpvObjID, LPIID * lplpGUIDs, DWORD dwcGUIDs, D3DRMLOADOPTIONS d3drmLOFlags, D3DRMLOADCALL-BACK d3drmLoadProc, LPVOID lpArgLP, D3DRMLOAD-TEXTURECALLBACK d3drmLoadTextureProc, LPVOID lpArgLTP, LPDIRECT3DRMFRAME lpParentFrame);`
Description	Loads an object.
`lpvObjSource`	Source for the object to be loaded. This source can be a file, resource, memory block, or stream, depending on the source flags specified in the d3drmLOFlags parameter.
`lpvObjID`	Object name or position to be loaded. The use of this parameter depends on the identifier flags specified in the d3drmLOFlags parameter. If the D3DRMLOAD_BYPOSITION flag is specified, this parameter is a pointer to a DWORD value that gives the object's order in the file. If this parameter is NULL, the first object will be loaded.
`lplpGUIDs`	Address of an array of interface identifiers to be loaded. For example, if this parameter is a two-element array containing IID_IDirect3DMeshBuilder and IID_IDirect3DRMAnimationSet, this method loads all the AnimationSet and MeshBuilder objects.
`dwcGUIDs`	Number of elements specified in the lplpGUIDs parameter.
`d3drmLOFlags`	Value of the D3DRMLOADOPTIONS type describing the load options.
`d3drmLoadProc`	A D3DRMLOADCALLBACK callback function called when the system reads the specified object.

`lpArgLP`	Address of application-defined data passed to the D3DRMLOAD-CALLBACK callback function.
`d3drmLoad-TextureProc`	A D3DRMLOADTEXTURECALLBACK callback function called to load any textures used by an object.
`lpArgLTP`	Address of application-defined data passed to the D3DRMLOAD-TEXTURECALLBACK callback function.
`lpParentFrame`	Address of a parent frame. This information is useful when loading Direct3DRMAnimationSet or Direct3DRMFrame objects because these objects would be created with a NULL parent otherwise. This value can be NULL, in which case a loaded frame would be a new scene.
Object::Method	**IDirect3DRM::LoadTexture**
Example	`HRESULT LoadTexture(const char * lpFileName, LPDIRECT3DRMTEXTURE* lplpD3DRMTexture);`
Description	Loads a texture from the Windows bitmap (.bmp) or Portable Pixmap (.ppm) P6 file. This texture can have 8, 24, or 32 bits per pixel.
`lpFileName`	Name of the required .bmp or .ppm file.
`lplpD3DRMTexture`	Address of a pointer to be initialized with a valid Direct3DRM-Texture pointer if the call succeeds.
Object::Method	**IDirect3DRM::LoadTextureFromResource**
Example	`HRESULT LoadTextureFromResource(HRSRC rs, LPDIRECT3DRMTEXTURE * lplpD3DRMTexture);`
Description	Loads a texture from a resource.
`rs`	Handle of the resource.
`lplpD3DRMTexture`	Address of a pointer to be initialized with a valid Direct3DRM-Texture object if the call succeeds.
Object::Method	**IDirect3DRM::SetDefaultTextureColors**
Example	`HRESULT SetDefaultTextureColors(DWORD dwColors);`
Description	Sets the number of colors to be used for textures subsequently created with IDirect3DRM::CreateTexture. It has no effect on textures that have already been created.
`dwColors`	Number of colors.
Object::Method	**IDirect3DRM::SetDefaultTextureShades**
Example	`HRESULT SetDefaultTextureShades(DWORD dwShades);`

Chapter 18 Retained Mode Reference

Description	Sets the number of shades to be used for textures subsequently created with IDirect3DRM::CreateTexture. It has no effect on textures that have already been created.
`dwShades`	Number of shades.
Object::Method	**IDirect3DRM::SetSearchPath**
Example	`HRESULT SetSearchPath(LPCSTR lpPath);`
Description	Sets the current file's search path from a list of directories. The default search path is specified in the D3DPATH environment variable. If this is not set, the search path will be empty. When opening a file, the system first looks for the file in the current working directory. If the file is not found there, it then checks every directory in the search path.
`lpPath`	Address of a NULL-terminated string specifying the path to set as the current search path.
Object::Method	**IDirect3DRM::Tick**
Example	`RESULT Tick(D3DVALUE d3dvalTick);`
Description	Performs the Direct3DRM system heartbeat. When this method is called, the positions of all moving frames are updated according to their current motion attributes, the scene is rendered to the current device, and relevant callback functions are called at their appropriate times. Control is returned when the rendering cycle is complete.
`d3dvalTick`	Velocity and rotation step for the IDirect3DRMFrame::SetRotation and IDirect3DRMFrame::SetVelocity methods.

IDirect3DRMAnimation Interface

Object::Method	**IDirect3DRMAnimation::AddPositionKey**
Example	`HRESULT AddPositionKey(D3DVALUE rvTime, D3DVALUE rvX, D3DVALUE rvY, D3DVALUE rvZ);`
Description	Adds a position key to the animation.
`rvTime`	The time in the animation at which to store the position key.
`rvX, rvY, and rvZ`	Position.
Object::Method	**IDirect3DRMAnimation::AddRotateKey**
Example	`HRESULT AddRotateKey(D3DVALUE rvTime, D3DRMQUATERNION *rqQuat);`
Description	Adds a rotate key to the animation.

`rvTime`	The time in the animation at which to store the rotate key.
`rqQuat`	Quaternion representing the rotation.
Object::Method	**IDirect3DRMAnimation::AddScaleKey**
Example	`HRESULT AddScaleKey(D3DVALUE rvTime, D3DVALUE rvX, D3DVALUE rvY, D3DVALUE rvZ);`
Description	Adds a scale key to the animation.
`rvTime`	The time in the animation at which to store the scale key.
`rvX`, `rvY`, and `rvZ`	Scale factor.
Object::Method	**IDirect3DRMAnimation::DeleteKey**
Example	`HRESULT DeleteKey(D3DVALUE rvTime);`
Description	Removes a key from an animation. You have to know the time of the key in order to delete it. There is no method that enumerates the keys in an animation.
`rvTime`	The time identifying the key that will be removed from the animation.
Object::Method	**IDirect3DRMAnimation::GetOptions**
Example	`D3DRMANIMATIONOPTIONS GetOptions();`
Description	Returns animation options.
Object::Method	**IDirect3DRMAnimation::SetFrame**
Example	`HRESULT SetFrame(LPDIRECT3DRMFRAME lpD3DRMFrame);`
Description	Sets the frame for the animation.
`lpD3DRMFrame`	Address of a variable representing the frame to set for the animation.
Object::Method	**IDirect3DRMAnimation::SetOptions**
Example	`HRESULT SetOptions(D3DRMANIMATIONOPTIONS d3drmanimFlags);`
Description	Sets the animation options.
`d3drmanimFlags`	`D3DRMANIMATIONOPTIONS` flags.
Object::Method	**IDirect3DRMAnimation::SetTime**
Example	`HRESULT SetTime(D3DVALUE rvTime);`
Description	Sets the current time for this animation.
`rvTime`	New current time for the animation.

IDirect3DRMAnimationSet

Object::Method	**IDirect3DRMAnimationSet::AddAnimation**
Example	`HRESULT AddAnimation(LPDIRECT3DRMANIMATION lpD3DRMAnimation);`
Description	Adds an animation to the AnimationSet.
`lpD3DRMAnimation`	Address of the Direct3DRMAnimation object to be added to the AnimationSet.
Object::Method	**IDirect3DRMAnimationSet::DeleteAnimation**
Example	`HRESULT DeleteAnimation(LPDIRECT3DRMANIMATION lpD3DRMAnimation);`
Description	Removes a previously added animation from the AnimationSet. To use this method, you need to know what animations you have added to the AnimationSet. There is no method that returns this information.
`lpD3DRMAnimation`	Address of the Direct3DRMAnimation object to be removed from the AnimationSet.
Object::Method	**IDirect3DRMAnimationSet::Load**
Example	`HRESULT Load(LPVOID lpvObjSource, LPVOID lpvObjID, D3DRMLOADOPTIONS d3drmLOFlags, D3DRMLOADTEXTURECALLBACK d3drmLoadTextureProc, LPVOID lpArgLTP, LPDIRECT3DRMFRAME lpParentFrame);`
Description	Loads an AnimationSet.
`lpvObjSource`	Source for the object to be loaded. This source can be a file, resource, memory block, or stream, depending on the source flags specified in the d3drmLOFlags parameter.
`lpvObjID`	Object name or position to be loaded. The use of this parameter depends on the identifier flags specified in the d3drmLOFlags parameter. If the D3DRMLOAD_BYPOSITION flag is specified, this parameter is a pointer to a DWORD value that gives the object's order in the file. If this parameter is NULL, the first AnimationSet in the source is loaded by default.
`d3drmLOFlags`	Value of the D3DRMLOADOPTIONS type describing the load options.
`d3drmLoadTextureProc`	A D3DRMLOADTEXTURECALLBACK callback function called to load any textures used by the object.
`lpArgLTP`	Address of application-defined data passed to the D3DRMLOADTEXTURECALLBACK callback function.

`lpParentFrame`	Address of a parent Direct3DRMFrame object. Specifying a parent frame prevents the frames referred to by the AnimationSet from being created with a NULL parent.
Object::Method	**IDirect3DRMAnimationSet::SetTime**
Example	`HRESULT SetTime(D3DVALUE rvTime);`
Description	Sets the time for this AnimationSet.
`rvTime`	New time of the AnimationSet.

IDirect3DRMDevice

Object::Method	**IDirect3DRMDevice::AddUpdateCallback**
Example	`HRESULT AddUpdateCallback(D3DRMUPDATECALLBACK d3drmUpdateProc, LPVOID arg);`
Description	Adds a callback function that is called by the renderer when a change occurs to the device. The system calls this callback function whenever the application calls the IDirect3DRMDevice::Update method.
`d3drmUpdateProc`	Address of an application-defined callback function, D3DRMUPDATECALLBACK.
`arg`	Private data to be passed to the update callback function.
Object::Method	**IDirect3DRMDevice::DeleteUpdateCallback**
Example	`HRESULT DeleteUpdateCallback(D3DRMUPDATECALL-BACK d3drmUpdateProc, LPVOID arg);`
Description	Removes an update callback function that was added with IDirect3DRMDevice::AddUpdateCallback.
`d3drmUpdateProc`	Address of an application-defined callback function, D3DRMUPDATECALLBACK.
`arg`	Private data that was passed to the update callback function.
Object::Method	**IDirect3DRMDevice::GetBufferCount**
Example	`DWORD GetBufferCount();`
Description	Returns the value set with IDirect3DRMDevice::SetBufferCount.
Object::Method	**IDirect3DRMDevice::GetColorModel**
Example	`D3DCOLORMODEL GetColorModel();`
Description	Returns the color model of a device.

Chapter 18 Retained Mode Reference

Object::Method	**IDirect3DRMDevice::GetDirect3DDevice**
Example	`HRESULT GetDirect3DDevice(LPDIRECT3DDEVICE * lplpD3DDevice);`
Description	Returns a pointer to the immediate mode device that is associated with this retained mode device.
`lplpD3Ddevice`	Address of a pointer that is initialized with a pointer to an immediate mode device object.

Object::Method	**IDirect3DRMDevice::GetDither**
Example	`BOOL GetDither();`
Description	Returns the dither flag for the device (TRUE = set).

Object::Method	**IDirect3DRMDevice::GetHeight**
Example	`DWORD GetHeight();`
Description	Returns the height, in pixels, of a device.

Object::Method	**IDirect3DRMDevice::GetTrianglesDrawn**
Example	`DWORD GetTrianglesDrawn();`
Description	Returns the number of triangles drawn to a device since its creation. Includes triangles that were passed to the renderer but were not drawn because they were backfacing. Does not include triangles that were rejected for lying outside of the viewing frustum.

Object::Method	**IDirect3DRMDevice::GetQuality**
Example	`D3DRMRENDERQUALITY GetQuality();`
Description	Returns the rendering quality for the device.

Object::Method	**IDirect3DRMDevice::GetShades**
Example	`DWORD GetShades();`
Description	Returns the number of shades per rendered color used in the ramp color mode.

Object::Method	**IDirect3DRMDevice::GetTextureQuality**
Example	`D3DRMTEXTUREQUALITY GetTextureQuality();`
Description	Returns the current texture quality for the device. Texture quality is relevant only for an RGB device, not a ramp device.

Object::Method	**IDirect3DRMDevice::GetViewports**

Example	`HRESULT GetViewports(LPDIRECT3DRMVIEWPORT-ARRAY* lplpViewports);`
Description	Returns a Direct3DRMViewportArray object containing all the viewports that have been created for a device.
`lplpViewports`	Address of a pointer that is initialized with a valid Direct3DRMViewportArray object if the call succeeds.
Object::Method	**IDirect3DRMDevice::GetWidth**
Example	`DWORD GetWidth();`
Description	Returns the width, in pixels, of a device.
Object::Method	**IDirect3DRMDevice::GetWireframeOptions**
Example	`DWORD GetWireframeOptions();`
Description	Returns the wireframe options of a device: D3DRMWIRE-FRAME_CULL (backfacing faces are not drawn) and/or D3DRMWIREFRAME_HIDDENLINE (wireframe-rendered lines are obscured by nearer objects).
Object::Method	**IDirect3DRMDevice::Init**
Example	`HRESULT Init(ULONG width, ULONG height);`
Description	Currently unimplemented under Windows.
Object::Method	**IDirect3DRMDevice::InitFromClipper**
Example	`HRESULT InitFromClipper(LPDIRECTDRAWCLIPPER lpDDClipper, LPGUID lpGUID, int width, int height);`
Description	Initializes a device from a specified DirectDrawClipper object.
`lpDDClipper`	Address of the DirectDrawClipper object to use as an initializer.
`lpGUID`	Address of the GUID used as the interface identifier.
`width` and `height`	Width and height of the device.
Object::Method	**IDirect3DRMDevice::InitFromD3D**
Example	`HRESULT InitFromD3D(LPDIRECT3D lpD3D, LPDIRECT3DDEVICE lpD3DIMDev);`
Description	Initializes a retained mode device from a specified Direct3D immediate mode object and immediate mode device.
`lpD3D`	Address of the Direct3D immediate mode object to use to initialize the retained mode device.

`lpD3DIMDev`	Address of the immediate mode device to use to initialize the retained mode device.
Object::Method	**IDirect3DRMDevice::SetBufferCount**
Example	`HRESULT SetBufferCount(DWORD dwCount);`
Description	Sets the number of buffers currently being used by the application. An application that employs double-buffering or triple-buffering must use this method to inform the system of how many buffers it is using so that the system can calculate how much of the window to clear and update on each frame.
`dwCount`	Specifies the number of buffers—one for single-buffering, two for double-buffering, and so on. The default is 1, which is correct only for a single-buffered window operation.
Object::Method	**IDirect3DRMDevice::SetDither**
Example	`HRESULT SetDither(BOOL bDither);`
Description	Sets the dither flag for the device.
`bDither`	New dithering mode for the device. The default is TRUE.
Object::Method	**IDirect3DRMDevice::SetQuality**
Example	`HRESULT SetQuality (D3DRMRENDERQUALITY rqQuality);`
Description	Sets the rendering quality of a device. The rendering quality is the maximum quality at which rendering can take place on the rendering surface of that device. The quality for each mesh can be set individually with IDirect3DRMMesh::SetGroupQuality and IDirect3DRMMeshBuilder::SetQuality, but the maximum rendering quality of the device will override higher individual mesh settings.
`rqQuality`	One or more D3DRMRENDERQUALITY flags. The default is D3DRMRENDER_FLAT.
Object::Method	**IDirect3DRMDevice::SetShades**
Example	`HRESULT SetShades(DWORD ulShades);`
Description	Sets the number of shades in a ramp of colors used for shading.
`ulShades`	New number of shades. This parameter must be a power of 2. The default is 32.
Object::Method	**IDirect3DRMDevice::SetTextureQuality**
Example	`HRESULT SetTextureQuality(D3DRMTEXTUREQUALITY tqTextureQuality);`

Description	Sets the texture quality for the device.
`tqTextureQuality`	D3DRMTEXTUREQUALITY type. The default is D3DRM-TEXTURE_NEAREST.
Object::Method	**IDirect3DRMDevice::Update**
Example	`HRESULT Update();`
Description	Copies the image that has been rendered to the display. It also provides a heartbeat function to the device driver. Each call to this method causes the system to call the application-defined callback function, D3DRMUPDATECALLBACK, if the callback function has been added with IDirect3DRMDevice::AddUpdateCallback.

IDirect3DRMFace

Object::Method	**IDirect3DRMFace::AddVertex**
Example	`HRESULT AddVertex(D3DVALUE x, D3DVALUE y, D3DVALUE z);`
Description	Adds a vertex to a Direct3DRMFace object.
`x, y, and z`	The *x*-, *y*-, and *z*-position values of the new vertex.
Object::Method	**IDirect3DRMFace::AddVertexAndNormalIndexed**
Example	`HRESULT AddVertexAndNormalIndexed(DWORD vertex, DWORD normal);`
Description	Adds a vertex and a normal to a Direct3DRMFace object, using an index for the vertex and an index for the normal in the containing MeshBuilder. The face, vertex, and normal must already be part of a MeshBuilder object.
`vertex and normal`	Indexes of the vertex and normal to add.
Object::Method	**IDirect3DRMFace::GetColor**
Example	`D3DCOLOR GetColor();`
Description	Returns the color of the face.
Object::Method	**IDirect3DRMFace::GetMaterial**
Example	`HRESULT GetMaterial(LPDIRECT3DRMMATERIAL* lplpMaterial);`
Description	Returns the material of the face.
`lplpMaterial`	Address of a variable that will be filled with a pointer to the Direct3DRMMaterial object applied to the face.

Object::Method	**IDirect3DRMFace::GetNormal**
Example	`HRESULT GetNormal(D3DVECTOR *lpNormal);`
Description	Returns the normal of the face.
`lpNormal`	Address of a D3DVECTOR structure that will be filled with the normal vector of the face.
Object::Method	**IDirect3DRMFace::GetTexture**
Example	`HRESULT GetTexture(LPDIRECT3DRMTEXTURE* lplpTexture);`
Description	Returns the Direct3DRMTexture object attached to the face.
`lplpTexture`	Address of a variable that will be filled with a pointer to the texture applied to the face.
Object::Method	**IDirect3DRMFace::GetTextureCoordinateIndex**
Example	`int GetTextureCoordinateIndex(DWORD dwIndex);`
Description	Returns the index of the vertex for texture coordinates in the face's mesh.
`dwIndex`	Index within the face of the vertex.
Object::Method	**IDirect3DRMFace::GetTextureCoordinates**
Example	`HRESULT GetTextureCoordinates(DWORD index, D3DVALUE *lpU, D3DVALUE *lpV);`
Description	Returns the texture coordinates of a vertex of the face.
`index`	Index of the vertex.
`lpU` and `lpV`	Addresses of variables that are filled with the texture coordinates of the vertex.
Object::Method	**IDirect3DRMFace::GetTextureTopology**
Example	`HRESULT GetTextureTopology(BOOL *lpU, BOOL *lpV);`
Description	Returns the texture topology.
`lpU` and `lpV`	Addresses of variables that are set or cleared depending on how the cylindrical wrapping flags are set for the face.
Object::Method	**IDirect3DRMFace::GetVertex**
Example	`HRESULT GetVertex(DWORD index, D3DVECTOR *lpPosition, D3DVECTOR *lpNormal);`
Description	Returns the position and normal of a vertex in a Direct3DRMFace object.

`index`	Index of the vertex.
`lpPosition` and `lpNormal`	Addresses of D3DVECTOR structures that will be filled with the position and normal of the vertex, respectively.
Object::Method	**IDirect3DRMFace::GetVertexCount**
Example	`int GetVertexCount();`
Description	Returns the number of vertices in a Direct3DRMFace object.
Object::Method	**IDirect3DRMFace::GetVertexIndex**
Example	`int GetVertexIndex (DWORD dwIndex);`
Description	Returns the index of the vertex in the face's mesh.
`dwIndex`	Index within the face of the vertex.
Object::Method	**IDirect3DRMFace::GetVertices**
Example	`HRESULT GetVertices(DWORD *lpdwVertexCount, D3DVECTOR *lpPosition, D3DVECTOR *lpNormal);`
Description	Returns the position and normal of each vertex in a Direct3DRM-Face object.
`lpdwVertexCount`	Address of a variable that is filled with the number of vertices. This parameter cannot be NULL.
`lpPosition` and `lpNormal`	Arrays of D3DVECTOR structures that will be filled with the positions and normal vectors of the vertices, respectively. If both of these parameters are NULL, the method will fill the lpdwVertex-Count parameter with the number of vertices that will be returned.
Object::Method	**IDirect3DRMFace::SetColor**
Example	`HRESULT SetColor(D3DCOLOR color);`
Description	Sets the color of a face.
`color`	Color to set.
Object::Method	**IDirect3DRMFace::SetColorRGB**
Example	`HRESULT SetColorRGB(D3DVALUE red, D3DVALUE green, D3DVALUE blue);`
Description	Sets the color of a face.
`red, green,` and `blue`	The red, green, and blue components of the color.
Object::Method	**IDirect3DRMFace::SetMaterial**
Example	`HRESULT SetMaterial(LPDIRECT3DRMMATERIAL lpD3DRMMaterial);`

Description	Sets the material of a face.
`lpD3DRMMaterial`	Address of the material.
Object::Method	**IDirect3DRMFace::SetTexture**
Example	`HRESULT SetTexture(LPDIRECT3DRMTEXTURE lpD3DRMTexture);`
Description	Sets the texture of a face.
`lpD3DRMTexture`	Address of the texture.
Object::Method	**IDirect3DRMFace::SetTextureCoordinates**
Example	`HRESULT SetTextureCoordinates(DWORD vertex, D3DVALUE u, D3DVALUE v);`
Description	Sets the texture coordinates of a vertex of a face.
`vertex`	Index of the vertex to be set. For a triangle, the possible vertex indices would be 0, 1, and 2.
`u` and `v`	Texture coordinates to assign to the vertex.
Object::Method	**IDirect3DRMFace::SetTextureTopology**
Example	`HRESULT SetTextureTopology(BOOL cylU, BOOL cylV);`
Description	Sets the texture topology of a face.
`cylU` and `cylV`	Specify whether the texture has a cylindrical topology in the **u** and **v** dimensions.

IDirect3DRMFrame

Object::Method	**IDirect3DRMFrame::AddChild**
Example	`HRESULT AddChild(LPDIRECT3DRMFRAME lpD3DRMFrameChild);`
Description	Adds a child frame to a frame hierarchy. If the frame being added as a child already has a parent, this method removes the frame from its previous parent before adding it to the new parent.
`lpD3DRMFrameChild`	Address of the Direct3DRMFrame object that will be added as a child.
Object::Method	**IDirect3DRMFrame::AddLight**
Example	`HRESULT AddLight(LPDIRECT3DRMLIGHT lpD3DRMLight);`
Description	Adds a light to a frame.

`lpD3DRMLight`	Address of a variable that represents the Direct3DRMLight object to be added to the frame.
Object::Method	**IDirect3DRMFrame::AddMoveCallback**
Example	`HRESULT AddMoveCallback(D3DRMFRAMEMOVECALLBACK d3drmFMC, VOID * lpArg);`
Description	Adds a callback function that will be called on the move traversal.
`d3drmFMC`	Application-defined D3DRMFRAMEMOVECALLBACK callback function.
`lpArg`	Application-defined data to be passed to the callback function.
Object::Method	**IDirect3DRMFrame::AddRotation**
Example	`HRESULT AddRotation(D3DRMCOMBINETYPE rctCombine, D3DVALUE rvX, D3DVALUE rvY, D3DVALUE rvZ, D3DVALUE rvTheta);`
Description	Adds a rotation about (*rvX*, *rvY*, *rvZ*) by the number of radians specified in rvTheta. This is a one-time rotation applied to the frame. IDirect3DRMFrame::SetRotation, in contrast, causes an additional rotation with every render tick.
`rctCombine`	A D3DRMCOMBINETYPE flag that specifies how to combine the new rotation with any current frame transformation.
`rvX, rvY, and rvZ`	Axis about which to rotate.
`rvTheta`	Angle of rotation, in radians.
Object::Method	**IDirect3DRMFrame::AddScale**
Example	`HRESULT AddScale(D3DRMCOMBINETYPE rctCombine, D3DVALUE rvX, D3DVALUE rvY, D3DVALUE rvZ);`
Description	Scales a frame's local transformation by (*rvX*, *rvY*, *rvZ*).
`rctCombine`	A D3DRMCOMBINETYPE flag that specifies how to combine the new scale with any current frame transformation.
`rvX, rvY, and rvZ`	Define the scale factors in the *x*-, *y*-, and z-directions.
Object::Method	**IDirect3DRMFrame::AddTransform**
Example	`HRESULT AddTransform(D3DRMCOMBINETYPE rctCombine, D3DRMMATRIX4D rmMatrix);`
Description	Transforms the local coordinates of the frame by the given affine transformation according to the value of the rctCombine parameter. Although a 4 × 4 matrix is given, the last column must be the transpose of [0 0 0 1] for the transformation to be affine.

`rctCombine`	A D3DRMCOMBINETYPE flag that specifies how to combine the new transformation with any current frame transformation.
`rmMatrix`	Member of the D3DRMMATRIX4D array that defines the transformation matrix to be combined.
Object::Method	**IDirect3DRMFrame::AddTranslation**
Example	`HRESULT AddTranslation(D3DRMCOMBINETYPE rctCombine, D3DVALUE rvX, D3DVALUE rvY, D3DVALUE rvZ);`
Description	Adds a translation by (*rvX*, *rvY*, *rvZ*) to a frame's local coordinate system.
`rctCombine`	A D3DRMCOMBINETYPE flag that specifies how to combine the new translation with any current frame transformation.
`rvX, rvY, and rvZ`	Define the position changes in the *x*-, *y*-, and *z*-directions.
Object::Method	**IDirect3DRMFrame::AddVisual**
Example	`HRESULT AddVisual(LPDIRECT3DRMVISUAL lpD3DRMVisual);`
Description	Adds a Visual object to a frame. Visual objects include meshes and textures. When a Visual object is added to a frame, it becomes visible if the frame is in view. The object is referenced by the frame, which means you can attach the same Visual to multiple frames and no copies of it will be made.
`lpD3DRMVisual`	Address of a variable that represents the Direct3DRMVisual object to be added to the frame.
Object::Method	**IDirect3DRMFrame::DeleteChild**
Example	`HRESULT DeleteChild(LPDIRECT3DRMFRAME lpChild);`
Description	Removes a frame from the hierarchy. If the frame is not referenced, it is destroyed along with any child frames, lights, and meshes.
`lpChild`	Address of a variable that represents the Direct3DRMFrame object to be used as the child.
Object::Method	**IDirect3DRMFrame::DeleteLight**
Example	`HRESULT DeleteLight(LPDIRECT3DRMLIGHT lpD3DRMLight);`
Description	Removes a light from a frame, destroying it if it is no longer referenced.

`lpD3DRMLight`	Address of a variable that represents the Direct3DRMLight object to be removed.
Object::Method	**IDirect3DRMFrame::DeleteMoveCallback**
Example	`HRESULT DeleteMoveCallback(D3DRMFRAMEMOVECALL-BACK d3drmFMC, VOID * lpArg);`
Description	Removes a callback function that performed special movement processing.
`d3drmFMC`	Application-defined D3DRMFRAMEMOVECALLBACK callback function.
`lpArg`	Application-defined data that was passed to the callback function.
Object::Method	**IDirect3DRMFrame::DeleteVisual**
Example	`HRESULT DeleteVisual(LPDIRECT3DRMVISUAL lpD3DRMVisual);`
Description	Removes a Visual object from a frame, destroying it if it is no longer referenced.
`lpD3DRMVisual`	Address of a variable that represents the Direct3DRMVisual object to be removed.
Object::Method	**IDirect3DRMFrame::GetChildren**
Example	`HRESULT GetChildren(LPDIRECT3DRMFRAMEARRAY* lplpChildren);`
Description	Returns a list of child frames in the form of a Direct3DRMFrameArray object.
`lplpChildren`	Address of a pointer to be initialized with a valid Direct3DRMFrameArray pointer if the call succeeds.
Object::Method	**IDirect3DRMFrame::GetColor**
Example	`D3DCOLOR GetColor();`
Description	Returns the default color of the frame.
Object::Method	**IDirect3DRMFrame::GetLights**
Example	`HRESULT GetLights(LPDIRECT3DRMLIGHTARRAY* lplpLights);`
Description	Returns a Direct3DRMLightArray of lights attached to a frame.
`lplpLights`	Address of a pointer to be initialized with a valid Direct3DRMLightArray pointer if the call succeeds.

Object::Method	**IDirect3DRMFrame::GetMaterialMode**
Example	`D3DRMMATERIALMODE GetMaterialMode();`
Description	Returns the material mode of the frame: D3DRMMATERIAL_FROMMESH, D3DRMMATERIAL_FROMPARENT, or D3DRMMATERIAL_FROMFRAME.
Object::Method	**IDirect3DRMFrame::GetOrientation**
Example	`HRESULT GetOrientation(LPDIRECT3DRMFRAME lpRef, LPD3DVECTOR lprvDir, LPD3DVECTOR lprvUp);`
Description	Returns the orientation of a frame relative to the given reference frame.
`lpRef`	Address of a variable that represents the Direct3DRMFrame object to be used as the reference.
`lprvDir` and `lprvUp`	Addresses of D3DVECTOR structures that will be filled with the directions of the frame's *z*- and *y*-axes, respectively.
Object::Method	**IDirect3DRMFrame::GetParent**
Example	`HRESULT GetParent(LPDIRECT3DRMFRAME* lplpParent);`
Description	Returns the parent frame of the current frame.
`lplpParent`	Address of a pointer that will be filled with the pointer to the Direct3DRMFrame object representing the frame's parent. Returns NULL if the current frame is the root frame of a scene (i.e., it has no parent).
Object::Method	**IDirect3DRMFrame::GetPosition**
Example	`HRESULT GetPosition(LPDIRECT3DRMFRAME lpRef, LPD3DVECTOR lprvPos);`
Description	Returns the position of a frame relative to the given reference frame. You can calculate the distance from the frame to the reference frame by using the D3DRMVectorModulus function on the returned vector.
`lpRef`	Address of a variable that represents the Direct3DRMFrame object to be used as the reference.
`lprvPos`	Address of a D3DVECTOR structure that will be filled with the frame's position.

Object::Method	**IDirect3DRMFrame::GetRotation**
Example	HRESULT GetRotation(LPDIRECT3DRMFRAME lpRef, LPD3DVECTOR lprvAxis, LPD3DVALUE lprvTheta);
Description	Returns the rotation of the frame relative to the given reference frame.
lpRef	Address of a variable that represents the Direct3DRMFrame object to be used as the reference.
lprvAxis	Address of a D3DVECTOR structure that will be filled with the frame's axis of rotation.
lprvTheta	Address of a variable that will be the frame's rotation, in radians.
Object::Method	**IDirect3DRMFrame::GetScene**
Example	HRESULT GetScene(LPDIRECT3DRMFRAME* lplpRoot);
Description	Returns the root frame of the hierarchy containing the given frame.
lplpRoot	Address of the pointer that will be filled with the pointer to the Direct3DRMFrame object representing the scene's root frame.
Object::Method	**IDirect3DRMFrame::GetSceneBackground**
Example	D3DCOLOR GetSceneBackground();
Description	Returns the background color of a scene.
Object::Method	**IDirect3DRMFrame::GetSceneBackgroundDepth**
Example	HRESULT GetSceneBackgroundDepth(LPDIRECTDRAW-SURFACE * lplpDDSurface);
Description	Returns the current background-depth buffer for the scene.
lplpDDSurface	Address of a pointer that will be initialized with the address of a DirectDraw surface representing the current background-depth buffer.
Object::Method	**IDirect3DRMFrame::GetSceneFogColor**
Example	D3DCOLOR GetSceneFogColor();
Description	Returns the fog color of a scene.
Object::Method	**IDirect3DRMFrame::GetSceneFogEnable**
Example	BOOL GetSceneFogEnable();
Description	Returns whether fog is currently enabled for this scene (TRUE = fog enabled).

Object::Method	**IDirect3DRMFrame::GetSceneFogMode**
Example	`D3DRMFOGMODE GetSceneFogMode();`
Description	Returns the current fog mode for this scene.
Object::Method	**IDirect3DRMFrame::GetSceneFogParams**
Example	`HRESULT GetSceneFogParams(D3DVALUE * lprvStart, D3DVALUE * lprvEnd, D3DVALUE * lprvDensity);`
Description	Returns the current fog parameters for this scene.
`lprvStart`, `lprvEnd`, and `lprvDensity`	Addresses of variables that will be the fog start, end, and density values.
Object::Method	**IDirect3DRMFrame::GetSortMode**
Example	`D3DRMSORTMODE GetSortMode();`
Description	Returns the sorting mode used to process child frames.
Object::Method	**IDirect3DRMFrame::GetTexture**
Example	`HRESULT GetTexture(LPDIRECT3DRMTEXTURE* lplpTexture);`
Description	Returns the texture of the given frame.
`lplpTexture`	Address of the pointer that will be filled with the address of the Direct3DRMTexture object representing the frame's texture.
Object::Method	**IDirect3DRMFrame::GetTextureTopology**
Example	`HRESULT GetTextureTopology(BOOL * lpbWrap_u, BOOL * lpbWrap_v);`
Description	Returns the topological properties of a texture when mapped onto objects in the given frame.
`lpbWrap_u` and `lpbWrap_v`	Addresses of variables that are set to TRUE if the texture is mapped in the *u*- and *v*-directions, respectively.
Object::Method	**IDirect3DRMFrame::GetTransform**
Example	`HRESULT GetTransform(D3DRMMATRIX4D rmMatrix);`
Description	Returns the local transformation of the frame as a 4 × 4 affine matrix.
`rmMatrix`	A D3DRMMATRIX4D array that will be filled with the frame's transformation. Because this is an array, this value is actually an address.

Object::Method	**IDirect3DRMFrame::GetVelocity**
Example	HRESULT GetVelocity(LPDIRECT3DRMFRAME lpRef, LPD3DVECTOR lprvVel, BOOL fRotVel);
Description	Returns the velocity of the frame relative to the given reference frame.
lpRef	Address of a variable that represents the Direct3DRMFrame object to be used as the reference.
lprvVel	Address of a D3DVECTOR structure that will be filled with the frame's velocity.
fRotVel	Flag specifying whether the rotational velocity of the object is taken into account when retrieving the linear velocity. If this parameter is TRUE, the object's rotational velocity is included in the calculation.
Object::Method	**IDirect3DRMFrame::GetVisuals**
Example	HRESULT GetVisuals(LPDIRECT3DRMVISUALARRAY* lplpVisuals);
Description	Returns a list of Visuals in the frame.
lplpVisuals	Address of a pointer to be initialized with a valid Direct3DRM-VisualArray pointer if the call succeeds.
Object::Method	**IDirect3DRMFrame::GetZbufferMode**
Example	D3DRMZBUFFERMODE GetZbufferMode();
Description	Returns the z-buffer mode (whether z-buffering is enabled or disabled).
Object::Method	**IDirect3DRMFrame::InverseTransform**
Example	HRESULT InverseTransform(D3DVECTOR *lprvDst, D3DVECTOR *lprvSrc);
Description	Transforms the vector in the lprvSrc parameter in world coordinates to frame coordinates and returns the result in the lprvDst parameter.
lprvDst	Address of a D3DVECTOR structure that will be filled with the result of the transformation.
lprvSrc	Address of a D3DVECTOR structure that is the source of the transformation.
Object::Method	**IDirect3DRMFrame::Load**
Example	HRESULT Load(LPVOID lpvObjSource, LPVOID lpvObjID, D3DRMLOADOPTIONS d3drmLOFlags, D3DRMLOADTEXTURECALLBACK d3drmLoadTextureProc, LPVOID lpArgLTP);

Description	Loads a Direct3DRMFrame object. The frame that you call this method on is used as the parent of the new frame hierarchy.
`lpvObjSource`	Source for the object to be loaded. This source can be a file, resource, memory block, or stream, depending on the source flags specified in the d3drmLOFlags parameter.
`lpvObjID`	Object name or position to be loaded. The use of this parameter depends on the identifier flags specified in the d3drmLOFlags parameter. If the D3DRMLOAD_BYPOSITION flag is specified, this parameter is a pointer to a DWORD value that gives the object's order in the file. This parameter can be NULL.
`d3drmLOFlags`	Value of the D3DRMLOADOPTIONS type describing the load options.
`d3drmLoad-TextureProc`	A D3DRMLOADTEXTURECALLBACK callback function called to load any textures used by the object.
`lpArgLTP`	Address of application-defined data passed to the D3DRMLOAD-TEXTURECALLBACK callback function.
Object::Method	**IDirect3DRMFrame::LookAt**
Example	`HRESULT LookAt(LPDIRECT3DRMFRAME lpTarget, LPDIRECT3DRMFRAME lpRef, D3DRMFRAMECONSTRAINT rfcConstraint);`
Description	Faces the frame toward the target frame, relative to the given reference frame, locking the rotation by the given constraints.
`lpTarget` and `lpRef`	Addresses of variables that represent the Direct3DRMFrame objects to be used as the target and reference, respectively.
`rfcConstraint`	A D3DRMFRAMECONSTRAINT flag that specifies the axis of rotation to constrain.
Object::Method	**IDirect3DRMFrame::Move**
Example	`HRESULT Move(D3DVALUE delta);`
Description	Applies the rotations and velocities for all frames in the given hierarchy.
`delta`	Amount by which to change the velocity and rotation.
Object::Method	**IDirect3DRMFrame::SetColor**
Example	`HRESULT SetColor(D3DCOLOR rcColor);`
Description	Sets the default color for meshes of a frame when its D3DRM-MATERIALMODE is set to D3DRMMATERIAL_FROMFRAME.
`rcColor`	New color for the frame.

Object::Method	**IDirect3DRMFrame::SetColorRGB**
Example	`HRESULT SetColorRGB(D3DVALUE rvRed, D3DVALUE rvGreen, D3DVALUE rvBlue);`
Description	Sets the default color for meshes of a frame when its D3DRMMATERIALMODE is set to D3DRMMATERIAL_FROMFRAME.
`rvRed, rvGreen, and rvBlue`	New color for the frame.
Object::Method	**IDirect3DRMFrame::SetMaterialMode**
Example	`HRESULT SetMaterialMode(D3DRMMATERIALMODE rmmMode);`
Description	Sets the material mode for a frame. The material mode specifies from where Visuals in a frame get their materials: D3DRMMATERIAL_FROMMESH, D3DRMMATERIAL_FROMPARENT, or D3DRMMATERIAL_FROMFRAME.
`rmmMode`	A D3DRMMATERIALMODE flag.
Object::Method	**IDirect3DRMFrame::SetOrientation**
Example	`HRESULT SetOrientation(LPDIRECT3DRMFRAME lpRef, D3DVALUE rvDx, D3DVALUE rvDy, D3DVALUE rvDz, D3DVALUE rvUx, D3DVALUE rvUy, D3DVALUE rvUz);`
Description	Aligns a frame so that its *z*-direction points along the direction vector [*rvDx, rvDy, rvDz*] and its *y*-direction aligns with the vector [*rvUx, rvUy, rvUz*]. The default orientation of a frame has a direction vector of [0, 0, 1] and an up vector of [0, 1, 0]. The [*rvUx, rvUy, rvUz*] vector passed is projected onto the plane that is perpendicular to [*rvDx, rvDy, rvDz*]. If the two vectors are parallel, D3DRMERR_BADVALUE is returned.
`lpRef`	Address of a variable that represents the Direct3DRMFrame object to be used as the reference.
`rvDx, rvDy, and rvDz`	New *z*-axis for the frame.
`rvUx, rvUy, and rvUz`	New *y*-axis for the frame.
Object::Method	**IDirect3DRMFrame::SetPosition**
Example	`HRESULT SetPosition(LPDIRECT3DRMFRAME lpRef, D3DVALUE rvX, D3DVALUE rvY, D3DVALUE rvZ);`

Description	Sets the position of a frame relative to the frame of reference. It places the frame a distance of [*rvX, rvY, rvZ*] from the reference. When a child frame is created within a parent, it is placed at [0, 0, 0] in the parent frame.
`lpRef`	Address of a variable that represents the Direct3DRMFrame object to be used as the reference.
`rvX, rvY, and rvZ`	New position for the frame.
Object::Method	**IDirect3DRMFrame::SetRotation**
Example	`HRESULT SetRotation(LPDIRECT3DRMFRAME lpRef, D3DVALUE rvX, D3DVALUE rvY, D3DVALUE rvZ, D3DVALUE rvTheta);`
Description	Sets a frame rotating by the given angle around the given vector at each call to the IDirect3DRM::Tick or IDirect3DRMFrame::Move method. The direction vector [*rvX, rvY, rvZ*] is defined in the reference frame. The specified rotation changes the matrix with every render tick, unlike the IDirect3DRMFrame::AddRotation method, which changes the objects in the frame only once.
`lpRef`	Address of a variable that represents the Direct3DRMFrame object to be used as the reference.
`rvX, rvY, and rvZ`	Vector about which rotation occurs.
`rvTheta`	Rotation angle, in radians.
Object::Method	**IDirect3DRMFrame::SetSceneBackground**
Example	`HRESULT SetSceneBackground(D3DCOLOR rcColor);`
Description	Sets the background color of a scene.
`rcColor`	New color for the background.
Object::Method	**IDirect3DRMFrame::SetSceneBackgroundDepth**
Example	`HRESULT SetSceneBackgroundDepth(LPDIRECTDRAW-SURFACE lpImage);`
Description	Specifies a background-depth buffer for a scene. The image must have a depth of 16. If the image and viewport sizes are different, the image is scaled first. Best performance when animating the background-depth buffer is achieved when the image is the same size as the viewport. This enables the depth buffer to be updated directly from the image memory without incurring extra overhead.
`lpImage`	Address of a DirectDraw surface that will store the new background depth for the scene.

Object::Method	**IDirect3DRMFrame::SetSceneBackgroundImage**
Example	`HRESULT SetSceneBackgroundImage(LPDIRECT3DRM-TEXTURE lpTexture);`
Description	Specifies a background image for a scene. If the image is a different size or color depth than the viewport, the image will first be scaled or converted to the correct depth, so for best performance both the image and the viewport should be the same size and color depth.
`lpTexture`	Address of a Direct3DRMTexture object that will be set to the new background scene.
Object::Method	**IDirect3DRMFrame::SetSceneBackgroundRGB**
Example	`HRESULT SetSceneBackgroundRGB(D3DVALUE rvRed, D3DVALUE rvGreen, D3DVALUE rvBlue);`
Description	Sets the background color of a scene.
`rvRed, rvGreen, and rvBlue`	New color for the background.
Object::Method	**IDirect3DRMFrame::SetSceneFogColor**
Example	`HRESULT SetSceneFogColor(D3DCOLOR rcColor);`
Description	Sets the fog color of a scene.
`rcColor`	New color for the fog.
Object::Method	**IDirect3DRMFrame::SetSceneFogEnable**
Example	`HRESULT SetSceneFogEnable(BOOL bEnable);`
Description	Sets the fog enable state.
`bEnable`	New fog enable state.
Object::Method	**IDirect3DRMFrame::SetSceneFogMode**
Example	`HRESULT SetSceneFogMode(D3DRMFOGMODE rfMode);`
Description	Sets the fog mode.
`rfMode`	A D3DRMFOGMODE flag that specifies the new fog mode.
Object::Method	**IDirect3DRMFrame::SetSceneFogParams**
Example	`HRESULT SetSceneFogParams(D3DVALUE rvStart, D3DVALUE rvEnd, D3DVALUE rvDensity);`
Description	Sets the current fog parameters for this scene.
`rvStart` and `rvEnd`	Fog start and end points for linear fog mode. These settings determine the distance from the camera at which fog effects first become visible and the distance at which fog reaches its maximum density.

Chapter 18 Retained Mode Reference

`rvDensity`	Fog density for the exponential fog modes. This value should be in the range of 0 through 1.
Object::Method	**IDirect3DRMFrame::SetSortMode**
Example	`HRESULT SetSortMode(D3DRMSORTMODE d3drmSM);`
Description	Sets the sorting mode used to process child frames. You can use this method to change the properties of hidden-surface-removal algorithms. If z-buffering is on, it is faster to have polygons sorted front to back (it is faster if z-buffer compares usually find something already closer on the screen, since it is slower to read/compare/write than just read/compare). If z-buffering is off, polygons must be sorted back to front (so the closest polygons will be on top).
`d3drmSM`	A D3DRMSORTMODE flag specifying the sorting mode. Default is D3DRMSORT_FROMPARENT.
Object::Method	**IDirect3DRMFrame::SetTexture**
Example	`HRESULT SetTexture(LPDIRECT3DRMTEXTURE lpD3DRMTexture);`
Description	Sets the texture of the frame. The texture is used for meshes in the frame when the D3DRMMATERIALMODE flag is D3DRM-MATERIAL_FROMFRAME. To disable the frame's texture, use a NULL texture.
`lpD3DRMTexture`	Address of a variable that represents the Direct3DRMTexture object to be used.
Object::Method	**IDirect3DRMFrame::SetTextureTopology**
Example	`HRESULT SetTextureTopology(BOOL bWrap_u, BOOL bWrap_v);`
Description	Defines the topological properties of the texture coordinates across objects in the frame.
`bWrap_u` and `bWrap_v`	Variables that are set to TRUE to map the texture in the *u*- and *v*-directions, respectively.
Object::Method	**IDirect3DRMFrame::SetVelocity**
Example	`HRESULT SetVelocity(LPDIRECT3DRMFRAME lpRef, D3DVALUE rvX, D3DVALUE rvY, D3DVALUE rvZ, BOOL fRotVel);`
Description	Sets the velocity of the frame relative to the reference frame. The frame will be moved by the vector [*rvX, rvY, rvZ*] with respect to the reference frame at each successive call to the IDirect3DRM::Tick or IDirect3DRMFrame::Move method.

`lpRef`	Address of a variable that represents the Direct3DRMFrame object to be used as the reference.
`rvX`, `rvY`, and `rvZ`	New velocity for the frame.
`fRotVel`	Flag specifying whether the rotational velocity of the object is taken into account when setting the linear velocity. If TRUE, the object's rotational velocity is included in the calculation.

Object::Method	**IDirect3DRMFrame::SetZbufferMode**
Example	`HRESULT SetZbufferMode(D3DRMZBUFFERMODE d3drmZBM);`
Description	Sets whether z-buffering is enabled or disabled.
`d3drmZBM`	A D3DRMZBUFFERMODE flag specifying the z-buffer mode. The default is D3DRMZBUFFER_FROMPARENT.

Object::Method	**IDirect3DRMFrame::Transform**
Example	`HRESULT Transform(D3DVECTOR *lpd3dVDst, D3DVECTOR *lpd3dVSrc);`
Description	Transforms the vector in the lpd3dVSrc parameter in frame coordinates to world coordinates, returning the result in the lpd3dVDst parameter.
`lpd3dVDst`	Address of a D3DVECTOR structure that will be filled with the result of the transformation operation.
`lpd3dVSrc`	Address of a D3DVECTOR structure that is the source of the transformation operation.

IDirect3DRMLight

Object::Method	**IDirect3DRMLight::GetColor**
Example	`D3DCOLOR GetColor();`
Description	Returns the color of a light.

Object::Method	**IDirect3DRMLight::GetConstantAttenuation**
Example	`D3DVALUE GetConstantAttenuation();`
Description	Returns the constant attenuation factor for a light. The constant attenuation value is inverse (doubling it halves the intensity of the light).

Object::Method	**IDirect3DRMLight::GetEnableFrame**
Example	`HRESULT GetEnableFrame(LPDIRECT3DRMFRAME * lplpEnableFrame);`

Chapter 18 Retained Mode Reference 315

Description	Returns the enable frame for a light. The enable frame is the frame to which a light applies.
`lplpEnableFrame`	Address of a pointer that will be set to the enable frame for the current Direct3DRMFrame object.
Object::Method	**IDirect3DRMLight::GetLinearAttenuation**
Example	`D3DVALUE GetLinearAttenuation();`
Description	Returns the linear attenuation factor for a light.
Object::Method	**IDirect3DRMLight::GetPenumbra**
Example	`D3DVALUE GetPenumbra();`
Description	Returns the penumbra angle of a spotlight.
Object::Method	**IDirect3DRMLight::GetQuadraticAttenuation**
Example	`D3DVALUE GetQuadraticAttenuation();`
Description	Returns the quadratic attenuation factor for a light.
Object::Method	**IDirect3DRMLight::GetRange**
Example	`D3DVALUE GetRange();`
Description	Returns the range of a light.
Object::Method	**IDirect3DRMLight::GetType**
Example	`D3DRMLIGHTTYPE GetType();`
Description	Returns the type of a light.
Object::Method	**IDirect3DRMLight::GetUmbra**
Example	`D3DVALUE GetUmbra();`
Description	Returns the umbra angle of a light.
Object::Method	**IDirect3DRMLight::SetColor**
Example	`HRESULT SetColor(D3DCOLOR rcColor);`
Description	Sets the color of a light.
`rcColor`	New color.
Object::Method	**IDirect3DRMLight::SetColorRGB**
Example	`HRESULT SetColorRGB(D3DVALUE rvRed, D3DVALUE rvGreen, D3DVALUE rvBlue);`

Description	Sets the color of a light.
`rvRed`, `rvGreen`, and `rvBlue`	The new color.
Object::Method	**IDirect3DRMLight::SetConstantAttenuation**
Example	`HRESULT SetConstantAttenuation(D3DVALUE rvAtt);`
Description	Sets the constant attenuation factor for a light. The constant attenuation value is inverse (that is, doubling it halves the intensity of the light).
`rvAtt`	New attenuation factor.
Object::Method	**IDirect3DRMLight::SetEnableFrame**
Example	`HRESULT SetEnableFrame(LPDIRECT3DRMFRAME lpEnableFrame);`
Description	Sets the enable frame for a light. The enable frame is the frame to which a light applies.
`lpEnableFrame`	Address of the light's enable frame. Child frames of this frame are also enabled for this light source.
Object::Method	**IDirect3DRMLight::SetLinearAttenuation**
Example	`HRESULT SetLinearAttenuation(D3DVALUE rvAtt);`
Description	Sets the linear attenuation factor for a light.
`rvAtt`	New attenuation factor.
Object::Method	**IDirect3DRMLight::SetPenumbra**
Example	`HRESULT SetPenumbra(D3DVALUE rvAngle);`
Description	Sets the penumbra angle for a light.
`rvAngle`	New penumbra angle of the cone. The default is 0.5 radians. This angle must be greater than or equal to the angle of the umbra; otherwise, the umbra angle will be set equal to the penumbra angle.
Object::Method	**IDirect3DRMLight::SetQuadraticAttenuation**
Example	`HRESULT SetQuadraticAttenuation(D3DVALUE rvAtt);`
Description	Sets the quadratic attenuation factor for a light.
`rvAtt`	New attenuation factor.

Chapter 18 Retained Mode Reference

Object::Method	**IDirect3DRMLight::SetRange**
Example	`HRESULT SetRange(D3DVALUE rvRange);`
Description	Sets the range of a light. A light affects only objects that are within the range.
`rvRange`	New range. The default is 256.
Object::Method	**IDirect3DRMLight::SetType**
Example	`HRESULT SetType(D3DRMLIGHTTYPE d3drmtType);`
Description	Changes the type of a light.
`d3drmtType`	New light type.
Object::Method	**IDirect3DRMLight::SetUmbra**
Example	`HRESULT SetUmbra(D3DVALUE rvAngle);`
Description	Sets the angle of the umbra cone.
`rvAngle`	New umbra angle. This angle must be less than or equal to the angle of the penumbra. If you try to set the umbra angle to greater than the penumbra angle, the penumbra angle will be set equal to the umbra angle. The default is 0.4 radians.

IDirect3DRMMaterial

Object::Method	**IDirect3DRMMaterial::GetEmissive**
Example	`HRESULT GetEmissive(D3DVALUE *lpr, D3DVALUE *lpg, D3DVALUE *lpb);`
Description	Returns the setting for the emissive property of a material (the color and intensity of the light the object emits).
`lpr, lpg, and lpb`	Addresses that will be set to the red, green, and blue components of the emissive color.
Object::Method	**IDirect3DRMMaterial::GetPower**
Example	`D3DVALUE GetPower();`
Description	Returns the power used for the specular exponent of a material.
Object::Method	**IDirect3DRMMaterial::GetSpecular**
Example	`HRESULT GetSpecular(D3DVALUE *lpr, D3DVALUE *lpg, D3DVALUE *lpb);`
Description	Returns the color of the specular highlights of a material.
`lpr, lpg, and lpb`	Addresses that will be set to the red, green, and blue components of the color of the specular highlights.

Object::Method	**IDirect3DRMMaterial::SetEmissive**
Example	`HRESULT SetEmissive(D3DVALUE r, D3DVALUE g, D3DVALUE b);`
Description	Sets the emissive property of a material. The emissive property is the color and intensity of the light the object emits.
`r, g,` and `b`	The emissive color.
Object::Method	**IDirect3DRMMaterial::SetPower**
Example	`HRESULT SetPower(D3DVALUE rvPower);`
Description	Sets the power used for the specular exponent in a material.
`rvPower`	New specular exponent.
Object::Method	**IDirect3DRMMaterial::SetSpecular**
Example	`HRESULT SetSpecular(D3DVALUE r, D3DVALUE g, D3DVALUE b);`
Description	Sets the color of the specular highlights for a material.
`r, g,` and `b`	The color of the specular highlights.

IDirect3DRMMesh

Object::Method	**IDirect3DRMMesh::AddGroup**
Example	`HRESULT AddGroup(unsigned vCount, unsigned fCount, unsigned vPerFace, unsigned *fData, D3DRMGROUPINDEX *returnId);`
Description	Groups a collection of faces and returns an identifier for the group. A newly added group will be white, with no texture or specular reflection, and each vertex has position, normal, and color equal to 0. You set the vertices with IDirect3DRMMesh::SetVertices.
`vCount` and `fCount`	Number of vertices and faces in the group.
`vPerFace`	Number of vertices per face in the group. If the group contains faces with varying vertex counts, set this parameter to 0.
`fData`	Address of face data. If each face contains the same number of vertices (i.e., if the vPerFace parameter is not set to 0), this data is simply a list of indices into the group's vertex array. If vPerFace is 0, the vertex indices should be preceded by an integer giving the number of vertices in that face. For example, if vPerFace is 0 and the group is made up of triangular and quadrilateral faces, the data might be in the following form: 3 *index index index* 4 *index index index index* 3 *index index index* ...

`returnId`	Address of a variable that will identify the group when the method returns.
Object::Method	**IDirect3DRMMesh::GetBox**
Example	`HRESULT GetBox(D3DRMBOX * lpD3DRMBox);`
Description	Returns the bounding box containing a mesh (the minimum and maximum model *x*-, *y*-, and *z*-coordinates).
`lpD3DRMBox`	Address of a D3DRMBOX structure that will be filled with the bounding box coordinates.
Object::Method	**IDirect3DRMMesh::GetGroup**
Example	`HRESULT GetGroup(D3DRMGROUPINDEX id, unsigned *vCount, unsigned *fCount, unsigned *vPerFace, DWORD *fDataSize, unsigned *fData);`
Description	Returns the vertex and face data of a group.
`id`	Identifier of the group.
`vCount` and `fCount`	Addresses of variables that will be set to the number of vertices and the number of faces for the group. These parameters can be NULL, in which case no values will be filled in.
`vPerFace`	Address of a variable that will be set to the number of vertices per face for the group. This parameter can be NULL.
`fDataSize`	Address of a variable that specifies the number of unsigned elements in the buffer pointed to by the fData parameter. This parameter cannot be NULL.
`fData`	Address of a buffer that will be set to the face data for the group. The format of this data is the same as was specified in the call to the IDirect3DRMMesh::AddGroup method. If this parameter is NULL, the method returns the required size of the buffer in the fDataSize parameter.
Object::Method	**IDirect3DRMMesh::GetGroupColor**
Example	`D3DCOLOR GetGroupColor(D3DRMGROUPINDEX id);`
Description	Returns the color for a group.
`id`	Identifier of the group.
Object::Method	**IDirect3DRMMesh::GetGroupCount**
Example	`unsigned GetGroupCount();`
Description	Returns the number of groups that have been created in the Mesh object (with IDirect3DRMMesh::AddGroup).

Object::Method	**IDirect3DRMMesh::GetGroupMapping**
Example	`D3DRMMAPPING GetGroupMapping(D3DRMGROUPINDEX id);`
Description	Returns the texture mapping setting for a group.
`id`	Identifier of the group.
Object::Method	**IDirect3DRMMesh::GetGroupMaterial**
Example	`HRESULT GetGroupMaterial(D3DRMGROUPINDEX id, LPDIRECT3DRMMATERIAL *returnPtr);`
Description	Returns a pointer to the material for a group.
`id`	Identifier of the group.
`returnPtr`	Address of a pointer to a variable that will be set to the IDirect3DRMMaterial for the group.
Object::Method	**IDirect3DRMMesh::GetGroupQuality**
Example	`D3DRMRENDERQUALITY GetGroupQuality(D3DRM-GROUPINDEX id);`
Description	Returns the rendering quality flags for a group.
`id`	Identifier of the group.
Object::Method	**IDirect3DRMMesh::GetGroupTexture**
Example	`HRESULT GetGroupTexture(D3DRMGROUPINDEX id, LPDIRECT3DRMTEXTURE *returnPtr);`
Description	Returns an address of the texture of a group.
`id`	Identifier of the group.
`returnPtr`	Address of a pointer to a variable that will be set to the IDirect3DRMTexture for the group.
Object::Method	**IDirect3DRMMesh::GetVertices**
Example	`HRESULT GetVertices(D3DRMGROUPINDEX id, DWORD index, DWORD count, D3DRMVERTEX *returnPtr);`
Description	Returns the vertex positions for a group.
`id`	Identifier of the group.
`index`	Index into the array of D3DRMVERTEX structures at which to begin returning vertex positions.
`count`	Number of D3DRMVERTEX structures (vertices) to retrieve following the index given in the index parameter. This parameter cannot be NULL.

returnPtr	Array of D3DRMVERTEX structures that will be set to the vertex positions. If this parameter is NULL, the method returns the required number of D3DRMVERTEX structures in the count parameter.
Object::Method	**IDirect3DRMMesh::Scale**
Example	`HRESULT Scale(D3DVALUE sx, D3DVALUE sy, D3DVALUE sz);`
Description	Scales a mesh in the *x*-, *y*-, and *z*-directions in model coordinates.
`sx`, `sy`, and `sz`	Scaling factors that are applied along the *x*-, *y*-, and *z*-axes.
Object::Method	**IDirect3DRMMesh::SetGroupColor**
Example	`HRESULT SetGroupColor(D3DRMGROUPINDEX id, D3DCOLOR value);`
Description	Sets the color of a group.
`id`	Identifier of the group.
`value`	Color of the group.
Object::Method	**IDirect3DRMMesh::SetGroupColorRGB**
Example	`HRESULT SetGroupColorRGB(D3DRMGROUPINDEX id, D3DVALUE red, D3DVALUE green, D3DVALUE blue);`
Description	Sets the color of a group.
`id`	Identifier of the group.
`red`, `green`, and `blue`	Red, green, and blue components of the group color.
Object::Method	**IDirect3DRMMesh::SetGroupMapping**
Example	`HRESULT SetGroupMapping(D3DRMGROUPINDEX id, D3DRMMAPPING value);`
Description	Sets the texture mapping for a group in a Direct3DRMMesh object.
`id`	Identifier of the group.
`value`	A D3DRMMAPPING flag.
Object::Method	**IDirect3DRMMesh::SetGroupMaterial**
Example	`HRESULT SetGroupMaterial(D3DRMGROUPINDEX id, LPDIRECT3DRMMATERIAL value);`
Description	Sets the material associated with a group.
`id`	Identifier of the group.

`value`	Address of the IDirect3DRMMaterial interface for the Direct3DRMMesh object.
Object::Method	**IDirect3DRMMesh::SetGroupQuality**
Example	`HRESULT SetGroupQuality(D3DRMGROUPINDEX id, D3DRMRENDERQUALITY value);`
Description	Sets the rendering quality for a group.
`id`	Identifier of the group.
`value`	D3DRMRENDERQUALITY flags.
Object::Method	**IDirect3DRMMesh::SetGroupTexture**
Example	`HRESULT SetGroupTexture(D3DRMGROUPINDEX id, LPDIRECT3DRMTEXTURE value);`
Description	Sets the texture of a group.
`id`	Identifier of the group.
`value`	Address of the IDirect3DRMTexture object.
Object::Method	**IDirect3DRMMesh::SetVertices**
Example	`HRESULT SetVertices(D3DRMGROUPINDEX id, unsigned index, unsigned count, D3DRMVERTEX *values);`
Description	Sets the vertex positions for a group.
`id`	Identifier of the group.
`index`	Index into the array specified in the values parameter at which to begin setting vertex positions.
`count`	Number of vertices to set following the index given in the index parameter.
`values`	Array of D3DRMVERTEX structures specifying the vertex positions to be set.
Object::Method	**IDirect3DRMMesh::Translate**
Example	`HRESULT Translate(D3DVALUE tx, D3DVALUE ty, D3DVALUE tz);`
Description	Adds the specified offsets to all the vertex positions in a mesh.
`tx, ty, and tz`	Offsets that are added to the x-, y-, and z-coordinates of each vertex position.

IDirect3DRMMeshBuilder

Object::Method	**IDirect3DRMMeshBuilder::AddFace**
Example	`HRESULT AddFace(LPDIRECT3DRMFACE lpD3DRMFace);`
Description	Adds a face to a MeshBuilder object. A face can be a part of only one MeshBuilder.
`lpD3DRMFace`	Address of the face being added.
Object::Method	**IDirect3DRMMeshBuilder::AddFaces**
Example	`HRESULT AddFaces(DWORD dwVertexCount, D3DVECTOR * lpD3DVertices, DWORD normalCount, D3DVECTOR *lpNormals, DWORD *lpFaceData, LPDIRECT3DRMFACEARRAY* lplpD3DRMFaceArray);`
Description	Adds faces to a MeshBuilder object.
`dwVertexCount`	Number of vertices.
`lpD3DVertices`	Base address of an array of D3DVECTOR structures that stores the vertex positions.
`normalCount`	Number of normals.
`lpNormals`	Base address of an array of D3DVECTOR structures that stores the normal positions.
`lpFaceData`	For each face, this parameter should contain a vertex count followed by the indices into the vertices array. If normalCount is nonzero, this parameter should contain a vertex count followed by pairs of indices, with the first index of each pair indexing into the array of vertices and the second indexing into the array of normals. The list of indices must terminate with a 0.
`lplpD3DRM-FaceArray`	Address of a pointer to an IDirect3DRMFaceArray interface that will be filled with a pointer to the newly created faces.
Object::Method	**IDirect3DRMMeshBuilder::AddFrame**
Example	`HRESULT AddFrame(LPDIRECT3DRMFRAME lpD3DRMFrame);`
Description	Adds the contents of a frame to a MeshBuilder object. The meshes of the source frame are not changed; a copy of their content is copied over to the MeshBuilder.
`lpD3DRMFrame`	Address of the frame whose contents are being added.

Object::Method	**IDirect3DRMMeshBuilder::AddMesh**
Example	`HRESULT AddMesh(LPDIRECT3DRMMESH lpD3DRMMesh);`
Description	Adds a mesh to a MeshBuilder object.
`lpD3DRMMesh`	Address of the mesh being added.
Object::Method	**IDirect3DRMMeshBuilder::AddMeshBuilder**
Example	`HRESULT AddMeshBuilder(LPDIRECT3DRMMESHBUILDER lpD3DRMMeshBuild);`
Description	Adds a copy of the contents of one MeshBuilder object to another MeshBuilder object. The source MeshBuilder is unchanged.
`lpD3DRMMeshBuild`	Address of the Direct3DRMMeshBuilder object whose contents are being added.
Object::Method	**IDirect3DRMMeshBuilder::AddNormal**
Example	`int AddNormal(D3DVALUE x, D3DVALUE y, D3DVALUE z);`
Description	Adds a normal to a MeshBuilder object and returns an index into the MeshBuilders normal table for that normal.
`x, y, and z`	The *x*, *y*, and *z* of the direction of the new normal.
Object::Method	**IDirect3DRMMeshBuilder::AddVertex**
Example	`int AddVertex(D3DVALUE x, D3DVALUE y, D3DVALUE z);`
Description	Adds a vertex to a MeshBuilder object and returns an index into the MeshBuilders vertex table for that normal.
`x, y, and z`	The *x*-, *y*-, and *z*-positions of the new vertex.
Object::Method	**IDirect3DRMMeshBuilder::CreateFace**
Example	`HRESULT CreateFace(LPDIRECT3DRMFACE* lplpD3DRMFace);`
Description	Creates a new face with no vertices and adds it to a MeshBuilder object.
`lplpD3DRMFace`	Address of a pointer to an IDirect3DRMFace interface that will be filled with a pointer to the face that was created.
Object::Method	**IDirect3DRMMeshBuilder::CreateMesh**
Example	`HRESULT CreateMesh(LPDIRECT3DRMMESH* lplpD3DRMMesh);`

Description	Creates a new Mesh object from a MeshBuilder object.
`lplpD3DRMMesh`	Address to be filled with a pointer to an IDirect3DRMMesh interface.
Object::Method	**IDirect3DRMMeshBuilder::GenerateNormals**
Example	`HRESULT GenerateNormals();`
Description	Calculates the normal vectors at each vertex (i.e., the vertex normals) in a MeshBuilder object. The normals for each face that uses the vertex are averaged together. Two back-to-back faces would produce a normal of 0 length at each vertex.
Object::Method	**IDirect3DRMMeshBuilder::GetBox**
Example	`HRESULT GetBox(D3DRMBOX *lpD3DRMBox);`
Description	Returns the bounding box (the minimum and maximum model coordinates) of a MeshBuilder object.
`lpD3DRMBox`	Address of a D3DRMBOX structure that will be filled with the bounding box coordinates.
Object::Method	**IDirect3DRMMeshBuilder::GetColorSource**
Example	`D3DRMCOLORSOURCE GetColorSource();`
Description	Returns the color source for a MeshBuilder object. The color source is either a face or a vertex.
Object::Method	**IDirect3DRMMeshBuilder::GetFaceCount**
Example	`int GetFaceCount();`
Description	Returns the number of faces in a MeshBuilder object.
Object::Method	**IDirect3DRMMeshBuilder::GetFaces**
Example	`HRESULT GetFaces(LPDIRECT3DRMFACEARRAY* lplpD3DRMFaceArray);`
Description	Returns the faces of a MeshBuilder object.
`lplpD3DRMFaceArray`	Address of a pointer to an IDirect3DRMFaceArray interface that is filled with an address of the faces.
Object::Method	**IDirect3DRMMeshBuilder::GetPerspective**
Example	`BOOL GetPerspective();`
Description	Returns the perspective correction setting for a MeshBuilder object (TRUE = perspective correction is on).

Object::Method	**IDirect3DRMMeshBuilder::GetQuality**
Example	`D3DRMRENDERQUALITY GetQuality();`
Description	Returns the rendering quality of a MeshBuilder object.
Object::Method	**IDirect3DRMMeshBuilder::GetTextureCoordinates**
Example	`HRESULT GetTextureCoordinates(DWORD index, D3DVALUE *lpU, D3DVALUE *lpV);`
Description	Returns the texture coordinates of a specified vertex in a MeshBuilder object.
`index`	Index of the vertex.
`lpU` and `lpV`	Addresses of variables that will be filled with the texture coordinates of the vertex.
Object::Method	**IDirect3DRMMeshBuilder::GetVertexColor**
Example	`D3DCOLOR GetVertexColor(DWORD index);`
Description	Returns the color of a specified vertex in a MeshBuilder object.
`index`	Index of the vertex.
Object::Method	**IDirect3DRMMeshBuilder::GetVertexCount**
Example	`int GetVertexCount();`
Description	Returns the number of vertices in a MeshBuilder object.
Object::Method	**IDirect3DRMMeshBuilder::GetVertices**
Example	`HRESULT GetVertices(DWORD *vcount, D3DVECTOR *vertices, DWORD *ncount, D3DVECTOR *normals, DWORD *face_data_size, DWORD *face_data);`
Description	Returns the vertices, normals, and face data for a MeshBuilder object.
`vcount`	Address of a variable that will be set to the number of vertices.
`vertices`	Address of an array of D3DVECTOR structures that will be set to the vertices for the Direct3DRMMeshBuilder object.
`ncount`	Address of a variable that will be set to the number of normals.
`normals`	Array of D3DVECTOR structures that will be set to the normals for the Direct3DRMMeshBuilder object.
`face_data_size`	Address of a variable that specifies the size of the buffer pointed to by the face_data parameter. The size is given in units of DWORD values. This parameter cannot be NULL.

Chapter 18 Retained Mode Reference 327

`face_data`	Address of the face data for the Direct3DRMMeshBuilder object. This data is in the same format as specified in the IDirect3DRMMesh::AddGroup method, except that it is NULL-terminated. If this parameter is NULL, the method returns the required size of the face-data buffer in the face_data_size parameter.
Object::Method	**IDirect3DRMMeshBuilder::Load**
Example	`HRESULT Load(LPVOID lpvObjSource, LPVOID lpvObjID, D3DRMLOADOPTIONS d3drmLOFlags, D3DRMLOADTEXTURECALLBACK d3drmLoadTextureProc, LPVOID lpvArg);`
Description	Loads a MeshBuilder object.
`lpvObjSource`	Source for the object to be loaded. This source can be a file, resource, memory block, or stream, depending on the source flags specified in the d3drmLOFlags parameter.
`lpvObjID`	Object name or position to be loaded. The use of this parameter depends on the identifier flags specified in the d3drmLOFlags parameter. If the D3DRMLOAD_BYPOSITION flag is specified, this parameter is a pointer to a DWORD value that gives the object's order in the file. If you set this parameter to NULL, the first mesh in the source will be loaded.
`d3drmLOFlags`	Value of the D3DRMLOADOPTIONS type describing the load options.
`d3drmLoad-TextureProc`	A D3DRMLOADTEXTURECALLBACK callback function called to load any textures used by an object.
`lpvArg`	Address of application-defined data passed to the D3DRMLOAD-TEXTURECALLBACK callback function.
Object::Method	**IDirect3DRMMeshBuilder::ReserveSpace**
Example	`HRESULT ReserveSpace(DWORD vertexCount, DWORD normalCount, DWORD faceCount);`
Description	Reserves space within a MeshBuilder object for the specified number of vertices, normals, and faces. This improves memory performance, since memory then does not have to be allocated for each individual addition of data to the MeshBuilder.
`vertexCount`, `normalCount`, and `faceCount`	Number of vertices, normals, and faces to allocate space for.

Object::Method	**IDirect3DRMMeshBuilder::Save**
Example	`HRESULT Save(const char * lpFilename, D3DRMXOFFORMAT d3drmXOFFormat, D3DRMSAVEOPTIONS d3drmSOContents);`
Description	Saves a MeshBuilder object.
`lpFilename`	Address specifying the name of the created file. This file must have an .x filename extension.
`d3drmXOFFormat`	The D3DRMXOF_TEXT value from the D3DRMXOFFORMAT enumerated type.
`d3drmSOContents`	A D3DRMSAVEOPTIONS flag describing the save options.
Object::Method	**IDirect3DRMMeshBuilder::Scale**
Example	`HRESULT Scale(D3DVALUE sx, D3DVALUE sy, D3DVALUE sz);`
Description	Scales a MeshBuilder object in the *x*-, *y*-, and *z*-directions in model coordinates.
`sx, sy,` and `sz`	Scaling factors that are applied along the *x*-, *y*-, and *z*-axes.
Object::Method	**IDirect3DRMMeshBuilder::SetColor**
Example	`HRESULT SetColor(D3DCOLOR color);`
Description	Sets all the faces of a MeshBuilder object to a given color.
`color`	Color of the faces.
Object::Method	**IDirect3DRMMeshBuilder::SetColorRGB**
Example	`HRESULT SetColorRGB(D3DVALUE red, D3DVALUE green, D3DVALUE blue);`
Description	Sets all the faces of a MeshBuilder object to a given color.
`red, green,` and `blue`	Red, green, and blue components of the color.
Object::Method	**IDirect3DRMMeshBuilder::SetColorSource**
Example	`HRESULT SetColorSource(D3DRMCOLORSOURCE source);`
Description	Sets the color source of a MeshBuilder object (either from a face or from a vertex).
`source`	A D3DRMCOLORSOURCE flag specifying the new color source to use.

Object::Method	**IDirect3DRMMeshBuilder::SetMaterial**
Example	`HRESULT SetMaterial(LPDIRECT3DRMMATERIAL lpIDirect3DRMMaterial);`
Description	Sets the material of all the faces of a MeshBuilder object.
`lpIDirect3DRM-Material`	Address of the IDirect3DRMMaterial interface for the Direct3DRMMeshBuilder object.
Object::Method	**IDirect3DRMMeshBuilder::SetNormal**
Example	`HRESULT SetNormal(DWORD index, D3DVALUE x, D3DVALUE y, D3DVALUE z);`
Description	Sets the normal vector of a specified vertex in a MeshBuilder object.
`index`	Index of the normal to be set.
`x, y, and z`	The *x*-, *y*-, and *z*-components of the vector to assign to the specified normal.
Object::Method	**IDirect3DRMMeshBuilder::SetPerspective**
Example	`HRESULT SetPerspective(BOOL perspective);`
Description	Turns on/off perspective-correct texture mapping for a MeshBuilder object.
`perspective`	Specify TRUE to turn on perspective correction.
Object::Method	**IDirect3DRMMeshBuilder::SetQuality**
Example	`HRESULT SetQuality(D3DRMRENDERQUALITY quality);`
Description	Sets the rendering quality of a MeshBuilder object.
`quality`	A D3DRMRENDERQUALITY flag specifying the new render quality.
Object::Method	**IDirect3DRMMeshBuilder::SetTexture**
Example	`HRESULT SetTexture(LPDIRECT3DRMTEXTURE lpD3DRMTexture);`
Description	Sets the texture of all the faces of a MeshBuilder object.
`lpD3DRMTexture`	Address of the Direct3DRMTexture object.
Object::Method	**IDirect3DRMMeshBuilder::SetTextureCoordinates**
Example	`HRESULT SetTextureCoordinates(DWORD index, D3DVALUE u, D3DVALUE v);`

Description	Sets the texture coordinates of a specified vertex in a MeshBuilder object.
`index`	Index of the vertex to be set.
`u` and `v`	Texture coordinates to assign to the vertex.
Object::Method	**IDirect3DRMMeshBuilder::SetTextureTopology**
Example	`HRESULT SetTextureTopology(BOOL cylU, BOOL cylV);`
Description	Sets the texture topology of a MeshBuilder object.
`cylU` and `cylV`	Specify TRUE for either or both of these parameters if you want the texture to have a cylindrical topology in the *u* and *v* dimensions respectively; otherwise, specify FALSE.
Object::Method	**IDirect3DRMMeshBuilder::SetVertex**
Example	`HRESULT SetVertex(DWORD index, D3DVALUE x, D3DVALUE y, D3DVALUE z);`
Description	Sets the position of a specified vertex in a MeshBuilder object.
`index`	Index of the vertex to be set.
`x, y,` and `z`	The new *x*-, *y*-, and *z*-positions.
Object::Method	**IDirect3DRMMeshBuilder::SetVertexColor**
Example	`HRESULT SetVertexColor(DWORD index, D3DCOLOR color);`
Description	Sets the color of a specified vertex in a MeshBuilder object.
`index`	Index of the vertex to be set.
`color`	The new color.
Object::Method	**IDirect3DRMMeshBuilder::SetVertexColorRGB**
Example	`HRESULT SetVertexColorRGB(DWORD index, D3DVALUE red, D3DVALUE green, D3DVALUE blue);`
Description	Sets the color of a specified vertex in a MeshBuilder object.
`index`	Index of the vertex to be set.
`red, green,` and `blue`	The new color.
Object::Method	**IDirect3DRMMeshBuilder::Translate**
Example	`HRESULT Translate(D3DVALUE tx, D3DVALUE ty, D3DVALUE tz);`

Description	Adds the specified position offset to all the vertices of a MeshBuilder object.
`tx, ty, and tz`	Offsets that are added to the *x*-, *y*-, and *z*-coordinates of each vertex position.

IDirect3DRMShadow

Object::Method	IDirect3DRMShadow::Init
Example	`HRESULT Init(LPDIRECT3DRMVISUAL lpD3DRMVisual, LPDIRECT3DRMLIGHT lpD3DRMLight, D3DVALUE px, D3DVALUE py, D3DVALUE pz, D3DVALUE nx, D3DVALUE ny, D3DVALUE nz);`
Description	Initializes a Direct3DRMShadow object.
`lpD3DRMVisual`	Address of the Direct3DRMVisual object casting the shadow.
`lpD3DRMLight`	Address of the Direct3DRMLight object that provides the light that defines the shadow.
`px, py, and pz`	Coordinates of a point on the plane on which the shadow is cast.
`nx, ny, and nz`	Coordinates of the normal vector of the plane on which the shadow is cast.

IDirect3DRMTexture

Object::Method	IDirect3DRMTexture::Changed
Example	`HRESULT Changed(BOOL bPixels, BOOL bPalette);`
Description	Tells the renderer that the application has changed the pixels or the palette of a texture.
`bPixels`	TRUE means the pixels have changed.
`bPalette`	TRUE means the palette has changed.
Object::Method	IDirect3DRMTexture::GetColors
Example	`DWORD GetColors();`
Description	Returns the maximum number of colors a texture has been quantitized to for rendering. This is not the same as the number of colors in the image from which the texture was created. Rather it means the values set with IDirect3DRM::SetDefaultTextureColors or IDirect3DRMTexture::SetColors.
Object::Method	IDirect3DRMTexture::GetDecalOrigin
Example	`HRESULT GetDecalOrigin(LONG * lplX, LONG * lplY);`

Description	Returns the current origin of the decal.
`lplX` and `lplY`	Addresses of variables that will be filled with the origin of the decal.
Object::Method	**IDirect3DRMTexture::GetDecalScale**
Example	`DWORD GetDecalScale();`
Description	Returns the scaling property of the given decal if successful or −1 otherwise.
Object::Method	**IDirect3DRMTexture::GetDecalSize**
Example	`HRESULT GetDecalSize(D3DVALUE *lprvWidth, D3DVALUE *lprvHeight);`
Description	Returns the size of the decal.
`lprvWidth` and `lprvHeight`	Addresses of variables that will be filled with the width and height of the decal.
Object::Method	**IDirect3DRMTexture::GetDecalTransparency**
Example	`BOOL GetDecalTransparency();`
Description	Returns the transparency setting for a decal (TRUE = decal has a transparent color).
Object::Method	**IDirect3DRMTexture::GetDecalTransparentColor**
Example	`D3DCOLOR GetDecalTransparentColor();`
Description	Returns the transparent color of the decal.
Object::Method	**IDirect3DRMTexture::GetImage**
Example	`D3DRMIMAGE * GetImage();`
Description	Returns an address of the image with which the texture was created.
Object::Method	**IDirect3DRMTexture::GetShades**
Example	`DWORD GetShades();`
Description	Returns the number of shades used to render each color in the texture.
Object::Method	**IDirect3DRMTexture::InitFromFile**
Example	`HRESULT InitFromFile(const char *filename);`
Description	Initializes a texture by using the information in a given file.
`filename`	Address of a string specifying the file from which initialization information is drawn.

Chapter 18 Retained Mode Reference

Object::Method	**IDirect3DRMTexture::InitFromResource**
Example	`HRESULT InitFromResource(HRSRC rs);`
Description	Initializes a texture from a specified resource.
`rs`	Handle of the specified resource.

Object::Method	**IDirect3DRMTexture::InitFromSurface**
Example	`HRESULT InitFromSurface(LPDIRECTDRAWSURFACE lpDDS);`
Description	Initializes a texture by using the data from a given DirectDraw surface.
`lpDDS`	Address of a DirectDraw surface from which initialization information is drawn.

Object::Method	**IDirect3DRMTexture::SetColors**
Example	`HRESULT SetColors(DWORD ulColors);`
Description	Sets the maximum number of colors used for rendering a texture. This method is relevant only in the ramp color model.
`ulColors`	Number of colors. The default is 8.

Object::Method	**IDirect3DRMTexture::SetDecalOrigin**
Example	`HRESULT SetDecalOrigin(LONG lX, LONG lY);`
Description	Sets the origin of the decal as an offset from the top left of the decal. The origin is the frame's position and location to which the decal is attached.
`lX` and `lY`	New origin, in decal coordinates, for the decal. The default origin is [0, 0].

Object::Method	**IDirect3DRMTexture::SetDecalScale**
Example	`HRESULT SetDecalScale(DWORD dwScale);`
Description	Sets the scaling property for a decal.
`dwScale`	If this parameter is TRUE, depth is taken into account when the decal is scaled. If it is FALSE, depth information is ignored. The default is TRUE.

Object::Method	**IDirect3DRMTexture::SetDecalSize**
Example	`HRESULT SetDecalSize(D3DVALUE rvWidth, D3DVALUE rvHeight);`

Description	Sets the size of the decal to be used if the decal is being scaled according to its depth in the scene.
`rvWidth` and `rvHeight`	New width and height, in model coordinates, of the decal. The default size is [1, 1].
Object::Method	**IDirect3DRMTexture::SetDecalTransparency**
Example	`HRESULT SetDecalTransparency(BOOL bTransp);`
Description	Sets the transparency property of the decal.
`bTransp`	TRUE = transparent color; FALSE = opaque color. The default is FALSE.
Object::Method	**IDirect3DRMTexture::SetDecalTransparentColor**
Example	`HRESULT SetDecalTransparentColor(D3DCOLOR rcTransp);`
Description	Sets the transparent color for a decal.
`rcTransp`	New transparent color. The default is black.
Object::Method	**IDirect3DRMTexture::SetShades**
Example	`HRESULT SetShades(DWORD ulShades);`
Description	Sets the maximum number of shades to use for each color for the texture when rendering. This method is relevant only in the ramp color model.
`ulShades`	New number of shades. The default is 16.

IDirect3DRMUserVisual

Object::Method	**IDirect3DRMUserVisual::Init**
Example	`HRESULT Init(D3DRMUSERVISUALCALLBACK d3drmUVProc, void * lpArg);`
Description	Initializes a Direct3DRMUserVisual object. Use only for a Visual created with IDirect3DRM::CreateObject.
`d3drmUVProc`	Application-defined D3DRMUSERVISUALCALLBACK callback function.
`lpArg`	Application-defined data to be passed to the callback function.

IDirect3DRMViewport

Object::Method	**IDirect3DRMViewport::Clear**
Example	`HRESULT Clear();`

Description	Clears the viewport to the current background color.
Object::Method	**IDirect3DRMViewport::Configure**
Example	`HRESULT Configure(LONG lX, LONG lY, DWORD dwWidth, DWORD dwHeight);`
Description	Sets the origin and dimensions of a viewport. Returns D3DRMERR_BADVALUE if lX + dwWidth or lY + dwHeight are greater than the width or height of the device or if any of lX, lY, dwWidth, or dwHeight is less than 0.
`lX` and `lY`	New position of the viewport.
`dwWidth` and `dwHeight`	New width and height of the viewport.
Object::Method	**IDirect3DRMViewport::ForceUpdate**
Example	`HRESULT ForceUpdate(DWORD dwX1, DWORD dwY1, DWORD dwX2, DWORD dwY2);`
Description	Forces an area of the viewport to be updated. The specified area will be copied to the screen at the next call to the IDirect3DRMDevice::Update method. The region that the renderer actually updates may be larger than the specified rectangle and may be the entire window.
`dwX1` and `dwY1`	Upper-left corner of the area to be updated.
`dwX2` and `dwY2`	Lower-right corner of the area to be updated.
Object::Method	**IDirect3DRMViewport::GetBack**
Example	`D3DVALUE GetBack();`
Description	Returns the position of the back clipping plane.
Object::Method	**IDirect3DRMViewport::GetCamera**
Example	`HRESULT GetCamera(LPDIRECT3DRMFRAME * lpCamera);`
Description	Returns the frame to which the viewport is attached.
`lpCamera`	Address of a variable that represents the Direct3DRMFrame object representing the camera frame.
Object::Method	**IDirect3DRMViewport::GetDevice**
Example	`HRESULT GetDevice(LPDIRECT3DRMDEVICE *lpD3DRMDevice);`
Description	Returns the device associated with a viewport.
`lpD3DRMDevice`	Address of a variable that represents the Direct3DRMDevice object.

Object::Method	**IDirect3DRMViewport::GetDirect3DViewport**
Example	`HRESULT GetDirect3DViewport(LPDIRECT3DVIEWPORT * lplpD3DViewport);`
Description	Returns the immediate mode viewport that corresponds to the retained mode viewport.
`lplpD3DViewport`	Address of a pointer that is initialized with a pointer to the Direct3DViewport object.
Object::Method	**IDirect3DRMViewport::GetField**
Example	`D3DVALUE GetField();`
Description	Returns the field of view.
Object::Method	**IDirect3DRMViewport::GetFront**
Example	`D3DVALUE GetFront();`
Description	Returns the position of the front clipping plane for a viewport.
Object::Method	**IDirect3DRMViewport::GetHeight**
Example	`DWORD GetHeight();`
Description	Returns the height, in pixels, of the viewport.
Object::Method	**IDirect3DRMViewport::GetPlane**
Example	`HRESULT GetPlane(D3DVALUE *lpd3dvLeft, D3DVALUE *lpd3dvRight, D3DVALUE *lpd3dvBottom, D3DVALUE *lpd3dvTop);`
Description	Returns the front clipping plane of the viewing frustum.
`lpd3dvLeft`, `lpd3dvRight`, `lpd3dvBottom`, and `lpd3dvTop`	Addresses of variables that will be filled to represent the front clipping plane.
Object::Method	**IDirect3DRMViewport::GetProjection**
Example	`D3DRMPROJECTIONTYPE GetProjection();`
Description	Returns the projection type for the viewport (orthographic or perspective projection).
Object::Method	**IDirect3DRMViewport::GetUniformScaling**
Example	`BOOL GetUniformScaling();`
Description	Returns the scaling property used to scale the viewing volume into the larger dimension of the window. TRUE = viewport scales uniformly.

Object::Method	**IDirect3DRMViewport::GetWidth**
Example	`DWORD GetWidth();`
Description	Returns the width, in pixels, of the viewport.
Object::Method	**IDirect3DRMViewport::GetX**
Example	`LONG GetX();`
Description	Returns the *x*-offset of the start of the viewport on a device.
Object::Method	**IDirect3DRMViewport::GetY**
Example	`LONG GetY();`
Description	Returns the *y*-offset of the start of the viewport on a device.
Object::Method	**IDirect3DRMViewport::Init**
Example	`HRESULT Init(LPDIRECT3DRMDEVICE lpD3DRMDevice, LPDIRECT3DRMFRAME lpD3DRMFrameCamera, DWORD xpos, DWORD ypos, DWORD width, DWORD height);`
Description	Initializes a Direct3DRMViewport object.
`lpD3DRMDevice`	Address of the DirectD3DRMDevice object associated with this viewport.
`lpD3DRMFrameCamera`	Address of the camera frame associated with this viewport.
`xpos` and `ypos`	The *x*- and *y*-coordinates of the upper-left corner of the viewport.
`width` and `height`	Width and height of the viewport.
Object::Method	**IDirect3DRMViewport::InverseTransform**
Example	`HRESULT InverseTransform(D3DVECTOR * lprvDst, D3DRMVECTOR4D * lprvSrc);`
Description	Transforms the vector in the lprvSrc parameter in screen coordinates to world coordinates and returns the result in the lprvDst parameter.
`lprvDst`	Address of a D3DVECTOR structure that will be filled with the result of the operation.
`lprvSrc`	Address of a D3DRMVECTOR4D structure representing the source of the operation.
Object::Method	**IDirect3DRMViewport::Pick**
Example	`HRESULT Pick(LONG lX, LONG lY, LPDIRECT3DRMPICKEDARRAY* lplpVisuals);`
Description	Finds a depth-sorted list of objects (and faces, if relevant) that includes the path taken in the hierarchy from the root down to the frame that contained the object.

`1X` and `1Y`	Coordinates to be used for picking.
`lplpVisuals`	Address of a pointer to be initialized with a valid pointer to the IDirect3DRMPickedArray interface if the call succeeds. |”

Object::Method   **IDirect3DRMViewport::Render**

Example   `HRESULT Render(LPDIRECT3DRMFRAME lpD3DRMFrame);`

Description   Renders a frame hierarchy to the given viewport. It renders only this frame and frames attached to it, so you can render part of a scene. To render a whole scene, specify the root frame of the scene.

`lpD3DRMFrame`   Address of a variable that represents the Direct3DRMFrame object that represents the frame hierarchy to be rendered.

Object::Method   **IDirect3DRMViewport::SetBack**

Example   `HRESULT SetBack(D3DVALUE rvBack);`

Description   Sets the position of the back clipping plane for a viewport.

`rvBack`   New position of the back clipping plane.

Object::Method   **IDirect3DRMViewport::SetCamera**

Example   `HRESULT SetCamera(LPDIRECT3DRMFRAME lpCamera);`

Description   Sets the frame in a scene to which a viewport is attached. A viewport's position, direction, and orientation come from the camera frame to which the viewport is attached. The viewport looks out the positive *z*-axis of the camera frame, with the up direction along the positive *y*-axis.

`lpCamera`   Address of a variable that represents the Direct3DRMFrame object that represents the camera.

Object::Method   **IDirect3DRMViewport::SetField**

Example   `HRESULT SetField(D3DVALUE rvField);`

Description   Sets the field of view for a viewport. The default is 0.5. The new value must be greater than 0 or D3DRMERR_BADVALUE is returned.

`rvField`   New field of view.

Object::Method   **IDirect3DRMViewport::SetFront**

Example   `HRESULT SetFront(D3DVALUE rvFront);`

Description	Sets the position of the front clipping plane for a viewport. The default is 1.0. The new value must be greater than 0 or D3DRMERR_BADVALUE is returned.
`rvFront`	New position of the front clipping plane.
Object::Method	**IDirect3DRMViewport::SetPlane**
Example	`RESULT SetPlane(D3DVALUE rvLeft, D3DVALUE rvRight, D3DVALUE rvBottom, D3DVALUE rvTop);`
Description	Sets the front clipping plane of the viewing frustum by supplying the coordinates of the four sides, relative to the camera's *z*-axis.
`rvLeft`, `rvRight`, `rvBottom`, and `rvTop`	New front clipping plane.
Object::Method	**IDirect3DRMViewport::SetProjection**
Example	`HRESULT SetProjection(D3DRMPROJECTIONTYPE rptType);`
Description	Sets the projection type for a viewport (orthographic or perspective projection).
`rptType`	The D3DRMPROJECTIONTYPE enumerated type.
Object::Method	**IDirect3DRMViewport::SetUniformScaling**
Example	`HRESULT SetUniformScaling(BOOL bScale);`
Description	Sets the scaling property used to scale the viewing volume into the larger dimension of the window. This method is typically used with the IDirect3DRMViewport::SetPlane method to support banding.
`bScale`	New scaling property. If this parameter is TRUE, the same horizontal and vertical scaling factor is used to scale the viewing volume. Otherwise, different scaling factors are used to scale the viewing volume exactly into the window. The default is TRUE.
Object::Method	**IDirect3DRMViewport::Transform**
Example	`HRESULT Transform(D3DRMVECTOR4D * lprvDst, D3DVECTOR * lprvSrc);`
Description	Transforms the vector in the lprvSrc parameter in world coordinates to screen coordinates and returns the result in the lprvDst parameter. The result of the transformation is a four-element homogeneous vector to avoid dividing by 0 when the vector is close to the camera's position. Perhaps a future version of Direct3D could return a flag indicating the result of this calculation.

IDirect3DRMWinDevice

Object::Method	IDirect3DRMWinDevice::HandleActivate
Example	`HRESULT HandleActivate(WORD wParam);`
Description	Responds to a Windows WM_ACTIVATE message, ensuring that rendering uses the correct color palette.
wParam	wParam parameter passed to the message-processing procedure with the WM_ACTIVATE message.
Object::Method	IDirect3DRMWinDevice::HandlePaint
Example	`HRESULT HandlePaint(HDC hDC);`
Description	Responds to a Windows WM_PAINT message. The hDC parameter should be taken from the PAINTSTRUCT structure given to the Windows BeginPaint function. This method should be called before repainting any application areas in the window because it may repaint areas outside the viewports that have been created on the device.
hDC	Handle of the device context (DC).

IDirect3DRMWrap

Object::Method	IDirect3DRMWrap::Apply
Example	`HRESULT Apply(LPDIRECT3DRMOBJECT lpObject);`
Description	Applies a Direct3DRMWrap object to the destination face or a mesh.
lpObject	Address of the destination object.
Object::Method	IDirect3DRMWrap::ApplyRelative
Example	`HRESULT ApplyRelative(LPDIRECT3DRMFRAME frame, LPDIRECT3DRMOBJECT mesh);`
Description	Applies the wrap to the vertices of the object after first transforming each vertex by the frame's world transformation and the wrap's reference frame's inverse world transformation.
frame	Direct3DRMFrame object containing the object to wrap.
mesh	Direct3DRMWrap object to apply.

(continued from previous page)

lprvDst	Address of a D3DRMVECTOR4D structure that acts as the destination for the transformation operation.
lprvSrc	Address of a D3DVECTOR structure that acts as the source for the transformation operation.

Chapter 18 Retained Mode Reference

Object::Method	**IDirect3DRMWrap::Init**
Example	`HRESULT Init(D3DRMWRAPTYPE d3drmwt, LPDIRECT3DRMFRAME lpd3drmfRef, D3DVALUE ox, D3DVALUE oy, D3DVALUE oz, D3DVALUE dx, D3DVALUE dy, D3DVALUE dz, D3DVALUE ux, D3DVALUE uy, D3DVALUE uz, D3DVALUE ou, D3DVALUE ov, D3DVALUE su, D3DVALUE sv);`
Description	Initializes a Direct3DRMWrap object.
`d3drmwt`	The AD3DRMWRAPTYPE enumerated type.
`lpd3drmfRef`	Address of a Direct3DRMFrame object representing the reference frame for this Direct3DRMWrap object.
`ox, oy,` and `oz`	Origin of the wrap.
`dx, dy,` and `dz`	The *z*-axis of the wrap.
`ux, uy,` and `uz`	The *y*-axis of the wrap.
`ou` and `ov`	Origin in the texture.
`su` and `sv`	Scale factor in the texture.

RM Arrays

Object::Method	**IDirect3DRMXXXArray::GetSize**
Example	`DWORD GetSize();`
Description	Returns the size, in objects, of the Direct3DRMXXXArray object.

Object::Method	**IDirect3DRMDeviceArray::GetElement**
Example	`HRESULT GetElement(DWORD index, LPDIRECT3DRMDEVICE * lplpD3DRMDevice);`
Description	Returns a specified element in a Direct3DRMDeviceArray object.
`index`	Element in the array.
`lplpD3DRMDevice`	Address to be filled with a pointer to an IDirect3DRMDevice interface.

Object::Method	**IDirect3DRMFaceArray::GetElement**
Example	`HRESULT GetElement(DWORD index, LPDIRECT3DRMFACE * lplpD3DRMFace);`
Description	Returns a specified element in a Direct3DRMFaceArray.
`index`	Element in the array.
`lplpD3DRMFace`	Address to be filled with a pointer to an IDirect3DRMFace interface.

Object::Method	**IDirect3DRMFrameArray::GetElement**
Example	`HRESULT GetElement(DWORD index, LPDIRECT3DRMFRAME * lplpD3DMFrame);`
Description	Returns a specified element in a Direct3DRMFrameArray object.
`index`	Element in the array.
`lplpD3DRMFrame`	Address to be filled with a pointer to an IDirect3DRMFrame interface.
Object::Method	**IDirect3DRMLightArray::GetElement**
Example	`HRESULT GetElement(DWORD index, LPDIRECT3DRMLIGHT * lplpD3DRMLight);`
Description	Returns a specified element in a Direct3DRMLightArray object.
`index`	Element in the array.
`lplpD3DRMLight`	Address to be filled with a pointer to an IDirect3DRMLight interface.
Object::Method	**IDirect3DRMPickedArray::GetPick**
Example	`HRESULT GetPick(DWORD index, LPDIRECT3DRMVISUAL * lplpVisual, LPDIRECT3DRMFRAMEARRAY * lplpFrameArray, LPD3DRMPICKDESC lpD3DRMPickDesc);`
Description	Returns the Direct3DRMVisual and Direct3DRMFrame objects intersected by the specified pick.
`index`	Index into the pick array identifying the pick for which information will be retrieved.
`lplpVisual`	Address that will be set to a pointer to the Direct3DRMVisual object associated with the specified pick.
`lplpFrameArray`	Address that will be set to a pointer to the Direct3DRMFrameArray object associated with the specified pick.
`lpD3DRMPickDesc`	Address of a D3DRMPICKDESC structure specifying the pick position and face and group identifiers of the objects being retrieved.
Object::Method	**IDirect3DRMViewportArray::GetElement**
Example	`HRESULT GetElement(DWORD index, LPDIRECT3DRMVIEWPORT * lplpD3DRMViewport);`
Description	Returns a specified element in a Direct3DRMViewportArray object.
`index`	Element in the array.
`lplpD3DRMViewport`	Address to be filled with a pointer to an IDirect3DRMViewport interface.

Chapter 18 Retained Mode Reference

Object::Method	**IDirect3DRMVisualArray::GetElement**
Example	`HRESULT GetElement(DWORD index, LPDIRECT3DRMVISUAL * lplpD3DRMVisual);`
Description	Returns a specified element in a Direct3DRMVisualArray object.
`index`	Element in the array.
`lplpD3DRMVisual`	Address to be filled with a pointer to an IDirect3DRMVisual interface.

Structures

Structure	**D3DRMBOX**

Example	`typedef struct _D3DRMBOX {`
	`D3DVECTOR min, max;`
	`}D3DRMBOX;`
	`typedef D3DRMBOX *LPD3DRMBOX;`

Description	Describes the bounding box of an object (the minimum and maximum model x-, y-, and z-coordinates).
Used by	IDirect3DRMMesh::GetBox, IDirect3DRMMeshBuilder::GetBox.
`min` and `max`	D3DVECTOR values defining the bounds of the box. Min is the minimum x-, y-, and z-values; max is the maximum x-, y-, and z-values.
Structure	**D3DRMIMAGE**

Example	`typedef struct _D3DRMIMAGE {`
	`int   width, height;`
	`int   aspectx, aspecty;`
	`int   depth;`
	`int   rgb;`
	`int   bytes_per_line;`
	`void*buffer1;`
	`void*buffer2;`
	`unsigned long red_mask;`
	`unsigned long green_mask;`
	`unsigned long blue_mask;`
	`unsigned long alpha_mask;`
	`int   palette_size;`
	`D3DRMPALETTEENTRY* palette;`
	`}D3DRMIMAGE;`
	`typedef D3DRMIMAGE, *LPD3DRMIMAGE;`

Description	Describes the image that is attached to a texture.

Used by	IDirect3DRM::CreateTexture, IDirect3DRMTexture::GetImage (returns address of image).
`width` and `height`	Width and height of the image, in pixels.
`aspectx` and `aspecty`	Aspect ratio for nonsquare pixels.
`depth`	Bits per pixel.
`rgb`	If this member FALSE, pixels are indices into a palette. Otherwise, pixels encode RGB values.
`bytes_per_line`	Number of bytes of memory for a scanline. This value must be a multiple of 4.
`buffer1`	Memory to render into (first buffer).
`buffer2`	Second rendering buffer for double buffering. Set this member to NULL for single buffering.
`red_mask`, `green_mask`, `blue_mask`, and `alpha_mask`	If rgb is TRUE, these members are masks for the red, green, blue, and alpha parts of a pixel. Otherwise, they are masks for the significant bits of the red, green, and blue elements in the palette. For example, most SVGA displays use 64 intensities of red, green, and blue, so the masks should all be set to 0xfc.
`palette_size`	Number of entries in the palette.
`palette`	If rgb is FALSE, this member is the address of a D3DRMPALETTE-ENTRY structure describing the palette entry.
Structure	**D3DRMLOADMEMORY**

Example	`typedef struct _D3DRMLOADMEMORY {`
	`LPVOID lpMemory;`
	`DWORD  dSize;`
	`} D3DRMLOADMEMORY, *LPD3DRMLOADMEMORY;`

Description	Describes a resource to be loaded from memory.
Used by	IDirect3DRM::Load or other Load method when D3DRMLOAD_FROMMEMORY is specified.
`lpMemory`	Address of a block of memory to be loaded.
`dSize`	Size, in bytes, of the block of memory to be loaded.
Structure	**D3DRMLOADRESOURCE**

Example	`typedef struct _D3DRMLOADRESOURCE {`
	`HMODULE hModule;`
	`LPCTSTR lpName;`
	`LPCTSTR lpType;`
	`} D3DRMLOADRESOURCE, *LPD3DRMLOADRESOURCE;`

Description	Describes a resource to be loaded.
Used by	IDirect3DRM::Load or other Load method when D3DRMLOAD_FROMRESOURCE is specified.
Note	You do not need to find or unlock any resources; the system handles this automatically.
`hModule`	Handle of the module containing the resource to be loaded. If this member is NULL, the resource must be attached to the calling executable file.
`lpName`	Name of the resource to be loaded. For example, if the resource is a mesh, this member should specify the name of the mesh file.
`lpType`	User-defined type identifying the resource.
	If the high-order word of the lpName or lpType member is 0, the low-order word specifies the integer identifier of the name or type of the given resource. Otherwise, those parameters are long pointers to NULL-terminated strings. If the first character of the string is a pound sign (#), the remaining characters represent a decimal number that specifies the integer identifier of the resource's name or type. For example, the string "#258" represents the integer identifier 258. An application should reduce the amount of memory required for the resources by referring to them by integer identifier instead of by name.
Structure	**D3DRMPALETTEENTRY**

Example	`typedef struct _D3DRMPALETTEENTRY {`
	`unsigned char red;`
	`unsigned char green;`
	`unsigned char blue;`
	`unsigned char flags;`
	`}D3DRMPALETTEENTRY;`
	`typedef D3DRMPALETTEENTRY, *LPD3DRMPALETTE-`
	`ENTRY;`

Description	Describes a color palette.
Used by	D3DRMIMAGE.
Usage	Used only if the rgb member of D3DRMIMAGE is FALSE (otherwise, rgb values are used and no color palette is needed).
`red, green, and blue`	Values defining the primary color components that define the palette. Range: 0 through 255.
`flags`	A D3DRMPALETTEFLAGS flag: D3DRMPALETTE_FREE, D3DRMPALETTE_READONLY, or D3DRMPALETTE_RESERVED.

Structure	**D3DRMPICKDESC**
Example	```typedef struct _D3DRMPICKDESC {
ULONG   ulFaceIdx;
LONG   lGroupIdx;
D3DVECTOR vPosition;
} D3DRMPICKDESC, *LPD3DRMPICKDESC;```
Description	Describes results of a pick operation (identifying objects at an x, y screen location).
Used by	Objects retrieved with the IDirect3DRMPickedArray::GetPick.
`ulFaceIdx`	Face index of the retrieved object.
`lGroupIdx`	Group index of the retrieved object.
`vPosition`	A D3DVECTOR describing the position of the retrieved object.
Structure	**D3DRMQUATERNION**
Example	```typedef struct _D3DRMQUATERNION {
D3DVALUE s;
D3DVECTOR v;
}D3DRMQUATERNION;
typedef D3DRMQUATERNION, *LPD3DRMQUATERNION;```
Description	Describes a unit quaternion (an orientation described by a direction vector and a rotation around that vector).
Used by	IDirect3DRMAnimation::AddRotateKey and several retained mode math functions.
`s`	Rotation around the direction vector.
`v`	Direction vector.
Structure	**D3DRMVECTOR4D**
Example	```typedef struct _D3DRMVECTOR4D {
D3DVALUE x;
D3DVALUE y;
D3DVALUE z;
D3DVALUE w;
}D3DRMVECTOR4D;
typedef D3DRMVECTOR4D, *LPD3DRMVECTOR4D;```
Description	Homogeneous x, y, and z. These values define the result of a transformation.
Used by	Destination of a transformation IDirect3DRMViewport::Transform, source of a transformation IDirect3DRMViewport::InverseTransform.

Chapter 18 Retained Mode Reference

Usage	Divide *x*, *y*, and *z* by *w* to get straight *x*, *y*, and *z*.
`x, y, z, and w`	D3DVALUEs describing homogeneous values.
Structure	**D3DRMVERTEX**

Example	`typedef struct _D3DRMVERTEX{`
	`D3DVECTOR position;`
	`D3DVECTOR normal;`
	`D3DVALUE  tu, tv;`
	`D3DCOLOR  color;`
	`} D3DRMVERTEX;`

Description	Describes a vertex and the data associated with it.
Used by	Direct3DRMMesh.
`position`	Position of the vertex.
`normal`	Normal vector for the vertex.
`tu` and `tv`	Horizontal and vertical texture coordinates, respectively, for the vertex.
`color`	Vertex color.

Enumerated Types

Type	**D3DRMCOLORSOURCE**

Example	`typedef enum _D3DRMCOLORSOURCE{`
	`D3DRMCOLOR_FROMFACE,`
	`D3DRMCOLOR_FROMVERTEX`
	`} D3DRMCOLORSOURCE;`

Description	Indicates where color for the faces in a MeshBuilder comes from: the color of faces or the colors of the individual vertices.
Used by	IDirect3DRMMeshBuilder::SetColorSource, IDirect3DRMMesh-Builder::GetColorSource.
D3DRMCOLOR_FROMFACE	Color source is a face.
D3DRMCOLOR_FROMVERTEX	Color source is a vertex.
Type	**D3DRMCOMBINETYPE**

Example	`typedef enum _D3DRMCOMBINETYPE{`
	`D3DRMCOMBINE_REPLACE,`
	`D3DRMCOMBINE_BEFORE,`
	`D3DRMCOMBINE_AFTER`
	`} D3DRMCOMBINETYPE;`

Description	Tells how to combine two matrices. The order of the supplied and current matrices when they are multiplied together is important because matrix multiplication is not commutative ($a \times b$ is not the same as $b \times a$).
Used by	Frame methods.

D3DRMCOMBINE_REPLACE

The supplied matrix replaces the frame's current matrix.

D3DRMCOMBINE_BEFORE

The supplied matrix is multiplied with the frame's current matrix and precedes the current matrix in the calculation.

D3DRMCOMBINE_AFTER

The supplied matrix is multiplied with the frame's current matrix and follows the current matrix in the calculation.

Type	**D3DRMFILLMODE**
Example	```typedef enum _D3DRMFILLMODE {
D3DRMFILL_POINTS = 0 * D3DRMLIGHT_MAX,
D3DRMFILL_WIREFRAME = 1 * D3DRMLIGHT_MAX,
D3DRMFILL_SOLID = 2 * D3DRMLIGHT_MAX,
D3DRMFILL_MASK = 7 * D3DRMLIGHT_MAX,
D3DRMFILL_MAX   = 8 * D3DRMLIGHT_MAX
} D3DRMFILLMODE;```
Description	Describes rendering types.
Used by	In the definition of the D3DRMRENDERQUALITY type.
D3DRMFILL_POINTS	Fill points only; minimum fill mode.

D3DRMFILL_WIREFRAME

Fill wireframes.

D3DRMFILL_SOLID	Fill solid objects.
D3DRMFILL_MASK	Fill using a mask.
D3DRMFILL_MAX	Maximum value for fill mode.
Type	**D3DRMFOGMODE**
Example	```typedef enum _D3DRMFOGMODE{
D3DRMFOG_LINEAR,
D3DRMFOG_EXPONENTIAL,
D3DRMFOG_EXPONENTIALSQUARED
} D3DRMFOGMODE;```

Chapter 18 Retained Mode Reference

Description	Describes different ways fog intensifies with distance from the camera.
Used by	IDirect3DRMFrame::SetSceneFogParams.
Usage	Only linear fog is supported for DirectX 2.
Note	*e* is the base of the natural logarithms; approximately 2.71828.
D3DRMFOG_LINEAR	The fog effect intensifies linearly between the start and end points; based on the formula.
D3DRMFOG_EXPONENTIAL	
	The fog effect intensifies exponentially; based on the formula.
D3DRMFOG_EXPONENTIALSQUARED	
	The fog effect intensifies exponentially with the square of the distance; based on the formula.

Type	**D3DRMFRAMECONSTRAINT**

Example	`typedef enum _D3DRMFRAMECONSTRAINT {`
	`D3DRMCONSTRAIN_Z,`
	`D3DRMCONSTRAIN_Y,`
	`D3DRMCONSTRAIN_X`
	`} D3DRMFRAMECONSTRAINT;`

Description	The axes of rotation to constrain when viewing a Direct3DRM-Frame object.
Used by	IDirect3DRMFrame::LookAt.
D3DRMCONSTRAIN_Z	Use only *x*- and *y*-rotations.
D3DRMCONSTRAIN_Y	Use only *x*- and *z*-rotations.
D3DRMCONSTRAIN_X	Use only *y*- and *z*-rotations.

Type	**D3DRMLIGHTMODE**

Example	`typedef enum _D3DRMLIGHTMODE {`
	`D3DRMLIGHT_OFF  = 0 * D3DRMSHADE_MAX,`
	`D3DRMLIGHT_ON   = 1 * D3DRMSHADE_MAX,`
	`D3DRMLIGHT_MASK = 7 * D3DRMSHADE_MAX,`
	`D3DRMLIGHT_MAX  = 8 * D3DRMSHADE_MAX`
	`} D3DRMLIGHTMODE;`

Description	Describes light type.
Used by	D3DRMRENDERQUALITY type.
D3DRMLIGHT_OFF	Lighting is off.
D3DRMLIGHT_ON	Lighting is on.

D3DRMLIGHT_MASK   Lighting uses a mask.

D3DRMLIGHT_MAX   Maximum lighting mode.

Type	**D3DRMLIGHTTYPE**
Example	`typedef enum _D3DRMLIGHTTYPE{ D3DRMLIGHT_AMBIENT, D3DRMLIGHT_POINT, D3DRMLIGHT_SPOT, D3DRMLIGHT_DIRECTIONAL, D3DRMLIGHT_PARALLELPOINT } D3DRMLIGHTTYPE;`
Description	Describes the type of a light.
Used by	IDirect3DRM::CreateLight.

D3DRMLIGHT_AMBIENT
   Light is ambient.

D3DRMLIGHT_POINT   Light is a point source.

D3DRMLIGHT_SPOT   Light is a spotlight source.

D3DRMLIGHT_DIRECTIONAL
   Light is a directional source.

D3DRMLIGHT_PARALLELPOINT
   Light is a parallel source.

Type	**D3DRMMATERIALMODE**
Example	`typedef enum _D3DRMMATERIALMODE{ D3DRMMATERIAL_FROMMESH, D3DRMMATERIAL_FROMPARENT, D3DRMMATERIAL_FROMFRAME } D3DRMMATERIALMODE;`
Description	Indicates where a mesh gets its material.
Used by	IDirect3DRMFrame::GetMaterialMode, IDirect3DRMFrame::SetMaterialMode.

D3DRMMATERIAL_FROMMESH
   Material comes from the mesh (default).

D3DRMMATERIAL_FROMPARENT
   Material inherited from the parent frame.

D3DRMMATERIAL_FROMFRAME
   Material inherited from the current frame.

Type	**D3DRMPALETTEFLAGS**

Example	`typedef enum _D3DRMPALETTEFLAGS {`
	`D3DRMPALETTE_FREE,`
	`D3DRMPALETTE_READONLY,`
	`D3DRMPALETTE_RESERVED`
	`} D3DRMPALETTEFLAGS;`

Description	Tells how a color may be used in a palette.
Used by	D3DRMPALETTEENTRY.

D3DRMPALETTE_FREE
Renderer may use this entry freely.

D3DRMPALETTE_READONLY
Fixed but may be used by the renderer.

D3DRMPALETTE_RESERVED
May not be used by the renderer.

Type	**D3DRMPROJECTIONTYPE**

Example	`typedef enum _D3DRMPROJECTIONTYPE{`
	`D3DRMPROJECT_PERSPECTIVE,`
	`D3DRMPROJECT_ORTHOGRAPHIC`
	`} D3DRMPROJECTIONTYPE;`

Description	Defines the type of projection used in a Direct3DRMViewport object.
Used by	IDirect3DRMViewport::GetProjection, IDirect3DRMViewport::SetProjection.

D3DRMPROJECT_PERSPECTIVE
The projection is perspective.

D3DRMPROJECT_ORTHOGRAPHIC
The projection is orthographic.

Type	**D3DRMRENDERQUALITY**

Example	`typedef enum _D3DRMSHADEMODE {`
	`D3DRMSHADE_FLAT = 0,`
	`D3DRMSHADE_GOURAUD = 1,`
	`D3DRMSHADE_PHONG= 2,`
	`D3DRMSHADE_MASK = 7,`
	`D3DRMSHADE_MAX = 8`
	`} D3DRMSHADEMODE;`

```
typedef enum _D3DRMLIGHTMODE {
D3DRMLIGHT_OFF = 0 * D3DRMSHADE_MAX,
D3DRMLIGHT_ON = 1 * D3DRMSHADE_MAX,
D3DRMLIGHT_MASK = 7 * D3DRMSHADE_MAX,
D3DRMLIGHT_MAX = 8 * D3DRMSHADE_MAX
} D3DRMLIGHTMODE;
typedef enum _D3DRMFILLMODE {
D3DRMFILL_POINTS = 0 * D3DRMLIGHT_MAX,
D3DRMFILL_WIREFRAME = 1 * D3DRMLIGHT_MAX,
D3DRMFILL_SOLID = 2 * D3DRMLIGHT_MAX,
D3DRMFILL_MASK = 7 * D3DRMLIGHT_MAX,
D3DRMFILL_MAX = 8 * D3DRMLIGHT_MAX
} D3DRMFILLMODE;

typedef DWORD D3DRMRENDERQUALITY;

#define D3DRMRENDER_WIREFRAME
(D3DRMSHADE_FLAT+D3DRMLIGHT_OFF+D3DRMFILL_
WIREFRAME)
#define D3DRMRENDER_UNLITFLAT
(D3DRMSHADE_FLAT+D3DRMLIGHT_OFF+D3DRMFILL_
SOLID)
#define D3DRMRENDER_FLAT
(D3DRMSHADE_FLAT+D3DRMLIGHT_ON+D3DRMFILL_
SOLID)
#define D3DRMRENDER_GOURAUD
(D3DRMSHADE_GOURAUD+D3DRMLIGHT_ON+D3DRMFILL_
SOLID)
#define
D3DRMRENDER_PHONG(D3DRMSHADE_PHONG+D3DRM-
LIGHT_ON+D3DRMFILL_SOLID)
```

Description	Describes shading, lighting, and filling modes.
Used by	Direct3DRMMesh objects.
D3DRMSHADEMODE	Shade mode.
D3DRMLIGHTMODE	Light mode.
D3DRMFILLMODE	Fill mode.

D3DRMRENDER_WIREFRAME
Display edge lines.

D3DRMRENDER_UNLITFLAT
Flat shading, no lighting.

D3DRMRENDER_FLAT Flat shaded.

D3DRMRENDER_GOURAUD
    Gouraud shaded.

D3DRMRENDER_PHONG
    Phong shaded (not supported for DirectX 2).

Type	**D3DRMSHADEMODE**

Example	`typedef enum _D3DRMSHADEMODE {`
	`D3DRMSHADE_FLAT = 0,`
	`D3DRMSHADE_GOURAUD = 1,`
	`D3DRMSHADE_PHONG = 2,`
	`D3DRMSHADE_MASK = 7,`
	`D3DRMSHADE_MAX = 8`
	`} D3DRMSHADEMODE;`

Description	Describes shading modes.
Used by	D3DRMRENDERQUALITY.

Type	**D3DRMSORTMODE**

Example	`typedef enum _D3DRMSORTMODE {`
	`D3DRMSORT_FROMPARENT,`
	`D3DRMSORT_NONE,`
	`D3DRMSORT_FRONTTOBACK,`
	`D3DRMSORT_BACKTOFRONT`
	`}D3DRMSORTMODE;`

Description	Describes how child frames are sorted in a scene.
Used by	IDirect3DRMFrame::GetSortMode, IDirect3DRMFrame::SetSortMode.
Usage	If z-buffering is on, it is faster to have polygons sorted front to back (it is faster if z-buffer compares usually find something already closer on the screen, since it is slower to read/compare/write than just to read/compare). If z-buffering is off, polygons must be sorted back to front (so the closest polygons will be on top).

D3DRMSORT_FROMPARENT
    Child frames inherit the sorting order of their parents. This is the default.

D3DRMSORT_NONE   Child frames are not sorted.

D3DRMSORT_FRONTTOBACK
    Child frames are sorted front to back.

D3DRMSORT_BACKTOFRONT
    Child frames are sorted back to front.

Type	**D3DRMTEXTUREQUALITY**

Example	`typedef enum _D3DRMTEXTUREQUALITY{`
	`D3DRMTEXTURE_NEAREST,`
	`D3DRMTEXTURE_LINEAR,`
	`D3DRMTEXTURE_MIPNEAREST,`
	`D3DRMTEXTURE_MIPLINEAR,`
	`D3DRMTEXTURE_LINEARMIPNEAREST,`
	`D3DRMTEXTURE_LINEARMIPLINEAR`
	`} D3DRMTEXTUREQUALITY;`

Description	Describes the texture filtering quality
Used by	IDirect3DRMDevice::SetTextureQuality, IDirect3DRMDevice::GetTextureQuality.

D3DRMTEXTURE_NEAREST
  Choose the nearest pixel in the texture. Also called point sampling.

D3DRMTEXTURE_LINEAR
  Linearly interpolate the 4 nearest pixels. Also called bilinear filtering.

D3DRMTEXTURE_MIPNEAREST
  Similar to D3DRMTEXTURE_NEAREST but uses the appropriate mipmap instead of the texture. Simple mipmapping.

D3DRMTEXTURE_MIPLINEAR
  Similar to D3DRMTEXTURE_LINEAR but uses the appropriate mipmap instead of the texture. Mipmapping with bilinear filtering on one mipmap.

D3DRMTEXTURE_LINEARMIPNEAREST
  Similar to D3DRMTEXTURE_MIPNEAREST but interpolates between the two nearest mipmaps. Mipmapping with bilinear filtering on two mipmaps.

D3DRMTEXTURE_LINEARMIPLINEAR
  Similar to D3DRMTEXTURE_MIPLINEAR but interpolates between the two nearest mipmaps. Trilinear mipmapping.

Type	**D3DRMUSERVISUALREASON**

Example	`typedef enum _D3DRMUSERVISUALREASON {`
	`D3DRMUSERVISUAL_CANSEE,`
	`D3DRMUSERVISUAL_RENDER`
	`} D3DRMUSERVISUALREASON;`

Description	Tells a UserVisual object why it was called by the renderer.
Used by	D3DRMUSERVISUALCALLBACK.

Chapter 18 Retained Mode Reference

D3DRMUSERVISUAL_CANSEE

The callback should return TRUE if the UserVisual object is visible in the viewport. In this case, the callback uses the device specified in the lpD3DRMview parameter to determine visibility.

D3DRMUSERVISUAL_RENDER

The callback should render the UserVisual element. In this case, the callback uses the device specified in the lpD3DRMDev parameter to do its own immediate mode rendering.

Type	**D3DRMWRAPTYPE**

Example	`typedef enum _D3DRMWRAPTYPE{`
	`D3DRMWRAP_FLAT,`
	`D3DRMWRAP_CYLINDER,`
	`D3DRMWRAP_SPHERE,`
	`D3DRMWRAP_CHROME`
	`} D3DRMWRAPTYPE;`

Description	Describes the wrapping method for a texture around a mesh.
Used by	IDirect3DRM::CreateWrap, IDirect3DRMWrap::Init.

D3DRMWRAP_FLAT   The wrap is flat.

D3DRMWRAP_CYLINDER

The wrap is cylindrical.

D3DRMWRAP_SPHERE

The wrap is spherical.

D3DRMWRAP_CHROME

The wrap allocates texture coordinates so that the texture appears to be reflected onto the objects.

Type	**D3DRMXOFFORMAT**

Example	`typedef enum _D3DRMXOFFORMAT{`
	`D3DRMXOF_BINARY,`
	`D3DRMXOF_COMPRESSED,`
	`D3DRMXOF_TEXT`
	`} D3DRMXOFFORMAT;`

Description	Defines the .x file type.
Used by	IDirect3DRMMeshBuilder::Save.

D3DRMXOF_BINARY   Not currently supported.

D3DRMXOF_COMPRESSED

Not currently supported.

D3DRMXOF_TEXT   File is in text format. This is the only file type that is currently supported.

Type	**D3DRMZBUFFERMODE**

Example	`typedef enum _D3DRMZBUFFERMODE {`
	`D3DRMZBUFFER_FROMPARENT,`
	`D3DRMZBUFFER_ENABLE,`
	`D3DRMZBUFFER_DISABLE`
	`} D3DRMZBUFFERMODE;`

Description	Describes z-buffering enabling.
Used by	IDirect3DRMMesh.

D3DRMZBUFFER_FROMPARENT
　　　　The frame inherits the z-buffer setting from its parent frame. This is the default.

D3DRMZBUFFER_ENABLE
　　　　Z-buffering is enabled.

D3DRMZBUFFER_DISABLE
　　　　Z-buffering is disabled.

Other Types

Type	**D3DRMANIMATIONOPTIONS**

Example	`typedef DWORD D3DRMANIMATIONOPTIONS;`
	`#define D3DRMANIMATION_CLOSED 0x02L`
	`#define D3DRMANIMATION_LINEARPOSITION 0x04L`
	`#define D3DRMANIMATION_OPEN 0x01L`
	`#define D3DRMANIMATION_POSITION 0x00000020L`
	`#define D3DRMANIMATION_SCALEANDROTATION 0x00000010L`
	`#define D3DRMANIMATION_SPLINEPOSITION 0x08L`

Description	Describes animation playback options.
Used by	IDirect3DRMAnimation::GetOptions, IDirect3DRMAnimation::SetOptions.

D3DRMANIMATION_CLOSED
　　　　The animation plays continually, looping back to the beginning whenever it reaches the end.

D3DRMANIMATION_LINEARPOSITION
　　　　The animation's position is set linearly.

D3DRMANIMATION_OPEN
　　　　The animation plays once and stops.

D3DRMANIMATION_POSITION
　　　　The animation's position matrix should overwrite any transformation matrices that could be set by other methods.

D3DRMANIMATION_SCALEANDROTATION
The animation's scale and rotation matrix should overwrite any transformation matrices that could be set by other methods.

D3DRMANIMATION_SPLINEPOSITION
The animation's position is set using splines.

Type	**D3DRMCOLORMODEL**
Example	`typedef D3DCOLORMODEL D3DRMCOLORMODEL;`
Description	Describes the color model.
Used by	D3DCOLORMODEL enumerated type.

Type	**D3DRMLOADOPTIONS**

Example	`typedef DWORD D3DRMLOADOPTIONS;`
	`#define D3DRMLOAD_FROMFILE 0x00L`
	`#define D3DRMLOAD_FROMRESOURCE 0x01L`
	`#define D3DRMLOAD_FROMMEMORY 0x02L`
	`#define D3DRMLOAD_FROMSTREAM 0x03L`
	`#define D3DRMLOAD_BYNAME 0x10L`
	`#define D3DRMLOAD_BYPOSITION 0x20L`
	`#define D3DRMLOAD_BYGUID 0x30L`
	`#define D3DRMLOAD_FIRST 0x40L`
	`#define D3DRMLOAD_INSTANCEBYREFERENCE 0x100L`
	`#define D3DRMLOAD_INSTANCEBYCOPYING 0x200L`

Description	Describes load options.
Used by	IDirect3DRM::Load, IDirect3DRMAnimationSet::Load, IDirect3DRMFrame::Load, IDirect3DRMMeshBuilder::Load.

D3DRMLOAD_FROMFILE
Load from a file. This is the default.

D3DRMLOAD_FROMRESOURCE
Load from a resource. If this flag is specified, the lpvObjSource parameter of the calling Load method must point to a D3DRM-LOADRESOURCE structure.

D3DRMLOAD_FROMMEMORY
Load from memory. If this flag is specified, the lpvObjSource parameter of the calling Load method must point to a D3DRM-LOADMEMORY structure.

D3DRMLOAD_FROMSTREAM
Load from a stream.

D3DRMLOAD_BYNAME
Load using a specified name.

D3DRMLOAD_BYPOSITION
Load using a specified 0-based position (that is, the *n*th object in the file).

D3DRMLOAD_BYGUID Load using a specified GUID.

D3DRMLOAD_FIRST Load the first top-level object of the given type (for example, a mesh if the application calls IDirect3DRMMeshBuilder::Load). This is the default setting.

D3DRMLOAD_INSTANCEBYREFERENCE
Check whether an object already exists with the same name as specified and, if so, use an instance of that object instead of creating a new one.

D3DRMLOAD_INSTANCEBYCOPYING
Check whether an object already exists with the same name as specified and, if so, copy that object.

Each of the Load methods uses an lpvObjSource parameter to specify the source of the object and an lpvObjID parameter to identify the object. The system interprets the contents of the lpvObjSource parameter based on the choice of source flags, and it interprets the contents of the lpvObjID parameter based on the choice of identifier flags.

The instance flags do not change the interpretation of any of the parameters. By using the D3DRMLOAD_INSTANCEBYREFERENCE flag, an application may possibly load the same file twice without creating any new objects. If an object does not have a name, setting the D3DRMLOAD_INSTANCEBYREFERENCE flag has the same effect as setting the D3DRMLOAD_INSTANCEBYCOPYING flag. That is, the loader creates each unnamed object as a new one, even if some of the objects are identical.

Type	**D3DRMMAPPING**

Example	```typedef DWORD D3DRMMAPPING, D3DRMMAPPINGFLAG;```
	 ```static const D3DRMMAPPINGFLAG```
	 ```D3DRMMAP_WRAPU = 1;```
	 ```static const D3DRMMAPPINGFLAG```
	 ```D3DRMMAP_WRAPV = 2;```
	 ```static const D3DRMMAPPINGFLAG```
	 ```D3DRMMAP_PERSPCORRECT = 4;```

Description	Describes how textures are mapped to a group.
Used by	IDirect3DRMMesh::GetGroupMapping, IDirect3DRMMesh::SetGroupMapping.

D3DRMMAPPINGFLAG Type equivalent to D3DRMMAPPING.

D3DRMMAP_WRAPU	Texture wraps in the *u* direction.
D3DRMMAP_WRAPV	Texture wraps in the *v* direction.
D3DRMMAP_PERSPCORRECT	
	Texture wrapping is perspective-corrected.

The D3DRMMAP_WRAPU and D3DRMMAP_WRAPV flags determine how the rasterizer interprets texture coordinates. The rasterizer always interpolates the shortest distance between texture coordinates, that is, a line. The path taken by this line, and the valid values for the *u*- and *v*-coordinates, varies with the use of the wrapping flags. If either or both flags are set, the line can wrap around the texture edge in the *u*- or *v*-direction, as if the texture had a cylindrical or toroidal topology.

Type	**D3DRMMATRIX4D**
Example	`typedef D3DVALUE D3DRMMATRIX4D[4][4];`
Description	Expresses a transformation matrix as an array.
Usage	D3DRMMATRIX4D[*row*][*column*].

Type	**D3DRMSAVEOPTIONS**

Example	`typedef DWORD D3DRMSAVEOPTIONS;`
	`#define D3DRMXOFSAVE_NORMALS 1`
	`#define D3DRMXOFSAVE_TEXTURECOORDINATES 2`
	`#define D3DRMXOFSAVE_MATERIALS 4`
	`#define D3DRMXOFSAVE_TEXTURENAMES 8`
	`#define D3DRMXOFSAVE_ALL 15`

Description	Gives mesh save options.
Used by	IDirect3DRMMeshBuilder::Save.

D3DRMXOFSAVE_NORMALS
  Save normal vectors in addition to the basic geometry.

D3DRMXOFSAVE_TEXTURECOORDINATES
  Save texture coordinates in addition to the basic geometry.

D3DRMXOFSAVE_MATERIALS
  Save materials in addition to the basic geometry.

D3DRMXOFSAVE_TEXTURENAMES
  Save texture names in addition to the basic geometry.

D3DRMXOFSAVE_ALL Save normal vectors, texture coordinates, materials, and texture names in addition to the basic geometry.

Retained Mode Functions

Function	**Direct3DRMCreate**
Example	`HRESULT Direct3DRMCreate(LPDIRECT3DRM FAR * lplpD3DRM);`
Description	Creates an instance of a Direct3DRM object.
Usage	This is the initializing function to start Direct3D retained mode. It returns a pointer to a COM object (a Direct3DRM), which gets the COM ball rolling. This function is linked into your application to avoid your having to load and run OLE in order to create COM objects.
`lplpD3DRM`	Address of a pointer that will be initialized with a valid Direct3DRM pointer if the call succeeds.

Function	**D3DRMColorGetAlpha**
Example	`D3DVALUE D3DRMColorGetAlpha(D3DCOLOR d3drmc);`
Description	Returns the alpha component of a color.

Function	**D3DRMColorGetBlue**
Example	`D3DVALUE D3DRMColorGetBlue(D3DCOLOR d3drmc);`
Description	Returns the blue component of a color.

Function	**D3DRMColorGetGreen**
Example	`D3DVALUE D3DRMColorGetGreen(D3DCOLOR d3drmc);`
Description	Returns the green component of a color.

Function	**D3DRMColorGetRed**
Example	`D3DVALUE D3DRMColorGetRed(D3DCOLOR d3drmc);`
Description	Returns the red component of a color.

Function	**D3DRMCreateColorRGB**
Example	`D3DVALUE D3DRMCreateColorRGB(D3DVALUE red, D3DVALUE green, D3DVALUE blue);`
Description	Creates an RGB color.

Function	**D3DRMCreateColorRGBA**
Example	`D3DVALUE D3DRMCreateColorRGBA(D3DVALUE red, D3DVALUE green, D3DVALUE blue, D3DVALUE alpha);`

Description	Creates an RGB color with alpha.
Function	**D3DRMFREEFUNCTION**
Example	`typedef VOID (*D3DRMFREEFUNCTION)(LPVOID lpArg);` `typedef D3DRMFREEFUNCTION *LPD3DRMFREEFUNCTION;`
Description	Application-defined function to free memory. You can define your own memory functions if you do not want to use standard C runtime routines.
`lpArg`	Address of application-defined data.
Function	**D3DRMMALLOCFUNCTION**
Example	`typedef LPVOID (*D3DRMMALLOCFUNCTION)(DWORD dwSize);` `typedef D3DRMMALLOCFUNCTION *LPD3DRMMALLOC-FUNCTION;`
Description	Allocates memory. This function is application-defined. It returns the address of the allocated memory if successful or 0 otherwise.
`dwSize`	Specifies the size, in bytes, the memory that will be allocated.
Function	**D3DRMMatrixFromQuaternion**
Example	`void D3DRMMatrixFromQuaternion (D3DRMMATRIX4D mat,LPD3DRMQUATERNION lpquat);`
Description	Calculates the matrix for the rotation that a unit quaternion represents.
`mat`	Address that will be set to the calculated matrix when the function returns. (The D3DRMMATRIX4D type is an array.)
`lpquat`	Address of the D3DRMQUATERNION structure.
Function	**D3DRMQuaternionFromRotation**
Example	`LPD3DRMQUATERNION 3DRMQuaternionFromRotation(LPD3DRMQUATERNION lpquat, LPD3DVECTOR lpv, D3DVALUE theta);`
Description	Returns a unit quaternion that represents a rotation of a specified number of radians around the given axis. It returns the address of the unit quaternion that was passed as the first parameter if successful or 0 otherwise.
`lpquat`	Address of a D3DRMQUATERNION structure that will be set to the result of the operation.
`lpv`	Address of a D3DVECTOR structure specifying the axis of rotation.

`theta`	Number of radians to rotate around the axis specified by the lpv parameter.
Function	**D3DRMQuaternionMultiply**
Example	`LPD3DRMQUATERNION D3DRMQuaternionMultiply(LPD3DRMQUATERNION lpq, LPD3DRMQUATERNION lpa, LPD3DRMQUATERNION lpb);`
Description	Calculates the product of two quaternions. It returns the address of the quaternion that was passed as the first parameter if successful or 0 otherwise.
`lpq`	Address of the D3DRMQUATERNION structure that will be set to the product of the multiplication.
`lpa` and `lpb`	Addresses of the D3DRMQUATERNION structures that will be multiplied together.
Function	**D3DRMQuaternionSlerp**
Example	`LPD3DRMQUATERNION D3DRMQuaternionSlerp(LPD3DRMQUATERNION lpq, LPD3DRMQUATERNION lpa, LPD3DRMQUATERNION lpb, D3DVALUE alpha);`
Description	Interpolates between two quaternion structures, using spherical linear interpolation. Returns the address of the quaternion that was passed as the first parameter if successful, or zero otherwise.
`lpq`	Address of the D3DRMQUATERNION structure that will be set to the interpolation.
`lpa` and `lpb`	Addresses of the D3DRMQUATERNION structures that are used as the starting and ending points for the interpolation, respectively.
`alpha`	Value between 0 and 1 that specifies how far to interpolate between lpa and lpb.
Function	**D3DRMREALLOCFUNCTION**
Example	`typedef LPVOID (*D3DRMREALLOCFUNCTION) (LPVOID lpArg, DWORD dwSize); typedef D3DRMREALLOCFUNCTION *LPD3DRMREALLOCFUNCTION;`
Description	Reallocates memory. This function is application-defined. Returns an address of the reallocated memory if successful, or zero otherwise.
`lpArg`	Address of application-defined data.
`dwSize`	Size, in bytes, of the reallocated memory.

Function	**D3DRMVectorAdd**
Example	`LPD3DVECTOR D3DRMVectorAdd(LPD3DVECTOR lpd, LPD3DVECTOR lps1, LPD3DVECTOR lps2);`
Description	Adds two vectors. Returns the address of the vector that was passed as the first parameter if successful, or zero otherwise.
`lpd`	Address of a D3DVECTOR structure that will be set to the result of the addition.
`lps1` and `lps2`	Addresses of the D3DVECTOR structures that will be added together.
Function	**D3DRMVectorCrossProduct**
Example	`LPD3DVECTOR D3DRMVectorCrossProduct(LPD3DVECTOR lpd, LPD3DVECTOR lps1, LPD3DVECTOR lps2);`
Description	Calculates the cross product of the two vector arguments. Returns the address of the vector that was passed as the first parameter if successful, or zero otherwise.
`lpd`	Address of a D3DVECTOR structure that will be set to the result of the cross product.
`lps1` and `lps2`	Addresses of the D3DVECTOR structures from which the cross product is produced.
Function	**D3DRMVectorDotProduct**
Example	`D3DVALUE D3DRMVectorDotProduct(LPD3DVECTOR lps1, LPD3DVECTOR lps2);`
Description	Returns the vector dot product. Returns the result of the dot product if successful, or zero otherwise.
`lps1` and `lps2`	Addresses of the D3DVECTOR structures from which the dot product is produced.
Function	**D3DRMVectorModulus**
Example	`D3DVALUE D3DRMVectorModulus(LPD3DVECTOR lpv);`
Description	Returns the length of a vector (sqrt(x*x + y*y + z*z)). Returns the length of the D3DVECTOR structure if successful, or zero otherwise.
`lpv`	Address of the D3DVECTOR structure whose length is returned.
Function	**D3DRMVectorNormalize**

Example	`LPD3DVECTOR D3DRMVectorNormalize(LPD3DVECTOR lpv);`
Description	Scales a vector so that its length is 1. Returns the address of the vector that was passed as the first parameter if successful, or zero if an error occurs. Passing this method a vector of zero length would be an error.
`lpv`	Address of a D3DVECTOR structure that will be set to the result of the scaling operation.

Function	**D3DRMVectorRandom**
Example	`LPD3DVECTOR D3DRMVectorRandom(LPD3DVECTOR lpd);`
Description	Returns a random unit vector. Returns the address of the vector that was passed as the first parameter if successful, or zero otherwise.
`lpd`	Address of a D3DVECTOR structure that will be set to a random unit vector.

Function	**D3DRMVectorReflect**
Example	`LPD3DVECTOR D3DRMVectorReflect(LPD3DVECTOR lpd, LPD3DVECTOR lpRay, LPD3DVECTOR lpNorm);`
Description	Reflects a ray about a given normal. Returns the address of the vector that was passed as the first parameter if successful, or zero otherwise.
`lpd`	Address of a D3DVECTOR structure that will be set to the result of the operation.
`lpRay`	Address of a D3DVECTOR structure that will be reflected about a normal.
`lpNorm`	Address of a D3DVECTOR structure specifying the normal about which the vector specified in lpRay is reflected.

Function	**D3DRMVectorRotate**
Example	`LPD3DVECTOR D3DRMVectorRotate(LPD3DVECTOR lpr, LPD3DVECTOR lpv, LPD3DVECTOR lpaxis, D3DVALUE theta);`
Description	Rotates a vector around a given axis. Returns the address of the vector that was passed as the first parameter if successful, or zero otherwise.
`lpr`	Address of a D3DVECTOR structure that will be set to the result of the operation.
`lpv`	Address of a D3DVECTOR structure that will be rotated around the given axis.

Chapter 18 Retained Mode Reference

`lpaxis`	Address of a D3DVECTOR structure that is the axis of rotation.
`theta`	The rotation in radians.
Function	**D3DRMVectorScale**
Example	`LPD3DVECTOR D3DRMVectorScale(LPD3DVECTOR lpd, LPD3DVECTOR lps, D3DVALUE factor);`
Description	Scales a vector uniformly in all three axes. Returns the address of the vector that was passed as the first parameter if successful, or zero otherwise.
`lpd`	Address of a D3DVECTOR structure that will be set to the result of the operation.
`lps`	Address of a D3DVECTOR structure that this function scales.
`factor`	Scaling factor. A value of 1 does not change the scaling; a value of 2 doubles it, and so on.
Function	**D3DRMVectorSubtract**
Example	`LPD3DVECTOR D3DRMVectorSubtract(LPD3DVECTOR lpd, LPD3DVECTOR lps1, LPD3DVECTOR lps2);`
Description	Subtracts two vectors. Returns the address of the vector that was passed as the first parameter if successful, or zero otherwise.
`lpd`	Address of a D3DVECTOR structure that will be set to the result of the operation.
`lps1`	Address of the D3DVECTOR structure from which lps2 is subtracted.
`lps2`	Address of the D3DVECTOR structure that is subtracted from lps1.

Callback Functions

Function	**D3DRMDEVICEPALETTECALLBACK**
Example	`void (*D3DRMDEVICEPALETTECALLBACK) (LPDIRECT3DRMDEVICE lpDirect3DRMDev, LPVOID lpArg, DWORD dwIndex, LONG red, LONG green, LONG blue);`
Description	Enumerates palette entries. This callback function is application-defined.
`lpDirect3DRMDev`	Address of the IDirect3DRMDevice interface for this device.
`lpArg`	Address of application-defined data passed to this callback function.
`dwIndex`	Index of the palette entry being described.

red, green, and blue	Red, green, and blue components of the color at the given index in the palette.
Function	**D3DRMFRAMEMOVECALLBACK**
Example	`void (*D3DRMFRAMEMOVECALLBACK) (LPDIRECT3DRMFRAME lpD3DRMFrame, LPVOID lpArg, D3DVALUE delta);`
Used by	IDirect3DRMFrame::AddMoveCallback, IDirect3DRMFrame::DeleteMoveCallback.
Description	Enables an application to apply customized algorithms when a frame is moved or updated. You can use this callback function to compensate for changing frame rates. This callback function is application-defined, and returns no value. When determining the order in which to call callback functions, the system searches the objects highest in the hierarchy first, and then calls their callback functions in the order in which they were created.
lpD3DRMFrame	Address of the Direct3DRMFrame object that is being moved.
lpArg	Address of application-defined data passed to this callback function.
delta	Amount of change to apply to the movement. There are two components to the change in position of a frame: linear and rotational. The change in each component is equal to *velocity_of_component* $\leftrightarrow$ *delta*. Although either or both of these velocities can be set relative to any frame, the system automatically converts them to velocities relative to the parent frame for the purpose of applying time deltas.
Function	**D3DRMLOADCALLBACK**
Example	`void (*D3DRMLOADCALLBACK) (LPDIRECT3DRMOBJECT lpObject, REFIID ObjectGuid, LPVOID lpArg);`
Used by	IDirect3DRM::Load.
Description	Loads objects named in a call to the method. This callback function is application-defined.
lpObject	Address of the Direct3DRMObject being loaded.
ObjectGuid	GUID of the object being loaded.
lpArg	Address of application-defined data passed to this callback function.
Function	**D3DRMLOADTEXTURECALLBACK**
Example	`HRESULT (*D3DRMLOADTEXTURECALLBACK) (char *tex_name, void *lpArg, LPDIRECT3DRMTEXTURE * lpD3DRMTex);`
Used by	IDirect3DRM::Load, other load methods.

Description	Loads texture maps from a file or resource named in a call to one of the Load methods. Application-defined function to implement support for textures that are not in the Windows bitmap (.bmp) or Portable Pixmap (.ppm) P6 format.
`tex_name`	Address of a string containing the name of the texture.
`lpArg`	Address of application-specific data.
`lpD3DRMTex`	Address of the Direct3DRMTexture object.
Function	**D3DRMOBJECTCALLBACK**
Example	`void (*D3DRMOBJECTCALLBACK)(LPDIRECT3DRMOBJECT lpD3DRMobj, LPVOID lpArg);`
Used by	IDirect3DRM::EnumerateObjects.
Description	Application-defined function for processing each enumerated object.
`lpD3DRMobj`	Address of an IDirect3DRMObject interface for the object being enumerated. The application must call the Release method for each enumerated object.
`lpArg`	Address of application-defined data passed to this callback function.
Function	**D3DRMUPDATECALLBACK**
Example	`void (*D3DRMUPDATECALLBACK)(LPDIRECT3DRMDEVICE lpobj, LPVOID lpArg, int x, LPD3DRECT d3dRectUpdate);`
Used by	IDirect3DRMDevice::AddUpdateCallback.
Description	Application-defined function called whenever the device changes.
`lpobj`	Address of the Direct3DRMDevice object to which this callback function applies.
`lpArg`	Address of application-defined data passed to this callback function.
`x`	Number of rectangles specified in the d3dRectUpdate parameter.
`d3dRectUpdate`	Array of one or more D3DRECT structures that describe the area to be updated. The coordinates are specified in device units.
Function	**D3DRMUSERVISUALCALLBACK**
Example	`int (*D3DRMUSERVISUALCALLBACK)(LPDIRECT3DRM-USERVISUAL lpD3DRMUV, LPVOID lpArg, D3DRMUSERVISUALREASON lpD3DRMUVreason, LPDIRECT3DRMDEVICE lpD3DRMDev, LPDIRECT3DRMVIEWPORT lpD3DRMview);`

Description	Called to tell a UserVisual object that it should execute the execute buffer. It should return TRUE if the lpD3DRMUVreason parameter is D3DRMUSERVISUAL_CANSEE and the UserVisual object is visible in the viewport; returns FALSE otherwise. If the lpD3DRMUVreason parameter is D3DRMUSERVISUAL_RENDER, the return value is application-defined. It is always safe to return TRUE.
`lpD3DRMUV`	Address of the Direct3DRMUserVisual object.
`lpArg`	Address of application-defined data passed to this callback function.
`lpD3DRMUVreason`	An AD3DRMUSERVISUALREASON enumerated type.
`lpD3DRMDev`	Address of a Direct3DRMDevice object used to render the Direct3DRMUserVisual object.
`lpD3DRMview`	Address of a Direct3DRMViewport object used to determine whether the Direct3DRMUserVisual object is visible.

RM Return Values

D3DRM_OK	No error.
D3DRMERR_BADALLOC	Out of memory.
D3DRMERR_BADDEVICE	Device is not compatible with renderer.
D3DRMERR_BADFILE	Data file is corrupt.
D3DRMERR_BADMAJORVERSION	Bad DLL major version.
D3DRMERR_BADMINORVERSION	Bad DLL minor version.
D3DRMERR_BADOBJECT	Object expected in argument.
D3DRMERR_BADTYPE	Bad argument type passed.
D3DRMERR_BADVALUE	Bad argument value passed.
D3DRMERR_FACEUSED	Face already used in a mesh.
D3DRMERR_FILENOTFOUND	File cannot be opened.
D3DRMERR_NOTDONEYET	Unimplemented.
D3DRMERR_NOTFOUND	Object not found in specified place.
D3DRMERR_UNABLETOEXECUTE	Unable to carry out procedure.

Chapter 19

Immediate Mode Reference

To use the Direct 3D immediate mode, you need to set up the immediate mode objects, build an execute buffer, and pass it through the transform, lighting, and rasterization modules. But how things work can get very confusing. A starting point is to learn the execute buffer instructions. The guts of the immediate mode complexities, however, are in low-level flags, so be sure to examine D3DDEVICEDESC.

Because immediate mode objects are COM objects, all of them support the AddRef, QueryInterface, and Release methods in exactly the same way as described in the retained mode section. (They also support an Initialize method for COM compatibility. However, they are initialized upon creation. This means Initialize will always return an error if you call it—so why bother?)

IDirect3D

Description	The main manager object of the immediate mode.
How to create	It's an interface off the DirectDraw object.
	```lpDirectDraw->QueryInterface(```
	```IID_IDirect3D, // IDirect3D interface ID```
	```lpD3D); // Address of a Direct3D object```
Usage	Create other IM objects; find devices.
What the object contains	A list of viewports, lights, materials, and devices.
What are handles?	The data resides on the hardware and can be manipulated by it.

Table 19-1. IDirect3D methods

Category	Methods
Creation	CreateLight CreateMaterial CreateViewport
Enumeration and Initialization	EnumDevices FindDevice

IDirect3DDevice

Description	Represents the display device.
How to create	Call IDirect3D::QueryInterface on the DirectDraw surface object that was created as a 3D-capable, back-buffer surface. You then need to initialize the device object with IDirect3DDevice::Initialize.
Matrix handles	Reference transformation matrices indirectly by handle instead of by pointer to a matrix data structure or by a COM object that encapsulates a matrix. This is to isolate you from internal optimizations that may be done on the matrix that would be lost if you could directly set the values of the matrix. (For example, the immediate mode might check to see if some of the values in the matrix were 1, in which case it would know to skip certain multiply operations.) You create a new matrix and get a handle to it with IDirect3DDevice::CreateMatrix. Thereafter, you set the matrix by passing this handle and an actual matrix data structure to IDirect3DDevice::SetMatrix.

Table 19-2. IDirect3DDevice methods

Category	Methods
Execution	CreateExecuteBuffer Execute
Information	EnumTextureFormats GetCaps GetDirect3D GetPickRecords GetStats
Matrices	CreateMatrix DeleteMatrix GetMatrix SetMatrix

Chapter 19 Immediate Mode Reference

Table 19-2. IDirect3DDevice methods *(continued)*

Category	Methods
Miscellaneous	Pick SwapTextureHandles
Scenes	BeginScene EndScene
Viewports	AddViewport DeleteViewport NextViewport

IDirect3DExecuteBuffer

Description	Manages an execute buffer.
What is an execute buffer?	A block of memory that contains a list of vertex data and instructions (opcodes) about how to render it. The list may be read by hardware DMA into VRAM for processing. All display primitives in the buffer that have indices to vertices must also have those vertices in the same buffer.
How to create	Call lpD3DDevice::CreateExecuteBuffer with a D3DEXECUTE-BUFFERDESC data structure that specifies the execute buffer's size and address and whether it is in system or video memory.
Primitives	Geometry primitives (triangles, points, and lines) described in the buffer must have their vertices described in the same buffer.
How to change	Call IDirect3DExecuteBuffer::Lock to gain access (you lock it to your use).
Where's the data?	Not in the ExecuteBuffer object. The execute buffer COM object contains only pointers and some descriptions of the format of the buffer. The contents of the buffer are dynamically allocated and can reside in the memory of the graphics card.

Table 19-3. IDirect3DExecuteBuffer methods

Category	Methods
Execute Data	GetExecuteData SetExecuteData
Lock and Unlock	Lock Unlock
Miscellaneous	Optimize Validate

IDirect3DLight

Description	An immediate mode light.
How to create	IDirect3D::CreateLight.
How to set values	You pass the object the address of a D3DLight data structure with a call to IDirect3DLight:SetLight.
How to show light	You add the light to a viewport with IDirect3DViewport::AddLight:

```
lpDirect3D->CreateLight(
lplpDirect3DLight,   // Address of a new light
pUnkOuter);  // NULL
```

Table 19-4. IDirect3DLight methods

Category	Methods
Get and Set	GetLight
	SetLight

IDirect3DMaterial

Description   An immediate mode material.

Table 19-5. IDirect3DMaterial methods

Category	Methods
Color Reservation	Reserve
	Unreserve
Materials	GetMaterial
	SetMaterial
Miscellaneous	GetHandle

IDirect3DTexture

Description	Direct3D textures are not distinct object types, but rather another interface of DirectDrawSurface objects. The following example obtains a Direct3D texture interface from a DirectDrawSurface object.
How to create	Create a DirectDraw surface.
How to get this interface	Call IDirect3D::QueryInterface on the DirectDraw surface object that was created as a texture map, specifying IID_IDirect3DTexture.

```
LPDIRECTDRAWSURFACE lpDDSurface;
LPDIRECT3DTEXTURE   lpD3DTexture;
ddres = lpDD->CreateSurface(&ddsd,
&lpDDSurface, NULL);
ddres = lpDDSurface->QueryInterface(IID_
IDirect3DTexture, &lpD3DTexture);
```

Table 19-6. IDirect3DTexture methods

Category	Methods
Handles	GetHandle
Loading	Load Unload
Palette Information	PaletteChanged

IDirect3DViewport

Description	Represents the screen region to which to draw.
How to create	Call IDirect3D::CreateViewport. Then attach the viewport to a device with IDirect3DDevice::AddViewport.
Usage	Get and set backgrounds and viewports; add and delete lights; transform vertices.
How to set values	Pass the viewport object a D3DVIEWPORT data structure with IDirect3DViewport::SetViewport.

Table 19-7. IDirect3DViewport methods

Category	Methods
Backgrounds	GetBackground GetBackgroundDepth SetBackground SetBackgroundDepth
Lights	AddLight DeleteLight LightElements NextLight
Materials and Viewports	Clear GetViewport SetViewport
Transformation	TransformVertices

IDirect3D Interface

Object::Method	**IDirect3D::CreateLight**
Example	`HRESULT CreateLight(LPDIRECT3DLIGHT* lplpDirect3Dlight, IUnknown* pUnkOuter);`
Description	Creates a Direct3DLight object. Use IDirect3DViewport::AddLight to attach this light to a viewport.
`lplpDirect3DLight`	Address that will be filled with a pointer to an IDirect3DLight interface.
`pUnkOuter`	Must by NULL (provided for future compatibility with COM aggregation).
Object::Method	**IDirect3D::CreateMaterial**
Example	`HRESULT CreateMaterial(LPDIRECT3DMATERIAL* lplpDirect3DMaterial, IUnknown* pUnkOuter);`
Description	Allocates a Direct3DMaterial object.
`lplpDirect3D-Material`	Address that will be filled with a pointer to an IDirect3DMaterial interface.
`pUnkOuter`	Must by NULL (provided for future compatibility with COM aggregation).
Object::Method	**IDirect3D::CreateViewport**
Example	`HRESULT CreateViewport(LPDIRECT3DVIEWPORT* lplpD3DViewport, IUnknown* pUnkOuter);`
Description	Creates a Direct3DViewport object. Use IDirect3DDevice::AddViewport to associate the viewport with a Direct3DDevice object.
`lplpD3DViewport`	Address that will be filled with a pointer to an IDirect3DViewport interface.
`pUnkOuter`	Must by NULL (provided for future compatibility with COM aggregation).
Object::Method	**IDirect3D::EnumDevices**
Example	`HRESULT EnumDevices(LPD3DENUMDEVICESCALLBACK pEnumDevicesCallback, LPVOID lpUserArg);`
Description	Enumerates all Direct3D device drivers installed on the system.

lpEnumDevices-Callback	Address of the D3DENUMDEVICESCALLBACK callback function that will be called for each match.
lpUserArg	Address of application-defined data passed to the callback function.
Object::Method	**IDirect3D::FindDevice**
Example	`HRESULT FindDevice(LPD3DFINDDEVICESEARCH lpD3DFDS, LPD3DFINDDEVICERESULT lpD3DFDR);`
Description	Finds a device that has specified characteristics and retrieves a description of it.
lpD3DFDS	Address of the D3DFINDDEVICESEARCH structure describing the device to be located.
lpD3DFDR	Address of the D3DFINDDEVICERESULT structure describing the device if it is found.

IDirect3DDevice Interface

Object::Method	**IDirect3DDevice::AddViewport**
Example	`HRESULT AddViewport(LPDIRECT3DVIEWPORT lpDirect3DViewport);`
Description	Attaches the viewport to the device. Multiple viewports can be attached to a device.
lpDirect3DViewport	Address of IDirect3DViewport interface to be associated with the Direct3DDevice object.
Object::Method	**IDirect3DDevice::BeginScene**
Example	`HRESULT BeginScene();`
Description	Begins a scene. You must call this method before you start rendering and then call IDirect3DDevice::EndScene when rendering is complete.
Object::Method	**IDirect3DDevice::CreateExecuteBuffer**
Example	`HRESULT CreateExecuteBuffer(LPDIRECT3DEXECUTE-BUFFERDESC lpDesc, LPDIRECT3DEXECUTEBUFFER* lplpDirect3DExecute-Buffer, IUnknown* pUnkOuter);`
Description	Creates an ExecuteBuffer object. The Create method does not necessarily allocate memory for the execute buffer itself; you can pass information about the execute buffer in the D3DEXECUTE-

BUFFERDESC structure, including the size and address of the block of memory that you want to use for the execute buffer. At a minimum, you must specify the size of the execute buffer. If you specify DEBCAPS_VIDEO_MEMORY in the capabilities member, Direct3D will attempt to keep the execute buffer in video memory.

You can move a memory block for the execute buffer by calling IDirect3DExecuteBuffer::Lock. You then change the contents of EXECUTEBUFFERDESC structure.

`lpDesc` Address of a D3DEXECUTEBUFFERDESC structure that describes the Direct3DExecuteBuffer object to be created. In this structure, you must at least specify the size of the execute buffer.

`lplpDirect3D-ExecuteBuffer` Address of a pointer that will be filled with the address of the new Direct3DExecuteBuffer object.

`pUnkOuter` Must by NULL (provided for future compatibility with COM aggregation).

Object::Method	**IDirect3DDevice::CreateMatrix**
Example	`HRESULT CreateMatrix(LPD3DMATRIXHANDLE lpD3DMatHandle);`
Description	Creates a matrix. You set the matrix with IDirect3DDevice::SetMatrix.
`lpD3DMatHandle`	Address of a variable that will contain a handle to the matrix that is created. The call will fail if a buffer of at least the size of the matrix cannot be created.
Object::Method	**IDirect3DDevice::DeleteMatrix**
Example	`HRESULT DeleteMatrix(D3DMATRIXHANDLE d3dMatHandle);`
Description	Deletes a matrix handle.
`d3dMatHandle`	Matrix handle to be deleted.
Object::Method	**IDirect3DDevice::DeleteViewport**
Example	`HRESULT DeleteViewport(LPDIRECT3DVIEWPORT lpDirect3DViewport);`
Description	Unattaches the viewport from the device.
`lpDirect3DViewport`	Address of the Direct3DViewport object to be detached.
Object::Method	**IDirect3DDevice::EndScene**
Example	`HRESULT EndScene();`

Chapter 19 Immediate Mode Reference

Description	Ends a scene that was begun by calling the IDirect3DDevice::BeginScene method.
Object::Method	**IDirect3DDevice::EnumTextureFormats**

Example	`HRESULT EnumTextureFormats(`
	`LPD3DENUMTEXTUREFORMATSCALLBACK`
	`lpd3dEnumTextureProc,`
	`LPVOID lpArg);`

Description	Returns a list of supported texture formats.
`lpd3dEnum-TextureProc`	Address of the D3DENUMTEXTUREFORMATSCALLBACK callback function that the enumeration procedure will call for each texture format.
`lpArg`	Address of application-defined data passed to the callback function.
Object::Method	**IDirect3DDevice::Execute**

Example	`HRESULT Execute(LPDIRECT3DEXECUTEBUFFER`
	`lpDirect3DExecuteBuffer,`
	`LPDIRECT3DVIEWPORT lpDirect3DViewport, DWORD`
	`dwFlags);`

Description	Executes a buffer (i.e., submits the contents of the execute buffer to the renderer for processing).
`lpDirect3D-ExecuteBuffer`	Address of the execute buffer to be executed.
`lpDirect3DViewport`	Address of the Direct3DViewport object that describes the transformation context into which the execute buffer will be rendered.
`dwFlags`	Flags specifying whether objects in the buffer should be clipped: D3DEXECUTE_CLIPPED means clip any primitives in the buffer that are outside or partially outside the viewport. D3DEXECUTE_UNCLIPPED means all primitives in the buffer are contained within the viewport.
Object::Method	**IDirect3DDevice::GetCaps**

Example	`HRESULT GetCaps(LPD3DDEVICEDESC`
	`lpD3DHWDevDesc,`
	`LPD3DDEVICEDESC lpD3DHELDevDesc);`

Description	Returns the capabilities of the Direct3DDevice object. To get the capabilities of the display device, call IDirectDraw::GetCaps.
`lpD3DHWDevDesc`	Address of a D3DDEVICEDESC structure that will contain the hardware features of the device.
`lpD3DHELDevDesc`	Address of a D3DDEVICEDESC structure that will contain the software emulation being provided.

Object::Method	**IDirect3DDevice::GetDirect3D**
Example	`HRESULT GetDirect3D(LPDIRECT3D* lpD3D);`
Description	Returns the current IDirect3D interface.
`lpD3D`	Address that will contain the interface when the method returns.
Object::Method	**IDirect3DDevice::GetMatrix**
Example	`HRESULT GetMatrix(D3DMATRIXHANDLE lpD3DMatHandle, LPD3DMATRIX lpD3DMatrix);`
Description	Returns a matrix from a matrix handle.
`lpD3DMatHandle`	Address of a variable that contains the handle of a matrix to be returned.
`lpD3DMatrix`	Address of a D3DMATRIX structure that contains the matrix when the method returns.
Object::Method	**IDirect3DDevice::GetPickRecords**
Example	`HRESULT GetPickRecords(LPDWORD lpCount, LPD3DPICKRECORD lpD3DPickRec);`
Description	Returns the pick records for a device. You call this method twice, after first calling IDirect3DDevice::Pick. In the first call, you set the second parameter (lpD3DPickRec) to NULL, and the first parameter returns a count of all relevant D3DPICKRECORD structures. You then allocate sufficient memory for those structures and call the method again, specifying the newly allocated memory for the second parameter.
`lpCount`	Address of a variable that contains the number of D3DPICKRECORD structures to return.
`lpD3DPickRec`	Address that will contain an array of D3DPICKRECORD structures when the method returns.
Object::Method	**IDirect3DDevice::GetStats**
Example	`HRESULT GetStats(LPD3DSTATS lpD3DStats);`
Description	Returns the number of triangles, lines, points, and spans drawn since the device was created.
`lpD3DStats`	Address of a D3DSTATS structure that will be filled with the statistics.

Object::Method	**IDirect3DDevice::Initialize**

Example	`HRESULT Initialize(LPDIRECT3D lpd3d,`
	`LPGUID lpGUID,`
	`LPD3DDEVICEDESC lpd3ddvdesc);`

Description	Initializes a device. To find the values to put in 3DDEVICEDESC, use IDirect3D::EnumDevices or IDirect3D::FindDevice.
`lpd3d`	Address of the Direct3D device to use as an initializer.
`lpGUID`	Address of the GUID used as the interface identifier.
`lpd3ddvdesc`	Address of a D3DDEVICEDESC structure describing the Direct3DDevice object to be initialized.
Object::Method	**IDirect3DDevice::NextViewport**

Example	`HRESULT NextViewport(LPDIRECT3DVIEWPORT`
	`lpDirect3DViewport,`
	`LPDIRECT3DVIEWPORT* lplpDirect3DViewport,`
	`DWORD dwFlags);`

Description	Walks through the list of viewport objects attached to the device.
`lpDirect3DViewport`	Address of a viewport in the list of viewports associated with this Direct3DDevice object.
`lplpDirect3D-Viewport`	Address of the next viewport in the list of viewports associated with this Direct3DDevice object.
`dwFlags`	Flags specifying which viewport in the list to get: D3DNEXT_NEXT (the default), D3DNEXT_HEAD, or D3DNEXT_TAIL.
Object::Method	**IDirect3DDevice::Pick**

Example	`HRESULT Pick(LPDIRECT3DEXECUTEBUFFER`
	`lpDirect3DExecuteBuffer,`
	`LPDIRECT3DVIEWPORT lpDirect3DViewport,`
	`DWORD dwFlags,`
	`LPD3DRECT lpRect);`

Description	Executes a buffer without performing any rendering, but returns a z-ordered list of offsets to the primitives that cover the rectangle specified by lpRect. This call will fail if the execute buffer object is locked (will return the error D3DERR_EXECUTE_LOCKED). If the x1 and x2 members of the structure specified in the lpRect parameter are equal, and the y1 and y2 members are equal, a single pixel is used for picking. The coordinates are specified in device-pixel space.

	All Direct3DExecuteBuffer objects must be attached to a Direct3DDevice object in order for this method to succeed.
`lpDirect3D-ExecuteBuffer`	Address of an execute buffer from which the z-ordered list is retrieved.
`lpDirect3DViewport`	Address of a viewport in the list of viewports associated with this Direct3DDevice object.
`dwFlags`	No flags are currently defined.
`lpRect`	Address of a D3DRECT structure specifying the range of device coordinates to be picked.
Object::Method	**IDirect3DDevice::SetMatrix**
Example	`HRESULT SetMatrix(D3DMATRIXHANDLE d3dMatHandle, LPD3DMATRIX lpD3DMatrix);`
Description	Applies a matrix to a matrix handle. Transformations inside the execute buffer include a handle of a matrix. The IDirect3DDevice::SetMatrix method enables an application to change this matrix without having to lock and unlock the execute buffer.
`d3dMatHandle`	Matrix handle to be set.
`lpD3DMatrix`	Address of a D3DMATRIX structure that describes the matrix to be set.
Object::Method	**IDirect3DDevice::SwapTextureHandles**
Example	`HRESULT SwapTextureHandles(LPDIRECT3DTEXTURE lpD3DTex1, LPDIRECT3DTEXTURE lpD3DTex2);`
Description	Swaps two texture handles. This is useful if you want to change all the textures in a complicated object.
`lpD3DTex1` and `lpD3DTex2`	Addresses of the textures whose handles will be swapped when the method returns.

IDirect3DExecuteBuffer Interface

Object::Method	**IDirect3DExecuteBuffer::GetExecuteData**
Example	`HRESULT GetExecuteData(LPD3DEXECUTEDATA lpData);`
Description	Returns the execute data state of the Direct3DExecuteBuffer object. The execute data is used to describe the contents of the Direct3DExecuteBuffer object. This method will fail if the execute buffer object is locked (will return D3DERR_EXECUTE_LOCKED).

lpData	Address of a D3DEXECUTEDATA structure that will be filled with the current execute data state of the Direct3DExecuteBuffer object.
Object::Method	**IDirect3DExecuteBuffer::Lock**
Example	`HRESULT Lock(LPD3DEXECUTEBUFFERDESC lpDesc);`
Description	Obtains a direct pointer to the commands in the execute buffer. Will fail if the execute buffer object is locked (D3DERR_EXECUTE_LOCKED) or if a IDirect3DDevice::Execute call has not yet completed (DDERR_WASSTILL DRAWING).
lpDesc	Address of a D3DEXECUTEBUFFERDESC structure. When the method returns, the lpData member will be set to point to the actual data the application has access to. This data may reside in system or video memory and is specified by the dwCaps member. The application may use the IDirect3DExecuteBuffer::Lock method to request that Direct3D move the data between system or video memory.
Object::Method	**IDirect3DExecuteBuffer::Optimize**
Example	`HRESULT Optimize();`
Description	Not currently supported.
Object::Method	**IDirect3DExecuteBuffer::SetExecuteData**
Example	`HRESULT SetExecuteData(LPD3DEXECUTEDATA lpData);`
Description	Sets the execute data state of the Direct3DExecuteBuffer object. The execute data is used to describe the contents of the Direct3D-ExecuteBuffer object. This method will fail if the execute buffer object is locked.
lpData	Address of a D3DEXECUTEDATA structure that describes the execute buffer layout.
Object::Method	**IDirect3DExecuteBuffer::Unlock**
Example	`HRESULT Unlock();`
Description	Releases the direct pointer to the commands in the execute buffer. This must be done prior to calling the IDirect3DDevice::Execute method for the buffer, and the method will fail if the buffer is not already locked (D3DERR_EXECUTE_NOT_LOCKED).
Object::Method	**IDirect3DExecuteBuffer::Validate**
Example	`HRESULT Validate(LPDWORD lpdwOffset, LPD3DVALIDATECALLBACK lpFunc, LPVOID lpUserArg, DWORD dwReserved);`

Description	A debugging routine that checks an execute buffer and returns an offset into the buffer when any errors are encountered. The callback function specified in the lpFunc parameter is called whenever an error is detected in the execute buffer. The callback function is passed the value specified in lpUserArg and the offset is passed into the execute buffer where the error was detected. This method will fail if the execute buffer object is locked (D3DERR_EXECUTE_LOCKED).
`lpdwOffset`	Address of a variable that will be filled with the offset into the execute buffer at which an error was first detected. This parameter is filled in only if NULL is specified for the lpFunc parameter. If a callback function is specified for lpFunc, the offset for each error is passed to the callback function and the lpdwOffset parameter is not set.
`lpFunc`	Address of an application-defined D3DVALIDATECALLBACK callback function. If this parameter is NULL, checking stops when the first error is detected.
`lpUserArg`	Address of application-defined data passed to the callback function.
`dwReserved`	Reserved for future use.

IDirect3DLight Interface

Object::Method	**IDirect3DLight::GetLight**
Example	`HRESULT GetLight(LPD3DLIGHT lpLight);`
Description	Returns the light information for the Direct3DLight object.
`lpLight`	Address of a D3DLIGHT structure that will be filled with the current light data.
Object::Method	**IDirect3DLight::SetLight**
Example	`HRESULT SetLight(LPD3DLIGHT lpLight);`
Description	Sets the light information for the Direct3DLight object.
`lpLight`	Address of a D3DLIGHT structure that will be used to set the current light data.

IDirect3DMaterial Interface

Object::Method	**IDirect3DMaterial::GetHandle**
Example	`HRESULT GetHandle(LPDIRECT3DDEVICE lpDirect3DDevice, LPD3DMATERIALHANDLE lpHandle);`

Description	Obtains the material handle for the Direct3DMaterial object. This handle is used in all immediate mode calls where a material is to be referenced. A material can be used by only one device at a time. If the device is destroyed, the material is disassociated from the device.
`lpDirect3DDevice`	Address of the Direct3DDevice object in which the material is being used.
`lpHandle`	Address of a variable that will be filled with the material handle corresponding to the Direct3DMaterial object.
Object::Method	**IDirect3DMaterial::GetMaterial**
Example	`HRESULT GetMaterial(LPD3DMATERIAL lpMat);`
Description	Returns the material data for the Direct3DMaterial object.
`lpMat`	Address of a D3DMATERIAL structure that will be filled with the current material properties.
Object::Method	**IDirect3DMaterial::Reserve**
Example	`HRESULT Reserve();`
Description	Not currently implemented.
Object::Method	**IDirect3DMaterial::SetMaterial**
Example	`HRESULT SetMaterial(LPD3DMATERIAL lpMat);`
Description	Sets the material data for the Direct3DMaterial object.
`lpMat`	Address of a D3DMATERIAL structure that contains the material properties.
Object::Method	**IDirect3DMaterial::Unreserve**
Example	`HRESULT Unreserve();`
Description	Not currently implemented.

IDirect3DTexture Interface

Object::Method	**IDirect3DTexture::GetHandle**
Example	`HRESULT GetHandle(LPDIRECT3DDEVICE lpDirect3DDevice, LPD3DTEXTUREHANDLE lpHandle);`
Description	Obtains the texture handle for the Direct3DTexture object. This handle is used in all Direct3D API calls where a texture is to be referenced.

lpDirect3DDevice	Address of the Direct3DDevice object into which the texture is to be loaded.
lpHandle	Address that will contain the texture handle corresponding to the Direct3DTexture object.
Object::Method	**IDirect3DTexture::Load**
Example	`HRESULT Load(LPDIRECT3DTEXTURE lpD3DTexture);`
Description	Loads a texture that was created with the DDSCAPS_ALLOCONLOAD flag, which indicates that memory for the DirectDraw surface is not allocated until the surface is loaded by using this method.
lpD3DTexture	Address of the texture to load.
Object::Method	**IDirect3DTexture::PaletteChanged**
Example	`HRESULT PaletteChanged(DWORD dwStart, DWORD dwCount);`
Description	Informs the driver that the palette has changed on a surface; for example, if you are playing a video clip into a texture and therefore require palette-changing capabilities.
dwStart	Index of the first palette entry that has changed.
dwCount	Number of palette entries that have changed.
Object::Method	**IDirect3DTexture::Unload**
Example	`HRESULT Unload();`
Description	Unloads the current texture.

IDirect3DViewport Interface

Object::Method	**IDirect3DViewport::AddLight**
Example	`HRESULT AddLight(LPDIRECT3DLIGHT lpDirect3DLight);`
Description	Adds a light to the list of lights attached to this viewport.
lpDirect3DLight	Address of the Direct3DLight object.
Object::Method	**IDirect3DViewport::Clear**
Example	`HRESULT Clear(DWORD dwCount, LPD3DRECT lpRects, DWORD dwFlags);`
Description	Clears the viewport or a set of rectangles in the viewport to the current background material.
dwCount	Number of rectangles pointed to by lpRects.

Chapter 19 Immediate Mode Reference

`lpRects`	Address of an array of D3DRECT structures.
`dwFlags`	Flags indicating what to clear (can be both): D3DCLEAR_TARGET (the rendering target) or D3DCLEAR_ZBUFFER (the z-buffer).
Object::Method	**IDirect3DViewport::DeleteLight**
Example	`HRESULT DeleteLight(LPDIRECT3DLIGHT lpDirect3DLight);`
Description	Removes the light object from the list of lights attached to this viewport.
`lpDirect3DLight`	Address of the Direct3DLight object.
Object::Method	**IDirect3DViewport::GetBackground**
Example	`HRESULT GetBackground(LPD3DMATERIALHANDLE lphMat, LPBOOL lpValid);`
Description	Returns the handle of a material that represents the current background associated with the viewport.
`lphMat`	Address that will contain the handle of the material being used as the background.
`lpValid`	Address of a variable that will be filled to indicate whether a background is associated with the viewport. If this parameter is FALSE, then no background will be associated with the viewport.
Object::Method	**IDirect3DViewport::GetBackgroundDepth**
Example	`HRESULT GetBackgroundDepth(LPDIRECTDRAWSURFACE* lplpDDSurface, LPBOOL lpValid);`
Description	Returns a DirectDraw surface that represents the current background-depth field associated with the viewport.
`lplpDDSurface`	Address that will be initialized to point to a DirectDrawSurface object representing the background depth.
`lpValid`	Address of a variable that is set to FALSE if no background depth is associated with the viewport.
Object::Method	**IDirect3DViewport::GetViewport**
Example	`HRESULT GetViewport(LPD3DVIEWPORT lpData);`
Description	Returns the viewport registers of the viewport.
`lpData`	Address of a D3DVIEWPORT structure representing the viewport.

Object::Method	**IDirect3DViewport::LightElements**
Example	`HRESULT LightElements(DWORD dwElementCount, LPD3DLIGHTDATA lpData);`
Description	Calculates light intensities and colors for rendering a geometry.
`dwElementCount`	Number of elements to be lit.
`lpData`	Address of a D3DLIGHTDATA structure that contains the points to be lit and the resulting colors.
Object::Method	**IDirect3DViewport::NextLight**
Example	`HRESULT NextLight(LPDIRECT3DLIGHT lpDirect3DLight, LPDIRECT3DLIGHT* lplpDirect3DLight, DWORD dwFlags);`
Description	Enumerates the Direct3DLight objects associated with the viewport.
`lpDirect3DLight`	Address of a light in the list of lights associated with this Direct3DDevice object.
`lplpDirect3DLight`	Address of a pointer that will contain the requested light in the list of lights associated with this Direct3DDevice object. The requested light is specified in the dwFlags parameter.
`dwFlags`	Flags specifying which light in the list to get: D3DNEXT_NEXT (the default), D3DNEXT_HEAD, or D3DNEXT_TAIL.
Object::Method	**IDirect3DViewport::SetBackground**
Example	`HRESULT SetBackground(D3DMATERIALHANDLE hMat);`
Description	Sets the background associated with the viewport.
`hMat`	Material handle that will be used as the background.
Object::Method	**IDirect3DViewport::SetBackgroundDepth**
Example	`HRESULT SetBackgroundDepth(LPDIRECTDRAWSURFACE lpDDSurface);`
Description	Sets the background-depth field for the viewport. The z-buffer is filled with the specified depth field when the IDirect3DViewport::Clear method is called and the D3DCLEAR_ZBUFFER flag is specified. The bit depth must be 16 bits.
`lpDDSurface`	Address of the DirectDrawSurface object representing the background depth.
Object::Method	**IDirect3DViewport::SetViewport**
Example	`HRESULT SetViewport(LPD3DVIEWPORT lpData);`

Description	Sets the viewport registers of the viewport.
`lpData`	Address of a D3DVIEWPORT structure that contains the new viewport.
Object::Method	**IDirect3DViewport::TransformVertices**
Example	`HRESULT TransformVertices(DWORD dwVertexCount, LPD3DTRANSFORMDATA lpData, DWORD dwFlags, LPDWORD lpOffscreen);`
Description	Transforms a set of vertices by the transformation matrix. You can use this method to do high-level bounding box or bounding sphere tests on your objects before transforming all the vertices, so you can skip whole meshes that are out of view. If you turn clipping on for this method, the dwClip member of D3DTRANSFORMDATA can help the transformation module determine whether the geometry will need clipping against the viewing volume.
`dwVertexCount`	Number of vertices to transform.
`lpData`	Address of a D3DTRANSFORMDATA structure that contains the vertices to transform.
`dwFlags`	D3DTRANSFORM_CLIPPED or D3DTRANSFORM_UNCLIPPED. If you request clipped, the current transformation matrix is used to transform a set of vertices and each vertex is checked to see if it is visible in the viewing frustum. The homogeneous part of the D3DTLVERTEX structure within lpData will be set if the vertex is clipped; otherwise, only the screen coordinates will be set. The clip intersection of all the vertices transformed is returned in lpOffscreen. That is, if lpOffscreen is nonzero, all the vertices were off-screen and not straddling the viewport. The drExtent member of the D3DTRANSFORMDATA structure will also be set to the 2D bounding rectangle of the resulting vertices.
	If you request unclipped, the system assumes that all the resulting coordinates will be within the viewing frustum. The drExtent member of the D3DTRANSFORMDATA structure will be set to the bounding rectangle of the resulting vertices.
`lpOffscreen`	Address of a variable that is set to nonzero if the resulting vertices are all off-screen.

Macros

Macro	**D3DDivide**
Example	`D3DDivide(a, b)(float)((double) (a) / (double) (b))`

Description	Divides two values, returning the quotient (a is the dividend; b is the divisor).
Macro	**D3DMultiply**
Example	`D3DMultiply(a, b)((a) * (b))`
Description	Multiplies two values and returns the product.
Macro	**D3DRGB**
Example	`D3DRGB(r, g, b) \` `(0xff000000L	(((long)((r) * 255)) << 16)	\` `(((long)((g) * 255)) << 8)	(long)((b) * 255))`
Description	Returns an RGB D3DCOLOR from red, green, and blue floating-point values from 0 to 1.
Macro	**D3DRGBA**
Example	`D3DRGBA(r, g, b, a) \` `((((long)((a) * 255)) << 24)	(((long)((r) * 255)) << 16)	` `(((long)((g) * 255)) << 8)	(long)((b) * 255))`
Description	Returns an RGBA D3DCOLOR from red, green, blue, and alpha floating-point values from 0 to 1.
Macro	**D3DSTATE_OVERRIDE**
Example	`D3DSTATE_OVERRIDE(type) ((DWORD) (type) + D3DSTATE_OVERRIDE_BIAS)`
Description	Overrides the state of the rasterization, lighting, or transformation module. Applications can use this macro to lock and unlock a state.
type	State to override. This parameter should be one of the members of the D3DTRANSFORMSTATETYPE, D3DLIGHTSTATETYPE, or D3DRENDERSTATETYPE enumerated types.
Macro	**D3DVAL**
Example	`D3DVAL(val)((float)val)`
Description	Creates a D3DVALUE with 16 bits of precision for the fractional part.
Macro	**D3DVALP**
Example	`D3DVALP(val, prec)((float)val)`

Description	Creates a value of the specified precision.
`val`	Value to be converted.
`prec`	Precision.
Macro	**RGB_GETBLUE**
Example	`RGB_GETBLUE(rgb)((rgb) & 0xff)`
Description	Returns the blue component of an RGB D3DCOLOR.
Macro	**RGB_GETGREEN**
Example	`RGB_GETGREEN(rgb)(((rgb) >> 8) & 0xff)`
Description	Returns the green component of an RGB D3DCOLOR.
Macro	**RGB_GETRED**
Example	`RGB_GETRED(rgb)(((rgb) >> 16) & 0xff)`
Description	Returns the red component of an RGB D3DCOLOR.
Macro	**RGB_MAKE**
Example	`RGB_MAKE(r, g, b)((D3DCOLOR) (((r) << 16)	((g) << 8)	(b)))`
Description	Creates an RGB color from red, green, and blue components (integers of 0 to 255).
Macro	**RGB_TORGBA**
Example	`RGB_TORGBA(rgb)((D3DCOLOR) ((rgb)	0xff000000))`
Description	Converts an RGB color into an RGBA color (i.e., adds an alpha component of 0).
Macro	**RGBA_GETALPHA**
Example	`RGBA_GETALPHA(rgb)((rgb) >> 24)`
Description	Returns the alpha component of an RGBA D3DCOLOR.
Macro	**RGBA_GETBLUE**
Example	`RGB_GETBLUE(rgb)((rgb) & 0xff)`
Description	Returns the blue component of an RGBA D3DCOLOR.
Macro	**RGBA_GETGREEN**
Example	`RGB_GETGREEN(rgb)(((rgb) >> 8) & 0xff)`
Description	Returns the green component of an RGBA D3DCOLOR.

Macro	**RGBA_GETRED**
Example	`RGB_GETRED(rgb)(((rgb) >> 16) & 0xff)`
Description	Returns the red component of an RGBA D3DCOLOR value.
Macro	**RGBA_MAKE**
Example	`RGBA_MAKE(r, g, b, a)    \` `(D3DCOLOR) (((a) << 24)	((r) << 16)`   `| ((g) << 8)	(b)))`
Description	Creates an RGB color from red, green, blue, and alpha components (integers of 0 to 255).
Macro	**RGBA_SETALPHA**
Example	`2RGBA_SETALPHA(rgba, x)(((x) << 24)	((rgba) & 0x00ffffff))`
Description	Sets the alpha component of an RGBA D3DCOLOR.
Macro	**RGBA_TORGB**
Example	`RGBA_TORGB(rgba)((D3DCOLOR) ((rgba) & 0xffffff))`
Description	Converts an RGBA D3DCOLOR into an RGB D3DCOLOR by stripping off the alpha component.

Callback Functions

Function	**D3DENUMDEVICESCALLBACK**

Example	`typedef HRESULT (FAR PASCAL * LPD3DENUM-DEVICESCALLBACK)`
	 `(LPGUID lpGuid, LPSTR lpDeviceDescription, LPSTR lpDeviceName, LPD3DDEVICEDESC lpD3DHWDeviceDesc,`
	 `LPD3DDEVICEDESC lpD3DHELDeviceDesc, LPVOID lpUserArg);`

Description	Defines the callback function for enumerating devices.
Called by	IDirect3D::EnumDevices.
Usage	Called by IDirect3D::EnumDevices for each Direct3D device installed in the system.
Should return	D3DENUMRET_CANCEL or D3DENUMRET_OK to tell the system to cancel or continue enumerating the devices.

`lpGuid`	Address of a GUID.
`lpDevice-Description`	Address of a textual description of the device.
`lpDeviceName`	Address of the device name.
`lpD3DHWDeviceDesc`	Address containing the hardware capabilities of the Direct3D device.
`lpD3DHELDeviceDesc`	Address containing the software-emulated capabilities of the Direct3D device.
`lpUserArg`	Address of application-defined data passed to this callback function.
Function	**D3DENUMTEXTUREFORMATSCALLBACK**
Example	`typedef HRESULT (WINAPI* LPD3DENUMTEXTURE-FORMATSCALLBACK) (LPDDSURFACEDESC lpDdsd, LPVOID lpUserArg);`
Description	Defines the callback function for enumerating supported texture formats.
Called by	IDirect3D::EnumTextureFormats.
Usage	Called by IDirect3D::EnumTextureFormats for each supported texture format.
`lpDdsd`	Address of the DirectDrawSurface object containing the texture information.
`lpUserArg`	Address of application-defined data passed to this callback function.
Function	**D3DVALIDATECALLBACK**
Example	`typedef HRESULT (WINAPI* LPD3DVALIDATE-CALLBACK) (LPVOID lpUserArg, DWORD dwOffset);`
Description	A debugging routine that is called when you validate the contents of an execute buffer.
Called by	IDirect3DExecuteBuffer::Validate.
Usage	If the Validate method finds an error in the execute buffer, it calls this routine specifying the offset into the execute buffer where the error was found. It does not tell you the nature of the error.
`lpUserArg`	Address of application-defined data passed to this callback function.
`dwOffset`	Offset into the execute buffer at which the system found an error.

Structures

Structure	**D3DCOLORVALUE**
| **Example** | ```
typedef struct _D3DCOLORVALUE {
union {
D3DVALUE r;
D3DVALUE dvR;
};
union {
D3DVALUE g;
D3DVALUE dvG;
};
union {
D3DVALUE b;
D3DVALUE dvB;
};
union {
D3DVALUE a;
D3DVALUE dvA;
};
} D3DCOLORVALUE;
``` |
Description	Describes the color values for the D3DLIGHT and D3D-MATERIAL structures.
dvR	Red.
dvG	Green.
dvB	Blue.
dvA	Alpha.
Structure	**D3DDEVICEDESC**
| **Example** | ```
typedef struct _D3DDeviceDesc {
DWORD dwSize;
DWORD dwFlags;
D3DCOLORMODEL dcmColorModel;
DWORD dwDevCaps;
D3DTRANSFORMCAPS dtcTransformCaps;
BOOL bClipping;
D3DLIGHTINGCAPS dlcLightingCaps;
D3DPRIMCAPS dpcLineCaps;
D3DPRIMCAPS dpcTriCaps;
DWORD dwDeviceRenderBitDepth;
DWORD dwDeviceZBufferBitDepth;
DWORD dwMaxBufferSize;
``` |

	`DWORD dwMaxVertexCount;` `} D3DDEVICEDESC, *LPD3DDEVICEDESC;`
Description	Describes the current device.
Used by	IDirect3DDevice::GetCaps.
`dwSize`	Size, in bytes, of this structure.
`dwFlags`	Flags indicating which fields in this structure contain valid data: D3DDD_BCLIPPING D3DDD_COLORMODEL D3DDD_DEVCAPS D3DDD_LIGHTINGCAPS D3DDD_LINECAPS D3DDD_MAXBUFFERSIZE D3DDD_MAXVERTEXCOUNT D3DDD_TRANSFORMCAPS D3DDD_TRICAPS
`dcmColorModel`	Color model (D3DCOLORMODEL): D3DCOLOR_MONO = 1, D3DCOLOR_RGB = 2.
`dwDevCaps`	Device capability flags:

D3DDEVCAPS_EXECUTESYSTEMMEMORY
　　　　　　Execute buffers can be in system memory.

D3DDEVCAPS_EXECUTEVIDEOMEMORY
　　　　　　Execute buffers can be in video memory.

D3DDEVCAPS_FLOATTLVERTEX
　　　　　　Floating-point posttransform vertex data allowed.

D3DDEVCAPS_SORTDECREASINGZ
　　　　　　Data must be sorted for decreasing depth.

D3DDEVCAPS_SORTEXACT
　　　　　　Data must be sorted exactly.

D3DDEVCAPS_SORTINCREASINGZ
　　　　　　Data must be sorted for increasing depth.

D3DDEVCAPS_TEXTURESYSTEMMEMORY
　　　　　　Textures can be in system memory.

D3DDEVCAPS_TEXTUREVIDEOMEMORY
　　　　　　Textures can be in video memory.

D3DDEVCAPS_TLVERTEXSYSTEMMEMORY
　　　　　　Transformed and lit vertices can be in system memory.

D3DDEVCAPS_TLVERTEXVIDEOMEMORY
　　　　　　Transformed and lit vertices can be in video memory.

`dtcTransformCaps`	Transformation capabilities (D3DTRANSFORMCAPS).

`bClipping`	TRUE if the device can perform 3D clipping.
`dlcLightingCaps`	Lighting capabilities (D3DLIGHTINGCAPS).
`dpcLineCaps`	Line-drawing capabilities (D3DPRIMCAPS).
`dpcTriCaps`	Triangle-drawing capabilities (D3DPRIMCAPS).
`dwDeviceRender-BitDepth`	Bit-depth: DDBD_8, DDBD_16, DDBD_24, or DDBD_32.
`dwDeviceZBuffer-BitDepth`	Z-buffer bit-depth: DDBD_8, DDBD_16, DDBD_24, or DDBD_32.
`dwMaxBufferSize`	Maximum execute buffer size (0 = any size).
`dwMaxVertexCount`	Maximum vertex count.
Structure	**D3DEXECUTEBUFFERDESC**

Example	```typedef struct _D3DExecuteBufferDesc {```
	 ```DWORD dwSize;```
	 ```DWORD dwFlags;```
	 ```DWORD dwCaps;```
	 ```DWORD dwBufferSize;```
	 ```LPVOID lpData;```
	 ```} D3DEXECUTEBUFFERDESC;```
	 ```typedef D3DEXECUTEBUFFERDESC *LPD3DEXECUTE-BUFFERDESC;```

Description	Describes the execute buffer.
Used by	IDirect3DDevice::CreateExecuteBuffer and IDirect3DExecute-Buffer::Lock.
Usage	Lock the execute buffer object, change the contents of the memory pointed to by lpData, and then unlock the execute buffer object.
`dwSize`	Size of this structure, in bytes.
`dwFlags`	Flags identifying which members of this structure contain valid data: D3DDEB_BUFSIZE, D3DDEB_CAPS, and/or D3DDEB_LPDATA.
`dwCaps`	Location of the execute buffer: D3DDEBCAPS_SYSTEM-MEMORY, D3DDEBCAPS_VIDEOMEMORY, or D3DDEBCAPS_MEM (either system or video memory).
`dwBufferSize`	Size of the execute buffer, in bytes.
`lpData`	Address of the buffer data.
Structure	**D3DEXECUTEDATA**
Example	```typedef struct _D3DEXECUTEDATA {``` ```DWORD dwSize;```

```
                DWORD dwVertexOffset;
                DWORD dwVertexCount;
                DWORD dwInstructionOffset;
                DWORD dwInstructionLength;
                DWORD dwHVertexOffset;
                D3DSTATUS dsStatus;
                } D3DEXECUTEDATA, *LPD3DEXECUTEDATA;
```

Description	Structure to tell the main execute buffer processing method (IDirect3DDevice::Execute) what to do.
Usage	After transformation of vertices is complete, IDirect3DDevice::Execute starts its parsing and rendering at the offset into the execute buffer specified by dwInstructionOffset.
`dwSize`	Size of this structure, in bytes.
`dwVertexOffset`	Offset into the list of vertices.
`dwVertexCount`	Number of vertices to execute.
`dwInstruction-Offset`	Offset into the list of instructions to execute.
`dwInstructionLength`	Length of the instructions to execute.
`dwHVertexOffset`	Offset into the list of vertices for the homogeneous vertex used when the application is supplying screen coordinate data that needs clipping.
`dsStatus`	Value storing the screen extent of the rendered geometry for use after the transformation is complete. This value is a D3DSTATUS structure.

Structure Example	**D3DFINDDEVICERESULT**
	`typedef struct _D3DFINDDEVICERESULT {`
	`DWORD dwSize;`
	`GUID guid;`
	`D3DDEVICEDESC ddHwDesc;`
	`D3DDEVICEDESC ddSwDesc;`
	`} D3DFINDDEVICERESULT, *LPD3DFINDDEVICERESULT;`

Description	Describes the device found by a call to IDirect3D::FindDevice.
`dwSize`	Size, in bytes, of the structure.
`guid`	GUID of the device that was found.
`ddHwDesc`	D3DDEVICEDESC structure for the hardware device found.
`ddSwDesc`	D3DDEVICEDESC structure for the software device found.

Structure	**D3DFINDDEVICESEARCH**

Example	`typedef struct _D3DFINDDEVICESEARCH {`
	`DWORD dwSize;`
	`DWORD dwFlags;`
	`BOOL bHardware;`
	`D3DCOLORMODEL dcmColorModel;`
	`GUID guid;`
	`DWORD dwCaps;`
	`D3DPRIMCAPS dpcPrimCaps;`
	`} D3DFINDDEVICESEARCH, *LPD3DFINDDEVICESEARCH;`

Description	Describes the device to be found with IDirect3D::FindDevice.
`dwSize`	Size, in bytes, of this structure.
`dwFlags`	Flags defining the type of device the application wants to find:

D3DFDS_ALPHACMPCAPS
    Match dwAlphaCmpCaps of D3DPRIMCAPS with dpcPrimCaps.

D3DFDS_COLORMODEL
    Match by color model in dcmColorModel.

D3DFDS_DSTBLENDCAPS
    Match dwDestBlendCaps of D3DPRIMCAPS with dpcPrimCaps.

D3DFDS_GUID	Match by GUID in guid.
D3DFDS_HARDWARE	Match by hardware or software by bHardware.
D3DFDS_LINES	Match the D3DPRIMCAPS in dpcLineCaps.
D3DFDS_MISCCAPS	Match dwMiscCaps of D3DPRIMCAPS with dpcPrimCaps.
D3DFDS_RASTERCAPS	Match dwRasterCaps of D3DPRIMCAPS with dpcPrimCaps.
D3DFDS_SHADECAPS	Match dwShadeCaps of D3DPRIMCAPS with dpcPrimCaps.

D3DFDS_SRCBLEND-CAPS
    Match dwSrcBlendCaps of D3DPRIMCAPS with dpcPrimCaps.

D3DFDS_TEXTUREBLENDCAPS
    Match dwTextureBlendCaps of D3DPRIMCAPS with dpcPrimCaps.

D3DFDS_TEXTURECAPS
    Match dwTextureCaps of D3DPRIMCAPS with dpcPrimCaps.

D3DFDS_TEXTUREFILTERCAPS
    Match dwTextureFilterCaps of D3DPRIMCAPS with dpcPrimCaps.

D3DFDS_TRIANGLES	Match D3DPRIMCAPS structure specified by the dpcTriCaps member of the D3DDEVICEDESC structure.
D3DFDS_ZCMPCAPS	Match dwZCmpCaps of D3DPRIMCAPS with dpcPrimCaps.
`bHardware`	Flag specifying whether the device to find is implemented as hardware or software. If this member is TRUE, the device to search for

Chapter 19 Immediate Mode Reference 397

	has hardware rasterization and may also provide other hardware acceleration. Applications that use this flag should set the D3DFDS_HARDWARE bit in the dwFlags member.
dcmColorModel	D3DCOLORMODEL specifying whether the device to find should use the ramp or RGB color model.
guid	GUID of the device to find.
dwCaps	Capability flags.
dpcPrimCaps	Specifies a D3DPRIMCAPS structure defining the device's capabilities for each primitive type.
Structure	**D3DHVERTEX**

Example	`typedef struct _D3DHVERTEX {`
	`DWORD dwFlags;`
	`union {`
	`D3DVALUE hx;`
	`D3DVALUE dvHX;`
	`};`
	`union {`
	`D3DVALUE hy;`
	`D3DVALUE dvHY;`
	`};`
	`union {`
	`D3DVALUE hz;`
	`D3DVALUE dvHZ;`
	`};`
	`} D3DHVERTEX, *LPD3DHVERTEX;`

Description	Defines a homogeneous vertex used when the application is supplying screen coordinate data that needs clipping.
Usage	Part of the D3DTRANSFORMDATA.
dwFlags	Clip status of the homogeneous vertex (the dwClip member of the D3DTRANSFORMDATA).
dvHX, dvHY, and dvHZ	D3DVALUEs describing transformed homogeneous coordinates of the vertex.
Structure	**D3DLIGHT**

Example	`typedef struct _D3DLIGHT {`
	`DWORD dwSize;`
	`D3DLIGHTTYPE dltType;`
	`D3DCOLORVALUE dcvColor;`
	`D3DVECTOR dvPosition;`
	`D3DVECTOR dvDirection;`

```
                D3DVALUE dvRange;
                D3DVALUE dvFalloff;
                D3DVALUE dvAttenuation0;
                D3DVALUE dvAttenuation1;
                D3DVALUE dvAttenuation2;
                D3DVALUE dvTheta;
                D3DVALUE dvPhi;
                } D3DLIGHT, *LPD3DLIGHT;
```

Description	Describes a light.
Used by	IDirect3DLight::SetLight and IDirect3DLight::GetLight.
Usage	The system uses all three of the attenuation settings to determine how the effect of a light decreases with distance from the source.
`dwSize`	Size, in bytes, of this structure.
`dltType`	Light type (D3DLIGHTTYPE).
`dcvColor`	Light color (D3DCOLORVALUE).
`dvPosition`	Light position in world space.
`dvDirection`	Light direction in world space.
`dvRange`	Maximum distance of light's effect.
`dvFalloff`	Decrease in illumination between the umbra (dvTheta) and the outer edge of the penumbra (dvPhi).
`dvAttenuation0`	Constant light intensity. Specifies a light level that does not decrease between the light and the cutoff point given by the dvRange member.
`dvAttenuation1`	Light intensity that decreases linearly. The light intensity is 50 percent of this value halfway between the light and the cutoff point given by the dvRange member.
`dvAttenuation2`	Light intensity that decreases according to a quadratic attenuation factor.
`dvTheta`	Angle, in radians, of the spotlight's umbra (the fully illuminated spotlight cone).
`dvPhi`	Angle, in radians, of the outer edge of the spotlight's penumbra. Points outside this cone are not lit by the spotlight.
Structure	**D3DLIGHTDATA**
Example	```typedef struct _D3DLIGHTDATA {
DWORD dwSize;
LPD3DLIGHTINGELEMENT lpIn;
DWORD dwInSize;
LPD3DTLVERTEX lpOut;
DWORD dwOutSize;
} D3DLIGHTDATA, *LPD3DLIGHTDATA;```

Description	Describes a point to be lit and the resulting colors.
Used by	IDirect3DViewport::LightElements.
`dwSize`	Size, in bytes, of this structure.
`lpIn`	Address of a D3DLIGHTINGELEMENT structure specifying the input positions and normal vectors.
`dwInSize`	Amount to skip from one input element to the next. This allows the application to store extra data inline with the element.
`lpOut`	Address of a D3DTLVERTEX structure specifying the output colors.
`dwOutSize`	Amount to skip from one output color to the next. This allows the application to store extra data inline with the color.
Structure	**D3DLIGHTINGCAPS**

Example	`typedef struct _D3DLIGHTINGCAPS {`
	`DWORD dwSize;`
	`DWORD dwCaps;`
	`DWORD dwLightingModel;`
	`DWORD dwNumLights;`
	`} D3DLIGHTINGCAPS, *LPD3DLIGHTINGCAPS;`

Description	Describes lighting capabilities of a device.
Used by	This structure is part of the D3DDEVICEDESC structure.
`dwSize`	Size, in bytes, of this structure.
`dwCaps`	Light types supported by the lighting module:

D3DLIGHTCAPS_DIRECTIONAL
   Directional lights.

D3DLIGHTCAPS_GLSPOT
   OpenGL-style spotlights.

D3DLIGHTCAPS_PARALLELPOINT
   Parallel point lights.

D3DLIGHTCAPS_POINT
   Point lights.

D3DLIGHTCAPS_SPOT Spotlights.

`dwLightingModel`	Lighting models supported: D3DLIGHTINGMODEL_MONO or D3DLIGHTINGMODEL_RGB.
`dwNumLights`	Number of lights that can be handled.
Structure	**D3DLIGHTINGELEMENT**
Example	`typedef struct _D3DLIGHTINGELEMENT {` `D3DVECTOR dvPosition;`

```
                  D3DVECTOR dvNormal;
                  } D3DLIGHTINGELEMENT, *LPD3DLIGHTINGELEMENT;
```

Description   Describes points in model space to be lit.

Used by   Part of the D3DLIGHTDATA structure.

`dvPosition`   A D3DVECTOR specifying the lightable point in model space.

`dvNormal`   A D3DVECTOR specifying the normalized unit vector.

Structure   **D3DLINEPATTERN**

Example
```
typedef struct _D3DLINEPATTERN {
WORD wRepeatFactor;
WORD wLinePattern;
} D3DLINEPATTERN;
```

Description   Describes a line pattern.

Used by   D3DRENDERSTATE_LINEPATTERN in D3DRENDERSTATE-TYPE.

`wRepeatFactor`   Number of bits in the pattern in wLinePattern to use before repeating the pattern (16 = use all of wLinePattern).

`wLinePattern`   Bit pattern for the line. A dotted line: 1100110011001100.

Structure   **D3DLVERTEX**

Example
```
typedef struct _D3DLVERTEX {
union {
D3DVALUE x;
D3DVALUE dvX;
};
union {
D3DVALUE y;
D3DVALUE dvY;
};
union {
D3DVALUE z;
D3DVALUE dvZ;
};
DWORD dwReserved;
union {
D3DCOLOR color;
D3DCOLOR dcColor;
};
union {
D3DCOLOR specular;
D3DCOLOR dcSpecular;
};
```

Chapter 19 Immediate Mode Reference

```
                    union {
                    D3DVALUE tu;
                    D3DVALUE dvTU;
                    };
                    union {
                    D3DVALUE tv;
                    D3DVALUE dvTV;
                    };
                    } D3DLVERTEX, *LPD3DLVERTEX;
```

Description	Describes an untransformed and lit vertex with color, in model coordinates.
Usage	Use if the hardware supports vertex transformations.
`dvX, dvY,` and `dvZ`	D3DVALUEs specifying the homogeneous coordinates of the vertex.
`dwReserved`	Reserved; must be 0.
`dcColor` and `dcSpecular`	D3DCOLORs for the color and specular component of the vertex.
`dvTU` and `dvTV`	D3DVALUEs for the texture coordinates of the vertex.
Structure	**D3DMATERIAL**
Example	

```
                    typedef struct _D3DMATERIAL {
                    DWORD dwSize;
                    union {
                    D3DCOLORVALUE diffuse;
                    D3DCOLORVALUE dcvDiffuse;
                    };
                    union {
                    D3DCOLORVALUE ambient;
                    D3DCOLORVALUE dcvAmbient;
                    };
                    union {
                    D3DCOLORVALUE specular;
                    D3DCOLORVALUE dcvSpecular;
                    };
                    union {
                    D3DCOLORVALUE emissive;
                    D3DCOLORVALUE dcvEmissive;
                    };
                    union {
                    D3DVALUE power;
                    D3DVALUE dvPower;
                    };
```

|  | ```
D3DTEXTUREHANDLE hTexture;
DWORD dwRampSize;
} D3DMATERIAL, *LPD3DMATERIAL;
``` |
Description	Describes a material.
Used by	IDirect3DMaterial::GetMaterial and IDirect3DMaterial::SetMaterial.
Usage	The texture handle is acquired from Direct3D by loading a texture into the device. The texture handle may be used only when it has been loaded into the device.
`dwSize`	Size, in bytes, of this structure.
`dcvDiffuse`	Diffuse color.
`dcvAmbient`	Ambient color.
`dcvSpecular`	Specular color.
`dcvEmissive`	Emissive color.
`dvPower`	Sharpness of specular highlights.
`hTexture`	Handle of the texture map.
`dwRampSize`	Size of the color ramp. For the monochromatic (ramp) driver, this value must be less than or equal to 1 for materials assigned to the background; otherwise, the background is not displayed. This behavior also occurs when a texture that is assigned to the background has an associated material whose dwRampSize member is greater than 1.
Structure	**D3DMATRIX**
| **Example** | ```
typedef struct _D3DMATRIX {
D3DVALUE _11, _12, _13, _14;
D3DVALUE _21, _22, _23, _24;
D3DVALUE _31, _32, _33, _34;
D3DVALUE _41, _42, _43, _44;
} D3DMATRIX, *LPD3DMATRIX;
``` |
Description	Describes a 4 × 4 matrix.
Used by	IDirect3DDevice::GetMatrix and IDirect3DDevice::SetMatrix.
Structure	**D3DPICKRECORD**
| **Example** | ```
typedef struct _D3DPICKRECORD {
BYTE bOpcode;
BYTE bPad;
DWORD dwOffset;
D3DVALUE dvZ;
} D3DPICKRECORD, *LPD3DPICKRECORD;
``` |
```

Description	Describes a picked primitive in an execute buffer.
Used by	IDirect3DDevice::GetPickRecords.
Usage	You specify the *x*- and *y*-screen coordinates when you call IDirect3DDevice::Pick. The geometric primitives in the specified execute buffer at that screen location are returned with IDirect3DDevice::GetPickRecords and described by D3DPICKRECORDs.
`bOpcode`	Opcode of the picked primitive.
`bPad`	Pad byte.
`dwOffset`	Offset from the start of the execute buffer in which the picked primitive was found.
`dvZ`	Depth of the picked primitive.
Structure	**D3DPRIMCAPS**

Example	``typedef struct _D3DPrimCaps {``
	 ``DWORD dwSize;``
	 ``DWORD dwMiscCaps;``
	 ``DWORD dwRasterCaps;``
	 ``DWORD dwZCmpCaps;``
	 ``DWORD dwSrcBlendCaps;``
	 ``DWORD dwDestBlendCaps;``
	 ``DWORD dwAlphaCmpCaps;``
	 ``DWORD dwShadeCaps;``
	 ``DWORD dwTextureCaps;``
	 ``DWORD dwTextureFilterCaps;``
	 ``DWORD dwTextureBlendCaps;``
	 ``DWORD dwTextureAddressCaps;``
	 ``DWORD dwStippleWidth;``
	 ``DWORD dwStippleHeight;``
	 ``} D3DPRIMCAPS, *LPD3DPRIMCAPS;``

Description	Describes capabilities for different primitive types.
Used by	Several fields in the D3DDEVICEDESC structure.
`dwSize`	Size, in bytes, of this structure.
`dwMiscCaps`	General capabilities the device supports for this primitive:

D3DPMISCCAPS_CONFORMANT
    OpenGL compatible.

D3DPMISCCAPS_CULLCCW
    Supports counterclockwise culling of triangles through the D3DRENDERSTATE_CULLMODE state. Corresponds to D3DCULL_CCW in D3DCULL.

D3DPMISCCAPS_CULLCW
: Supports clockwise culling of triangles through the D3DRENDERSTATE_CULLMODE state. Corresponds to D3DCULL_CW in D3DCULL.

D3DPMISCCAPS_CULLNONE
: Does not cull triangles. Corresponds to D3DCULL_NONE of D3DCULL.

D3DPMISCCAPS_LINEPATTERNREP
: For line-drawing primitives, values other than 1 are supported for the wRepeatFactor member of the D3DLINEPATTERN.

D3DPMISCCAPS_MASKPLANES
: Device can perform a bitmask of color planes.

D3DPMISCCAPS_MASKZ
: Device can enable and disable modification of the z-buffer on pixel operations.

`dwRasterCaps` Raster-drawing capabilities:

D3DPRASTERCAPS_DITHER
: Device can dither.

D3DPRASTERCAPS_FOGTABLE
: Device calculates the fog value by referring to a lookup table containing fog values that are indexed to the depth of a given pixel.

D3DPRASTERCAPS_FOGVERTEX
: Device calculates the fog value during the lighting operation, places the value into the alpha component of the D3DCOLOR value given for the specular member of the D3DTLVERTEX structure, and interpolates the fog value during rasterization.

D3DPRASTERCAPS_PAT
: Device can perform patterned drawing (lines or fills with D3DRENDERSTATE_LINEPATTERN or one of the D3DRENDERSTATE_STIPPLEPATTERN render states) for the primitive being queried.

D3DPRASTERCAPS_ROP2
: Device can support raster operations other than R2_COPYPEN.

D3DPRASTERCAPS_STIPPLE
: Device can stipple polygons to simulate translucency.

D3DPRASTERCAPS_SUBPIXEL
: Device performs subpixel placement of z, color, and texture data, rather than working with the nearest integer pixel coordinate. This helps avoid bleed-through due to z imprecision and jitter of color and texture values for pixels. Note that there is no corresponding state that can be enabled and disabled; the device either performs subpixel placement or it does not, and this bit is present only to describe rendering quality.

D3DPRASTERCAPS_SUBPIXELX
> The device is subpixel accurate along the *x*-axis only and is clamped to an integer *y*-axis scanline.

D3DPRASTERCAPS_XOR
> The device can support XOR operations. If this flag is not set but D3DPRIM_RASTER_ROP2 is, then XOR operations must still be supported.

D3DPRASTERCAPS_ZTEST
> The device can perform z-test operations. This effectively renders a primitive and indicates whether any z pixels would have been rendered.

`dwZCmpCaps`   Z-buffer comparison tests the driver can perform:

D3DPCMPCAPS_ALWAYS
> z test always succeeds.

D3DPCMPCAPS_EQUAL
> New z = current z.

D3DPCMPCAPS_GREATER
> New z > current z.

D3DPCMPCAPS_GREATEREQUAL
> New z > or = current z.

D3DPCMPCAPS_LESS   New z < current z.

D3DPCMPCAPS_LESSEQUAL
> New z < or = current z.

D3DPCMPCAPS_NEVER
> z test always fails.

D3DPCMPCAPS_NOTEQUAL
> New z not = current z.

`dwSrcBlendCaps`   Source blending capabilities (*s* = source, *d* destination):

D3DPBLENDCAPS_BOTHINVSRCALPHA
> Source blend factor is ($1-A_s$, $1-A_s$, $1-A_s$, $1-A_s$) and destination blend factor is (A_s, A_s, A_s, A_s); the destination blend selection is overridden.

D3DPBLENDCAPS_BOTHSRCALPHA
> Source blend factor is (A_s, A_s, A_s, A_s) and destination blend factor is ($1-A_s$, $1-A_s$, $1-A_s$, $1-A_s$); the destination blend selection is overridden.

D3DPBLENDCAPS_DESTALPHA
> Blend factor: A_d, A_d, A_d, A_d.

D3DPBLENDCAPS_DESTCOLOR
> R_d, G_d, B_d, A_d.

D3DPBLENDCAPS_INVDESTALPHA
> $1-A_d$, $1-A_d$, $1-A_d$, $1-A_d$.

D3DPBLENDCAPS_INVDESTCOLOR
    $1-R_d$, $1-G_d$, $1-B_d$, $1-A_d$.

D3DPBLENDCAPS_INVSRCALPHA
    $1-A_s$, $1-A_s$, $1-A_s$, $1-A_s$.

D3DPBLENDCAPS_INVSRCCOLOR
    $1-R_d$, $1-G_d$, $1-B_d$, $1-A_d$.

D3DPBLENDCAPS_ONE
    1, 1, 1, 1.

D3DPBLENDCAPS_SRCALPHA
    A_s, A_s, A_s, A_s.

D3DPBLENDCAPS_SRCALPHASAT
    $f, f, f, 1$; $f = \min(A_s, 1-A_d)$.

D3DPBLENDCAPS_SRCCOLOR
    R_s, G_s, B_s, A_s.

D3DPBLENDCAPS_ZERO
    0, 0, 0, 0.

`dwDestBlendCaps`	Destination blending capabilities (same flags as dwSrcBlendCaps).
`dwAlphaCmpCaps`	Alpha-test comparison tests the driver can perform (same flags as dwZCmpCaps).
`dwShadeCaps`	Shading operations that the device can perform. It is assumed, in general, that if a device supports a given command (such as D3DOP_TRIANGLE) at all, it supports the D3DSHADE_FLAT mode (as specified in the D3DSHADEMODE). This flag specifies whether the driver can also support Gouraud and Phong shading and whether alpha color components are supported for each of the three color-generation modes. When alpha components are not supported in a given mode, the alpha value of colors generated in that mode is implicitly 255 (the maximum, full-intensity alpha).

D3DPSHADECAPS_ALPHAFLATBLEND and D3DPSHADECAPS_ALPHAFLATSTIPPLED
    Device can support an alpha component for flat-blended and stippled transparency, respectively (the D3DSHADE_FLAT state for the D3DSHADEMODE). In these modes, the alpha color component for a primitive is provided as part of the color for the first vertex of the primitive.

D3DPSHADECAPS_ALPHAGOURAUDBLEND and D3DPSHADECAPS_ALPHAGOURAUDSTIPPLED
    Device can support an alpha component for Gouraud-blended and -stippled transparency, respectively (the D3DSHADE_GOURAUD state for the D3DSHADEMODE). In these modes, the alpha color component for a primitive is provided at vertices and interpolated across a face along with the other color components.

D3DPSHADECAPS_ALPHAPHONGBLEND and D3DPSHADECAPS_ALPHAPHONGSTIPPLED

Device can support an alpha component for Phong-blended and -stippled transparency, respectively (the D3DSHADE_PHONG state for the D3DSHADEMODE). In these modes, vertex parameters are reevaluated on a per-pixel basis, applying lighting effects for the red, green, and blue color components. Phong shading is not supported for DirectX 2.

D3DPSHADECAPS_COLORFLATMONO and D3DPSHADECAPS_COLORFLATRGB

Device can support colored flat shading in the D3DCOLOR_MONO and D3DCOLOR_RGB color models, respectively. In these modes, the color component for a primitive is provided as part of the color for the first vertex of the primitive. In monochromatic lighting modes, only the blue component of the color is interpolated. In RGB lighting modes, of course, the red, green, and blue components are interpolated.

D3DPSHADECAPS_COLORGOURAUDMONO and D3DPSHADECAPS_COLORGOURAUDRGB

Device can support colored Gouraud shading in the D3DCOLOR_MONO and D3DCOLOR_RGB color models, respectively. In these modes, the color component for a primitive is provided at vertices and interpolated across a face along with the other color components. In monochromatic lighting modes, only the blue component of the color is interpolated. In RGB lighting modes, of course, the red, green, and blue components are interpolated.

D3DPSHADECAPS_COLORPHONGMONO and D3DPSHADECAPS_COLORPHONGRGB

Device can support colored Phong shading in the D3DCOLOR_MONO and D3DCOLOR_RGB color models, respectively. In these modes, vertex parameters are reevaluated on a per-pixel basis. Lighting effects are applied for the red, green, and blue color components in RGB mode, and for the blue component only for monochromatic mode. Phong shading is not supported for DirectX 2.

D3DPSHADECAPS_FOGFLAT, D3DPSHADECAPS_FOGGOURAUD, and D3DPSHADECAPS_FOGPHONG

Device can support fog in the flat, Gouraud, and Phong shading models, respectively. Phong shading is not supported for DirectX 2.

D3DPSHADECAPS_SPECULARFLATMONO and D3DPSHADECAPS_SPECULARFLATRGB

Device can support specular highlights in flat shading in the D3DCOLOR_MONO and D3DCOLOR_RGB color models, respectively.

D3DPSHADECAPS_SPECULARGOURAUDMONO and
D3DPSHADECAPS_SPECULARGOURAUDRGB
> Device can support specular highlights in Gouraud shading in the D3DCOLOR_MONO and D3DCOLOR_RGB color models, respectively.

D3DPSHADECAPS_SPECULARPHONGMONO and
D3DPSHADECAPS_SPECULARPHONGRGB
> Device can support specular highlights in Phong shading in the D3DCOLOR_MONO and D3DCOLOR_RGB color models, respectively. Phong shading is not supported for DirectX 2.

`dwTextureCaps`   Texture-mapping capabilities:

D3DPTEXTURECAPS_ALPHA
> RGBA textures are supported in the D3DTEX_DECAL and D3DTEX_MODULATE texture filtering modes. If this capability is not set, then only RGB textures are supported in those modes. Regardless of the setting of this flag, alpha must always be supported in D3DTEX_DECAL_MASK, D3DTEX_DECAL_ALPHA, and D3DTEX_MODULATE_ALPHA filtering modes whenever those filtering modes are available.

D3DPTEXTURECAPS_BORDER
> Texture mapping along borders supported.

D3DPTEXTURECAPS_PERSPECTIVE
> Perspective correction supported.

D3DPTEXTURECAPS_POW2
> All non-mipmapped textures must have widths and heights specified as powers of 2 if this flag is set. (Note that all mipmapped textures must always have dimensions that are powers of 2.)

D3DPTEXTURECAPS_SQUAREONLY
> All textures must be square.

D3DPTEXTURECAPS_TRANSPARENCY
> Texture transparency is supported. (Only those texels that are not the current transparent color are drawn.)

`dwTexture-FilterCaps`   Texture-mapping capabilities. This member can be one or more of the following:

D3DPTFILTERCAPS_LINEAR
> A weighted average of a 2 × 2 area of texels surrounding the desired pixel is used. This applies to both zooming in and zooming out. If either zooming in or zooming out is supported, then both must be supported.

D3DPTFILTERCAPS_LINEARMIPLINEAR
> Similar to D3DPRIM_TEX_MIP_LINEAR, but interpolates between the two nearest mipmaps.

Chapter 19 Immediate Mode Reference

D3DPTFILTERCAPS_LINEARMIPNEAREST

Similar to D3DPRIM_TEX_MIP_NEAREST, but interpolates between the two nearest mipmaps.

D3DPTFILTERCAPS_MIPLINEAR

Similar to D3DPRIM_TEX_LINEAR, but uses the appropriate mipmap for texel selection.

D3DPTFILTERCAPS_MIPNEAREST

Similar to D3DPRIM_TEX_NEAREST, but uses the appropriate mipmap for texel selection.

D3DPTFILTERCAPS_NEAREST

The texel with the coordinates nearest to the desired pixel value is used. This applies to both zooming in and zooming out. If either zooming in or zooming out is supported, then both must be supported.

`dwTextureBlendCaps` Texture-blending capabilities. See D3DTEXTUREBLEND for discussions of the various texture-blending modes. This member can be one or more of the following:

D3DPTBLENDCAPS_COPY

Copy mode texture-blending (D3DTBLEND_COPY from D3DTEXTUREBLEND) is supported.

D3DPTBLENDCAPS_DECAL

Decal texture-blending mode (D3DTBLEND_DECAL from D3DTEXTUREBLEND) is supported.

D3DPTBLENDCAPS_DECALALPHA

Decal-alpha texture-blending mode (D3DTBLEND_DECALALPHA from D3DTEXTUREBLEND) is supported.

D3DPTBLENDCAPS_DECALMASK

Decal-mask texture-blending mode (D3DTBLEND_DECALMASK from D3DTEXTUREBLEND) is supported.

D3DPTBLENDCAPS_MODULATE

Modulate texture-blending mode (D3DTBLEND_MODULATE from D3DTEXTUREBLEND) is supported.

D3DPTBLENDCAPS_MODULATEALPHA

Modulate-alpha texture-blending mode (D3DTBLEND_MODULATEALPHA from D3DTEXTUREBLEND) is supported.

D3DPTBLENDCAPS_MODULATEMASK

Modulate-mask texture-blending mode (D3DTBLEND_MODULATEMASK from the D3DTEXTUREBLEND) is supported.

`dwTextureAddressCaps` Texture-addressing capabilities:

D3DPTADDRESSCAPS_CLAMP
Device can clamp textures to addresses.

D3DPTADDRESSCAPS_MIRROR
Device can mirror textures to addresses.

D3DPTADDRESSCAPS_WRAP
Device can wrap textures to addresses.

`dwStippleWidth` — Maximum stipple width (up to 32).

`dwStippleHeight` — Maximum stipple height (up to 32).

Structure	**D3DRECT**
Example	```typedef struct _D3DRECT {
union {
LONG x1;
LONG lX1;
};
union {
LONG y1;
LONG lY1;
};
union {
LONG x2;
LONG lX2;
};
union {
LONG y2;
LONG lY2;
};
} D3DRECT, *LPD3DRECT;```
Description	Describes a rectangle.
`lX1` and `lY1`	Coordinates of the upper-left corner of the rectangle.
`lX2` and `lY2`	Coordinates of the lower-right corner of the rectangle.
Structure	**D3DSTATS**
Example	```typedef struct _D3DSTATS {
DWORD dwSize;
DWORD dwTrianglesDrawn;
DWORD dwLinesDrawn;
DWORD dwPointsDrawn;
DWORD dwSpansDrawn;
DWORD dwVerticesProcessed;
} D3DSTATS, *LPD3DSTATS;```

Chapter 19 Immediate Mode Reference 411

Description	Structure containing the number of triangles, lines, points, and spans drawn and the number of vertices processed.
Period	Since the device was created.
Used by	IDirect3DDevice::GetStats.
`dwSize`	Size, in bytes, of this structure.
`dwTrianglesDrawn`	Triangles.
`dwLinesDrawn`	Lines.
`dwPointsDrawn`	Points.
`dwSpansDrawn`	Spans.
`dwVerticesProcessed`	Vertices.

Structure

Example

D3DTLVERTEX

```
typedef struct _D3DTLVERTEX {
union {
D3DVALUE sx;
D3DVALUE dvSX;
};
union {
D3DVALUE sy;
D3DVALUE dvSY;
};
union {
D3DVALUE sz;
D3DVALUE dvSZ;
};
union {
D3DVALUE rhw;
D3DVALUE dvRHW;
};
union {
D3DCOLOR color;
D3DCOLOR dcColor;
};
union {
D3DCOLOR specular;
D3DCOLOR dcSpecular;
};
union {
D3DVALUE tu;
D3DVALUE dvTU;
};
```

```
union {
D3DVALUE tv;
D3DVALUE dvTV;
};
} D3DTLVERTEX, *LPD3DTLVERTEX;
```

Description Defines a transformed and lit vertex (i.e., in screen coordinates with color).

Used by D3DLIGHTDATA.

`dvSX` Screen *x*.

`dvSY` Screen *y*.

`dvSZ` Screen *z*.

`dvRHW` The reciprocal of homogeneous *w*: 1 divided by the distance from the origin to the object along the *z*-axis.

`dcColor` Color of the vertex.

`dcSpecular` Specular value of the vertex.

`dvTU` and `dvTV` Texture coordinates of the vertex.

Structure **D3DTRANSFORMCAPS**

Example
```
typedef struct _D3DTransformCaps {
DWORD dwSize;
DWORD dwCaps;
} D3DTRANSFORMCAPS, *LPD3DTRANSFORMCAPS;
```

Description Describes the transformation capabilities of a device.

Used by Part of D3DDEVICEDESC.

`dwSize` Size, in bytes, of this structure.

`dwCaps` If D3DTRANSFORMCAPS_CLIP, the system clips while transforming.

Structure **D3DTRANSFORMDATA**

Example
```
typedef struct _D3DTRANSFORMDATA {
DWORD dwSize;
LPVOID lpIn;
DWORD dwInSize;
LPVOID lpOut;
DWORD dwOutSize;
LPD3DHVERTEX lpHOut;
DWORD dwClip;
DWORD dwClipIntersection;
DWORD dwClipUnion;
D3DRECT drExtent;
} D3DTRANSFORMDATA, *LPD3DTRANSFORMDATA;
```

Description	Describes a transformation operation.
Used by	IDirect3DViewport::TransformVertices.
Note	Each input vertex represents *x, y, z* in model space.
Precision	The transformation module generates 16-bit precision results.
Clip	The clip is treated as an integer bitfield that is set to the inclusive OR of the viewing volume planes that clip a given transformed vertex.
`dwSize`	Size of the structure, in bytes.
`lpIn`	Address of the vertices to be transformed.
`dwInSize`	Stride of the vertices to be transformed (the amount to skip between vertices, allowing the application to store extra data inline with each vertex).
`lpOut`	Address used to store the transformed vertices.
`dwOutSize`	Stride of output vertices.
`lpHOut`	Address of a value that contains homogeneous transformed vertices.
`dwClip`	Flags specifying by which planes of the viewing frustum the vertices are to be clipped:
D3DCLIP_BACK	Back plane.
D3DCLIP_BOTTOM	Bottom plane.
D3DCLIP_FRONT	Front plane.
D3DCLIP_LEFT	Left plane.
D3DCLIP_RIGHT	Right plane.
D3DCLIP_TOP	Top plane.
D3DCLIP_GEN0 through D3DCLIP_GEN5	Application-defined clipping planes.
`dwClipIntersection`	Flags denoting the intersection of the clip flags:
D3DSTATUS_CLIPINTERSECTIONLEFT	Logical AND of the clip flags for the vertices compared to the left side of the viewing frustum.
D3DSTATUS_CLIPINTERSECTIONRIGHT	Logical AND of the clip flags for the vertices compared to the right side of the viewing frustum.
D3DSTATUS_CLIPINTERSECTIONTOP	Logical AND of the clip flags for the vertices compared to the top of the viewing frustum.
D3DSTATUS_CLIPINTERSECTIONBOTTOM	Logical AND of the clip flags for the vertices compared to the bottom of the viewing frustum.

D3DSTATUS_CLIPINTERSECTIONFRONT
: Logical AND of the clip flags for the vertices compared to the front clipping plane of the viewing frustum.

D3DSTATUS_CLIPINTERSECTIONBACK
: Logical AND of the clip flags for the vertices compared to the back clipping plane of the viewing frustum.

D3DSTATUS_CLIPINTERSECTIONGEN0 through
D3DSTATUS_CLIPINTERSECTIONGEN5
: Logical AND of the clip flags for application-defined clipping planes.

`dwClipUnion` Flags denoting the union of the clip flags:

D3DSTATUS_CLIPUNIONLEFT
: Equal to D3DCLIP_LEFT.

D3DSTATUS_CLIPUNIONRIGHT
: Equal to D3DCLIP_RIGHT.

D3DSTATUS_CLIPUNIONTOP
: Equal to D3DCLIP_TOP.

D3DSTATUS_CLIPUNIONBOTTOM
: Equal to D3DCLIP_BOTTOM.

D3DSTATUS_CLIPUNIONFRONT
: Equal to D3DCLIP_FRONT.

D3DSTATUS_CLIPUNIONBACK
: Equal to D3DCLIP_BACK.

D3DSTATUS_CLIPUNIONGEN0 through
D3DSTATUS_CLIPUNIONGEN5
: Equal to D3DCLIP_GEN0 through D3DCLIP_GEN5.

`drExtent` D3DRECT structure that defines the extent of the transformed vertices. This structure is filled by the transformation module with the screen extent of the transformed geometry. For geometries that are clipped, this extent will include only vertices that are inside the viewing volume.

Structure **D3DVECTOR**

Example
```
typedef struct _D3DVECTOR {
union {
D3DVALUE x;
D3DVALUE dvX;
};
union {
D3DVALUE y;
D3DVALUE dvY;
};
```

Chapter 19 Immediate Mode Reference

```
union {
D3DVALUE z;
D3DVALUE dvZ;
};
} D3DVECTOR, *LPD3DVECTOR;
```

Description Defines a vector.

dvX, dvY, and dvZ   Coordinates of the vector.

Structure **D3DVERTEX**

Example
```
typedef struct _D3DVERTEX {
union {
D3DVALUE x;
D3DVALUE dvX;
};
union {
D3DVALUE y;
D3DVALUE dvY;
};
union {
D3DVALUE z;
D3DVALUE dvZ;
};
union {
D3DVALUE nx;
D3DVALUE dvNX;
};
union {
D3DVALUE ny;
D3DVALUE dvNY;
};
union {
D3DVALUE nz;
D3DVALUE dvNZ;
};
union {
D3DVALUE tu;
D3DVALUE dvTU;
};
union {
D3DVALUE tv;
D3DVALUE dvTV;
};
} D3DVERTEX, *LPD3DVERTEX;
```

Description	Defines an untransformed and unlit vertex (model coordinates with normal direction vector).
`dvX`, `dvY`, and `dvZ`	Homogeneous vertex coordinates.
`dvNX`, `dvNY`, and `dvNZ`	The vertex normal.
`dvTU` and `dvTV`	Texture coordinates of the vertex.

Structure	**D3DVIEWPORT**
	 ```typedef struct _D3DVIEWPORT {```
	 ```DWORD dwSize;```
	 ```DWORD dwX;```
	 ```DWORD dwY;```
	 ```DWORD dwWidth;```
	 ```DWORD dwHeight;```
	 ```D3DVALUE dvScaleX;```
	 ```D3DVALUE dvScaleY;```
	 ```D3DVALUE dvMaxX;```
	 ```D3DVALUE dvMaxY;```
	 ```D3DVALUE dvMinZ;```
	 ```D3DVALUE dvMaxZ;```
	 ```} D3DVIEWPORT, *LPD3DVIEWPORT;```

Period	Sets the visible 3D volume and the 2D screen area that a 3D volume projects.
Used by	IDirect3DViewport::GetViewport and IDirect3DViewport::SetViewport.
Effect	When you change the viewport, the system builds a new transformation matrix.
Note	Viewport values are relative to the top left of the device.
`dwSize`	Size of this structure, in bytes.
`dwX` and `dwY`	Coordinates of the top-left corner of the viewport.
`dwWidth` and `dwHeight`	Dimensions of the viewport.
`dvScaleX` and `dvScaleY`	Scaling quantities homogeneous to screen.
`dvMaxX`, `dvMaxY`, `dvMinZ`, and `dvMaxZ`	Maximum and minimum homogeneous coordinates of x, y, and z.

Enumerated Types

Type	**D3DBLEND**
Example	```typedef enum _D3DBLEND {
D3DBLEND_ZERO = 1,
D3DBLEND_ONE = 2,
D3DBLEND_SRCCOLOR = 3,
D3DBLEND_INVSRCCOLOR = 4,
D3DBLEND_SRCALPHA = 5,
D3DBLEND_INVSRCALPHA = 6,
D3DBLEND_DESTALPHA = 7,
D3DBLEND_INVDESTALPHA = 8,
D3DBLEND_DESTCOLOR = 9,
D3DBLEND_INVDESTCOLOR = 10,
D3DBLEND_SRCALPHASAT = 11,
D3DBLEND_BOTHSRCALPHA = 12,
D3DBLEND_BOTHINVSRCALPHA = 13,
} D3DBLEND;```
Description	Defines the supported blend modes for the D3DRENDERSTATE_DSTBLEND values in the D3DRENDERSTATETYPE.
Note	Subscripts *s* and *d* mean "source" and "destination."

D3DBLEND_ZERO Blend factor is (0, 0, 0, 0).

D3DBLEND_ONE Blend factor is (1, 1, 1, 1).

D3DBLEND_SRCCOLOR
Blend factor is (R_s, G_s, B_s, A_s).

D3DBLEND_INVSRCCOLOR
Blend factor is (A_s, A_s, A_s, A_s, $1-A_s$).

D3DBLEND_SRCALPHA
Blend factor is (A_s, A_s, A_s, A_s).

D3DBLEND_INVSRCALPHA
Blend factor is ($1-A_s$, $1-A_s$, $1-A_s$, $1-A_s$).

D3DBLEND_DESTALPHA
Blend factor is (A_d, A_d, A_d, A_d).

D3DBLEND_INVDESTALPHA
Blend factor is ($1-A_d$, $1-A_d$, $1-A_d$, $1-A_d$).

D3DBLEND_DESTCOLOR
Blend factor is (R_d, G_d, B_d, A_d).

D3DBLEND_INVDESTCOLOR
Blend factor is (1-R_d, 1-G_d, 1-B_d, 1-A_d).

D3DBLEND_SRCALPHASAT
Blend factor is (f, f, f, 1); f = min(A_s, 1-A_d).

D3DBLEND_BOTHSRCALPHA
Source blend factor is (A_s, A_s, A_s, A_s), and destination blend factor is (1-A_s, 1-A_s, 1-A_s, 1-A_s); the destination blend selection is overridden.

D3DBLEND_BOTHINVSRCALPHA
Source blend factor is (1-A_s, 1-A_s, 1-A_s, 1-A_s), and destination blend factor is (A_s, A_s, A_s, A_s); the destination blend selection is overridden.

Type	**D3DCMPFUNC**
Example	```typedef enum _D3DCMPFUNC {
D3DCMP_NEVER = 1,
D3DCMP_LESS = 2,
D3DCMP_EQUAL = 3,
D3DCMP_LESSEQUAL = 4,
D3DCMP_GREATER = 5,
D3DCMP_NOTEQUAL = 6,
D3DCMP_GREATEREQUAL = 7,
D3DCMP_ALWAYS = 8,
} D3DCMPFUNC;```
Description	Defines the supported compare functions for the D3DRENDERSTATE_ZFUNC and D3DRENDERSTATE_ALPHAFUNC values of D3DRENDERSTATETYPE.
D3DCMP_NEVER	Always fail the test.
D3DCMP_LESS	Accept the new pixel if its value is less than the value of the current pixel.
D3DCMP_EQUAL	Accept the new pixel if its value equals the value of the current pixel.
D3DCMP_LESSEQUAL	Accept the new pixel if its value is less than or equal to the value of the current pixel.
D3DCMP_GREATER	Accept the new pixel if its value is greater than the value of the current pixel.
D3DCMP_NOTEQUAL	Accept the new pixel if its value does not equal the value of the current pixel.
D3DCMP_GREATER-EQUAL	Accept the new pixel if its value is greater than or equal to the value of the current pixel.

D3DCMP_ALWAYS	Always pass the test.
Type	**D3DCOLORMODEL**

Example	`typedef enum _D3DCOLORMODEL {`
	`D3DCOLOR_MONO = 1,`
	`D3DCOLOR_RGB = 2,`
	`} D3DCOLORMODEL;`

Description	Defines the color models.
D3DCOLOR_MONO	Use a monochromatic model (also called ramp model). In this model, the blue component of a vertex color is used to define the brightness of a lit vertex.
D3DCOLOR_RGB	Use a full RGB model.
Type	**D3DCULL**

Example	`typedef enum _D3DCULL {`
	`D3DCULL_NONE = 1,`
	`D3DCULL_CW = 2,`
	`D3DCULL_CCW = 3,`
	`} D3DCULL;`

Description	Describes supported cull modes.
What is a cull mode	How a face is considered to be facing away from the view (backfacing) and therefore should be removed from further processing by the renderer.
D3DCULL_NONE	Do not cull faces.
D3DCULL_CW	Cull faces with clockwise vertices.
D3DCULL_CCW	Cull faces with counterclockwise vertices.
Type	**D3DFILLMODE**

Example	`typedef enum _D3DFILLMODE {`
	`D3DFILL_POINT = 1,`
	`D3DFILL_WIREFRAME = 2,`
	`D3DFILL_SOLID = 3`
	`} D3DFILLMODE;`

Description	Describes fill modes.
Used by	The D3DRENDERSTATE_FILLMODE render state.
D3DFILL_POINT	Fill points.
D3DFILL_WIREFRAME	Fill wireframes.
D3DFILL_SOLID	Fill solids.

Type	**D3DFOGMODE**

Example	`typedef enum _D3DFOGMODE {`
	`D3DFOG_NONE = 0,`
	`D3DFOG_EXP = 1,`
	`D3DFOG_EXP2 = 2,`
	`D3DFOG_LINEAR = 3`
	`} D3DFOGMODE;`

Description	Describes fog modes.
Used by	The D3DRENDERSTATE_FOGTABLEMODE render state.
Formulas	See Chapter 18 for the fog interpolation formulas.
D3DFOG_NONE	No fog effect.
D3DFOG_EXP	The fog effect intensifies exponentially.
D3DFOG_EXP2	The fog effect intensifies exponentially with the square of the distance.
D3DFOG_LINEAR	The fog effect intensifies linearly between the start and endpoints. (This is the only fog mode supported for DirectX 2.)
Type	**D3DLIGHTTYPE**

Example	`typedef enum _D3DLIGHTTYPE {`
	`D3DLIGHT_POINT = 1,`
	`D3DLIGHT_SPOT = 2,`
	`D3DLIGHT_DIRECTIONAL = 3,`
	`D3DLIGHT_PARALLELPOINT = 4,`
	`D3DLIGHT_GLSPOT= 5,`
	`} D3DLIGHTTYPE;`

Description	Defines the light type.
Usage	Part of D3DLIGHT.
D3DLIGHT_POINT	Light is a point source.
D3DLIGHT_SPOT	Light is a spotlight source.
D3DLIGHT_DIRECTIONAL	Light is a directional source.
D3DLIGHT_PARALLELPOINT	Light is a parallel source.
D3DLIGHT_GLSPOT	Light is a GL-style spotlight.
Type	**3DSHADEMODE**
Example	`typedef enum _D3DSHADEMODE {` `D3DSHADE_FLAT = 1,`

	`D3DSHADE_GOURAUD = 2,`
	`D3DSHADE_PHONG = 3,`
	`} D3DSHADEMODE;`

Description	Describes the supported shade mode for the D3DRENDERSTATE_SHADEMODE render state.
D3DSHADE_FLAT	Flat shade mode. The color of the first vertex in the triangle is used to determine the color of the face.
D3DSHADE_GOURAUD	Gouraud shade mode. The color of the face is determined by a linear interpolation between all three of the triangle's vertices.
D3DSHADE_PHONG	Phong shade mode is not supported for DirectX 2.
Type	**D3DTEXTUREADDRESS**

Example	`typedef enum _D3DTEXTUREADDRESS {`
	`D3DTADDRESS_WRAP = 1,`
	`D3DTADDRESS_MIRROR = 2,`
	`D3DTADDRESS_CLAMP = 3,`
	`} D3DTEXTUREADDRESS;`

Description	Describes the supported texture address for the D3DRENDERSTATE_TEXTUREADDRESS render state in D3DRENDERSTATETYPE.
D3DTADDRESS_WRAP	The D3DRENDERSTATE_WRAPU and D3DRENDERSTATE_WRAPV render states of the D3DRENDERSTATETYPE enumerated type are used. This is the default setting.
D3DTADDRESS_MIRROR	
	Equivalent to a tiling texture-addressing mode (that is, when neither D3DRENDERSTATE_WRAPU nor D3DRENDERSTATE_WRAPV is used), except that the texture is flipped at every integer junction. For *u*-values between 0 and 1, for example, the texture is addressed normally, between 1 and 2 the texture is flipped (mirrored), between 2 and 3 the texture is normal again, and so on.
D3DTADDRESS_CLAMP	
	Texture coordinates greater than 1.0 are set to 1.0, and values less than 0.0 are set to 0.0.
Type	**D3DTEXTUREBLEND**

Example	`typedef enum _D3DTEXTUREBLEND {`
	`D3DTBLEND_DECAL = 1,`
	`D3DTBLEND_MODULATE = 2,`
	`D3DTBLEND_DECALALPHA = 3,`
	`D3DTBLEND_MODULATEALPHA = 4,`
	`D3DTBLEND_DECALMASK = 5,`
	`D3DTBLEND_MODULATEMASK = 6,`
	`D3DTBLEND_COPY = 7,`
	`} D3DTEXTUREBLEND;`

Description	Defines the supported texture-blending modes.
Usage	Used by the D3DRENDERSTATE_TEXTUREMAPBLEND render state in the D3DRENDERSTATETYPE.
Modulate	Modulation combines the effects of lighting and texturing. Because colors are specified as values between and including 0 and 1, modulating (multiplying) the texture and preexisting colors together typically produces colors that are less bright than either source. The brightness of a color component is undiminished when one of the sources for that component is white (1). The simplest way to ensure that the colors of a texture do not change when the texture is applied to an object is to ensure that the object is white (1, 1, 1).
D3DTBLEND_DECAL	Decal texture-blending mode is supported. In this mode, the RGB and alpha values of the texture replace the colors that would have been used with no texturing.
D3DTBLEND_MODULATE	Modulate texture-blending mode is supported. In this mode, the RGB values of the texture are multiplied with the RGB values that would have been used with no texturing. Any alpha values in the texture replace the alpha values in the colors that would have been used with no texturing.
D3DTBLEND_DECALALPHA	Decal-alpha texture-blending mode is supported. In this mode, the RGB and alpha values of the texture are blended with the colors that would have been used with no texturing, according to the formula $C = (1 - A_t)C_o + A_t C_t$, where C is the color, A is the alpha, t is the texture, and o is the original object (before blending). Any alpha values in the texture replace the alpha values in the colors that would have been used with no texturing.
D3DTBLEND_MODULATEALPHA	Modulate-alpha texture-blending mode is supported. In this mode, the RGB values of the texture are multiplied with the RGB values that would have been used with no texturing and the alpha values of the texture are multiplied with the alpha values that would have been used with no texturing.
D3DTBLEND_DECALMASK	Decal-mask texture-blending mode is supported.
D3DTBLEND_MODULATEMASK	Modulate-mask texture-blending mode is supported.
D3DTBLEND_COPY	Copy texture-blending mode is supported.
Structure	**D3DTEXTUREFILTER**
Example	`typedef enum _D3DTEXTUREFILTER {` `D3DFILTER_NEAREST = 1,`

```
D3DFILTER_LINEAR = 2,
D3DFILTER_MIPNEAREST = 3,
D3DFILTER_MIPLINEAR = 4,
D3DFILTER_LINEARMIPNEAREST = 5,
D3DFILTER_LINEARMIPLINEAR = 6,
} D3DTEXTUREFILTER;
```

Description	Defines the supported texture filter modes used by the D3DRENDERSTATE_TEXTUREMAG render state in D3DRENDERSTATETYPE.
D3DFILTER_NEAREST	The texel with coordinates nearest to the desired pixel value is used. This applies to both zooming in and zooming out. If either zooming in or zooming out is supported, then both must be supported.
D3DFILTER_LINEAR	A weighted average of a 2 × 2 area of texels surrounding the desired pixel is used. This applies to both zooming in and zooming out. If either zooming in or zooming out is supported, then both must be supported.
D3DFILTER_MIPNEAREST	Similar to D3DFILTER_NEAREST, but uses the appropriate mipmap for texel selection.
D3DFILTER_MIPLINEAR	Similar to D3DFILTER_LINEAR, but uses the appropriate mipmap for texel selection.
D3DFILTER_LINEARMIPNEAREST	Similar to D3DFILTER_MIPNEAREST, but interpolates between the two nearest mipmaps.
D3DFILTER_LINEARMIPLINEAR	Similar to D3DFILTER_MIPLINEAR, but interpolates between the two nearest mipmaps.

Other Types

Type	**D3DCOLOR**
Example	`typedef DWORD D3DCOLOR, D3DCOLOR, *LPD3DCOLOR;`
Description	A D3D color.
Type	**D3DVALUE**
Example	`typedef float D3DVALUE, *LPD3DVALUE;`
Description	A D3D value.

Return Values

D3D_OK
D3DERR_BADMAJORVERSION
D3DERR_BADMINORVERSION
D3DERR_EXECUTE_CLIPPED_FAILED
D3DERR_EXECUTE_CREATE_FAILED
D3DERR_EXECUTE_DESTROY_FAILED
D3DERR_EXECUTE_FAILED
D3DERR_EXECUTE_LOCK_FAILED
D3DERR_EXECUTE_LOCKED
D3DERR_EXECUTE_NOT_LOCKED
D3DERR_EXECUTE_UNLOCK_FAILED
D3DERR_LIGHT_SET_FAILED
D3DERR_MATERIAL_CREATE_FAILED
D3DERR_MATERIAL_DESTROY_FAILED
D3DERR_MATERIAL_GETDATA_FAILED
D3DERR_MATERIAL_SETDATA_FAILED
D3DERR_MATRIX_CREATE_FAILED
D3DERR_MATRIX_DESTROY_FAILED
D3DERR_MATRIX_GETDATA_FAILED
D3DERR_MATRIX_SETDATA_FAILED
D3DERR_SCENE_BEGIN_FAILED
D3DERR_SCENE_END_FAILED
D3DERR_SCENE_IN_SCENE
D3DERR_SCENE_NOT_IN_SCENE
D3DERR_SETVIEWPORTDATA_FAILED
D3DERR_TEXTURE_CREATE_FAILED
D3DERR_TEXTURE_DESTROY_FAILED
D3DERR_TEXTURE_GETSURF_FAILED
D3DERR_TEXTURE_LOAD_FAILED
D3DERR_TEXTURE_LOCK_FAILED
D3DERR_TEXTURE_LOCKED
D3DERR_TEXTURE_NO_SUPPORT
D3DERR_TEXTURE_NOT_LOCKED

D3DERR_TEXTURE_SWAP_FAILED

D3DERR_TEXTURE_UNLOCK_FAILED

Execute Buffer Instructions

Instruction	**D3DINSTRUCTION**

Example	```typedef struct _D3DINSTRUCTION {```
	 ```BYTE bOpcode;```
	 ```BYTE bSize;```
	 ```WORD wCount;```
	 ```} D3DINSTRUCTION, *LPD3DINSTRUCTION;```

Description	Describes an instruction in the execute buffer.
Layout	An instruction in the execute buffer starts with this header structure and is followed by a variable-length, instruction-specific block of data (see D3DOPCODE that follows).
`bOpcode`	Opcode for the instruction (D3DOPCODE).
`bSize`	Size of each instruction data unit. This member can be used to skip to the next instruction in the sequence.
`wCount`	Number of data units of instructions that follow. This allows you to batch similar instructions, such as triangles that make up a triangle mesh.
Instruction	**D3DOPCODE**

Example	```typedef enum _D3DOPCODE {```
	 ```D3DOP_POINT = 1,```
	 ```D3DPOINT```
	 ```D3DOP_LINE = 2,```
	 ```D3DLINE```
	 ```D3DOP_TRIANGLE = 3,```
	 ```D3DTRIANGLE```
	 ```D3DOP_MATRIXLOAD = 4,```
	 ```D3DMATRIXLOAD```
	 ```D3DOP_MATRIXMULTIPLY = 5,```
	 ```D3DMATRIXMULTIPLY```
	 ```D3DOP_STATETRANSFORM = 6,```
	 ```D3DSTATE```
	 ```D3DOP_STATELIGHT = 7,```
	 ```D3DSTATE```
	 ```D3DOP_STATERENDER = 8,```
	 ```D3DSTATE```
	 ```D3DOP_PROCESSVERTICES = 9,```

```
            D3DPROCESSVERTICES
            D3DOP_TEXTURELOAD = 10,
            D3DTEXTURELOAD
            D3DOP_EXIT = 11,
            D3DOP_BRANCHFORWARD = 12,
            D3DBRANCH
            D3DOP_SPAN= 13,
            D3DSPAN
            D3DOP_SETSTATUS = 14,
            D3DSTATUS
            } D3DOPCODE;
```

Description   The types of execute buffer instructions.

D3DOP_POINT   Sends a point to the renderer. See D3DPOINT.

D3DOP_LINE   Sends a line to the renderer. See D3DLINE.

D3DOP_TRIANGLE   Sends a triangle to the renderer. See D3DTRIANGLE.

D3DOP_MATRIXLOAD   Loads a matrix. See D3DMATRIXLOAD.

D3DOP_MATRIXMULTIPLY

    Multiplies two matrices. See D3DMATRIXMULTIPLY.

D3DOP_STATETRANSFORM

    Sets the internal state variables of the transformation module. See D3DSTATE and D3DTRANSFORMSTATETYPE.

D3DOP_STATELIGHT   Sets the internal state variables of the lighting module. See D3DSTATE and D3DLIGHTSTATETYPE.

D3DOP_STATERENDER

    Sets the internal state variables of the rendering module. See D3DSTATE and D3DRENDERSTATETYPE.

D3DOP_PROCESSVERTICES

    Sets both lighting and transformations for vertices. See D3DPROCESSVERTICES.

D3DOP_TEXTURELOAD

    Loads a texture to the rendering engine. See D3DTEXTURELOAD.

D3DOP_EXIT   Signals the end of the list of instructions. There is no following block of data for this instruction.

D3DOP_BRANCHFORWARD

    Causes a branch forward in the instruction list (skipping instructions). See D3DBRANCH.

D3DOP_SPAN   Sends a span to the renderer (a span is a list of points with the same *y*-value). See D3DSPAN.

D3DOP_SETSTATUS   Resets the status of the execute buffer. See D3DSTATUS.

Instruction	**D3DPOINT (1)**
Example	```typedef struct _D3DPOINT {
WORD wCount;
WORD wFirst;
} D3DPOINT, *LPD3DPOINT;```
Description	Data for D3DOP_POINT execute buffer instruction.
Usage	Points are rendered by using a list of vertices.
`wCount`	Number of points.
`wFirst`	Index of the first vertex.
Instruction	**D3DLINE (2)**
Example	```typedef struct _D3DLINE {
union {
WORD v1;
WORD wV1;
};
union {
WORD v2;
WORD wV2;
};
} D3DLINE, *LPD3DLINE;```
Description	Data for D3DOP_Line execute buffer instruction.
Usage	Describes a line, which can be a group of line segments.
Note	There will be one less line segment drawn than the number of vertices (because of endpoints).
`wV1` and `wV2`	Vertex indices of first and last vertex to be joined in a group of line segments.
Instruction	**D3DTRIANGLE (3)**
Example	```typedef struct _D3DTRIANGLE {
union {
WORD v1;
WORD wV1;
};
union {
WORD v2;
WORD wV2;
};
union {
WORD v3;
WORD wV3;
};```

```
        WORD wFlags;
} D3DTRIANGLE, *LPD3DTRIANGLE;
```

Description	Data for D3DOP_TRIANGLE.
Usage	Describes a triangle, the main rendering primitive.
What is an index	The three vertex indices v1, v2, and v3 are vertex indexes into the vertex list at the start of the execute buffer.
Shading	For flat shading, color and specular value of the triangle's face comes from the first vertex (v1).
Triangle strips	The flags for a strip of 5 triangles: D3DTRIFLAG_START D3DTRIFLAG_ODD D3DTRIFLAG_EVEN D3DTRIFLAG_ODD D3DTRIFLAG_EVEN The flags for a fan of 5 triangles: D3DTRIFLAG_START D3DTRIFLAG_EVEN D3DTRIFLAG_EVEN D3DTRIFLAG_EVEN D3DTRIFLAG_EVEN
`wV1`	Index of vertex 1.
`wV2`	Index of vertex 2.
`wV3`	Index of vertex 3.
`wFlags`	Describes triangle strips and fans. For wireframe mode, it specifies which triangle edges are enabled (visible). Edge flags: If two triangles share an edge (i.e., share two vertices), then only one edge should be enabled to avoid drawing the edge twice.

D3DTRIFLAG_EDGEENABLE1
> v1–v2 is an edge.

D3DTRIFLAG_EDGEENABLE2
> v2–v3 is an edge.

D3DTRIFLAG_EDGEENABLE3
> v3–v1 is an edge.

D3DTRIFLAG_EDGEENABLETRIANGLE
> All are edges.
> Strip and fan flags:

D3DTRIFLAG_EVEN   The v1–v2 edge of the current triangle is adjacent to the v3–v1 edge of the previous triangle. In other words, v1 is the previous v1, and v2 is the previous v3.

Chapter 19 Immediate Mode Reference 429

D3DTRIFLAG_ODD	The v1–v2 edge of the current triangle is adjacent to the v2–v3 edge of the previous triangle. In other words, v1 is the previous v3, and v2 is the previous v2.
D3DTRIFLAG_START	Begin the strip or fan, loading all three vertices.
D3DTRIFLAG_STARTFLAT(len)	Begin a flat (coplanar) triangle strip or fan. If this triangle is culled, also cull len subsequent triangles (0<len<30).

Instruction	**D3DMATRIXLOAD (4)**

Example	`typedef struct _D3DMATRIXLOAD {`
	`D3DMATRIXHANDLE hDestMatrix;`
	`D3DMATRIXHANDLE hSrcMatrix;`
	`} D3DMATRIXLOAD, *LPD3DMATRIXLOAD;`

Description	Data for D3DOP_MATRIXLOAD.
`hDestMatrix`	Destination matrix handle.
`hSrcMatrix`	Source matrix handle.

Instruction	**D3DMATRIXMULTIPLY (5)**

Example	`typedef struct _D3DMATRIXMULTIPLY {`
	`D3DMATRIXHANDLE hDestMatrix;`
	`D3DMATRIXHANDLE hSrcMatrix1;`
	`D3DMATRIXHANDLE hSrcMatrix2;`
	`} D3DMATRIXMULTIPLY, *LPD3DMATRIXMULTIPLY;`

Description	Data for D3DOP_MATRIXMULTIPLY.
`hDestMatrix`	Handle for the result.
`hSrcMatrix1`	Handle for the first matrix.
`hSrcMatrix2`	Handle for the second matrix.

Instruction	**D3DSTATE (6, 7, 8)**

Example	`typedef struct _D3DSTATE {`
	`union {`
	`D3DTRANSFORMSTATETYPE dtstTransformStateType;`
	`D3DLIGHTSTATETYPE dlstLightStateType;`
	`D3DRENDERSTATETYPEdrstRenderStateType;`
	`};`
	`union {`
	`DWORD dwArg[1];`
	`D3DVALUE dvArg[1];`
	`};`
	`} D3DSTATE, *LPD3DSTATE;`

Description	Data for D3DOP_STATETRANSFORM, D3DOP_STATELIGHT, and D3DOP_STATERENDER.

Usage	Sets internal state variables for the transformation, lighting, and render modules.
`dtstTransform-StateType`	D3DTRANSFORMSTATETYPE.
`dlstLightStateType`	D3DLIGHTSTATETYPE.
`drstRender-StateType`	D3DRENDERSTATETYPE.
`dvArg`	Value of the type specified in the first member of this structure.

D3DTRANSFORMSTATETYPE

Example	`typedef enum _D3DTRANSFORMSTATETYPE {`
	`D3DTRANSFORMSTATE_WORLD = 1,`
	`D3DTRANSFORMSTATE_VIEW = 2,`
	`D3DTRANSFORMSTATE_PROJECTION = 3,`
	`} D3DTRANSFORMSTATETYPE;`

Description	Data for D3DOP_STATETRANSFORM.
Default	Default matrices are NULL (the identity matrix).

D3DTRANSFORMSTATE_WORLD
Matrix for world transformation.

D3DTRANSFORMSTATE_VIEW
Matrix for view transformation.

D3DTRANSFORMSTATE_PROJECTION
Matrix for projection transformation.

D3DLIGHTSTATETYPE

Example	`typedef enum _D3DLIGHTSTATETYPE {`
	`D3DLIGHTSTATE_MATERIAL = 1,`
	`D3DLIGHTSTATE_AMBIENT = 2,`
	`D3DLIGHTSTATE_COLORMODEL = 3,`
	`D3DLIGHTSTATE_FOGMODE = 4,`
	`D3DLIGHTSTATE_FOGSTART = 5,`
	`D3DLIGHTSTATE_FOGEND = 6,`
	`D3DLIGHTSTATE_FOGDENSITY = 7,`
	`} D3DLIGHTSTATETYPE;`

Description	Data for D3DOP_STATELIGHT.
Usage	Defines the state of a light.
Note	Part of the D3DSTATE structure.

D3DLIGHTSTATE_MATERIAL
Sets the material associated with a light. (The default is NULL.)

D3DLIGHTSTATE_AMBIENT
Sets light to ambient. (The default is 0.)

D3DLIGHTSTATE_COLORMODEL
> D3DCOLORMODEL. (The default is D3DCOLOR_RGB.)

D3DLIGHTSTATE_FOGMODE
> D3DFOGMODE. (The default is D3DFOG_NONE.)

D3DLIGHTSTATE_FOGSTART
> Sets the starting value for fog. (The default is 1.0.)

D3DLIGHTSTATE_FOGEND
> Sets the ending value for fog. (The default is 100.0.)

D3DLIGHTSTATE_FOGDENSITY
> Sets the density setting for fog. (The default is 1.0.)

D3DRENDERSTATETYPE

Example

```
typedef enum _D3DRENDERSTATETYPE {
    D3DRENDERSTATE_TEXTUREHANDLE = 1,
    D3DRENDERSTATE_ANTIALIAS = 2,
    D3DRENDERSTATE_TEXTUREADDRESS = 3,
    D3DRENDERSTATE_TEXTUREPERSPECTIVE = 4,
    D3DRENDERSTATE_WRAPU = 5,
    D3DRENDERSTATE_WRAPV = 6,
    D3DRENDERSTATE_ZENABLE = 7,
    D3DRENDERSTATE_FILLMODE = 8,
    D3DRENDERSTATE_SHADEMODE = 9,
    D3DRENDERSTATE_LINEPATTERN = 10,
    D3DRENDERSTATE_MONOENABLE = 11,
    D3DRENDERSTATE_ROP2 = 12,
    D3DRENDERSTATE_PLANEMASK = 13,
    D3DRENDERSTATE_ZWRITEENABLE = 14,
    D3DRENDERSTATE_ALPHATESTENABLE = 15,
    D3DRENDERSTATE_LASTPIXEL = 16,
    D3DRENDERSTATE_TEXTUREMAG = 17,
    D3DRENDERSTATE_TEXTUREMIN = 18,
    D3DRENDERSTATE_SRCBLEND = 19,
    D3DRENDERSTATE_DESTBLEND = 20,
    D3DRENDERSTATE_TEXTUREMAPBLEND = 21,
    D3DRENDERSTATE_CULLMODE = 22,
    D3DRENDERSTATE_ZFUNC = 23,
    D3DRENDERSTATE_ALPHAREF = 24,
    D3DRENDERSTATE_ALPHAFUNC = 25,
    D3DRENDERSTATE_DITHERENABLE = 26,
    D3DRENDERSTATE_BLENDENABLE = 27,
    D3DRENDERSTATE_FOGENABLE = 28,
    D3DRENDERSTATE_SPECULARENABLE = 29,
    D3DRENDERSTATE_ZVISIBLE = 30,
```

```
             D3DRENDERSTATE_SUBPIXEL = 31,
             D3DRENDERSTATE_SUBPIXELX = 32,
             D3DRENDERSTATE_STIPPLEDALPHA = 33,
             D3DRENDERSTATE_FOGCOLOR = 34,
             D3DRENDERSTATE_FOGTABLEMODE = 35,
             D3DRENDERSTATE_FOGTABLESTART = 36,
             D3DRENDERSTATE_FOGTABLEEND = 37,
             D3DRENDERSTATE_FOGTABLEDENSITY = 38,
             D3DRENDERSTATE_STIPPLEENABLE = 39,
             D3DRENDERSTATE_STIPPLEPATTERN00 = 64,
                // Stipple patterns 01 through 30 omitted
             here.
             D3DRENDERSTATE_STIPPLEPATTERN31 = 95,
             } D3DRENDERSTATETYPE;
```

Description	Data for D3DOP_STATERENDER.
Usage	Defines render state variables.
Note	Part of the D3DSTATE structure.

D3DRENDERSTATE_TEXTUREHANDLE
:   Texture handle. (The default is NULL.)

D3DRENDERSTATE_ANTIALIAS
:   Antialiasing primitive edges. (The default is FALSE.)

D3DRENDERSTATE_TEXTUREADDRESS
:   D3DTEXTUREADDRESS. (The default is D3DTADDRESS_WRAP.)

D3DRENDERSTATE_TEXTUREPERSPECTIVE
:   TRUE for perspective correction. (The default is FALSE.)

D3DRENDERSTATE_WRAPU
:   TRUE for wrapping in *u*-direction. (The default is FALSE.)

D3DRENDERSTATE_WRAPV
:   TRUE for wrapping in *v*-direction. (The default is FALSE.)

D3DRENDERSTATE_ZENABLE
:   TRUE to enable the z-buffer comparison test when writing to the frame buffer. (The default is FALSE.)

D3DRENDERSTATE_FILLMODE
:   D3DFILLMODE. (The default is D3DFILL_SOLID.)

D3DRENDERSTATE_SHADEMODE
:   D3DSHADEMODE. (The default is D3DSHADE_GOURAUD.)

D3DRENDERSTATE_LINEPATTERN
:   The D3DLINEPATTERN structure. (The default is 0 for wRepeatPattern and wLinePattern.)

D3DRENDERSTATE_ROP2
: One of the 16 ROP2 binary raster operations specifying how the supplied pixels are combined with the pixels of the display surface. (The default is R2_COPYPEN.) Use the D3DPRASTERCAPS_ROP2 flag in dwRasterCaps of D3DPRIMCAPS to find out which raster operations are supported by the device.

D3DRENDERSTATE_PLANEMASK
: Physical plane mask, type ULONG. (The default is 0.)

D3DRENDERSTATE_ZWRITEENABLE
: TRUE to enable z writes. (The default is TRUE.) FALSE will stop the updating of the z-buffer with new z-values.

D3DRENDERSTATE_ALPHATESTENABLE
: TRUE to enable alpha tests. (The default is FALSE.)

D3DRENDERSTATE_LASTPIXEL
: TRUE to prevent drawing the last pixel in a line. (The default is FALSE.)

D3DRENDERSTATE_TEXTUREMAG
: D3DTEXTUREFILTER. (The default is D3DFILTER_NEAREST.)

D3DRENDERSTATE_TEXTUREMIN
: D3DTEXTUREFILTER. (The default is D3DFILTER_NEAREST.)

D3DRENDERSTATE_SRCBLEND
: D3DBLEND. (The default is D3DBLEND_ONE.)

D3DRENDERSTATE_DSTBLEND
: D3DBLEND. (The default is D3DBLEND_ZERO.)

D3DRENDERSTATE_TEXTUREMAPBLEND
: D3DTEXTUREBLEND. (The default is D3DTBLEND_MODULATE.)

D3DRENDERSTATE_CULLMODE
: D3DCULL. (The default is D3DCULL_CCW.) Software renderers have a fixed culling order and do not support changing the culling mode.

D3DRENDERSTATE_ZFUNC
: D3DCMPFUNC. (The default is D3DCMP_LESSEQUAL.) This sets the type of comparison the renderer makes with the z-buffer.

D3DRENDERSTATE_ALPHAREF
: D3DFIXED specifying a reference alpha value against which pixels are tested when alpha-testing is enabled. (The default is 0.)

D3DRENDERSTATE_ALPHAFUNC
: D3DCMPFUNC. (The default is D3DCMP_ALWAYS.) This sets the type of alpha comparison the renderer performs.

D3DRENDERSTATE_DITHERENABLE
    TRUE to enable dithering. (The default is FALSE.)

D3DRENDERSTATE_BLENDENABLE
    TRUE to enable alpha blending. (The default is FALSE.)

D3DRENDERSTATE_FOGENABLE
    TRUE to enable fog. (The default is FALSE.)

D3DRENDERSTATE_SPECULARENABLE
    TRUE to enable specular. (The default is TRUE.)

D3DRENDERSTATE_ZVISIBLE
    TRUE to enable z-checking. (The default is FALSE.) Z-checking is a culling technique in which a polygon representing the screen space of an entire group of polygons is tested against the z-buffer to discover whether any of the polygons should be drawn.

D3DRENDERSTATE_SUBPIXEL
    TRUE to enable subpixel correction. (The default is FALSE.)

D3DRENDERSTATE_SUBPIXELX
    TRUE to enable correction in X only. (The default is FALSE.)

D3DRENDERSTATE_STIPPLEDALPHA
    TRUE to enable stippled alpha. (The default is FALSE.)

D3DRENDERSTATE_FOGCOLOR
    Value whose type is D3DCOLOR. (The default is 0.)

D3DRENDERSTATE_FOGTABLEMODE
    D3DFOGMODE. (The default is D3DFOG_NONE.)

D3DRENDERSTATE_FOGTABLESTART
    Fog table start. This is the position at which fog effects begin for linear fog mode.

D3DRENDERSTATE_FOGTABLEEND
    Fog table end. This is the position at which fog effects reach their maximum density for linear fog mode.

D3DRENDERSTATE_FOGTABLEDENSITY
    Sets the maximum fog density for linear fog mode. This value can range from 0 to 1.

D3DRENDERSTATE_STIPPLEENABLE
    Enables stippling in the device driver. When stippled alpha is enabled, it must override the current stipple pattern. When stippled alpha is disabled, the stipple pattern must be returned.

D3DRENDERSTATE_STIPPLEPATTERN00 through
D3DRENDERSTATE_STIPPLEPATTERN31
    Stipple pattern. Each render state applies to a separate line of the stipple pattern.

Instruction	**D3DPROCESSVERTICES (9)**
Example	```typedef struct _D3DPROCESSVERTICES {
DWORD dwFlags;
WORD wStart;
WORD wDest;
DWORD dwCount;
DWORD dwReserved;
} D3DPROCESSVERTICES, *LPD3DPROCESSVERTICES;```
Description	Data for D3DOP_PROCESSVERTICES.
Usage	Describes how vertices in the execute buffer should be processed.
`dwFlags`	One or more processing options for the vertices:

D3DPROCESSVERTICES_COPY
> Just copy the vertices to the driver because they have already been transformed and lit.

D3DPROCESSVERTICES_NOCOLOR
> Vertices should not be colored.

D3DPROCESSVERTICES_OPMASK
> Specifies a bitmask of the other flags in the dwFlags member, exclusive of D3DPROCESSVERTICES_NOCOLOR and D3DPROCESSVERTICES_UPDATEEXTENTS.

D3DPROCESSVERTICES_TRANSFORM
> Vertices should be transformed.

D3DPROCESSVERTICES_TRANSFORMLIGHT
> Vertices should be transformed and lit.

D3DPROCESSVERTICES_UPDATEEXTENTS
> Extents of all transformed vertices should be updated. This information is returned in the drExtent member of the D3DSTATUS structure.

`wStart`	Index of the first vertex in the source.
`wDest`	Index of the first vertex in the local buffer.
`dwCount`	Number of vertices to be processed.
`dwReserved`	Reserved; must be 0.
Instruction	**D3DTEXTURELOAD (10)**
Example	```typedef struct _D3DTEXTURELOAD {
D3DTEXTUREHANDLE hDestTexture;
D3DTEXTUREHANDLE hSrcTexture;
} D3DTEXTURELOAD, *LPD3DTEXTURELOAD;```
Period	Data for D3DOP_TEXTURELOAD.

Usage	The source and destination textures must be the same size.
`hDestTexture`	Handle of the destination texture.
`hSrcTexture`	Handle of the source texture.
Instruction	**D3DBRANCH (12)**
| Example | ```
typedef struct _D3DBRANCH {
DWORD dwMask;
DWORD dwValue;
BOOL bNegate;
DWORD dwOffset;
} D3DBRANCH, *LPD3DBRANCH;
``` |
Description	Defines a branch operation in an execute buffer (i.e., tells the renderer to skip a specified amount of instructions forward in a list of execute buffer commands).
`dwMask`	Bitmask for the branch. This mask is combined with the driver-status mask by using the logical AND operator. If the result equals the value specified in the dwValue member and the bNegate member is FALSE, the branch is taken.
`dwValue`	Application-defined value to compare against the operation described in the dwMask member.
`bNegate`	TRUE to negate comparison.
`dwOffset`	How far to branch forward. Specify 0 to exit.
Instruction	**D3DSPAN (13)**
| Example | ```
typedef struct _D3DSPAN {
WORD wCount;
WORD wFirst;
} D3DSPAN, *LPD3DSPAN;
``` |
Description	Data for D3DOP_Span.
What is a span	A span is a list of points with the same *y* screen value. Rasterizers break triangles into spans, one span for each *y* pixel value on screen.
`wCount`	Number of spans.
`wFirst`	Index to first vertex.
Instruction	**D3DSTATUS (14)**
| Example | ```
typedef struct _D3DSTATUS {
DWORD dwFlags;
DWORD dwStatus;
D3DRECT drExtent;
} D3DSTATUS, *LPD3DSTATUS;
``` |
```

Description	Data for D3DOP_SETSTATUS.
Usage	Sets current status of the execute buffer.
Note	The status is a rolling status and is updated during each execution.
`dwFlags`	Status to set:

D3DSETSTATUS_STATUS
> Set the status.

D3DSETSTATUS_EXTENTS
> Set the extents specified in drExtent.

D3DSETSTATUS_ALL Set both status and extents.

`dwStatus`
> Clipping flags:
> Combination and General Flags:

D3DSTATUS_CLIPINTERSECTION
> Combination of all CLIPINTERSECTION flags.

D3DSTATUS_CLIPUNIONALL
> Combination of all CLIPUNION flags.

D3DSTATUS_DEFAULT
> Combination of D3DSTATUS_CLIPINTERSECTION and D3DSTATUS_ZNOTVISIBLE flags. This value is the default.

D3DSTATUS_ZNOTVISIBLE
> Clip Intersection Flags.

D3DSTATUS_CLIPINTERSECTIONLEFT
> Logical AND of the clip flags for the vertices compared to the left side of the viewing frustum.

D3DSTATUS_CLIPINTERSECTIONRIGHT
> Logical AND of the clip flags for the vertices compared to the right side of the viewing frustum.

D3DSTATUS_CLIPINTERSECTIONTOP
> Logical AND of the clip flags for the vertices compared to the top of the viewing frustum.

D3DSTATUS_CLIPINTERSECTIONBOTTOM
> Logical AND of the clip flags for the vertices compared to the bottom of the viewing frustum.

D3DSTATUS_CLIPINTERSECTIONFRONT
> Logical AND of the clip flags for the vertices compared to the front clipping plane of the viewing frustum.

D3DSTATUS_CLIPINTERSECTIONBACK
> Logical AND of the clip flags for the vertices compared to the back clipping plane of the viewing frustum.

D3DSTATUS_CLIPINTERSECTIONGEN0 through
D3DSTATUS_CLIPINTERSECTIONGEN5
: Logical AND of the clip flags for application-defined clipping planes.
Clip Union Flags:

D3DSTATUS_CLIPUNIONLEFT
: Equal to D3DCLIP_LEFT.

3DSTATUS_CLIPUNIONRIGHT
: Equal to D3DCLIP_RIGHT.

3DSTATUS_CLIPUNIONTOP
: Equal to D3DCLIP_TOP.

D3DSTATUS_CLIPUNIONBOTTOM
: Equal to D3DCLIP_BOTTOM.

D3DSTATUS_CLIPUNIONFRONT
: Equal to D3DCLIP_FRONT.

D3DSTATUS_CLIPUNIONBACK
: Equal to D3DCLIP_BACK.

D3DSTATUS_CLIPUNIONGEN0 through
D3DSTATUS_CLIPUNIONGEN5
: Equal to D3DCLIP_GEN0 through D3DCLIP_GEN5.
Basic Clipping Flags:

D3DCLIP_BACK	All vertices are clipped by the back plane of the viewing frustum.
D3DCLIP_BOTTOM	All vertices are clipped by the bottom plane of the viewing frustum.
D3DCLIP_FRONT	All vertices are clipped by the front plane of the viewing frustum.
D3DCLIP_LEFT	All vertices are clipped by the left plane of the viewing frustum.
D3DCLIP_RIGHT	All vertices are clipped by the right plane of the viewing frustum.
D3DCLIP_TOP	All vertices are clipped by the top plane of the viewing frustum.
D3DCLIP_GEN0 through D3DCLIP_GEN5	Application-defined clipping planes.
drExtent	A D3DRECT structure that defines a bounding box for all the relevant vertices. For example, the structure might define the area containing the output of the D3DOP_PROCESSVERTICES opcode, assuming the D3DPROCESSVERTICES_UPDATEEXTENTS flag is set in the D3DPROCESSVERTICES structure. The bounding box in the drExtent member can grow with each execution, but it does not shrink. It can be reset only via the D3DOP_SETSTATUS opcode.

Glossary

3 DOF. Three degrees of freedom. Three different directions that a sensor or input device can move: *x, y,* and *z* (but not orientation). Compare with **6 DOF.**

3D pipeline. The multiple-step process of converting 3D scene data into an image displayed on a 2D screen.

3DMF. 3D Meta File, Apple's 3D cross-platform 3D file format for QuickDraw3D.

6 DOF. Six degrees of freedom. Six different directions that a sensor or input device can move: location *(x, y,* and *z)* and orientation (roll, pitch, and yaw). Compare with **3 DOF.**

    absolute coordinate system. Same as **world coordinate system.**

    affine matrix. A matrix that specifies an affine transformation.

    affine transformation. A transformation that preserves parallel lines of the objects transformed. Scale, translate, and rotate transforms are affine transforms.

    AGP. Accelerated Graphics Port. A special-purpose bus to speed communication between the CPU and a graphics chip. See **PCI.**

    aliasing. Jarring visual imperfections in a pixel-based image. Caused by abrupt changes in color from pixel to pixel. Also called the "jaggies." Also includes moire patterns. *Temporal aliasing* is aliasing effects caused by small imperfections as an image changes over time.

    alpha. Transparency information about an image (which, if you think about it, you can also consider as opacity information).

    alpha blending. Blending two images based on their transparency. Some graphics hardware supports alpha blending.

alpha buffer. A memory buffer that stores transparency values for each pixel of an image. An 8-bit alpha channel might specify that 255 is opaque, 0 is completely transparent, and values in between represent relative transparency.

alpha channel. An alpha buffer.

ambient light. A default minimum amount of light that is arbitrarily assigned to an object in a 3D scene. Ambient light does not represent "real" light, since objects are not lit in the real world if no light is shining on them. Ambient light is a convenient way to simplify lighting and simulate natural diffuse light.

animation. Creating the illusion of movement and change by displaying a rapid sequence of images.

antialiasing. Removing the jaggies by creating more visually pleasing slanted lines. The main antialiasing technique is subpixel sampling, which means the renderer assumes that each screen pixel is a grid of subpixels.

API. Application Programming Interface. A toolkit of code and functions designed to provide support to an application programmer.

application framework. An API, playback engine, and associated file formats that describe the structure of an application. Multimedia authoring tools are application frameworks.

approximating spline. A spline where the line goes near but not through the control points. Compare with **interpolating spline.**

articulated figure. A simulation of a human, animal, robot, or avatar with moving joints.

articulated object. Any object with separately moveable parts.

articulated part. An attached part of an entity or object that can be moved separately from the object itself, such as with a joint or slider.

artifact. An unwanted visual feature in the rendering of an image. See **aliasing.**

atmospheric effects. Effects like fog and depth cueing that affect the rendering of a 3D scene. The basic atmospheric technique is to blend in a color based on the z depth (distance into the screen) at a particular pixel. Simple atmospheric effects are usually easy and quick to produce in hardware accelerators.

attenuation. The reduction of light intensity over distance.

avatar. A 3D model that represents a person in a multiuser 3D simulation.

axis. A line in 3D space around which an object may be rotated. Also, a line representing the x-, y-, or z-direction in 3D space.

back buffer. The buffer that is not being displayed on the screen when double buffering is occurring. Compare with **front buffer.**

back clipping plane. The plane that defines the farthest polygons that will be rendered. Polygons with a z-value in relation to the screen that is greater than the back clipping plane will not be rendered.

back end. Low-level system component.

backface culling. Also called *backface removal*. The process of removing from further rendering those polygons whose back sides face the viewer. Done in order to speed up overall rendering speed.

backfacing. A polygon facing away from the screen. This means that the surface normal of the polygon will be facing away from the camera.

behavior. Something that adds intelligence, movement, or interactivity to a 3D scene or an object in it.

behavioral animation. Simulating movement through algorithms such as collision avoidance and flocking (objects tending to stay near each other without bumping into each other).

best-effort service. A communication service in which transmitted data is not acknowledged. The data usually arrives in order, and without errors. If an error occurs, the packet is not automatically retransmitted. Multiuser 3D spaces sometimes rely on best effort services like PDU, rather than TCP/IP.

Bezier patch. A surface defined by interpolating the space between a set of Bezier splines.

Bezier spline. A type of spline with four control points. The ends of the spline start at the two end control points, and the shape of the spline is defined by the location of the two other control points. See **piecewise Bezier curve.**

bilinear filtering/sampling. A texture mapping technique that smooths out close-up views of textures that make each pixel in the texture map look blocky on the screen. The four closest texels in the texture map are sampled and then the average (bilinear interpolation) is used. Bilinear filtered textures look fuzzy instead of blocky; fuzzy looks better for things like walls, floors, and terrains. Compare with **trilinear mipmapping.**

billboard object. A 3D object that always faces in a particular direction, such as toward the screen, regardless of the orientation of the scene. Billboard objects are useful for displaying things like distant trees, which look similar from every side. A single texture of a tree could be used as a billboard object, and it would always face towards the screen.

blending function. The combining of two numbers into one number.

bounding box. A box that surrounds an object. Used for fast collision testing and visual culling.

bounding sphere. A sphere that surrounds an object. Used for fast collision testing and visual culling.

bounding volume. A bounding sphere or box.

B-spline. A type of spline.

bump map. A grid of height values that are used to render bump effects on the surface of an object.

bump mapping. A rendering technique that creates a bumpy-looking surface based on the values in a bump map. Bump mapping is occasionally attempted in real-time environments.

CAD. Computer-aided design.

CAE. Computer-aided engineering.

callback. A user-defined function that is called on traversal of the scene graph.

CAM. Computer-aided manufacturing.

Cartesian coordinates. In 2D, *x*- and *y*-values that define a location in a plane. In 3D, *x*-, *y*-, and *z*-values that define a location in space.

Catmull-Rom spline. An interpolating spline. The spline goes through all but the two end control points. Also called a *cardinal spline*.

cel animation. Traditional 2D animation. Each frame was traditionally painted on a clear acetate sheet called a cel or cell.

center of projection. The point where the projectors of a perspective projection intersect at the eye of the viewer.

CGF. Computer-generated force. An entity in a military simulation that is under the control of computer algorithms rather than humans.

CGI. Computer-generated image.

channel. (1) In motion capture data, a value that can be animated (changed) over time, like the *x*-location of an object. (2) In rasterization, another term for a memory buffer, as in alpha channel.

character animation. Animation of people, animals, and anything else lifelike.

chroma keying. Also called *blue screening*. A rasterization step whereby the color of a pixel is compared to a specified range (a minimum or maximum). If the color falls inside the range (or outside the range, depending on the effect desired), nothing is written to the frame buffer. Blue screening is chroma keying that tests for colors in the blue range.

clipping. Cutting out the parts of a scene outside of view.

clipping plane. A plane that is parallel to the image plane (the screen). Only objects between the front and back clipping planes are visible.

collision detection. Determination of when two objects have run into each other. Numerous algorithms exist, and the fastest involve bounding box and bounding sphere tests.

color model. One of two color modes of Direct3D. **Ramp color** (also called *index* or *monochromatic*) is 8-bit, palettized color. **RGB color** is 16-, 24-, or 32-bit colors specified by red, green, and blue components.

color space. Any method for specifying colors.

COM. Component object model. Microsoft's standard for binary-compatible interfaces to software components.

concave polygon. A polygon with an indentation (think of a cave). Concave polygons are generally no-nos in 3D (as are nonplanar polygons) because they are much harder to handle than convex polygons.

constant shading. See **flat shading.**

constructive simulation. A 3D simulation that is driven entirely by algorithms and data input, with no interactive participation by humans. See **HITL (human in the loop)** and **live simulation.**

control points. The points that define the shape of a spline or patch.

convex polygon. A polygon with all interior angles of less than 180 degrees. Compare with **concave polygon.** Rendering concave polygons is difficult, so many renderers do not allow them. Triangles are always convex, and Direct3D breaks all polygons into triangles before rendering.

coordinate. A location. Two common coordinate systems are Cartesian (x-, y-, and z-locations in space relative to an origin) and polar (locations on a sphere).

coordinate system. A set of x-, y-, and z-axes, with a 0, 0, 0 origin. The entire 3D scene has its own coordinate system. Each object within the scene has its own coordinate system, centered at the object's center and oriented based on the object's orientation.

coplanar. On the same plane. The three points of a triangle are always coplanar. This is one reason rendering software prefers to render triangles.

cracking. Space between polygons of a mesh. Cracking is a problem when adjacent surfaces (such as Bezier patches) are tessellated into polygons.

crawl. A temporal aliasing effect. If the edges are off slightly as an object moves, the edge pixels will appear to move.

cross product. A mathematical operation on two vectors, resulting in a third vector perpendicular to the first two. The cross product of vectors **u** and **v** is written **u** $\times$ **v**. The length of the resulting vector is equal to the product of the lengths of the other vectors times the sine of the angle between them.

culling. Removing polygons from further processing in the rendering pipeline because they are not visible. See **backface culling.**

dead reckoning. A method or algorithm for estimating the movement and location of an object based on a previously known location plus elapsed time and motion.

decal texture. A texture that is rendered without any mixing in of lighting effects. Also sometimes refers to rendering a texture without applying it to a polygon.

decimation. Reducing the number of polygons in a mesh, while keeping the same basic shape of the original mesh.

deformation. The changing of the shape of a surface.

degree of freedom (DOF). The number of ways that an object or point can be moved and oriented. 6 degrees of freedom (6 DOF) means x, y, z movement plus roll, pitch, and yaw orientation. 3 DOF means x, y, z movement, with no orientation. Sometimes, DOF means any number of adjustments that can be applied to an object, such as all the joint movements of a human figure.

depth buffer. A z-buffer.

depth complexity. The average number of pixels that can be drawn at each location screen by the renderer at a given frame rate and screen resolution.

depth cueing. Changing an object's color and intensity as it gets farther from the viewpoint. In essence, you lower the color intensity as the object gets farther away, as this reinforces a sense of depth in the scene.

diffuse reflection. Soft reflection off a surface in all directions, with no shininess. Also called *Lambertian reflection*. See **specular reflection.**

digitize. To convert an image into pixels. In 3D, creating a 3D model of a real-world object by sampling points on the surface of the object.

directional light. A light source whose rays all go in one parallel direction. The sun can be considered a directional light on the earth.

DIS. Distributed Interactive Simulation. The Department of Defense's simulation standard.

display list. A list of low-level graphics commands sent to a 3D back end. An intelligent 3D API will arrange and sort the display list it sends the back end in order to maximize performance.

dithering. Using a stippled pattern of pixels of different colors to represent an intermediate color. In index-color displays (like 256-color computer displays), dithering simulates the effect of having more than 256 colors. Dithering also can reduce the mach banding effect.

DOF. Degree of freedom.

dot product. The result of a mathematical operation on two vectors. The dot product is a value, not a vector. It is the sum of the x's multiplied together, plus the y's multiplied together, plus the z's multiplied together. The dot product of **u** and **v** is written **u** · **v**. The dot product of two perpendicular vectors is always 0. See **cross product**.

double buffer. Flipping back and forth between two memory buffers to represent the screen. One buffer (the front buffer) is displayed, while the other buffer (the back buffer) is being prepared (rendered into). When the back buffer is ready for display, it is flipped with the front buffer (which becomes the new back buffer). Double-buffering makes screen image changes look instantaneous.

DSI. Defense Simulation Internet. A military-sponsored, high-speed, secure version of the Internet used for military simulations.

dynamic terrain. Terrain that can be changed during the course of a simulation. Most simulations take the terrain as a static given.

edge. A line segment between two consecutive vertices of a polygon.

emitter. An object in a 3D scene that can send out signals. For example, radiation and sound.

entity. A thing in a 3D scene, such as a robot, car, or tree. An entity represents an abstraction of a physical thing and often has intelligence or the ability to change and move attached to it. Also called an *object* or "*thing*."

environment map. An image that looks like the scene from the viewpoint of a particular object. When used as a texture map on the object, it makes the object look like it has a mirror-like surface, reflecting the scene around it.

ESPDU. Entity State Protocol Data Unit (Distributed Interactive Simulation).

Euler angles. A set of three angles used to describe which way an object is facing in 3D space (its orientation). First, you rotate around one axis, then the next, and then the last. The order of rotation matters (x, y, z is different from z, y, x).

event. An occurrence that causes a change of state in a 3D scene. Defining how to transmit and handle events, and their effect on interpolated animations, is a fundamental design issue for 3D applications.

execute buffer. Direct3D's term for immediate mode display list. An execute buffer is a block of memory that contains vertices followed by a set of instructions that tells the rendering pipeline what to do with those vertices.

face. The filled-in part of a polygon.

face normal. A vector pointing straight out from the face of a polygon.

facet. A face.

fan. A set of triangles organized in a shape of a fan. Each additional vertex adds one more triangle to the fan by combining with the previous and first vertices in the list.

fidelity. The degree of realism of a simulation.

field-of-view. The angle of the visible volume through a camera.

filtering. Calculating the value of a pixel by sampling the region around it. Filtering tends to smooth out the rendering and reduce aliasing.

fixed point. A technique to describe a number with two integers. The value to the left of the decimal point is represented by one integer; the value to the right of the decimal point is the fractional part of the number. On pre-Pentium PCs, performing fixed-point math is faster than performing floating-point math.

flat shading. A shading technique that applies the same color to an entire polygon, with no gradation of color. Flat shading is the fastest shading, but it produces the lowest-quality image. Compare with **Gouraud shading** and **Phong shading**.

flatten. To convert a parent/child frame hierarchy of meshes into a single mesh. Flattening can speed up rendering because it eliminates layers of matrices from the geometry calculation. However, flattened meshes are much more difficult to manipulate because the intermediate frames have been removed.

floating point. A CPU register-level representation of numeric values.

flocking. Animation algorithms that make objects tend to stay near each other without bumping into each other like a herd of animals. Also called *particle system animation*.

fog. A rendering technique that causes colors to fade as the distance from the viewpoint increases. A fixed color (commonly white) is blended in with each rendered pixel based on its z depth. Fog blended in on a logarithmic scale usually looks best. A technique to hide the harsh look of polygons disappearing abruptly when they are beyond the renderer's back viewing plane.

FPS. Frames per second. Same as **frame rate.**

frame. The Direct3D retained mode object. The node in the scene graph structure. Meshes, lights, and cameras are attached to frames, which represent position and orientation in 3D space.

frame buffer. A block of graphics memory that represents the screen.

frame rate. The number of times per second the screen is re-rendered and redisplayed. Usually (although not always) the entire screen is re-rendered with each frame, although an intelligent renderer might try to re-render only the "dirty" (changed) areas. Thirty frames per second is generally considered the target rate for smooth, realtime 3D. Note that the screen refresh rate is the number of times per second that the display monitor refreshes itself. Screen refresh rates are typically 65 to 70 times/sec.

free-form deformation (FFD). An algorithm for changing the shape of 3D objects.

front buffer. The buffer that is currently being displayed on the screen when double-buffering. Compare with **back buffer.**

front face. The front side of a polygon (the side you are supposed to see). Sometimes only front faces are rendered, and sometimes both front and back faces are rendered (although this is slower). Production renderers often render both front and back faces. Realtime renderers often render only front faces.

frustum. A pyramid with the top cut off. The volume of space than can be seen from a particular viewpoint and camera width (after perspective transformation). Imagine a pyramid going out vertically from the camera: The part of the pyramid that is the visible area on screen is the frustum. Show you are in the know and don't call it "frustrum."

geometric primitive. Simple, fundamental graphic objects and shapes, such as lines, points, polygons, or spheres.

gesture. A specific motion of a character, such as a smile or wave. Gestures are sometimes distinguished from postures, such as sitting.

GIS. Global information system. Contains digital maps and geographically related data.

global coordinate system. Same as the **world coordinate system.**

Gouraud shading. A rendering technique to make polygons look smoothly shaded. Each vertex of a polygon is assigned a color, and the colors are blended together (linearly interpolated) across the face of the polygon.

GPS. Global Positioning System.

ground truth. A DIS design architecture concept. Each participant in the simulation broadcasts a continuing stream of messages, called the *ground truth,* about the entities it controls, such as their location, orientation, and velocity. Every other participant, as well as observers of the simulation, determines whether that entity is visible (such as in front of the camera, not hidden by fog or another object) based on evaluating the ground truth. In theory, this means that each participant can cheat because the computer knows more about other entities than a viewer of the simulation may be assumed to know.

haptic. Referring to the sense of touch. Haptic devices simulate the sense of touch in 3D simulations through physical sensors and force feedback devices.

hidden surface removal. The process of removing from display any polygons or pixels that are behind other polygons or pixels. See z-buffering and z-sorting.

hierarchical model. The conceptual organization of the objects in a 3D scene into a tree-like graph of parent, child, and sibling relationships.

hierarchy. The ordering of data as a tree of records, with parents, children, and siblings. Files and folders on a hard disk are a hierarchy.

hit. The intersection of a 2D point on the screen with an object in the 3D scene.

hither clipping plane. The front clipping plane.

HITL. Human in the loop. An entity that is controlled by a human.

homogeneous coordinates. A coordinate represented by [x y z w], where w is used to divide x, y, and z. Used primarily for perspective computations and clipping.

I/ITSEC. Interservice/Industry Training Simulation and Education Conference. A major trade show and conference for the DIS community.

immediate mode. A renderer that does not keep a copy of the data it is displaying. Each time the scene is rendered, all of the 3D data must be passed to it. This is characteristic of 3D back ends as opposed to retained-mode APIs.

in-betweens. The fill-in image between the key frame illustrations.

index color. A palette-based technique for representing color. Each number points into a palette that contains the actual color represented by the number. Eight-bit (256) color is an index color mode.

inheritance. The passing of properties from parent to child. Inheritance in a 3D scene database is a fundamental architectural issue.

inner product. A dot product.

instance. A copy of a previously defined object.

interactive renderer. A realtime renderer.

interface. A set of functions (methods) that can be called on a COM object.

interpolated shading. See **Gouraud shading.**

interpolating spline. A spline whereby the line goes through the control points.

interpolation. The calculation of an intermediate value between given values. For example, finding the color halfway between red and blue or the location a third of the way between two points in space.

IST. Institute for Simulation and Training.

jaggies. The visual artifact of aliasing. Slanted lines look like a jagged staircase because you can see the individual pixels.

keyframe. The state of a 3D object, scene, or value at a particular instance in time. 3D animation software generally is based on keyframe animation. The animator sets up positions for several keyframes and then the software interpolates values between the keyframes.

Lambertian reflection. Diffuse reflection.

latency. The delay between an action or event and a visual change on the screen. High frame rates and low latency go together, but they are not the same thing because high frame rates can be achieved by preprocessing data on the assumption that things won't change from frame to frame. Low latency is often considered to be 100 milliseconds between closely coupled interactions and 300 milliseconds between loosely coupled interactions.

leaf. In a scene graph or database, a type of node that does not have children.

left-hand coordinate system. z-values get bigger away from you.

level of detail (LOD). The technique of switching between different resolution versions of a model depending on how far away it is from the camera. Low-resolution versions of an object are used in the distance, and higher-resolution versions are switched in as the object moves closer. Level of detail conserves polygons by not wasting a lot of them on distant objects.

level-of-detail blending. An advanced level-of-detail technique that results in smoother-looking transitions between levels of detail.

lighted textures. Including lighting effects on top of a texture map. Some graphics hardware does not allow the combining of the two effects.

linear. A mathematical relationship like a straight line, where the formula has no squared or cubed values (a polynomial of degree 1).

linear interpolation. A straight-line relationship between two values (polynomial of degree 1). Usually, a linear relationship is expressed as a blending (adding) of the two values, one multiplied by a value n and the other by $(1-n)$, with n a value between 0 and 1.

live simulation. A 3D computer simulation of actual, real-world scenes and events as they happen.

LOD. Level of detail.

luminance. The intensity of light.

mach banding. Stripes that appear across a shaded surface if too few gradiants of color are used. For example, if a red ball is rendered with only four shades of red, the borders between the shades of red will be obvious. If, however, the same ball is rendered with 20 shades of red, it will look smoothly shaded. Mach banding is a problem for index-color rendering.

matrix. A rectangular grid of numbers. Used as a shorthand for the coefficients in a set of equations.

metadata. Data about data. Descriptive information that describes what a particular data file is supposed to represent, who created it, etc.

mipmapping. See **trilinear mipmapping.**

model. A 3D object or mesh.

modeling. The process of creating 3D objects, like an illustration in three dimensions.

morphing. Changing the shape of a mesh by moving the individual vertices.

motion blur. Purposely rendering an object as fuzzy or blurred when it is moving quickly. This improves the overall visual appeal of a rendered animation.

motion capture. Sampling movement on real people and converting it into a stream of 3D data.

multicast. A networking transmission mode in which a single message is sent to multiple locations, that is, one-to-many. See **unicast.**

near plane. The front clipping plane.

Newtonian Protocol. A DIS algorithm for handling collisions and other interactions between entities.

node. An object in a tree structure. Nodes can have children. Leaves are attached to nodes and have no children.

nonuniform rational. A rational B-spline.

normal. (1) Normal to a surface means perpendicular to a surface. (2) Shorthand for a normal vector.

normal vector. A vector pointing straight out from a point on a surface, usually assumed to be normalized (of unit length 1). A normal vector to the ground where you are sitting points straight up. [The term *normal vector* is confusing because it is shorthand for a normalized (of unit length 1), orthogonal (perpendicular) vector to a surface.]

normalized vector. Also known as a unit vector. A vector whose length is 1 unit. Any vector divided by its length is a normalized vector (a vector 3 units long divided by 3 is 1 unit long). It is easier to perform mathematical operations that compare vectors that are all normalized.

object. (1) An instance of a class in object-oriented programming. (2) In 3D, a representation of a thing or entity from the real world.

occluded. Covered up, as in when one polygon is behind another.

opacity. Opposite of transparency. The degree to which a surface does not let light go through it.

opacity map. A map that represents the opacity at each location on a surface.

origin. The center of a coordinate system. In 3D space, where (x, y, z) equals $(0, 0, 0)$.

orthogonal. Perpendicular (at a 90-degree angle).

overdraw. The number of pixels that are drawn to each pixel location on the screen. A well-designed 3D scene will have low overdraw. See **depth complexity.**

overlay. In rasterizing, an image that appears on the screen over the main image. An overlay is not actually in the frame buffer; it is simply displayed over the image in the frame buffer. Hardware sprites are overlays.

overlay plane. An overlay.

oversampling. Rendering more pixels than actually appear on screen and then filtering down.

painter's algorithm. A simple rendering technique where each polygon in the scene is rendered in reverse z order. Polygons farther from the screen are rendered first and then covered by closer polygons rendered on top of them. Same as **z-sorting.**

palette. A collection of colors.

panning. Moving the camera horizontally or vertically.

particle system. Algorithm-driven animation in which a set of objects such as smoke particles or a herd of animals moves as an interacting and partly random system of objects. Particles have a birth, lifetime, color, velocity, position, etc.

patch. A surface, such as a piece of paper.

PCI. Peripheral component interconnect. The bus that connects the CPU to peripheral devices, including the graphics chip.

PDU. Protocol data unit. A packet of information sent in a DIS simulation to update other computers participating in the simulation.

perspective foreshortening. The process of making objects look smaller as they get farther away.

perspective projection. A rendering in which parallel lines extend to a vanishing point.

Phong shading. Shading that uses the normal vectors at each vertex to calculate the shading of colors over a polygon. It produces a better-looking result than Gouraud shading does, but it takes more computation.

photorealistic rendering. High-quality rendering that is potentially as good as a photograph. Photorealistic rendering is more of a quest and a claim than a specific technique.

physically based modeling. Animation of a 3D scene and the objects in it through algorithmically generated changes, such as formulas, deformations, and dynamics.

picking. Selecting an object, polygon, or vertex, usually with a mouse. Picking is often a function of a 3D API rather than a 3D application.

piecewise Bezier curve. A set of joined Bezier curves that share endpoints such that the slope of every two Bezier curves is the same at the shared endpoint. This means that the tangent lines for the joined Bezier curves are parallel.

pitch. Roll to the side, pitch forward, and turn for yaw. Rotation about the x-axis.

pixel. The smallest dot that can be displayed on a screen.

pixel fill rate. The number of pixels a renderer or hardware accelerator can draw to the frame buffer per second.

pixel map. An image made of pixels.

planar. Flat (all in the same plane). All triangles are planar; quadrilaterals may not be. Many renderers need all polygons to be planar.

plane. A flat surface.

plane equation. A formula that describes the condition met by all the points of a plane: $ax + by + cz + d = 0$.

point. A location in 3D space. Has no size. Defined by its coordinates: (x, y, z). In row matrix form, a point is written as [x y z].

point light. A light that spreads out in all directions from one point.

polygon. A shape formed by connecting a series of points (vertices). A triangle is a polygon with three vertices; a square is a polygon with four vertices.

polygon budgets. The number of polygons you can have in your scene and still have the renderer achieve a target frame rate.

polygon mesh. A collection of polygons that shares vertices.

polygons per second. A notoriously fudgeable statistic to describe graphics performance. All polygons are not alike, so polygons-per-second speeds will vary depending on the polygons' size, shape, occlusion, and many other factors.

polynomial. A mathematical expression consisting of two or more terms, such as $x^2 + 3x + 7$. Also, one of the terms of a polynomial expression.

procedural animation. Animation driven by rules, procedures, or algorithms.

projection. The mathematical method for displaying 3D objects on a 2D screen (such as a shadow projected on a wall).

protocol. A set of rules and formats that describes communication between computers.

quad. A quadrilateral.

quad chain. A quad mesh.

quad mesh. A series of quadrilaterals organized so that each new quadrilateral shares two vertices with the previous quadrilaterals. Quadrilateral meshes (like tri meshes) speed up rendering by reducing the total number of vertices that need to be processed.

quad strip. A single row of quadrilaterals.

quadrilateral. A four-sided polygon. Some hardware accelerators support quadrilaterals, but Direct3D supports only triangles.

quaternion. A method of expressing an orientation in 3D space. A combination of a vector and a rotation. The vector defines the direction; the rotation defines the orientation around the vector.

radian. A unit measure of an angle. 2π radians is 360 degrees.

radiosity. A global illumination model that includes multiple diffuse light sources. A technique that produces softer and more realistic shadows than ray tracing.

ramp color. Index color.

rasterize. Convert to pixels. The last step in the 3D rendering pipeline, after a polygon has been converted from world coordinates to screen coordinates.

ray tracing. A high-quality rendering technique in which the paths of light rays are calculated as they bounce around in a 3D scene. Not a realtime 3D technique, at least for the current generation of computers.

realtime. Fast enough, that is, multiple frames per second of display, with a tolerable lag time between an event and its display on screen.

real-world time. Greenwich Mean Time (GMT), the actual time in Greenwich, England. Same as **sidereal time**.

refraction. The bending of light as it passes through a material such as glass.

reliable service. A communication service in which the received data is guaranteed to be exactly what was sent (through an acknowledgment of receipt protocol). Compare with **best-effort service**.

render. Convert data to an image.

renderer. Software or hardware that does all or part of the rendering pipeline. Final or production renderers create high-quality images and can take minutes or hours. Realtime renderers create the best quality they can in a fraction of a second.

RenderMan. The high-quality production renderer from Pixar, used for the movie *Toy Story* and many other well-known 3D animations. Actually, RenderMan is considered a specification for an interface between a modeler and a renderer, but this is a fine point for most purposes.

render pipeline. The multiple steps involved in rendering an image. 3D objects must be converted from world coordinates to screen coordinates and then lit, textured, and rasterized.

retained mode. A 3D API or renderer that keeps a copy of the 3D data it displays. See **immediate mode**.

RGB. Color value specified by its red, green, and blue components.

right-hand coordinate system. *z*-values get larger as they come right out of the screen toward you.

rigid body animation. Animation involving objects that move but don't change shape.

rotation. Movement around an axis.

rotoscoping. A traditional cel animation technique of filming live actors to define the movement for animated characters. Motion capture is the 3D equivalent of 2D rotoscoping.

scalar. A number or value.

scalar product. A dot product. See **dot product**.

scale. To change the size of something. When you scale an object, you make it bigger or smaller. Also, the ability of a software architecture to work well in different operating systems.

scene. A collection of 3D objects, lights, and cameras.

scene database. The data and its structure that describe a 3D scene and the objects in it.

scene graph. A hierarchical list of nodes and leaves that organize the scene database of a retained mode API.

scissor clip. A test in the rendering pipeline to discard from further render processing those polygons that lie outside a specified region.

screen coordinates. The x, y coordinates on the screen corresponding to a point in 3D space.

SGRAM. Synchronous Graphics RAM. A type of RAM, less expensive than VRAM, that supports fast reading, writing for graphics rasterization, and display operations.

shading. Calculating and applying colors to the face of a rendered polygon. Gouraud, flat, and Phong shading are common realtime shading techniques.

sidereal time. Absolute time, independent of time zones. Same as real-world time.

SIMNET. Simulator Networking. The predecessor to DIS.

simulation entity. An object in a DIS simulation, such as a tank, submarine, or airplane.

slow-in/slow-out. The traditional animation technique of starting and ending slowly a particular gesture. Slow-in/slow-out can be mimicked (but probably not artistically duplicated) by an interpolation algorithm.

span. The pixels on screen of a triangle at a single y-value.

specular highlight. A bright area on an object's surface that results from a specular reflection.

specular reflection. A shiny reflection (light bounces off at a complementary angle).

sphere. A ball. Mathematically defined by a center point and a radius distance.

spline. A curve that is mathematically defined by the relative influence of control points. Bezier, cardinal, B-spline, and NURBS are common splines.

spotlight. A light that shines out like a cone.

squash and stretch. A family of classic animation techniques. Shapes squash when they meet resistance and stretch with speed.

staircasing. The jaggies.

stencil buffer. A memory buffer that defines a mask for stenciling.

stenciling. Using a mask to block rendering in defined areas of the window. Think of a 3D scene outside a car's windshield. The shape of the edge of the windshield could be a stencil overlaying the screen.

stippling. A mask of on/off pixels that is applied over an image. Where the pixels are off, the image is not displayed (i.e., not rasterized into the frame buffer). A stipple pattern is usually small and stored in registers; a stencil pattern is big and stored in memory.

stretch. Hardware expansion of a small image so that it fills a larger area on screen. Good hardware stretching should not leave jagged edges.

STRICOM. Simulation, Training, and Instrumentation Command.

subpixel. Breaking a screen pixel into a set of pixels. Used for antialiasing.

supersampling. See **oversampling**.

surface normal. The normal at a given point on a surface.

synthetic environment. Classy-sounding term for a 3D simulation.

temporal aliasing. Artifacts that do not appear in a still, 3D-rendered image but do appear in a realtime, moving 3D scene.

teraflop. One trillion floating-point operations.

terrain. The ground in a simulation.

terrain following. An algorithm by which an object or camera automatically follows the ground as it moves.

tessellation. Converting a mathematically defined surface such as a patch into a set of polygons. Also, splitting a concave polygon into convex polygons or triangles.

texel. Texture element. A pixel, plus its texture and lighting values. Also, the texture value at a particular location in a texture map.

texture filtering. Techniques for improving the image quality of rendered textures, such as bilinear filtering and trilinear mipmapping.

texture mapping. A rendering technique for wrapping an image (the texture map) around a 3D object. In realtime 3D, texture mapping is a favored technique because it can be hardware-accelerated. The quality of texture mapping can be improved with bilinear filtering and mipmapping.

tiling. Repeating a texture over a surface or mesh, like a set of tiles.

torus. A donut-shaped graphics primitive.

transformation. A mathematical operation applied to a point in 3D space. Commonly, a matrix is used as a shorthand expression of the formula applied to a point when it is transformed.

translation. Movement in the x-, y-, and/or z-direction without rotation or scaling.

transparency. The ability of a surface to let light pass through it.

traversal. A pass through a scene graph that visits every node and leaf in parent/child/sibling order.

triangle mesh. Often called tristrip. A series of triangles organized so that each new triangle shares two vertices with the previous triangles. Triangle meshes (like quad meshes) speed up rendering by reducing the total number of vertices that need to be processed.

trilinear mipmapping. *Multum In Parvum*, Latin for "many in one." A rendering technique to improve the quality of texture mapping, particularly for objects in the distance. A series of increasingly smaller texture maps is created from the original texture map. The smaller texture maps are used as the object moves farther away from the camera. Once solely the province of high-end SGI workstations, mipmapping is showing up on consumer 3D graphics chips. A bilinear filter is applied to each of two mipmap resolutions, and the two resulting values are linearly interpolated to calculate a final, single value. Compare with **bilinear filtering.**

tristrip. A triangle mesh.

true color. Usually means 16-bit or 24-bit color, where each color value describes the actual color rather than an index into a color table. Calculations can be performed directly on a true color value without the need to look up the color it represents in a table. Compare with **index color.**

tweening. In-betweening.

UDP. User Datagram Protocol. The multicasting protocol of the Internet.

unicast. A networking transmission mode in which a single message is sent to one location, that is, one-to-one. See **multicast.**

unit vector. A **normalized vector** (a vector that is 1 unit long).

uv coordinates. In a texture map, **u** and **v** are like *x* and *y* on a graph. They define a particular location in the texture map. One corner of the texture map, **u, v** is 0, 0; the opposite corner is 1, 1.

vector. A mathematical quantity with magnitude and direction. Think of an arrow. It points in a direction, and its length is its magnitude. Vectors are specified as an *x, y, z* value, as if they always start at the origin (0, 0, 0).

vector product. See **cross product.**

vertex. A corner point of a polygon.

vertex normal. A normalized vector (same as a **unit vector**) that points straight out from a vertex of a polygon or polygon mesh. The vertex normal is the average of the normal vectors of each of the polygons that shares the vertex. Imagine a pyramid sitting on the ground. The top point is a vertex, and its vertex normal points straight up.

view vector. The (imaginary) vector pointing out of the camera's eye into the 3D scene.

viewing frustum. The part of the frustum that is between the front and back clipping planes and therefore visible.

viewpoint. The point from which your eyes are looking.

virtual reality. 3D graphics with an attitude (that if it gets good enough and you wear goggles, it will seem virtually real).

virtual set. A TV blue screen stage that is filled in with realtime 3D rendering so that live actors look like they are walking around in the rendered setting. A cool idea that is occasionally used on TV, but it is usually less expensive to use a real set than an expensive computer (perhaps in the future, the cost equation will change).

volume rendering. Unlike more common surface rendering, volume rendering displays a set of 3D points in space, called voxels, rather than surfaces between points. Volume rendering requires a large number of voxels to look good.

voxel. Volume pixel. A little chunk of 3D space. Voxels are what are usually rendered with volume rendering techniques.

VRML. Virtual Reality Modeling Language.

walk-through. What you do in a 3D scene when there is nothing else to do. Like wandering through a still life.

WGS 84. World Geodetic System 1984. A standard method for describing locations on Earth. A location-specifying system for the real Earth. The origin is the center of Earth. The positive x-axis passes through the Prime Meridian at the equator; the positive y-axis passes through 90 degrees east longitude at the equator; and the positive z-axis passes through the North Pole.

wireframe. Rendering only the edge lines of a 3D object, thereby allowing you to see through the object. Wireframe rendering is much faster than shaded rendering, which fills in the faces of the polygons.

world. A bigger-than-life word for a 3D scene.

world coordinate system. The coordinate values of objects in a 3D scene before they are converted into locations on the screen.

.x. The file format for Direct3D.

yon clipping plane. The back clipping plane.

z-buffer. A popular, fast, but memory-intensive technique for removing hidden surfaces when rendering (i.e., for not displaying surfaces that are hidden behind other surfaces). A z-buffer is a buffer of values (usually 16 bits) for each pixel on the screen. The z-buffer value represents the depth value (the z-value) for the object being displayed in that pixel. As the renderer renders each polygon, it checks the current z-buffer for each pixel where the polygon is on screen. If the z-value for the polygon being rendered is smaller (closer) than the current z-value, it is put on screen (and its z-value becomes the new z-value). Otherwise, that pixel for that polygon is ignored.

zoom. Same as **stretch**.

z-sorting. Same as **painter's algorithm**.

Index

.3DS. *See* 3DS binary file (.3ds file)
.bvh. *See* BioVision file format (.bvh file)
.dxf. *See* Drawing Interchange Format (.dxf file)
.x. *See* DirectX file format (.x file)
3D. *See* Realtime 3D
3D Artist magazine, 222
3D Cafe, 230
3D Computer Animation (Vince), 223
3D Design magazine, 223
3DDEVICEDESC structure, 122–123
3D Engines List, 225
3D/EYE, Inc., 228
3Dfx Interactive, Inc., 19, 220
3Dlabs, Inc., 19, 30, 220
   See also GLINT 3D chip; Permedia 3D chip
3DR, 21, 225
3DS binary file (.3ds file)
   chunk hierarchy, 234–248*t*
   defined, 233–234
3DSite, 230
3D Studio Max, 227
3Name3D, 229

A

Abrash, Michael, 31, 153
Acceleration, 7–8, 53–54, 219–232
ACM Transactions on Graphics, 222
ActiveMovie, 24
ActiveX technologies, 23
Actors, 133, 138–140
Acuris, Inc., 229
AddAttachedSurface method, 49–50
AddChild method, 83, 85
AddDestroyCallback method, 33, 75
AddFace method, 95, 98
AddGroup method, 95
AddMoveCallback method, 87, 136
AddRef method, 32, 74, 76, 83
AddVertexAndNormalIndexed method, 98
AddVisual method, 93, 110
Advanced Animation and Rendering Techniques (Watt), 223
AGP, 7, 56–59, 158
Alias animation package, 4
Alias Wavefront, 228
Alpha blending, 51

Amapi, 226
Ambient light, 90–91, 109
Animation and AnimationSets, 102–103, 196–197, 226–228
Animation Master, 226
Animation playback, 22
Animetix Technologies, Inc., 230
Antialiasing, 51
API access (.x file), 182
Apple, 10, 15
  See also QuickDraw3D
Application autonomy in DIS, 169
Application framework
  actors as things, 133, 138–140
  events as things, 133, 140–141
  godforces as things, 134, 141–143
  overview, 131–134
  traversal engine, 133, 135–138
  and the user, 134, 143–144
  variations, 144–145
Application independence (.x file), 181
Applications, 3D, 8
Arrays, 73, 341–343
ASCII, 174, 249
ATI Technologies, Inc., 18, 220
Autodesk, 20

B

BBC Micro, 30
Behavior, 132
Bell, Ian, 30
BioVision, 174
BioVision file format (.bvh file)
  hierarchy section, 175–176
  motion section, 177
  overview, 174–175, 175
  sample, 177–178
BioVision Motion Capture, 230
Blocks section (.dxf file), 253
Braben, David, 30
BRender, 30, 225
Bristol University, 30
British 3D invasion, 30–31
Broadcasting, 168

Brooktree, 220
Brown University, 231

C

Caching, 88
CAD
  beginning of 3D, role in, 4
  drawing interchange format (.dxf file), 250
  intelligent shapes, 139
  MFC wrapper, 132–133
  object-oriented database, 181
Callback functions, 365–367, 390–391
CAM, 9, 133
Cartesian coordinate system, 203–206
Center for Human Modeling and Simulation, 231
CGA and graphics programming, 18
Channels (.bvh file), 176
Children's software, 9
Chromatic Research, 220
Chrome wrapping, 101
Chunk (.3ds file), 233–234
Chunk hierarchy (.3ds file), 234–248*t*
Cirrus Logic, 18, 220
Clear, 80
Color interpolation, 66
Component Object Model (COM)
  and mesh component, 92
  model, 31–32
  and performance modeling, 76–77
  and performance programming, 34–35
  standard interfaces, 32–34
  See also Immediate mode; Retained mode
Computer Game Developers' Association, 224
Computer Game Developers' Conference, 224
Computer Graphics: Principles and Practice (Foley), 223
Computer Graphics Proceedings, 222
Computer Graphics World, 222
Connectivity interface, 166
Content and tools, 3D, 8
Cornell, 231
Coryphaeus Software, Inc., 228
Cosmo, 15
CPU power and memory, 8

CreateDeviceFromClipper method, 107
CreateExecuteBuffer method, 123–124
CreateFace method, 98
CreateFrame method, 108
CreateMesh method, 98
CreateShadow method, 100
CreateSurface method, 49–50
CreateTextureFromSurface method, 100
CreateTexture method, 100
CreateViewport method, 80, 108, 109
Crestline Software, 229
Crisis in Perspective, Inc., 225
Criterion Software, Ltd., 225
Culhane, Shamus, 174
Culling, 22, 88
   See also Infrastructure
Cylindrical wrapping, 101

D

D3DDEVICEDESC structure, 116
D3DEXECUTEBUFFERDESC structure, 124
D3DEXECUTEDATA structure, 124, 125
D3DINSTRUCTION structure, 127
D3DLIGHTINGELEMENT structure, 118
D3DOPCODE enumerated type, 126
D3DRMUSERVISUAL_RENDER flag, 129
D3DTLVERTEX structure, 125
D3DTRANSFORMDATA structure, 118
D3DVal, math conversion macro, 205
D3DValue, math value type, 205–206
Database management, 22
Data objects (.x file), 186
Data visualization, 9
Decals, 85, 100–101
   See also Textures
Defense Mapping Agency, 232
DeleteChild method, 83
Delta 3D chip, 57, 58, 59–61, 64
Depth complexity formula, 158–160
Depth cueing, 66
Depth test, 65
Desktop supercomputers, 5, 53
Device, 70, 78–79, 106–108, 120–122
Diamond Multimedia, 221
Direct3D, 8, 20, 31
   See also Immediate mode; Retained mode;
     specific object names

Direct3DRMCreate object, 70, 77
DirectDraw
   back ends, 21
   graphics hardware interface, 24, 25
   graphics memory, 78
   infrastructure, 19
   mipmap, 48–49
   overview, 29–30
   surface COM object, 119–122
   texture, 100
DirectDrawCreate, 106
Directed line segment, 206–207
Directional light, 91, 110
DirectPlay, 27, 166, 169–171
DirectX
   background, 26–27
   and British 3D invasion, 30–31
   Direct3D overview, 31
   graphics hardware interface, 24–25
   HAL/HEL philosophy, 27–29
   and media types, 25–26
   overview, 23
   user interface, 27
   See also Component Object Model (COM)
DirectX file format (.x file), 140
   animation set, 195–197
   example, complex, 192–194
   example, simple, 182–186
   file format failures, 179–180
   file-loading methods, retained mode, 190–191
   future, 191
   goals, 181–182
   hierarchy, representing, 195
   scene fundamentals, 180–181
   templates, retained mode, 186–190
DIS, 139, 168–169, 232
Display list 38
Dither, 66
DMA, 62
Doom, 3D game, 4, 202
Dot product
   described, 210–212
   and equation of plane, 215
   properties of, 212
   vector conversion, 212–213
Drawing. *See* Rendering
Drawing Interchange Format (.dxf file), 20, 249–260

binary format, 256–260
file structure, 250–251
overview, 249–250
polyline group codes, 254–255
reading a file, 253–254
sample file, 251–252
sections in file, 252–253
DXFOUT command, 256

E

EGA and graphics programming, 17–18
EISA bus, 54
Elite, 3D game, 30
Emissive, 99
End site (.bvh file), 176
Entertainment industry and 3D, 4, 9
Entities in DIS, 169
Entities section (.dxf file), 250, 253
EnumDevices method, 122
Events, 133, 140–141
Execute buffer
   COM and, 77
   data structures, 124–125
   defined, 116–119
   filling the buffer, 124
   immediate mode object, 123–128
   instructions, 126–128, 425–438
   lighting module, 114–115, 118
   methods, list of, 124t
   opcodes, list of, 126t
   rasterization module, 114–115, 118–119
   rendering concept, 38
   rendering loop, 128
   transform module, 114–115, 117–118
   See also Immediate mode
Execute method, 115
Extensibility (.x file), 181
Extreme3D, 227

F

Face, 98–99
FIFO pipeline, 61–63
File header (.x file), 183–184
Filtering, 37
FireWalker, 228

Flat shading, 43
Flat wrapping, 101
Fleischer, Max and Dave, 174
Flight simulators and 3D, 4, 9, 37
Fog and depth cueing, 51
Foley, J.D.
   Computer Graphics: Principles and Practice, 223
Forward/backward compatibility (.x file), 181
Fractal Design Corporation, 227
Framebuffer read and write, 65, 66
Frame hierarchy (.x file), 195
Frames, 82–90
   animation attachment, 87
   collapsing, 88
   default velocity and rotation application, 86–87
   and local transform, 84
   local transform change, 86
   move callback, 87
   moving a frame, 85–87
   and scene graph, 83–84
   transforming coordinates, 84–85
   and visuals, 85
   z-buffer and sort modes, 87–88
Frames (.bvh file), 177
Frame tree, 38, 39
   See also Scene graphs

G

Game Developer magazine, 222
Game Developer's Kit (GDK). *See* Game SDK
Games and entertainment, 9
Game SDK, 26–27
   See also DirectX
GDI and graphics programming, 17, 19, 24–25
Gemini, 229
Georgia Tech, 231
GetAppData method, 33, 75
GetCaps method, 116
GetChildren method, 83, 85
GetClassName method, 33, 75
GetColor method, 95
GetElement method, 73
GetFace method, 98

GetHeight method, 78
GetName method, 33, 74
GetPick method, 82
GetScene method, 83
Get/SetPosition method, 84, 85
Get/SetRotation method, 84
Get/SetSortMode method, 87
Get/SetVelocity method, 84
Get/SetZBufferMode method, 87
GetSize method, 73
GetVertices method, 95
GetWidth method, 78
GIF, 51
Glassner, Andrew
  Graphics Gems, 223
GLINT 3D chip, 57, 58
Godforces, 134, 141–143
Gouraud shading, 43, 91, 151
Graphics
  acceleration, 7–8, 53–54
  AGP 56–59
  hardware interface, 24–25
  memory, 78
  operating systems, 15–16, 20–21
  programming, 17–19, 24, 26, 61
Graphics Gems (Glassner), 223
Ground truth in DIS, 169
Groups in mesh component, 93–95
GUID
  as a COM class identifier, 35
  in DirectX file format, 182–183, 184, 186
  forward/backward compatibility, 181
  in immediate mode, 122
GWeb: An Electronic Trade Journal for Computer Animators, 230

H

HAL, 20, 24, 27–29, 122
Hardware
  AGP, 56–59
  Delta programming model, 59–61
  importance of, 53–54
  PCI bus, 54–56
  Permedia rasterization, 61–66
Hash, Inc., 227
Header section (.dxf file), 253

Header template (.x file), 184–185
HEL, 27–29, 122
Hierarchical relationships (.x file), 180–181
High-level culling, 88, 151
High-level rendering, 38, 39
Humanoid, 229

I

IBM, as PC standards leader, 18, 20
IDirect3D, 119–120
  interface and methods, 374–375
  object, 369–370
IDirect3DDevice, 115, 116, 122, 123
  interface and methods, 375–380
  object, 370–371
IDirect3DExecuteBuffer, 124
  interface and methods, 380–382
  object, 371
IDirect3DLight
  interface and methods, 382
  object, 372
IDirect3DMaterial
  interface and methods, 382–383
  object, 372
IDirect3DRM
  methods, 281–291
  object, 264–265
  in retained mode architecture, 71, 77, 78–79
IDirect3DRMAnimation
  methods, 291–292
  object, 266–267
  in retained mode architecture, 102–103
IDirect3DRMAnimationSet
  methods, 293–294
  object, 267
  in retained mode architecture, 102–103
IDirect3DRMArray
  arrays, types, 341–343
  object, 278–279
IDirect3DRMDevice, 108
  methods, 294–298
  object, 267–268
  in retained mode architecture, 78–79
IDirect3DRMFace
  methods, 298–301
  object, 268–269

in retained mode architecture, 98–99
IDirect3DRMFrame
  methods, 301–314
  object, 269–271
  in retained mode architecture, 82–90
  in traversals, 136
IDirect3DRMLight
  methods, 314–317
  object, 271–272
  in retained mode architecture, 90–92
IDirect3DRMMaterial
  methods, 317–318
  object, 272–273
  in retained mode architecture, 99
IDirect3DRMMesh
  methods, 318–322
  object, 273
  in retained mode architecture, 92–95
IDirect3DRMMeshBuilder
  methods, 323–331
  object, 274–275
  in retained mode architecture, 95–98
IDirect3DRM methods, overview, 279–280
IDirect3DRMObject
  interface, 265
  methods, defined, 280–281
  in retained mode architecture, 77–78
IDirect3DRM objects, overview, 263–264
IDirect3DRMShadow
  methods, 331
  object, 275
  in retained mode architecture, 99–100
IDirect3DRMTexture
  methods, 331–334
  object, 275–276
  in retained mode architecture, 100–101
IDirect3DRMUserVisual
  methods, 334
  object, 276
  in retained mode architecture, 102
IDirect3DRMViewport
  methods, 334–340
  object, 276–277
  in retained mode architecture, 80–82
IDirect3DRMWinDevice
  methods, 340

object, 277–278
in retained mode architecture, 78–79
IDirect3DRMWrap
  methods, 340–341
  object, 278
  in retained mode architecture, 101–102
IDirect3DTexture
  interface and methods, 383–384
  object, 372–373
IDirect3DViewport
  interface and methods, 384–387
  object, 373
ID tag (.3ds file), 233
IEEE Computer Graphics and Applications,
  222
Immediate mode
  background, 21
  callback functions, defined, 390–391
  and COM, 115–116
  COM components, 119–128
  and DirectX, 24–25, 28
  enumerated types, defined, 417–423
  macros, defined, 387–390
  methods of objects defined, 374–387
  objects defined, 369–373
  overview, 114–115
  performance, 152–153, 156–157
  renderers, 20–21
  return values, defined, 424–425
  structures, defined, 392–416
  types (other), defined, 423
  and UserVisuals, 128–129
  vs retained mode, 113–114
  See also Execute buffer; *specific object names*
Immediate mode COM components
  3DDEVICEDESC structure, 122–123
  device, 120–122
  execute buffer object, 123–128
  IDIRECT3D, 119–120
Imperial College London, 30
Infrastructure
  APIs and scene database, 21, 22
  application environments, 21–22
  back ends, 20–21
  component, overview, 16–17
  frame buffer and screen, 17–19, 20, 21
  future of, 22

Infrastructure (*continued*)
    hardware, 19–20
    importance of, 13–14
    multiuser 3D infrastructure, 166
    operating systems, companies role in, 15–16
    performance concerns, 14, 22
    perspective, 14–15
    and rendering pipeline, 38, 40
    scalability, 14
    uncertainty, 14
Initialize, 74
Initial point of vector, 206–207
Installed base, 8
Institute for Simulation and Training, 232
Intel, 7, 19, 224
Intel Architecture Labs, 21
InterChange, 3D clip art, 230
Interface, 31
Internet
    multiuser 3D, role in, 166–169
    PC revolution, role in, 6, 9, 27, 52
Intervista Software, 226
Intranet, 166–168
InverseTransform method, 85
IP, 168
ISA bus, 54
ISDN, 166
IUknown, 32, 74–76, 265–266

J

Java3D, 3D viewer, 10, 15
Joey, 225
Joint name (.bvh file), 176
Journal of Graphic Tools, 222

K

Kent, Osman, 30
Keondjian, Servan, 30, 31
Kinetix (Autodesk), 227

L

LAN, 166
Length value (.3ds file), 233
Lighting, 38

Lights
    defined, 42–43
    lighting module, 114–115, 118
    setting up, 109–110
    types of, 42–43
LightWave, 227
Linear 3D, 8
Linear (bilinear filtering), 47
LoadTexture method, 100
Lobby server, 166
Local coordinates, 84
Local transform, 84
Lockheed Martin, 19, 221
Lock method, 124
LOD
    and actors in Direct3D, 140
    performance, role in, 160
    rendering, 37, 45, 51
Logical operation, 66
LookAt method, 84
Low-level rendering, 38, 87

M

Macromedia, Inc., 227
Macromedia Director, 145
Magnetic Scrolls, 3D game company, 30
Material, 99, 100
Material addition (.x file), 193–194
Math, 3D
    background, 201–202
    coordinate systems, 203–204
    dot product, 210–213
    numeric values, 205–206
    planes, 213–216
    quaternions, 216–218
    vectors, 206–210
Matrices, 203
Matrox Graphics, Inc., 221
Mazar Software, 251
Medical imaging, 10
Mesh, 71, 92–95
Mesh Mart, 229
Meshbuilder, 71, 92–93, 95–98, 110
Message manager, 166
Methods, 31
MFC wrapper, 132–133
Microchannel, 54

Index

Microsoft
   3D Device Driver Interface (3DDI), 21, 24
   3D-enabling software, 10
   3D infrastructure building, 15
   3D viewers, 10
   Direct3D, 8, 20
   DirectPlay, 27, 166, 169–171
   DirectX file format, 191
   hardware abstraction layer, 20
   and immediate and retained modes, 157
   OLE, 31, 76, 140
   OpenGL, 58, 64, 224
   operating systems vendor, 7
   RenderMorphics Reality Lab, 21, 30, 31, 100
   Softimage, 227
   See also Component Object Model (COM); DirectDraw; Windows
Middlesex University, 30
Mipmapping, 37, 48–51, 152
MMX, 79
Model coordinates, 84
Modeling & Simulation Resource Repository, 232
Moore's law, 150–151
Motion capture issue
   background, 173–174
   data structures, building of, 178
   motion capture data, 174–178
   resources for, 230
Move method, 136–137
MPEG compression technique, 148
Multicasting, 166, 168
MultiGen, Inc., 228
Multimedia, 9
Multiple stream sources (.x file), 182
Multiuser 3D issue
   bandwidth issue, overview, 165–166
   design of, 166–168, 171
   DirectPlay, 169–171
   DIS, 168–169
   latency issue, overview, 165–166
   tools, 232
Myst, 3D game, 6

N

Net 3D, 9
Netscape Navigator, Live 3D, 10
Newtek, Incorporated, 227
Nichimen Graphics, 228
Normal vector
   and meshbuilder component, 95, 98
   and mesh component, 93–94
   planes, 213–216
   in rendering, 42
NPSNET virtual battlefield research group, 232
NURBs, 202
NVIDIA Corp., 19, 221

O

Oak Technology, USA, 221
Object interface, 33, 74–75
Object-oriented database (.x file), 181
Objects section (.dxf file), 253
Object storage (.x file), 180
Offset (.bvh file), 176
OnLine! Technologies, 226
Onyx computers, 20
OpenGL
   cheesy transparency, 64
   and Direct3D, 24, 25
   and GLINT chip, 58
   resources for, 224
OpenGVS, 228
OpenInventor, 225
Operating systems, 15–16, 20–21
Orchestration, 142
OSF DCE standard, 184
OS-level support, 8
Overlay, 30
Oxford University, 30
Oz Interactive Motion Capture mailing list, 230

P

Painters algorithm, 40–41
Parallel point light, 91
PCI bus
   in Delta chip, 58
   hardware, 54–56
   performance, 156
   in Permedia chip, 61
   and rasterizer, 64

PC industry
  adaptation of technologies, 37–52
  overview, 3–4
  retooling the PC, 7–8
  revolution and Internet, 9, 26, 27, 52
  into visual computer, 5–6
PDUs in DIS, 169
Pentium, 7
Penumbra, 91
Performance
  depth complexity, 158–160
  fast path, 161
  hardware stretch, 161
  high-level culling, 151
  immediate mode, 152–153, 156–157
  infrastructure, concerns with, 14, 22
  LOD, 160
  mesh optimization, 160–161
  mitmapping, 152
  modeling in COM, 76–77
  Moore's law, 150–151
  optimization, 153
  overview, 147–148
  palettes, 161
  pipeline balance, 154
  programming in COM, 34–35
  resource management, 153–156
  retained mode, 157–158
  scalable base, 149
  and scale frame rate, 151–152
  state thrash, 160
  texel/pixel ratio, 161
  z-buffering, 158
Performer API, 136, 152
Permedia 3D chip
  AGP, 57
  and delta programming model, 60–61
  fixed-point format, 59
  rasterization, 58, 61–66
  texture, 65
PFACE command, 254
PFACEVMAX system variable, 254
Phillips Semiconductors, 221
Phong shading, 44, 78
PhotoModeler, 227
Picking, 82
Plane equation, 214–215

Planes, 203, 213–216
Plastic Thought, Inc., 229
Point light, 91
Point sampling, 47
Polyline group codes, 254–255
Portable Pixmap (.ppm), 100
Pythagorean theorem, 208, 212

Q

Quake, 3D game, 4
Quaternions, 103, 203, 216–218
QueryInterface, 32, 74, 76
QueryInterface method, 119–122
QuickDraw3D
  back ends, 20
  cross-platform 3D infrastructure, 15
  as a Direct3D competitor, 224
  file format, unique, 180
  OS-level support, 8

R

Rabson, Doug, 30, 31
Ramp color model, 78
Rasterization
  module, 114–115, 118–119
  PCI bus, 64
  and Permedia chip, 58, 61–66
  pipeline, 62–64
  and z-buffering, 40–41
Ray Dream, 227
Ray Tracing News, 222
Real3D, 221, 227
RealityEngine2, 20
Realtime 3D
  application framework, 131–145
  computer companies strategies, 10–11
  defined, 4
  DirectX file format, 180–197
  hardware, 53–66
  infrastructure, 13–22, 40, 166
  math, 201–218
  motion capture issue, 173–178, 230
  multiuser 3D issue, 165–171, 232
  need for, 9–10
  performance, 13, 14, 22, 147–161

resources, 219–232
See also DirectX; Immediate mode; PC industry; Rendering; Retained mode (RM)
Realtime 3D resources
   accelerators and boards, 219–222
   APIs, 224–225
   books, 223
   chipmakers, 220–222
   conferences and trade shows, 223–224
   DIS, 232
   file converters, 230
   modeling and animation tools, 226–228
   models, 229–230
   motion capture, 230
   multiuser, 232
   newsgroups, 224
   periodicals, 222–223
   research, 231–232
   tools, 228–229
   VRML, 225–226
   web sites, 230–231
Reference, 85
Release method, 32, 74, 76, 106
Reliability, 166, 168
RemoveDestroyCallback method, 33, 75
RemoveMoveCallback method, 136
Rendering
   color models, 45–46
   and execute buffer, 128
   frame tree, 39
   key concepts of, 38–39
   lights, 42–43
   LOD, 37, 45, 51
   loop, 128
   meshes, 44–45, 85
   pipeline, 38, 40
   progressive transmission, 51–52
   quality in retained mode, 108
   rasterization, 40–41
   renderers in immediate mode, 20–21
   rendering frames, 4, 69–70, 85
   shading, 43–44
   textures, 46–51, 85, 93
   z-buffering, 40–42, 65, 87
   z-sorting, 40–41
Render method, 80
RenderMorphics' Reality Lab, 21, 30, 31, 100
RenderWare, 30, 225
Rendition, Inc., 19, 221
Retained mode
   animation and AnimationSets, 102–103
   array components, 73
   arrays, 341–343
   callback functions, defined, 365–367
   camera frame and viewport, creating, 108–109
   COM and performance programming, 34–35, 76–77
   components, 70–74
   device, 78–79
   device, creating, 106–108
   enumerated types, defined, 347–355
   face, 98–99
   file-loading methods in DirectX file, 190–191
   frames, 82–90
   functions, defined, 359–365
   initializing D3D, 106
   lights, 90–92
   lights, setting-up, 109–110
   loading a mesh, 110
   material, 99
   meshbuilder component, 95–98
   mesh component, 92–95
   methods of objects defined, 279–341
   objects defined, 263–279
   performance, 157–158
   quaternion support, 218
   render quality, setting of, 108
   return values, defined, 367–368
   scene, starting, 105–106
   scene graph, 69–70, 83–84
   shadow, 99–100
   standard interfaces, 74–75
   structures, defined, 343–347
   templates in DirectX file, 186–190
   texture, 100–101
   types (other), defined, 356–359
   UserVisual, 102
   vector support, 207–208
   viewports, 80–82
   vs immediate mode, 113–114
   wrap, 101–102
See also specific object names
Reynolds' boids, Craig, 231

RGBA, 20
RGB color model, 45, 65, 78–79, 107
RMMatrixFromQuaternion function, 103
RMQuaternionFromMatrix function, 103
RMQuaternionFromRotation function, 103
RMQuaternionMultiply function, 103
RMQuaternionSlerp function, 103
Robot Simulators on the Net, 231
Root name (.bvh file), 176
Rotoscoping, 173–174

S

S3, 18, 221
Samsung, 221
San Diego Supercomputer Center VRML, 225
Scaleable, 29
Scene graphs
    defined, 69–70, 83–90
    in DirectX file, 180–181
    rendering concept, 38, 39
    starting, 105–106
Scissor test, 64
SDK, 105–106
Seekings, Kate, 30, 31
Send/receive paradigm, 170
SetAppData method, 33, 75
SetBack method, 80
SetCamera method, 80
SetDefaultTextureShades method, 108
SetDither method, 108
SetExecuteData method, 124
SetField method, 80
SetFront method, 80
SetGroupColor method, 95
SetGroupMaterial method, 95, 99
SetGroupQuality method, 95
SetGroupTexture method, 95
SetGroupWrapping method, 95
SetMaterial method, 99
SetMaterialMode method, 99
SetName method, 33, 74
SetQuality method, 108
SetRotation method, 136
SetShades method, 108
SetTextureQuality method, 108
SetVelocity method, 136

SetVertices method, 95
SGI
    3D-enabling software, 10
    Cosmo, 15
    infrastructure building, 15
    Onyx computers, 20
    OpenGL, 8, 20
    OpenInventor, 225
    performance, 19
    Performer API, 136, 152
SGRAM, 57
Shading
    defined, 43–44
    flat, 43
    Gouraud, 43, 91, 151
    Phong, 44, 78
    rendering concept, 38
Shadow, 99–100
SIGGRAPH, 31, 222, 224
Silicon Graphics, 4
SMOS, 222
Softimage, 4, 227
Specular, 99
Spherical wrapping, 101
Spotlight, 91
St. Hughes College, 30
State sorting, 88
Stencil test, 65
Stipple test, 64
Sun, 10, 15, 17
Super VGA and graphics programming, 17
Syndesis Corporation, 230

T

Tables section (.dxf file), 253
TCP, 168
Technology base, 3D, 7
Template Graphics Software, 226
Terminal point of vector, 206–207
Terrain Modeling Project Office, 232
Textures
    address, 65
    map, 30
    rendering, 46–51, 85, 93
    in retained mode architecture, 100–101
    texture, fog, and blend, 66

Things, 132
Tick method, 136–137
Toy Story, 5, 147
Transforming coordinates, 82, 84–85
Traversal engine, 133, 135–138
Trispectives, 227
Tseng, 18

U

UDP, 168
Umbra, 91
Unicasting, 168
Unlock method, 124
Update method, 80
User, 134, 143–144
User interface, 3D, 10, 27
UserVisual, 85, 92, 102
UserVisual callback, 128–129

V

Vectors
   in math, 3D, 203, 206–218
   and meshbuilder component, 95–98
   and mesh component, 93–95
   transforming coordinates, 84
Vertex group (.dxf file), 257–260
Vertex structure, 124–125
VGA and graphics programming, 17–18, 19, 61
Viewing frustum, 80
Viewpoint DataLabs, 174, 229
Viewports, 70, 80–82
Vince, John
   3D Computer Animation, 223
Virtual cities, 9
Virtual Humans, 231
Virtual reality, 9
Virtual Reality Labs, 228
Virtus Corporation, 226
Vistapro Landscape Generator, 228
VisualArray, 73
Visual Reality, 228
Visuals, 73, 85, 99
Visual Software, 228

VRAIS, 224
VRAM, 57
VREAM, 226
VR industry, 9
VRML, 9, 22, 131, 225–226
V-table, 32

W

Watt, Alan and Mark
   Advanced Animation and Rendering Techniques, 223
Wavefront animation package, 4
Wave Report on Digital Media, 223
Windows
   device, 78
   event management, 141
   GDI, 25, 26
   graphics performance, early releases, 18
   modeling and animation tools, 141
   OS-level support, 8
Windows bitmap (.bmp), 100
Wireframe, 43
World, 132, 133
WorldRender, 230, 251
Wrap, 93, 101–102

X

XGA and graphics programming, 18

Y

Yamaha Systems Technology, Inc., 222
Yonowat, Inc., 226
YUV-RGB converter, 65

Z

Z-buffer, 30
   depth, 30, 65
   and rendering, 40–42, 158
   and sort modes, 87–88
ZD3D, 230
Z-sorting, 40–41
Zygote Media Group, 229

Addison-Wesley warrants the enclosed disc to be free of defects in materials and faulty workmanship under normal use for a period of ninety days after purchase. If a defect is discovered in the disc during this warranty period, a replacement disc can be obtained at no charge by sending the defective disc, postage prepaid, with proof of purchase to:

Addison-Wesley Developers Press
Editorial Department
One Jacob Way
Reading, MA 01867

After the 90-day period, a replacement will be sent upon receipt of the defective disc and a check or money order for $10.00, payable to Addison Wesley Longman, Inc.

Addison-Wesley makes no warranty or representation, either express or implied, with respect to this software, its quality, performance, merchantability, or fitness for a particular purpose. In no event will Addison-Wesley, its distributors, or dealers be liable for direct, indirect, special, incidental, or consequential damages arising out of the use or inability to use the software. The exclusion of implied warranties is not permitted in some states. Therefore, the above exclusion may not apply to you. This warranty provides you with specific legal rights. There may be other rights that you may have that vary from state to state.

The Microsoft DirectX 3 SDK contained on the enclosed CD-ROM is up-to-date as of September 1996, but may have been superseded by new releases during the production of this book. The DirectX SDK is continuing to evolve and is likely to be out of date by the time you purchase this book. Therefore, you are encouraged to check with Microsoft for any current revisions to the DirectX SDK. You may obtain additional information on the DirectX SDK and check on the status of updated materials by visiting the Microsoft Developers Network Media Developers web site on the Internet at http://www.microsoft.com/mediadev.

In addition, regular updates of the DirectX SDK may be obtained as part of the Microsoft Developer Network (MSDN) subscription program. Information about the MSDN subscription program may be obtained from the MSDN web site on the Internet at http://www.microsoft.com/msdn.

To join the Microsoft Developer Network in the United States and Canada, developers can call (800) 759-5474 between 6:30 a.m. and 5:30 p.m. (Pacific time), Monday through Friday. Outside North America developers can contact their local Microsoft subsidiary, or call (510) 275-0763 in the United States to obtain local contact information.